A WILDERNESS WITHIN

The University of Minnesota Press gratefully acknowledges the generous assistance provided for the publication of this book by the Hamilton P. Traub University Press Fund.

A WILDERNESS WITHIN

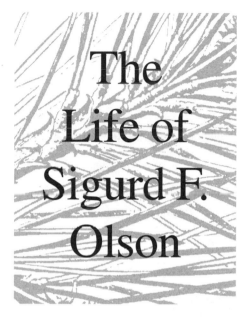

The Life of Sigurd F. Olson

DAVID BACKES

University of Minnesota Press
Minneapolis / London

Published by the University of Minnesota Press
111 Third Avenue South, Suite 290
Minneapolis, MN 55401-2520

Map on pages viii and ix provided by Cartographic Services Laboratory, University of Wisconsin, Milwaukee

Printed in the United States of America on acid-free paper.

Fourth Printing, 1999

Library of Congress Cataloging-in-Publication Data

Backes, David.
    A wilderness within : the life of Sigurd F. Olson / David Backes.
        p.   cm.
    Includes index.
    ISBN 0-8166-2842-4 (hc : alk. paper)
    ISBN 0-8166-2843-2 (pbk : alk. paper)
    1. Olson, Sigurd F., 1899–1982.   2. Naturalists—United States—
Biography.   3. Conservationists—United States—Biography.
    I. Title.
    QH31.O47B335   1997
    333.7'2'0092—dc21
    [B]   97-10891

The University of Minnesota is an equal-opportunity educator and employer.

To Judi
With love

By Sigurd F. Olson

The Singing Wilderness   (1956)

Listening Point   (1958)

The Lonely Land   (1961)

Runes of the North   (1963)

Open Horizons   (1969)

The Hidden Forest   (1969)

Wilderness Days   (1972)

Reflections from the North Country   (1976)

Of Time and Place   (1982)

❖ Contents ❖

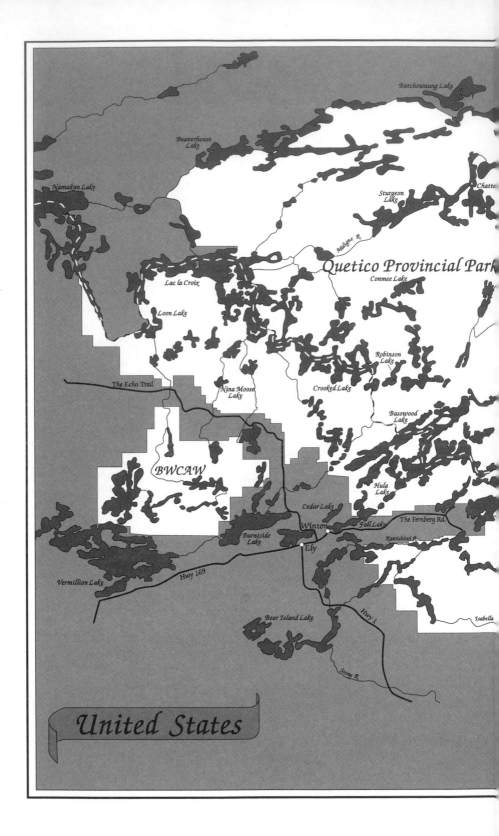

Batchewaung Lake

Beaverhouse Lake

Namakan Lake

Sturgeon Lake

Chatte

Quetico Provincial Park

Lac la Croix

Conmee Lake

Loon Lake

Robinson Lake

The Echo Trail

Nina Moose Lake

Crooked Lake

Basswood Lake

BWCAW

Hula Lake

Cedar Lake

Winton

Fall Lake

The Fernberg Rd.

Burntside Lake

Ely

Kawishiwi R.

Vermillion Lake

Hwy 169

Bear Island Lake

Hwy 1

Isabella

Stony R.

United States

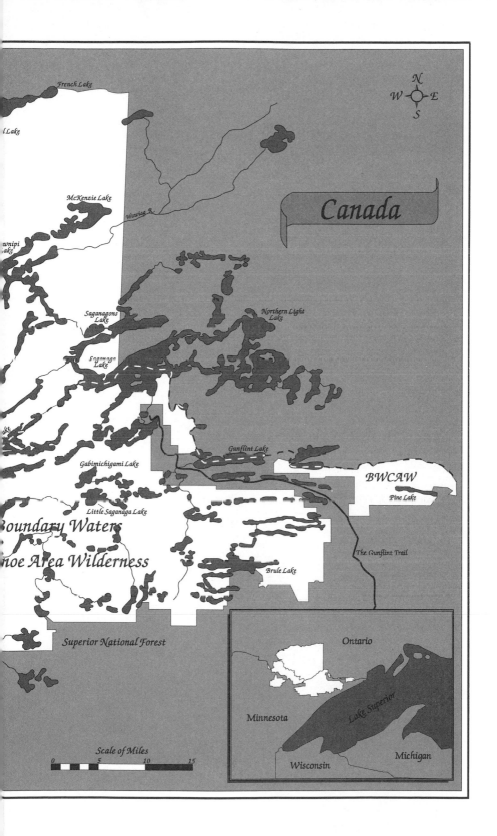

French Lake

l Lake

McKenzie Lake

Wawiag R.

wnipi
ake

Saganagons
Lake

Saganaga
Lake

Northern Light
Lake

Canada

N
W · E
S

Gunflint Lake

BWCAW

Gabimichigami Lake

Pine Lake

Little Saganaga Lake

Boundary Waters

noe Area Wilderness

The Gunflint Trail

Brule Lake

Superior National Forest

Ontario

Lake Superior

Minnesota

Michigan

Wisconsin

Scale of Miles

0   5   10   15

❖ Preface ❖

It was August 7, 1964. Sigurd Olson and five friends, known collectively as the Voyageurs, were paddling down the Hayes River toward Hudson Bay. They had begun their trip at the northeastern corner of Lake Winnipeg on July 25 and had proceeded without incident. But the weather had turned cold, with strong winds and freezing rain.

At the age of sixty-five, Olson was at the pinnacle of his career. He was vice president of the Wilderness Society, an adviser to the National Park Service and to Interior Secretary Stewart Udall, and an interpretive naturalist whose books of essays celebrating nature's effect on the human spirit had received acclaim across the United States and Canada. But the summer of 1964 had been difficult. The bill to create a national wilderness preservation system was nearing passage, and Olson was under intense pressure over a section of the bill related to the Boundary Waters Canoe Area, the wilderness outside his hometown of Ely, Minnesota. The group of conservationists who had paid his salary for the previous sixteen years expected him to affirm its position in favor of logging in the canoe country. Other conservationists, however, sent telegrams implying he would be a traitor if he did not advocate full wilderness protection. And in Ely, neighbors were publicly branding him a wilderness extremist. His canoe expedition with the Voyageurs promised to be a much-needed break from the stress.

And it was, for a while. But Sigurd's right shoulder, still not completely recovered from an accident more than a year earlier that had torn his ligaments and chipped a bone, became very sore. And then, on August 7, the Voyageurs' luck ran out. About noon, two of them dumped in their canoe while running a rapids. Amazingly—for these were canoeists with years of experience—they had not tied up the three packs they were carrying. They recovered two of them, the ones that held their personal gear, but the group's cook pack, with all the pots and utensils and much of the food, was gone forever. They were five days away from the end of their journey.

Sigurd and his canoe partner rescued the two who had dumped, and the Voyageurs went to shore to build a fire and dry out. It was a difficult task in the freezing rain, but essential to prevent hypothermia. After a long time, they were ready to set out again; they had more rapids to fight and portages to make if they were not to get too far behind schedule. By the end of the day Sigurd's shoulder was extremely sore. "We made a last portage over rocks and muskeg and I felt I could do no more," he wrote in the pocket notebook he carried along. "I lay down near the end for a while, then continued to a spruce where I lay down away from the rain and wind. The Voyageurs were worried and took good care of me."

It got worse. The next day, Sigurd paddled only when the Voyageurs were running rapids and needed his help. Late in the day, on an island portage around Berwick Falls, he slipped on an icy patch of rock and fell flat on his face. He gashed his lip and snapped off a tooth. The pain and blood made him sick to his stomach, and that night he vomited. During the final four days of their journey, Sigurd paddled only when it was absolutely necessary; he spent much of the time lying in the canoe in a sleeping bag while others paddled. He never again undertook a major canoe expedition.

What happened to the Voyageurs on that trip was more dramatic than anything that had occurred on any of the other trips in which Olson took part. It is curious that he, a writer, did not reconstruct the adventure for the public. His 1961 book, *The Lonely Land,* told the less dramatic story of an expedition the Voyageurs had taken along the Churchill River in 1955, and it had sold very well in both the United States and Canada. Surely the story of the Hudson Bay expedition would have fascinated those who had enjoyed the earlier book. But three sentences in an essay titled "Mementos" in his final book, *Of Time and Place,* provide his only description of the hardship he and his friends encountered on the Hayes River, and then he exaggerates:

"Somehow all six of us survived without food in the bitter cold for the next two weeks."

That is very much in keeping with what I have learned about Sigurd Olson during the past few years. He often was unconcerned with strict adherence to autobiographical facts in his essays, sometimes because he enjoyed adding drama, but often because he was more interested in making a larger point about nature and the human spirit. Even his autobiography, *Open Horizons,* published in 1969, rearranges events in his life to better suit his purpose, which, according to notes he jotted down at the time, was to offer his experience as an example to those who sought a deeper, more appreciative relationship with the natural world. The book ignores major aspects of Olson's career, and does not include dates. "The details of my life," he wrote in his notes, "are unimportant."

The lack of detail has not kept fans from constructing a mythology. During the last twenty years of his life Sigurd Olson achieved the status of a guru for those who seek deeper self-awareness and a sense of connectedness to the natural world, and the image has stuck. As in most lasting images, there is a solid core of truth in the depiction. But there also are sentimentality and wishful thinking on the part of an overly reverential core of followers. This is doubly unfortunate. First, Olson's accomplishments as a writer and as a conservationist (the term he preferred) are exceptional without any embellishment. For example, he not only received the highest award in nature writing, the John Burroughs Medal, but also is the only person to have received the highest honors of four of America's largest national conservation groups (see chapter 15).

Second, Sigurd Olson the man is much more interesting—and more inspiring—than Olson the icon. The latter is so optimistic, so peaceful, so wise, and seems to have acquired these gifts so easily, that he appears to be detached from the problems and circumstances of ordinary life. The real Sigurd Olson endured years of frustration, disappointment, and rejection. His life's story, as I hope to show, is about a sometimes agonizing inner journey, and about holding true to a dream in the face of tremendously long odds.

It is impossible to detail every aspect of a person's life without making far too long a book. I have chosen to emphasize Olson's search for meaning and fulfillment, the development of his ideas about ecology and about the importance of wilderness to the modern world, and the major events of his writing and conservation careers. There is much that, in the end, I decided I had to omit. In particular, I decided to pay little or no attention to many of the conservation issues in which he was involved from the 1950s through the 1970s. There are far too many of them, in a number of locations around the United States and Canada, and in many of them he did not play a key role. Even where his role *was* important—as in the creation of Point Reyes National Seashore in California and of Voyageurs National Park in Minnesota—I sometimes chose not to write about it, or to give only a little space to it. Instead, I tried to indicate the sweep of his activities and to give details mostly where they could help readers better understand a facet of Olson's life and character.

❖

I got to know Sigurd Olson and his wife, Elizabeth, during the late 1970s while I was an undergraduate at the University of Wisconsin in Madison. After I graduated in 1979 I lived in Ely for a short time and had several visits with the Olsons. I moved back to Madison in 1980, but stayed in touch with them; my master's thesis, which I began after Sigurd's death in 1982 and completed late in 1983, was a detailed study of his leading role in the effort to ban airplanes and fly-in resorts from the Superior National Forest Roadless Areas (now the Boundary Waters Canoe Area Wilderness). That battle at the end of the 1940s propelled him into the front ranks of the national conservation movement.

I used Olson's papers at the Minnesota Historical Society extensively for that study, and then again for my doctoral dissertation in mass communication at Madison. My dissertation, which was later revised and published in 1991 under the title *Canoe Country: An Embattled Wilderness,* was a cultural and environmental history of the Boundary Waters Canoe Area. It contained some analysis of Olson's role in the canoe country's history, but the focus was on the mass-mediated *images* of the area between 1920 and 1980.

Elizabeth Olson carefully guarded her late husband's image. She was very cautious about giving access to Sigurd's papers at the Minnesota Historical Society and often was not forthcoming with people who wanted to interview her. By 1990, however, she had known me for a dozen years, had read my research with care, and knew I had no axes to grind. Probably just as important, she had reached a point at which she was mentally ready to accept the idea of someone's writing her husband's biography. She was ninety-three years old, and perhaps thoughts of her own mortality spurred her to get Sigurd's biography under way while she was still capable of contributing to it. In any event, that fall she gave me permission to write this book. Between then and her death in 1994 she sat through many hours of interviews, and she gave me access not only to Sigurd's papers at the Minnesota Historical Society, but also to all of his private diaries and other papers and photographs at her home in Ely. She knew I would have to write about some difficult periods in her and her husband's life, and I am deeply grateful for her trust.

I also am tremendously thankful for the cooperation and encouragement given by Sigurd and Elizabeth's two sons, Sigurd T. Olson of Douglas, Alaska; and Robert K. Olson of Seeley, Wisconsin, and by Robert's wife, Yvonne. Many biographers have horror stories to tell about their relationships with the family of their subject, but I encountered only open minds and warm hearts. They placed no limits on my research or on my writing, even though some of what follows is deeply personal and painful.

A project such as this inevitably receives assistance from many people, and it is a pleasure to acknowledge those who helped me over the past seven years. Let me start by thanking Tom Klein, who convinced me that Elizabeth Olson probably would say yes if I asked her for permission to write this book, and who helped make possible my association with the University of Minnesota Press. I also would like to express my deep appreciation to the University of Wisconsin-Milwaukee Graduate School and to the Quetico-Superior Foundation for providing considerable financial support for this project, and to the Sigurd Olson Environmental Institute for facilitating the Quetico-Superior Foundation's grant.

I am very grateful to associate editor Todd Orjala of the University of Minnesota Press for his enthusiastic support of this project and for the many good conversations we've had. I also would like to thank managing editor Mary Byers, copy editor Lynn Marasco (who has given me newfound humility for my writing abilities), and the entire production team. This book also has benefited from the insights and suggestions of a number of other people—some known to me, some not—who read parts or all of the manuscript. I thank all of them, but can only acknowledge the readers I know of: Paul Gruchow, Bud Jordahl, Gerald Killan, Malcolm McLean, John Ross, and Ann Thering.

The staff members of the research facilities that I visited were invariably friendly and helpful. I especially want to thank Steve Nielsen, Ruth Ellen Bauer, and Dallas Lindgren at the Minnesota Historical Society Research Center in St. Paul; and Lisa Backman and Gary Goins at the Denver Public Library.

Many people, including some of those already mentioned, contributed to this book by sharing their memories of Sigurd Olson with me, by lending me material, or in some other way. I am grateful to Esther Ahonen, Don Albrecht, Durward Allen, Fred Bodsworth, Simon Bourgin, Jean Brewster, Bobbie Bristol, Paul Brooks, Bob Cary, Don Chase, Faye City, Fran Collin, Denis Coolican, Marla Dierkes, Annie Dillard, Jeff Evans, Tom Forecki, Michael Frome, Walt Goldsworthy, George Gould, Pat Groom, Robert Haraden, George Hartzog, John Kauffmann, Jim Klobuchar, Les and Jane Larsen, Arnell Lavasseur, Tony Lovink, Armin Luehrs, Dick Mackey, Wendy McLean, L. David Mech, Pat and Kate Miller, Michael Nadel, Karel Fraser Nelson, Pat Nelson, Mildred Olson, Susan Oman, Jean Packard, Bob Parsonage, Gerry Patterson, the Reverend Scott and Beth Pearson, Sheree Peterson, Kevin Proescholdt, Johanne Ranger, Tom Roberts Jr., Bill Rom, Ruth Rothman, Clayton Russell, R. Newell Searle, John Smrekar, Wallace Stegner, Chuck Stoddard, Charles and Bobs Strachan, Ted Swem, Stewart Udall, Dick Van Wagenen, Sister Noemi Weygant, Chuck Wick, Skip Wilke, Karlin Williams, Larry Wisner, Wendy Wong, Terry Wood, and Dave Zentner.

To Heidi, Tim, Jenny, and Andrew: I hope this book will always serve as a reminder to hold tight to your dreams and never let them go. And to Judi, who knew Sig and Elizabeth and understands about dreams: this one's for you.

❖ One ❖

Boyhood and Youth

1899–1916

November can be a treacherous time on the Great Lakes. Storms flare with little warning, whipping the waves, capsizing ships. Ida May Olson surely knew this as she boarded the boat in Chicago that November morning in 1906. She had reason for concern: the last time she had sailed on a ship she had nearly died. She was just nine, then, an immigrant on a small, storm-tossed vessel. Her parents and brother were with the other passengers in the ship's deckhold, which reeked of vomit. Ida May took a bucket to get some fresh water for the sick and climbed the ladder. When she reached the top deck a huge wave slapped the ship, nearly rolling it over, and she was thrown across the slippery deck. A sailor caught Ida May before she plummeted over the side.[1]

Twenty-five years later, Ida May once again had to trust herself, her family, and their few possessions to the skill of a ship's captain and to the winds of November. Sailing north out of Chicago, she and her husband, her mother, and her three sons were bound for Wisconsin's Door County peninsula, which juts into Lake Michigan like the thumb of a mitten. It must have been early evening when they reached the tip of the peninsula and crossed Death's Door, the narrow passage between the mainland and Washington Island. Over the years hundreds of boats had been dashed onto the rocks there by vicious crosswinds and a strong current. It would have been dark when the Olsons' ship docked in the harbor of their new hometown, Sister Bay.

Although the weather was good, it is hard to imagine that Ida May Olson was happy during that long day's travel up the Wisconsin coastline. She was leaving a nice Victorian home in Humboldt Park on Chicago's west side to live in—what? She would not have seen the house yet, but she had been in rural parsonages before, two of them, to be exact, in two states, and she could not have expected this one to be any better. It was so isolated. The Door County peninsula was reachable only by ship. Ida May had lived for eight years in the capital of Swedish America: Chicago was home to 60,000 Swedish-born citizens. She had enjoyed access to good doctors and well-stocked stores; she could not have expected to find either at Sister Bay. True, much of Chicago was ugly: streets full of horse manure, the river steeped in raw sewage. Upton Sinclair had just publicized the "hideous and bare" landscape of the South Side stockyards, the killing beds where poor immigrants were treated little better than the pigs and cattle they slaughtered. But this undoubtedly seemed a world away from Humboldt Park, and Chicago had given Ida May Olson amenities she could not have looked forward to leaving behind.

Her husband, Lawrence J. Olson, may also have gazed at the receding Chicago skyline with watery eyes. There is no record to indicate if he chose his new congregation freely or if he was assigned without regard to his wishes. But he was a single-minded man to whom his faith meant everything, and the thirty-seven-year-old minister certainly faced a challenge that may well have excited him. He was replacing the Reverend Charles Wassell, who had just retired after completing twenty-five years as the first pastor of Sister Bay's Swedish Baptist Church. The people had loved their heavyset, balding preacher who, with his dark eyebrows and a thick gray beard running ear to ear below his chin, perfectly fit the image of a distinguished church elder. The job of the thin, angular Lawrence Olson, with his naturally wavy brown hair combed up and back, and a thick mustache instead of the more traditional beard—he looked quite striking when he put on a little weight—was to modernize the practice of the faith in Door County by introducing English-language services. Second-generation Swedish Americans everywhere were embracing their new culture, and the Swedish Baptist Church did not want to lose its youth. This must have been a difficult task for Olson and a controversial one, for without the Old World language there was little to separate Swedish Baptists from any other northern Baptists. But he may well have foreseen his assignment as a step up in his career.[2]

Ida May's mother, Anna Cederholm, must have been miserable as the ship pulled out of the Chicago harbor. This was her third move in two years, and each one had been sorrowful. In 1904 she and her husband, Christian, had moved from Minnesota to California in a last-ditch effort to regain the health of their crippled twenty-eight-year-old son, Emil. During their journey west they lost all of their household goods in a flood. Then, three months after they arrived in California, Emil died. Anna and Christian moved to Chicago to be near Ida May, and Christian worked as a janitor in L. J.'s church. In 1906, as L. J. prepared to relocate to Sister Bay, Christian died. Anna moved in with her daughter and son-in-law, and prepared to go north with them. L. J. resented her presence. She was seventy years old, spoke only Swedish, and had no say in family decisions.

The children, no doubt, reacted to their voyage and new prospects much as children always do. Kenneth, age eleven, probably had good friends in Chicago whom he hated to leave. Leonard, age three, would have been too young to understand the full implications of their voyage up the lake. Of the whole family, only the middle child recorded any memories of the move. Sailing north to Sister Bay, he excitedly watched flocks of gulls, listened to their cries, and cast his eyes out over the broad, wind-swept waters of Lake Michigan. It was a taste of freedom. Seven-year-old Sigurd Olson, a second-generation Swedish American caught between Old World customs and New World possibilities, would seek out and savor open horizons for the rest of his life.

❖

To Lawrence J. Olson, only one thing was more important than following the tried and true ways of the Old World, and that was following the way of the Lord. When he converted to the Baptist faith during his childhood in Sweden, Lawrence, along with his family, broke custom and risked persecution.

The Baptist faith entered Sweden in the mid-nineteenth century, part of a general religious awakening that rebelled against the dry formalism of the state-enforced Lutheran faith and the widespread alcoholism that was contributing to the nation's demoralizing poverty. For a baptized Lutheran, raised to be suspicious of informal Bible reading at home and of prayers that did not come right out of the *Psalmbok*, it was a great shock to encounter a preacher who stirred some of his listeners to shout for joy, burst into prayer, or even be seized with spasms of religious rapture. For quite a few, that

3

initial shock was followed by a great longing to join in. But the state fought back, enforcing laws meant to keep the flock from straying. According to Swedish law, parents had to baptize their children in the Lutheran Church within eight days of birth; those who did not faced heavy fines and jail terms, and authorities often forcibly baptized the infants. A Swede who was not confirmed in the Lutheran Church could be prevented from getting a job, and could not marry.

Some of the strongest religious fervor, and some of the worst persecution, occurred in the central province of Dalarne. This was lake and mountain country, where poor soil made farming barely more than a subsistence occupation, and it was here, in the rugged village of Näs, that Lawrence Olson—Lars Jakob Olsson—was born on April 26, 1869. He was the third surviving child in a family of five boys and a girl.

Little is known of Lawrence's family, but it is clear that they were caught up in the religious awakening sweeping the province. His parents read the Bible daily and held prayer services in their home. Even if they had remained Lutheran, such behavior risked sanctions. Nearby in Dalarne's leading city, Falun, the jail was full to bursting with Lutherans who merely wanted to use hymn and prayer books that were different from the ones mandated by the church. But Baptists, their doctrine so far removed from Lutheranism, were treated the worst, their civil rights completely stripped away.

There is no evidence to indicate whether or not Lawrence's parents ever spent time in jail or were forced to pay fines. By the time Lawrence was born, the worst abuses were beginning to taper off, in part because of worldwide condemnation. But it was not unheard of for a Baptist preacher to be hauled into jail even as late as the 1880s, after Swedish laws had begun to grant more freedom. Lawrence converted to the Baptist faith at the age of twelve, so it is likely that his parents also had converted. Two of Lawrence's brothers became missionaries. One of them, Jon, spent his adult life in Jerusalem as a member of a Swedish group who believed that Christ would soon return to the ancient holy city.

Soon after Lawrence's conversion, he began meeting with other children to practice preaching; as a teenager working on one of the nearby small farms, he would stand on top of a stump and preach to the cows and sheep. But, while religious toleration improved significantly during his teen years, the economic picture was disheartening. The country was in the midst of an agricultural depression, caused primarily by inexpensive imported grain from the Americas, India, and Australia and made worse by changes in land-tenure laws and a rapidly growing population. A number of American states, especially in the Midwest, aggressively pursued Swedes by advertising in local newspapers, enticing young men with the prospects of higher wages, lower taxes, and free land. During the 1880s nearly three hundred and fifty thousand Swedes, 7 percent of the population, emigrated to the United States. In April 1888, at the age of nineteen, Lawrence, too, left behind his family and set sail for the land of opportunity.

Once in America, Lawrence sought out his mother's brother, who lived in the western Minnesota city of Alexandria, where he was an assistant masseur in a steam bath. Lawrence found work in Alexandria as a farm laborer and carpenter during the summers of 1888 and 1889; in between, he attended school, learned English, and paid his way by tending a doctor's horses.

But Lawrence's urge to preach was as strong as ever, and, with the recommendation of the Swedish Baptist Church of Alexandria, he was admitted into Chicago's Morgan Park Seminary in the fall of 1889. He graduated in the spring of 1892 and took his first assignment as pastor of the Swedish Baptist Church of St. Cloud, Minnesota, in the center of the state. He was now the Reverend Lawrence J. Olson, or L. J., as he preferred it, which, with a Swedish accent, became "Ell Yay."

Sixty miles north of St. Cloud, in Brainerd, lived a young woman from Malmö, Sweden, a large city on the southern coast. Her parents, Christian and Anna Cederholm, were devout Swedish Baptists, and so was she: Ida May Cederholm once had rejected a marriage proposal because the suitor was not a serious enough Christian. But in February 1894 Ida May fell in love with a visiting minister from St. Cloud. He was young, thin, mustachioed, and Swedish; furthermore, he was *very* serious in his faith. When the Reverend L. J. Olson and Ida May Cederholm married in July 1894, after a four-month courtship, they spent their honeymoon at a Swedish Baptist convention in Minneapolis.

❖

Before they celebrated their first anniversary, the Olsons were sent to Sioux Falls, South Dakota. The conditions were horrible. The region was in the midst of a drought as old as the state itself—seven years—and farmers were desperate. Many of the men were forced to leave their families behind while they traveled across South Dakota, Minnesota, and Nebraska, searching for any kind of work that could help pay the bills. The Olsons' congregation could not afford a parsonage, and could not always pay L. J.'s meager salary. But a church in Ohio had adopted the congregation as a special cause, and when Ida May delivered her first son in August 1895 the Ohioans sent a box of baby clothes. There was a catch, however: the ladies' aid society of the Ohio church asked for the honor of naming the boy. The Olsons already had chosen the name Sigurd, but renamed the baby Kenneth in accord with their benefactors' wishes.

About four years later and six hundred miles to the east, in Chicago, L. J. and Ida May got to use their first choice of a boy's name. Once again, they had just moved and Ida May was pregnant, but the Swedish Baptist congregation in Humboldt Park was larger and wealthier than any they had experienced, and they had a parsonage of their own that probably seemed luxurious in comparison to their recent quarters. The baby came two days after Easter, on April 4, 1899. (It must have been a tense Easter season, trying to get established in a new congregation and wondering if the baby would hold off its arrival until after the most important holy day of the Christian year.) They named him Sigurd Ferdinand Olson; the incongruous middle name, which he would always detest, belonged to a friend of the family.

Sigurd would have little memory of Chicago. He recalled walks in Humboldt Park, his surprise one day at seeing a mounted squirrel in a store window, and going to kindergarten. His father oversaw construction of a new church that seated six hundred and had a year or two to enjoy the new facility. Then came the new assignment at Sister Bay, and the Olsons moved to Wisconsin.

❖

Door County had been logged by the time the Olsons arrived in November 1906, and much of the land had been converted to agriculture. Farmers near Sister Bay grew peas, oats, corn, potatoes, hay; some raised hogs, sheep, or dairy cows. And there were many orchards: Door County cherry and apple trees were beginning to produce large amounts of delicious fruit and soon would draw national publicity. But the area's romantic quality derived primarily from another kind of harvest. Fishermen from Sister Bay and the other small towns up and down the peninsula caught and sold herring, whitefish, trout, chub, shad, and perch, and the sight of ships on the lake, of wharves and docks and ropes and sails, of fish markets and Friday fish boils, was beginning to draw tourists from Milwaukee and Chicago. Cool summer temperatures, white sand beaches, and spectacular limestone bluffs provided additional attractions that made Door County one of the most appealing places to visit in the Upper Midwest.

For seven-year-old Sigurd Olson, just reaching an age at which he had the desire and freedom to explore beyond the immediate neighborhood, it was ideal. His family's two-story rectangular frame home, half a mile east of town, was surrounded by farm fields, woods, and swampland. The dirt road passing in front of the house and the church next door cut straight across the peninsula to Appleport, three miles to the east. Sigurd got to know both sides of the peninsula: the deep harbor of Sister Bay, protected from west winds by wooded bluffs, the Sister Islands protruding thinly on the horizon; and the shallow waters and windswept shore of wide-open Appleport, where the constant pounding of waves left a beach of smooth stones, clumps of grasses, and hardy wildflowers such as the pigweed and beach pea. Just south of Sister Bay was Ephraim, where the harbor view centered on spectacular limestone cliffs that were bathed in a luminous gold by the early morning sun. Sigurd often visited Ephraim after his father began holding regular services in a log building there in 1907, and he occasionally accompanied L. J. on ministerial rounds to Bailey's Harbor, Gills Rock, and Washington Island (the latter by boat across Death's Door). On the way to Death's Door, the road they traveled with their horse and buggy took them steadily uphill to a high view of Ellison Bay and the broad expanses of Lake Michigan.

Sigurd learned to fish and built a small fort of branches in his yard. Each week he joined friends downtown to watch the stagecoach come in; its driver, knowing the children were watching (and waiting for the candy he handed out), always galloped the horses down the steep hill to the Sister Bay Post Office and Tavern. Fishermen brought the Olsons cold, shining catches in exchange for L. J.'s services, and orchard owners brought bushels of fruit. Sigurd would never forget the sweet autumn scent of apples in the cellar.

At night, lying in his bed, he could hear the moaning of foghorns, a sound that called to him as enticingly as would the howl of wolves or the wail of loons later in his life. When he was eight or nine he got the chance to follow that call, exploring nearby wooded paths by himself in an ever larger radius from home until one day he made it all the way to the lake. Half a century later, he described his experience at the end of an abandoned stone pier:

> A school of perch darted in and out of the rocks. They were green and gold and black, and I was fascinated by their beauty. Seagulls wheeled and cried above me. Waves crashed against the pier. I was alone in a wild and lovely place, part of the dark forest through which I had come, and of all the wild sounds and colors and feelings of the place I had found. That day I entered into a life of indescribable beauty and delight. There I believe I heard the singing wilderness for the first time.[3]

Although he never mentioned it in any of his writings, Sigurd certainly also came to intimately know nature's dark side at Sister Bay. It came roaring on November winds or with the storms of spring, churning the lake into a froth, tossing boats, hurling waves and debris in to the shore. Every year lives were lost: fathers, sons, husbands, lovers, sometimes disappearing without even a trace into a white squall. Sigurd's father undoubtedly officiated at some of their funerals. Even though Sigurd experienced this raw, powerful side of nature from the relatively safe perspective of the landlocked, it would not have been surprising if he had adopted the stoic view of life often found in harbor towns. In fact, however, the opposite occurred. Storms tended to bring out in him a joyous abandon that reflected two different, potentially contradictory, impulses: to become one with the forces of nature and, in surviving the encounter, to demonstrate his individuality and his own masculine power. He enjoyed the sensation of being part of a storm, as when he lay between the roots of an old white pine while it swayed violently and other trees crashed to the ground nearby. He also loved to laugh in the face of rough weather, as this 1935 journal entry shows:

I have stood on top of a wind swept hill, waved my hat at the breeze, shouted to the skies that I was alive, and I have fought the waves on gigantic lakes and enjoyed the slap of every one. I love the rain, the snow, thunder, storms, quiet, every change of the weather.[4]

The tension between the desire to lose himself in communion with the wild and to prove himself by doing things that set him apart from the wild and from other men would inform his life. At this point in his childhood, however, the first desire—to feel a sense of connectedness with nature—must have been intuitive. Sigurd Olson just naturally had an unusually passionate appreciation for the natural beauty around him. Later on, in college, he would unhappily find himself with a much more serious reason to seek such aesthetic experiences.

As for the second desire—to assert his individuality and value—this can be attributed in part to circumstances at his first two schools. In Chicago, Sigurd's teacher had been a mean-spirited woman named Mrs. Tubbs. As Sigurd and his father arrived for his first day of kindergarten, Mrs. Tubbs was beating a child with a ruler. The boy was screaming. When Mrs. Tubbs saw the Olsons in the doorway she threw down the other boy and shouted at Sigurd, "If you don't behave, you will be next!" L. J. left Sigurd cringing in a corner. At Sister Bay, Sigurd and his older brother attended a one-room school a mile down the road toward Appleport. It was run by Mr. Yates, another autocratic teacher who believed in punishing children for incorrect answers; Sigurd, who had trouble with spelling, often found himself standing in a corner with a dunce cap on his head. At his desk he frequently daydreamed. From where he sat he could see woods and farmland, and on warm days, when the seven tall, narrow windows lining the north wall were open, he could hear the faint cries of gulls in the distance, calling him to freedom.[5]

But school was not the only problem, nor was it the most important one. Sigurd's home life was deadening, too. His father was repressive: not abusive, but rigid, formal, and reserved, a generally grim man who seemed neither to know how to have fun nor to care, totally absorbed—driven—by his calling as a fundamentalist minister. He was a fire-and-brimstone preacher who led antialcohol campaigns and told his sons to turn their heads whenever they passed a Catholic church. Sigurd and his brother Kenneth once saved their money and bought a chess set; when L. J. discovered it he grabbed it away and threw it into the fire.

Sigurd's mother was just as devout a believer as his father, but she also was a charming woman who easily made friends. Ida May was not especially pretty, but she was full of fun, with a great sense of humor, a fine singing voice, and a way of making people feel comfortable and happy. Sunday school students liked the way she made Bible stories come alive, often ending a lesson with a cliffhanger that she would finish the following Sunday. By the time the Olsons moved to Sister Bay, Ida May had grown used to calming people who had been treated abruptly by her husband. At home, however, she could not eliminate the uneasy atmosphere created by L. J.'s excessive seriousness. Yet in her own way she contributed to the tension. Her flaw was a tendency toward overprotection, even possessiveness. Ida May loved her boys very much—so much, in fact, that it made her husband jealous.

The children had to adapt to an unapproachable father and a mother who at times was *too* close. Sigurd's childhood explorations of the woods, fields, and shorelines of Door County therefore were more than simple fun; they also served as an escape from the stifling atmosphere of school and home, and as an outlet to find and express his individuality. Decades later, in a draft of his memoirs, he would write:

> As I grew older, this need became a passion that could not be denied. Unless each day meant some contact with the out of doors, I was unhappy. As long as I could remember it had always been this way, needing to feel the wind and the rain on my face with open sky and vistas around me. I did not know at the time but this growing need was molding me in a way I did not fully understand. All I was aware of was the constant over-riding need and that when I was indoors it could never be too long or something would die within me.[6]

❖

The Reverend L. J. Olson succeeded in firmly establishing English-language services at Sister Bay. (There was irony in this task: the Olsons regularly spoke Swedish at home. In fact, Sigurd and his brothers learned Swedish before they learned English.) L. J. started slowly, just one Sunday a month at first, and during just one of the evening services. Eventually, he preached in a Swedish-accented English during all of the Sunday-evening services. His successors gradually extended the practice until eventually Swedish was used only on special occasions. Opponents of this cultural assimilation were proved right, too: once the transition to English was complete, the Sister Bay Swedish Baptist Church changed its name to First Baptist Church.

L. J.'s work earned him a promotion. On July 1, 1909, he resigned his position at Sister Bay to become state missionary for the Swedish Conference of the Wisconsin Baptist State Convention. For the next sixteen years he would oversee the operations of Swedish Baptist congregations around the state. Since most of them were in northwestern Wisconsin, the Olsons left Door County. They moved first to the village of Prentice, in Price County, and then three years later to the city of Ashland.

Prentice was a logging town, established along the Jump River in 1884 on land owned by the Jump River Lumber Company. At one time the town's two mills operated near their 100,000-foot daily capacity. By the time the Olsons arrived, however, the great pine and hemlock forests had been logged and burned, and only a few isolated white pines and scattered stands of hemlock remained.

It was no different anywhere else in northern Wisconsin. In little more than three decades loggers had taken 90 percent of the standing pine in twenty-seven counties. They took it any way they could, legally or illegally, and wasted much of it. By 1900 little remained. The Wisconsin Cutover was filling in with young aspen and birch, and thickets of alder and hazel. No longer a logging frontier, the northern counties became an agricultural frontier. Farmers, many of them immigrants beginning new lives, were moving in and clearing the land of stumps and slashings, enticed by cheap prices and false promises of good soil. "It must have seemed a raw and primitive place to mother and dad," Sigurd later said, "but to me it was beautiful and exciting."[7]

At Prentice, the ten-year-old Sigurd entered what he later called his "Daniel Boone days." Fishing became an almost daily activity. Early in the morning before school, Sigurd often left his house on the hill in the center of town and hurried down to the Jump River. From an old logging bridge he lowered his hook and worm and caught rock bass. An older boy eventually introduced him to trout fishing, taking him across a meadow to a tiny creek. Using a tamarack pole he had made himself, his mother's black thread for a line, and grasshoppers for bait, Sigurd caught his first brook trout.

He also was growing old enough to learn to trap and hunt. Excited by such popular adventure novels as Joseph Altsheler's *The Riflemen of the Ohio* and *The Dark and Bloody Ground,* Sigurd began imitating his fictional heroes. He built a primitive shelter of sticks next to a spring-fed brook at the edge of a stand of ancient hemlocks and used this as a base for his explorations. He killed squirrels and small birds such as Canada jays with a slingshot; he snared rabbits; he pulled crayfish, clams, and fish out of the brook. He brought the victims back to his shelter and skinned, plucked, shelled, or scaled them, then roasted or boiled them, and ate.

While the family was living in Prentice, Sigurd became acquainted with a man named Heine, a veteran of the Boer War of 1899 to 1902 in South Africa. Heine, or "Old John," as Olson called him in the final draft of *Open Horizons,* gave Sigurd—who probably was twelve at the time—his first opportunity to kill a deer. On a November day before the first snow, he brought Sigurd out to his farm fifteen miles from home, handed him a .30–30 Winchester rifle, showed him how to use it, and told him to choose a spot overlooking the valley. "When you shoot, I'll come," Heine said.

But no deer came within sight until that evening, as Heine and Sigurd were heading back under a red sky to Heine's cabin. As they came around a bend in the road, they found themselves fifty feet from a large buck. Heine stopped the horses, and Sigurd slowly pulled the rifle out from under a sack of oats in the wagon. He carefully loaded two bullets into the magazine, but when he opened the breech and sent a bullet into the chamber, the click startled the buck and it bounded away.

Disappointed but not deterred, Sigurd eventually saved up for his own rifle, a .22-caliber single-shot Stevens. And as soon as he bought it, he began practicing daily until he could hit a bull's-eye at fifty feet; then he began trying it out on the local grouse population. The Cutover was full of them, and Sigurd spent many autumn hours walking through a young aspen grove along a logging road, picking off grouse with shots through the head as they walked out of the brush.

Sigurd also used his rifle to shoot snowshoe hares; in fact, at Ashland he earned the nickname "Bunny" because he spent so much time pursuing them. By then he was using a shotgun; in autumn, if he was not out in a Lake Superior slough shooting mallards, he and a friend would go after hares. In the winter, he set traplines for weasels, whose fur had changed from the reddish brown of summer to a brilliant white, with black tail tips. "When I touched those wild furs," he wrote years later, "I somehow made contact with a life that had nothing to do with home or school or parents. I was in a world of my own, a free and beautiful world where all was fantasy and adventure."[8] In the context of the surrounding text, the quote naturally is interpreted as a typical child's love of imaginative play. In the context of other evidence about Sigurd's life, however, it can be seen as a rare public complaint about the repressive atmosphere of his childhood.

Hunting and trapping gave Sigurd something in common with most boys and at the same time made him different from his family. L. J. did not hunt or trap (although he sometimes fished); neither did Kenneth. They took little interest in the outdoors. Once Leonard was old enough he learned to hunt, but did not feel the passion for it that Sigurd felt. Ida May enjoyed picnics and walks and city parks, but had no desire to hunt or trap or explore the woods. Sigurd took comfort and pride in a family legend about a Swedish ancestor who shared his first name and had been a boar hunter for the king, but in his own house he was an enigma. "Nobody in the family understood why on earth I had to be running off in the woods all the time," he later recalled for the *Minneapolis Star.*[9]

That was not quite true. His grandmother understood. Anna Cederholm was a small, straight-backed pioneer woman who enjoyed raising chickens and hogs, canning fruit, and tending her herb garden. She enjoyed rubbing a pinch of soil between her fingers and smelling it. "To her," Sigurd would later recall, "the playing of bridge was a hopeless and criminal waste of time, coffee parties and frittering around with society a deplorable loss of precious hours that could much better have been spent out of doors."[10]

Sigurd especially loved the times—undoubtedly rare occasions—when both of his parents would go away for a few days and "Mormor" would take care of him and his brothers. She happily played along with their imaginative games; at night, for instance, they would pretend that lightning bugs in the nearby meadow were Indian campfires and that the whippoorwill calls were Indian scouts signaling to each other. More than anything else, she understood his need to explore and his love for trout fishing. "The rest of the family thought me slightly insane," Sigurd later recalled,

> getting up before dawn, rain or shine to hike for hours through the woods to some little creek and then at the end of the day bring home only a few six inchers, but Grandmother felt differently, knew instinctively that trout were worth all of the effort and more, that there was something other folks did not understand about the sound and feel of running water, the smell of bursting buds, no triumph after all as great as bringing home a mess of speckles.

After a successful trip, Sigurd would hurry back to show off his catch to his grandmother. He would tell her all about the creek he fished and about each fish he caught, and she would listen attentively, exclaiming over his victories and sympathizing when he told her about the ones that got away. Speaking in her native Swedish, she told him that trout were like flowers, the most beautiful fish in the world, and as she and Sigurd washed his catch, she would point out the colorful spots along the sides of the fish, glistening in the light. The red spots were rubies, she would say, the green spots emeralds, and the black spots black diamonds. Then she would sprinkle the trout with flour and salt, and lay them side by side in a sizzling pan. When the tails had curled and the skins turned golden she would say, "Nu lilla Sigurd, skall vi festa"—"Now, little Sigurd, we shall feast." Then they would sit down at the table "and talk of robins and spring and the eternal joy of fishing." Sigurd would always remember his grandmother with great fondness: "I loved her as only a small boy can, for she was a partner of the spirit."

❖

The Olsons moved ninety miles north from Prentice to Ashland in the summer of 1912. The reasons are not clear. Perhaps Ashland provided a more central location for L. J.'s travels, being closer to the northwestern corner of the state, where Swedish Americans were most heavily concentrated, while still not too far away from Swedish Baptist congregations in Price County and the western counties. Perhaps he and Ida May simply wanted to live in a larger community. Ashland had 15,000 people—not another Chicago by any means, but a metropolis in comparison to the communities where the Olsons had spent the previous six years. Perhaps Kenneth's June graduation from high school and desire for college played a role. They surely did not have the money to afford room and board as well as tuition, and, since L. J. was not tied to a specific congregation, moving to Ashland made economic sense. Their new home, a two-story white frame house on the northwest corner of Seventh Street and Second Avenue West, was just seven blocks from Northland College, where Kenneth enrolled in the fall.

That same fall, Sigurd entered ninth grade at Ashland High School. It must have been a little intimidating for a boy who was used to country schools where children of all grades were together in one room. Also, at thirteen, he was young for his class. But there is little record of his high school years, except that he received his first recognition for writing: he was given a five-dollar gold piece for best essay in the school's writing contest. The topic—ironically, in light of his eventual conservation career—was "The Function of the Chamber of Commerce."

Two anecdotes show that Sigurd also began to assert his independence in ways typical of boys his age. Once he and some friends staged a Halloween prank that got them into trouble. Under the cover of night, they pulled and pushed a heavy lumber wagon up the high school's front steps, intending to block the door with it. But just as they got it to the last step, the night watchman heard them and turned his light on them. Surprised and flustered, they let go of the wagon and it rolled all the way back down, chipping every step in two places. The next morning the principal fined Sigurd and each of his friends two dollars.

He also tried rolling and smoking cigarettes, which, of course, as the son of a Swedish Baptist minister, he knew was strictly forbidden. He almost got caught, too. He and his friends were sitting in a small clubhouse they had built, puffing away, when Sigurd noticed his father walking in their direction. Quickly, the boys snuffed out the cigarettes and began singing Sunday school hymns. L. J. had a very poor sense of smell, so all he noticed was the singing. "That's nice, boys," he said, and continued on his way.

Ashland, like Sister Bay, was a harbor town, but on a much larger scale, shipping millions of tons of timber and iron ore each year. The big timber was gone when the Olsons arrived, and the surrounding countryside bore the stump-filled, wide-open look of the Wisconsin Cutover. The mining industry was strong, however; ranges in northern Michigan and Minnesota produced more than half of the nation's iron ore. Four years after the Olsons arrived, construction began on a new concrete ore dock that ultimately became the world's largest: eighteen hundred feet long, eighty feet high, and fifty-nine feet wide. Sigurd regularly saw and heard the heavy industrial traffic of the harbor; he also enjoyed the beauty of Lake Superior, the world's largest freshwater lake, with its bold and rocky shoreline. As with Lake Michigan, every day brought a new perspective: some days the water might appear deep blue, other days blue with bands of green or violet; on dark, overcast days it would take on a milky cast, or sometimes the appearance of liquid steel. And Sigurd would have witnessed the power of Lake Superior, too. Chequamegon Bay, long and broad, could be blown into a frenzy unlike anything he had seen at Sister Bay. Downpours made roads impassable and leached the area's red soil into once-quiet creeks that became raging torrents of liquid earth, emptying into the bay until it took on the color of coffee, heavy on the cream.

Adjoining the lake near the west side of town was the Fish Creek slough, just two miles from Sigurd's house. Trumpeter swans nested there, and mallards and black ducks and blue-winged teal. The slough was probably Sigurd's favorite place near home. Farther afield was Star Lake, surrounded by an isolated stand of virgin white pine more than a hundred feet tall. Sigurd also occasionally got out onto Lake Superior and visited the Apostle Islands, which were becoming a popular tourist destination. And in the winter, under the right conditions of smooth ice and little snow, he skated on Chequamegon Bay.

After graduating from high school in 1916, Sigurd entered Northland College. Founded in 1892 by the Congregational Church as Northern Wisconsin Academy, it had provided the area's first high school education. In 1906 a liberal arts college was added and the name was changed to Northland. While the Congregational Church retained much of the managerial control, Northland billed itself as an interdenominational evangelical Protestant academy and college.[11]

Sigurd was one of 45 freshmen that fall, out of 65 college students and a total student body (including the academy) of 211. In a school that small, nobody remains anonymous, and Sigurd had the extra benefit—or burden—of following upon the heels of his older brother. Kenneth, who had graduated three months earlier, had been president of the student body, president of the Glee Club, on the cabinet of the YMCA, on the school newspaper and yearbook staffs, and had lettered in football. Nicknamed "Kinks" because of his curly hair, he had been one of the most popular young men on campus. Sigurd undoubtedly was greeted with high expectations. It is not possible to say how he felt about this, but later in life Sigurd's journals and letters show that, although he deeply loved and respected his big brother, he also compared their achievements to see if he measured up to Kenneth's high standards.

If Sigurd *had* been looking for a way to outshine Kenneth, football presented such an opportunity. Kenneth had lettered but had never played because he had dislocated his shoulder the first day of practice. Sigurd made the team, played left end, and, according to his later recollections, performed well. He would have earned a letter but for a fateful choice he made in November before the last game of the season. As Sigurd joined the team for practice on a Friday afternoon, the sky darkened and a north wind began to blow. Sigurd knew that a big storm was about to hit, and that it would force great flocks of migrating scaup—he called them bluebills—to take cover in the Fish Creek slough. The game was the next day, but the thought of missing the sight and what he called the "wild, canvas-tearing sounds" of the ducks as they poured out of the storm, wings outspread, was too much for him. Knowing he would be condemned for it, Sigurd skipped Saturday's game and hiked to the slough, where he watched the bluebills, the marsh reeds bent with new snow, and the white-capped waves of nearby Chequamegon Bay. Deserting the team cost Sigurd his varsity letter and some respect at Northland College. It also established a pattern for decisions he would make in the future.

But all was not lost. Sigurd was active in the YMCA, the glee club, and the quartet—he had an excellent singing voice and loved to use it. He had grown into a good-looking young man: nearly five feet, eleven inches tall, a hundred sixty-five pounds, dark brown hair parted in the middle and combed straight back in popular fashion. He had large ears but deep, sensitive eyes and an engaging smile. He also was naturally graceful. But despite these physical advantages, he was at a loss when it came to conversing with members of the opposite sex. Not long after the football fiasco, one of Sigurd's friends attempted to plant the seeds of a relationship by getting Sigurd to visit a young woman who was recuperating from pneumonia in the local hospital. He obliged, but found himself completely tongue-tied. Finally, out of sheer embarrassment and possibly hoping to break the ice, Sigurd picked up a pillow and threw it at her. "He certainly was a dandy!" she said afterward to her nurse.

This was the first time Elizabeth Uhrenholdt had met Sigurd, but she had seen him once before, the previous June, at Northland College's graduation ceremony. For the Olsons, of course, it was a big day. Kenneth gave one of the graduation speeches. (He took a strong and brave stand against anti-immigration laws, at a time when President Woodrow Wilson was receiving enthusiastic applause for saying that foreign-born Americans "have poured the poison of disloyalty into the very arteries of our national life.") And L. J. gave the invocation. During the ceremony, however, at least one person in the crowded auditorium seemed not to be suitably impressed. As Elizabeth Uhrenholdt recalled many years later, "I saw this kid sitting in an aisle seat, scrunched over, his leg way out in the aisle. I said, 'For goodness' sake, who's that? How rude!'" She discovered that it was a younger brother of the greatly respected Kenneth Olson, and that his name was Sigurd. She would have been shocked then had someone predicted that she would marry him.

❖ Two ❖

College Years

1916–1919

Soren Jensen Uhrenholdt was not one of the wealthiest farmers in Wisconsin in 1916, but he was one of the most respected. His potato and dairy farm along the Namekagon River some fifty miles southwest of Ashland was considered a model of progressive agriculture and forestry. The University of Wisconsin publicly honored him in 1916 for his inspiring example to other farmers, and the governor appointed him to represent the state at national farmers' conventions. He advised 4-H clubs and university professors and was quoted in agricultural and forestry journals. All of this and more, including an award presented in Texas, was a stunning achievement for someone who farmed in the poor soil of the Wisconsin Cutover. Soren Uhrenholdt was a gifted man, and he would become a second father to Sigurd Olson.[1]

Born in 1857 at Borup, Denmark, a northern village near Aalborg, Soren grew up on a farm. He undoubtedly would have stayed in Denmark but for one unfortunate fact: he was illegitimate, and therefore did not have the legal status to own a farm of his own. As a young teenager he left home to become a sailor, and in 1882, at the age of twenty-five, he emigrated from Denmark to the United States. He found his way to south central Wisconsin, where, after several years of saving, he bought a farm near Waupaca. All this time he corresponded with Kristine Thorn, a young Danish woman with whom he had fallen in love the year before he left Denmark. She came from a well-to-do family in Osteruttrup, another hamlet near Aalborg. In 1887 she agreed to marry Soren, over the strong objections of her father, a bank director who was not about to have his daughter marry an illegitimate, unlanded man with no future, and then take off with him to America. But her father had little say—Kristine had lived with her grandparents for years—so the wedding took place in Copenhagen, and the next day the couple sailed to America and traveled halfway across the continent to the little farm near Waupaca.

It was rich, fertile land. They prospered, and produced a large family. But by the time the seventh of their eight children—Elizabeth—was born, on November 13, 1897, the country had entered an economic depression that eventually broke the Uhrenholdts and forced them to sell. Intent to stay in farming on his own terms, rather than as someone else's hired hand—he was determined not to lose his status as a landed person in his adopted country—Soren discovered that railroad companies were selling land in northern Wisconsin's Cutover at bargain prices. In 1899 Soren spent most of what little money he had and bought 160 acres along the Namekagon River about ten miles north of Hayward at Seeley. It was the year of Sigurd Olson's birth. Friends built a one-room cabin (with a loft for the children), and on April 1, 1900, the Uhrenholdts moved in. They had no screens on the windows, no electricity, and no plumbing—not even a well.

That first summer Soren and his oldest son, Jens, cleared eight acres of stumps, slashings, and brush left behind by loggers, and planted potatoes; they built an open shed for the livestock and gathered hay for the winter from swamps and the edges of logging roads. "We did not really know we were poor," Elizabeth recalled. "We had cream, we had butter, we had lovely hams, we had lovely bacon, all these things, and our food was natural food."

At the time, Wisconsin was trying to solve the problems of the Cutover region—tax default lands, abandoned mills, loss of jobs—with a long-term vision of reforestation and a sustainable logging industry. In 1903 the legislature established a state forest system; over the next dozen years state forester Edward M. Griffith acquired Cutover lands and established a progressive program of scientific management and conservation.[2]

The northern counties, however, wanted immediate economic improvement and demanded that the state refocus its energies on agricultural settlement. They succeeded. In 1915 Wisconsin's Supreme Court declared most of Griffith's program unconstitutional, and he resigned. Meanwhile, northern boosters, with the help of agricultural experts at the University of Wisconsin, depicted the Cutover as rich farmland, and immigrants came and created ethnic enclaves in the north country.

The "stump farmers" of northern Wisconsin were true pioneers, scratching a living from soil that did not live up to the claims of county agents and the advertisements of railroad companies trying to dump their land. In Sawyer County, where the Uhrenholdts lived, agricultural experts had predicted that more than 60 percent of the land was suitable for farming. In truth, very little land was productive enough to sustain a farm family. Many farmers failed; many others, desperate for cash, gave in to pressure from logging companies and sold their stands of tall pine for five dollars a thousand board feet. The loggers would move in, take the trees, and leave behind a naked, stump-filled farm. The owners no longer had a hedge against future financial difficulties.

The Uhrenholdts had twenty thousand board feet of white pine on their land, but, although the family was badly in need of money, Soren refused to sell his stands to be clear-cut in exchange for quick cash. He cut pine for the family's needs and sometimes sold some of what he cut for profit, but he always cut selectively, so that the remaining trees grew better. Rather than give in to the offers of timber buyers, he hired out as a road boss for a couple of years, earning enough to pull the family through until their farm began to prosper. By the time Sigurd Olson came in contact with the family in 1916, the Uhrenholdts were enlarging their holdings to an eventual four hundred acres (containing three hundred thousand board feet of white pine), and Soren, without prospects in Denmark because of the circumstances of his birth, was a figure of great respect among the state's farmers and conservationists. In the Wisconsin Cutover, where agriculture and forestry were embroiled in politics, he had shown that the two were compatible.

When Olson entered Northland College in September 1916, the Uhrenholdts' fourth child, Andrew, was beginning his senior year in the academy. Although Andrew was completing his high school education, he was, at the age of twenty-three, six years older than Sigurd. They probably got to know each other through their participation in the campus YMCA. They became good friends, and early in 1917 Andrew invited Sigurd to the farm for Easter vacation.

Olson was majoring in agriculture, which was one of just three fields that received his father's blessing (the other two were teaching and, of course, the ministry). Northland College had a strong two-year agricultural program, which prepared students to transfer to the University of Wisconsin at Madison for their final two years. Besides receiving classroom training, students worked on the college's ninety-five acres under cultivation, plowing the fields, installing drain tiles, threshing grain, filling the silo. They also took care of the college's dairy herd. Sigurd enjoyed it and performed well, earning a B average in his courses. He thought that farming might be the life for him, so when Andrew Uhrenholdt invited him to visit, he jumped at the chance not only to join his friend for Easter, but also to see a model farm.

Full of enthusiasm, Sigurd impressed the whole family (including, this time, Elizabeth), and Soren offered him a summer job. As soon as school let out in June, Sigurd took the train down to Seeley. His major task over the next three months was to clear a marshy plot of land and plow it over. Armed with a double-bitted ax, a brush hook, and a crowbar, he chopped and dragged, chopped and dragged for hours a day, building big brush piles for burning. It was grimy, exhausting work, and Sigurd often was cut by thorns or sharp branch ends, but he thoroughly enjoyed himself. Every day he rose at 4:00 A.M. with the rest of the family and spent two hours on such chores as feeding the horses and sending the cows to pasture. Then he returned to the house for a big breakfast, after which he went out to clear his plot of land. He learned how to harness the horses (and nearly got kicked the first few times), and when he had cleared the plot of all the brush, Jens Uhrenholdt showed him how to use a team of logging horses to pull out the remaining stumps. By fall Sigurd had cleared the land, pulled the stumps, and plowed the clearing so it would be ready for planting the next spring.

Life along the Namekagon River was full of a vividness and purpose that contrasted markedly with the unreality Sigurd felt at home. For years afterward he would try, sometimes desperately, to regain the sense of authenticity he first felt while working at the Uhrenholdt farm. Here he met such outdoorsmen as Charley Hoffmann, who introduced him to fly-fishing; Olaf Cook, who taught him how to shoot by pointing rather than by aiming through the sights of a gun; and Jack Thompson, a logger who sang bunkhouse songs and told stories of the old days. He made a close friend in Dewey Sabin, a logger's son who lived north of the Uhrenholdts; he and Dewey fished the Totogatik River (pronounced TOE-bah-tick by the locals), explored the woods, and joined local men in shining deer, a practice that was simply taken for granted in a community where venison was an important part of the food supply. But above all of these rugged individuals, in Sigurd's estimation, stood Soren Uhrenholdt.

Soren was fifty-nine and in excellent health. His gnarled hands, tanned skin, sparkling blue eyes, and full beard gave him a physical presence to match his public prestige. Like many pioneers, he had so often of necessity performed tasks requiring strength and courage that these qualities were simply assumed as a matter of fact. There was the time, for instance, when an inexperienced woodcutter lost his grip on an ax and gashed Soren's thigh. Moving quickly before he lost too much blood, Soren plugged the wound with pitch from nearby balsam trees, then limped back to the barn, got a needle that he normally used on the livestock, and sewed stitches. After he finished, he made his way back to the house to lie down for a while.

Soren showed none of the repressive formality of L. J. Olson. He did have a temper, and when he lost it his blue eyes glittered with sparks of fire, but usually he was cheerful and engaging, a man who loved company and often invited strangers to the house. Sigurd, who could not speak to his own father about anything of consequence, found Soren most approachable, and they had many long talks, usually while strolling through the fields and woods of the Uhrenholdt farmstead.

It was during one of their first walks, on a Sunday morning in June 1917, that Sigurd learned his first lesson in conservation, and also discovered Soren's aesthetic side. Climbing high on a hill south of the farm and looking north toward the house, the Namekagon River sparkling in the sun as it wound past farm fields and stands of pine, Soren told Sigurd about his original dream for the farm. There had been practical reasons for not giving in to the timber buyers during the hard times of earlier years: the pines helped prevent erosion and kept moisture in the soil, making for better potato crops. And, by cutting selectively on his own terms, he sustained the resource while earning extra money when it was needed over a period of many years.

This was all common sense, learned in Denmark, a country famous for its tree plantations. But that morning Soren shared an additional perspective on the value of pine. Olson quoted him many years later:

> "Mother and I felt that a farmstead should be more than a place for the raising of crops and cattle," he told me. "It should have character and beauty. And we knew the pines, if they were taken care of, would give it both—a place our children would love."[3]

Soren, Sigurd wrote, "was an artist who painted with grander media than most, with fields and banks of trees, with rivers and creeks, skylines, silhouettes, and traceries of branches against the horizon."[4] He loved to sit on his back porch and watch the sunlight filter through the feathery needles of two massive white pines just a few feet away, and look out across the original clearing to a mixed stand of old-growth pine. His favorite quote was from a Danish poem: "Where the plow won't go, / And the scythe won't sing, / A tree should grow." Sigurd found in Soren Uhrenholdt an understanding father figure and his first mentor about the proper relationship between humans and the land. And he came to identify so strongly with farm living that when friends from Ashland visited him that summer he looked upon them as intruders, unfit in attire and attitude, people who did not belong.

Sigurd also noticed Elizabeth Uhrenholdt that summer. A year and a half his senior, she was slim, with wavy brown hair, striking blue eyes like her father's, and a warm smile. Elizabeth saw a more confident and engaging young man than the one who had thrown a pillow at her in the hospital—probably because at the farm Sigurd was in a setting that felt natural—and she was attracted to him. Soon they began to visit in the evenings and take long walks together. When Sigurd returned to Ashland for school in the fall, he often took the five o'clock train to Seeley to spend a couple of hours at the farm, and then took the nine o'clock train back home. On weekends he frequently went down for a whole day.

Not that Sigurd spent all of this time with Elizabeth. "He wasn't a man that just persisted in courtship to a girl," she recalled years later. "His passion was for the outdoors." He would often spend time hunting or fishing with Dewey Sabin or Andrew Uhrenholdt or some of his other friends before visiting Elizabeth. "I never really dated him," she recalled. "He was just visiting us at the farm. Then I'd visit him up at his own home." Still, she quickly grew attached to him, and assumed they would marry.

❖

Sigurd began his second year at Northland College in September 1917 against a backdrop of world war. The United States had entered "the war to end all wars" on April 6; on May 17 President Woodrow Wilson signed the Selective Service Act, mandating that men between the ages of twenty-one and thirty register for potential military service. Kenneth Olson was among those affected, and, like countless others, as the fighting grew more intense during the fall of 1917, he decided he could not wait any longer. On December 1 he enlisted as a private in the 409th Motor Supply Train of the Army's Sanitary Corps.[5]

Sigurd, who at eighteen was three years too young for the draft, remained active in a sophomore class that had shrunk to sixteen students from the forty-five freshmen of a year before. He was secretary of the YMCA, first bass in the Glee Club (which often practiced at Sigurd's house, his mother playing the piano), and assistant manager of the college newspaper. Northland had no football team that year, but Sigurd joined the basketball team and played second-string forward. None of these activities, however, had as much of an impact on him as did his participation in Northland's Dramatic Club. His association with this group possibly called into question for the first time the cultural and religious conventions under which he had been raised and threatened his budding relationship with Elizabeth Uhrenholdt.

During September and October, the club studied the history and technique of drama from the eighteenth century to modern times. Then, in November, the group began working on a production of Henrik Ibsen's *A Doll's House*. This was a daring choice at a conservative Christian college, for the play champions the testing of personal visions of truth against received truth of any kind. The director and faculty adviser to the group, Ruth Hitter, endured heavy criticism.[6]

The lead female role of Nora Helmer requires someone who can appear both girlish and seductive; Hitter chose freshman Kathryn Darke. With her dimpled chin, mischievous smile, and bedroom eyes, she made, as the school yearbook later put it, "an ideal Nora." The lead male role of Nora's husband, Torvald Helmer, demands someone who can convincingly display a narrow, rigid worldview, the epitome of the Victorian businessman. Hitter picked Sigurd Olson.

In unused portions of his memoirs Olson recalled just two points about his role in Ibsen's play. He described how he walked through the woods playacting the role of Torvald Helmer, and he recalled his excitement at receiving applause for his stage performance. But he hardly could have found a play that more strongly exposed the circumstances of his own upbringing. Ibsen's play, perceived by many as an attack on marriage and religion, portrayed a world in which most people—like Torvald Helmer—traded their individuality for rote formulas of thought and behavior. They allowed themselves to live like toys in a doll house, trapped in the enervating security of roles and stereotypes and social conventions. In Ibsen's view, only a relative few ultimately refused to be defined and delimited by other people's prescripted roles and beliefs. But while that refusal was necessary to gain freedom from the doll's house, it came at a cost, for with it came a sense of alienation that could not be cured until the individual created a new moral compass with which to chart his or her human destiny.[7]

During the final, climactic moments of the play, Nora decides to take a leap of faith into the void and leave Helmer and their children. Getting ready to go out the door, she tells Helmer that her duties to herself are just as sacred as her duties to them. Helmer, in desperation, appeals to her religious beliefs. The strategy fails:

> HELMER: Are you not clear about your place in your own home? Have you not an infallible guide in questions like these? Have you not religion?
> NORA: Oh, Torvald, I don't really know what religion is.
> HELMER: What do you mean?
> NORA: I know nothing but what Pastor Hansen told me when I was confirmed. He explained that religion was this and that. When I get away from all this and stand alone, I will look into that matter too. I will see whether what he taught me is right, or, at any rate, whether it is right for me.[8]

In Northland College's production of *A Doll's House,* Sigurd played the role of Torvald Helmer; his own experience, however, more closely resembled that of Nora. He knew what it was like to live in a house where "doing the right thing" meant following a prescribed formula, not the heart, where he was expected to live dutifully the role of a minister's son, to conform to the image created by others, and then, at adulthood, to assume one of the three careers prescribed by his father. He already had shown some small signs of rebellion, especially in his betrayal of the football team. It is quite possible that he did not sense this as a rebellion of any sort, but his recent experiences with the farmers and loggers of the Namekagon Valley *had* begun to open his eyes to the possibility of a richer, more genuine life than the one envisioned for him by his father. Ultimately, he would have to choose.

❖

Sigurd became infatuated with Kathryn Darke during that autumn of 1917. It is not unusual for performers in a stage production to develop romantic relationships; they work long and hard together under stressful conditions, and the emotions they are asked to unleash on stage can contribute to a charged atmosphere offstage as well. But it is also possible that he was attracted to her in her role as Nora, a woman who abandoned conventional norms for the open horizons of her dreams. Whatever the attraction, Sigurd wrote a breezy letter to Elizabeth Uhrenholdt, describing his new relationship and saying that Elizabeth would always be like a sister to him. Elizabeth was churning butter when the letter came. Her heartache was still painful to recall many years later.

Sigurd soon regretted the letter. When he went out on a date with Kathryn and some other friends, he was shocked and dismayed when she and the others pulled out some liquor and began drinking. Sigurd refused to join in; he left them and walked home in the cold night air. He was not prepared to take notions of freedom and free thinking so far as to break with the Swedish Baptist injunction against alcohol. But liberty and convention were at war within him, and he would complain of the conflict all his life.

Sigurd soon wrote Elizabeth Uhrenholdt an apologetic letter. She did not respond, nor did she answer any of the other letters he sent during the rest of the school year. They did not see each other again until Sigurd returned to the Uhrenholdt farm to work there the following summer. By then, as Elizabeth recalled years later, "he was a lot more attentive." Meanwhile, Sigurd experienced the pain of Elizabeth's rejection and also the loss of his beloved Grandmother Cederholm in March 1918. "Nu Sigurd, kan du inte fiska for mig mer," she said in her last words to him—"Now, Sigurd, you cannot fish for me any more."[9]

❖

During the fall of 1917, as Olson had begun practicing his role of Torvald Helmer, the news from Europe was bleak. The Germans and Austrians had captured more than a quarter of a million prisoners in Italy in October, and by the end of November the British had suffered three hundred thousand casualties in Flanders. The Bolshevik Revolution, meanwhile, took the Russians out of the war and left the Germans free to prepare for a massive assault on the western front. The United States responded to the pleas of its allies by greatly speeding up inductions and troop shipments. It was a deadly race: on March 21, 1918, the Germans began their offensive, and in three weeks took over twelve hundred square miles of French territory. Kenneth Olson, who got to France at the end of February, was a relatively early arrival. Soon U.S. troops began pouring in by the thousands every day, eventually reaching a total of two million.

The war was the most horrific ever seen, with single battles sometimes producing a couple of hundred thousand casualties. More Germans died in the four-month Battle of the Somme than Americans in the entire four years of the U.S. Civil War. New technology made the devastation possible. Submarines, warplanes, howitzers, and poison gas often killed as many civilians as combatants, while flame throwers, tanks, and machine guns made the battlefield far bloodier than ever before. Nevertheless, in America, far from the front, the war was romanticized as a glorious adventure and a noble crusade, and young men saw it as their chance to live the heroic life of their Civil War grandparents. The heady propaganda was everywhere: in such best-selling books as *The Glory of the Trenches,* in such movies as *Pershing's Crusaders,* and in song after popular song. *Over there, over there / Send the word, send the word, over there, / That the Yanks are coming . . .*

For the few who resisted the call, or even showed less than enthusiastic support, the romantic patriotism quickly became a gross caricature. At the most benign level of intimidation, those who did not enlist risked being called "slackers." In many cities around the country, thugs and "100 percenters"—encouraged by President Woodrow Wilson's claims that German spies filled America's "unsuspecting communities," and by federal actions that sharply curtailed civil liberties—attacked anything that smacked of German influence. Sometimes the actions were laughable, as when Pittsburgh banned Beethoven's music, or when a Milwaukee suburb changed its pronunciation from "New Ber-LIN" to "New BER-lin." Mostly, though, they were repugnant: people beaten up for not standing during the Pledge of Allegiance, horsewhipped for not subscribing to the Red Cross, imprisoned for circulating pamphlets critical of the draft.

Ashland and nearby towns were not immune to such acts. On February 19, 1918, someone broke into Bayfield High School and destroyed all the German textbooks. On April 1, a mob kidnapped a Northland College professor because of rumors that he had made disloyal comments. More likely, it was simply his German name, Schimler, that got him into trouble. Masked men took him a half mile out of town, tarred and feathered him, and then released him. The college, rather than defend the professor, fired him the next day. Within a week two more tar and featherings took place.

Sigurd Olson, by nature a romantic, got caught up in the war's popular mystique. He especially enjoyed the best-selling book of verse *Rhymes of a Red Cross Man* and began a lifelong devotion to the author, Robert Service. *Rhymes* was full of the terrors of war, but in the context of adventure, heroism, and romance:

> But if there's horror, there's beauty, wonder;
> The trench lights gleam and the rockets play.
> That flood of magnificent orange yonder
> Is a battery blazing miles away.
> With a rush and a singing a great shell passes,
> The rifles resentfully bicker and brawl,
> And here I crouch in the dew-drenched grasses,
> And look and listen and love it all.[10]

When Sigurd turned nineteen on April 4, 1918, he was still two years below draft age, but he had paid visits to the recruiting station in Ashland and wanted badly to enlist. His parents, however, were dead set against it. When school ended in June, he returned to the Uhrenholdt farm for another summer of work. Midway through the summer, though, a crisis developed: Andrew Uhrenholdt enlisted. Watching Andrew join the 333rd Machine Gun Battalion was more than Sigurd could stand; he *had* to enlist. A tense long-distance argument ensued between Sigurd and his parents in the days that followed. Ida May, fearing that Sigurd—momma's boy—would enlist despite her and L. J.'s opposition, ultimately played her trump card: she claimed she was having a heart attack. Sigurd hurried back to Ashland, getting a ride from Jens Uhrenholdt. When he got to his mother's bedside, she pleaded with him not to join the army. If he needed to do something patriotic, she said, he could spend the rest of the summer working at the nearby munitions plant, the Barksdale Works.[11]

Under enormous pressure, despite realizing that his mother was not as ill as she claimed, Sigurd agreed. But he resented her manipulation. As Sigurd's son Robert described it decades later, "*Big brother* went off to Europe, but not Sigurd. Sigurd was kept on a short leash. And all his pals, you know, going off to get themselves killed in a glorious fight over in France. Andrew had joined up. But he should not leave mother because he had promised." Elizabeth Uhrenholdt Olson vividly remembered the tension: "That was the hardest thing he ever held against his mother. That was very hard for him. That was *very* hard for him. He never quite forgave her, I think."

Olson easily found a job at the Barksdale Works. The factory was the world's largest producer of TNT, used in making dynamite. It began operating in 1905, supplying explosives for Minnesota's iron mines and Michigan's iron and copper mines. The war had necessitated a huge expansion, and 1918 was the factory's biggest year, so there were plenty of jobs. Sigurd was one of six thousand employees.[12]

If Ida May Olson thought her son's job at the Barksdale Works would be free from danger, she was gravely mistaken. Among the health problems were constant headaches from working in unventilated powder buildings. Chemicals often were poorly kept and easily misused. But such dangers were minor compared to the risk of explosions. When Sigurd began work as a lead burner's assistant, he noticed what must have been an uncomfortable sight: the TNT fortifying buildings were surrounded by gigantic rock and sand embankments to help keep explosions from destroying other buildings. The risk was much greater than he was likely to have realized: at about 10:00 A.M. on August 2 a TNT building was "blown to atoms," as the *Ashland Daily Press* put it. Two men in the building, and four nearby, were killed, five of them instantly. Sigurd worked the night shift, so he was not present that time, but one night a fortifying plant blew just as he was approaching. He dove to the ground, and in a moment bits of the building and the body of a man dropped down beside him. Surprisingly, the man was not dead, but his clothes had been burned off and he was in shock. Sigurd dragged him to a safer spot and then ran for help.

❖

In the fall of 1918, Sigurd was admitted to the University of Wisconsin at Madison, where he hoped to complete his agricultural degree. Meanwhile, in August, Congress extended the draft-eligible age brackets to cover all men ages eighteen to forty-five. This made thirteen million people suddenly eligible, and they were required to register September 12. Sigurd had one more chance to enter the war. The U.S. War Department, in need of officers and specialists, had arranged with two hundred and fifty colleges and universities to create a Students Army Training Corps (SATC), and the University of Wisconsin was one of the campuses involved in the program. Sigurd would get to enlist in the corps as soon as he got to school, while his parents could take some comfort in the knowledge that he would not go overseas until at least the following April and possibly much later, if he were among those chosen for additional officer training. Furthermore, the government would pay Olson's tuition and fees and provide room and board, plus a private's salary of thirty dollars a month.

More than twenty-two hundred men joined the SATC at the University of Wisconsin during registration week at the beginning of October. Sigurd rode the train down from Ashland, feeling nostalgic about the familiar sights he was leaving behind and undoubtedly excited about his entry into the military. The campus, frequently criticized during the previous two years for its wartime apathy and sometimes portrayed as a hotbed of disloyal radicals, was now almost completely militarized. Course offerings were cut but faculty teaching loads increased as the campus revamped its programs to offer the required military courses. In addition to a number of biological and physical science classes, the key courses included topography and map making, surveying, mechanical and freehand drawing, military law, hygiene, sanitation, and a course of pure propaganda called War Aims. SATC students operated under strict military discipline, wearing uniforms, living in barracks, and following a military schedule from reveille at 6:45 A.M. to lights out at 10:00 P.M.[13]

Olson received combat training from a sergeant who had spent two years in France and always referred to Germans as Krauts. Every day at Camp Randall, Sigurd's group practiced, learning how to fire rifles and Gatling guns, and how to fight with bayonets. A few photos of Olson in uniform survive. He looks bright and happy in all of them; in one, he has an especially broad smile on his face as he thrusts a bayoneted rifle at the camera. But the training was earnest and deadly and very real, for the United States at that time was engaged in the largest military offensive in its history. More than half a million American soldiers—along with nearly a hundred thousand horses and thousands of vehicles and artillery pieces—were attacking a twenty-four-mile front from the river Meuse to the Argonne forest in an attempt to cut off German rail lines. The Meuse-Argonne offensive was the American contribution to an enormous Allied assault along the entire Western front. The fighting went on for nearly fifty days, producing one hundred and seventeen thousand American casualties. The largest American graveyard in Europe would be built in the middle of the battlefield at Romagne Heights, with more than fourteen thousand soldiers buried there.

The Allied offensive was intended to produce a smashing, quick victory and end the war. It was not quick, but it did achieve the main goal. On November 11, 1918, the signing of the armistice brought closure to a war that was meant to end all wars but that would, in time, come to be called the *first* world war. There was joy in the streets and homes of America, but not for Sigurd Olson. Years later he recalled what he did upon hearing of the armistice: "I went to my bunk in the barracks and wept without shame for my dream of going to war was over."[14]

Olson's tour of duty as a private in the army officially ended on December 14, 1918, when he was discharged. He had served nine weeks and five days. Meanwhile, his big brother had achieved the rank of first lieutenant and was writing letters home about the elegant hotels he was staying at in France and the wonderful things he was seeing: Notre Dame and other cathedrals, museums, and parks. In fact, many Americans in France saw no fighting, and instead were treated to French wine, women, and song—under a modicum of military supervision, of course.

Had Sigurd gone to war perhaps he would have had his chance to be a hero, or, like his brother, the pleasure of experiencing French culture. But the odds of such a romantic fate were not as good as he preferred to imagine. For every ten American soldiers killed on the battlefield, eight died as victims of the worst worldwide influenza pandemic of modern times. Called the Spanish influenza because it was first publicly recognized in Spain, the flu and its related complications—pneumonia, mostly—killed at least twenty million people in its yearlong assault, which began in the spring of 1918. It hit its victims so fast that they often literally drowned in the fluids produced by their own bodies, gasping for breath with swollen lungs, their skin turning a color that gave the disease its other nickname, "the purple death." It claimed forty-three thousand American soldiers who had dreamed of the chance to be heroes. Among them was Andrew Uhrenholdt, who died in England at the end of September, en route to France. He had just turned twenty-five.

With the war over and his discharge imminent, Sigurd had to look for a job to help pay his tuition and had to find new living quarters. He got part-time work waiting on tables at fraternity houses and occasionally found other odd jobs, and he moved into the university's YMCA at 740 Langdon Street. This was a prime recruiting location for student religious groups, and Olson soon discovered and joined the Student Volunteers, American Protestantism's most important missionary organization. Formed in the late 1880s, the Student Volunteer Movement had vowed to evangelize the entire world within a generation. The Madison chapter's meetings sometimes featured missionaries who had just returned from the wilds of India, Africa, and the Amazon; their stories so excited Olson that he seriously began to consider becoming a missionary himself, and he became so enthusiastically active a member of the Student Volunteers that the chapter soon elected him to serve as its president. But at the very moment when it seemed as though he had found himself and his goal in life, he was assailed by doubts. As his junior year of college was coming to a close, Sigurd Olson opened the door of the doll's house for the first time and faced the void beyond.

The details are sketchy, but eleven years later, in the journal he had just started keeping, he recalled this period and wrote that "when new ideas of religion became mine" his faith and hope were "shattered."[15] What these ideas were and where they came from, he did not say. They do not seem to have come from his classes; he was taking an animal husbandry course called "Beef and Dairy Cattle," a course in modern European political history, a physics course called "Mechanics and Heat, Electricity and Magnetism," a basic soil science course about soil physics and fertility, and public speaking. No theory of evolution here, no modern psychological debates about the existence of the human soul or free will, no anthropological treatises on the cultural creation of God. Of course, just by attending the University of Wisconsin, Sigurd may have come into contact with these ideas, even if they were not part of his classes.[16]

Perhaps when he wrote about "new ideas of religion" he simply meant he was exposed to versions of Christianity that made him question his fundamentalist upbringing. Certainly the YMCA and the Student Volunteers were not only for Baptists. But his journal recollection makes the problem seem much deeper than that. He wrote that he would climb to the roof of the YMCA and look down on Lake Mendota and the city lights or up at the stars and "pray and battle with my God." He continued:

> Never will I forget the heights to which my exaltation brought me or the depths of despair that were mine. Upon descending from the pinnacle for a time my fancy carried me along the heights but not for long. Soon I was again in the commonplace and then came a sense of failure and futility. I wanted to know God. I wanted to see him. I could feel his presence but did not know.

As his doubts increased, Sigurd began to think that his excitement about the missionary life had more to do with his love of wild places than with a desire to save souls. The issue came to a head the night before he was to publicly declare his intent to become a missionary. Once again he climbed to the top of the YMCA to fight his inner battle. The pressure must have been tremendous: to change his mind now not only would upset his friends and advisers in the Student Volunteers, but also would make him L. J. Olson's second son to reject the ministry. Kenneth had decided he would go into journalism after completing his military service, despite L. J.'s strongly stated desire that he become a minister. (Late in life, Kenneth would write to Sigurd, "Dad and I never got along.")[17]

It was a story many young adults of the times would have understood. As a second-generation Swedish American, Sigurd was in conflict with his immigrant parents, trying to figure out his identity in a new world of American values, beliefs, and ways of life. His parents had grown up in Sweden and could live off the old culture. Sigurd had spent his childhood moving from one town to another, with no extended family or sense of place to keep him rooted in tradition. Growing up in a country where almost everything was called into question, Sigurd was at a loss for answers.

Before that night was over, Sigurd made his decision. The next morning he quit the Student Volunteers. As he recalled in his journal eleven years later:

> At last in despair I gave up my dream as a missionary and life's castles crashed around me. Doomed as it seemed to a commonplace existence I gave myself halfheartedly to my work and hung doggedly on. . . . I had not yet developed the philosophy that would have made it possible to override my despair.

❖ Three ❖

A Rolling Stone

1920–1923

Sigurd completed his course work at the university without any sense of direction. A summer job in 1919 with the Wisconsin Geological Survey gave him a new interest, which he pursued by taking a yearlong introductory geology course, but his major field of animal husbandry had lost its luster. In a draft of *Open Horizons,* he would recall his agricultural courses as "a far cry from what the farm had really meant, its romance and beauty, the feeling of being a pioneer."[1] Worse for him, however, was his loss of religious identity, because with it had gone his sense of mission in life. "Doomed to a commonplace existence," was how he put it, and Sigurd Olson never could stand the thought of being common. But in his last year at the university, with no career in mind that excited him, Olson did not distinguish himself. In his final semester he earned a C average, a full grade below his work of a year earlier.

Nevertheless, shortly before he graduated in June 1920, he was offered a job teaching animal husbandry, agricultural botany, and geology at high schools in the two neighboring northern Minnesota cities of Nashwauk and Keewatin. It may have been his only offer; there is no record of any others. Olson accepted and was excited to see on a map that the cities were surrounded by lakes and woods.

Located about sixty miles northwest of Duluth, Nashwauk and Keewatin were among the twenty cities built along the nation's mother lode of iron ore, the Mesabi Range. Starting southwest of Grand Rapids along the line separating Itasca and Cass Counties, the Mesabi zigzagged northeasterly for a hundred miles. In some places the band of ore was ten miles wide, although usually it was a narrower two or three miles wide. Three dozen mines operated on the Mesabi; by 1916 they accounted for half of the nation's total production of iron ore. In the sixty-year period from 1890 to 1950, Mesabi Range mines shipped 1.7 billion tons of ore, without which the United States could not have become a great industrial nation. Nashwauk and Keewatin were at the heart of that power, and their mines pumped ore down the railroad arteries to Duluth, where it was loaded on ships and sent eastward across the Great Lakes.[2]

In August 1920 Sigurd took the train from Madison to Nashwauk, his primary place of employment. He arrived late in the afternoon, found a room, and set out to explore the area. Just north of town he found a nice overlook on top of a high dump created by the excavation of an open pit iron ore mine. Looking back toward town, he could see the large brown brick high school, two white churches, and rows of modest houses built close together. All around he could see the ugliness of open pit mining: gaping holes, dumps, and treeless hills. But to the north he could see a lone dirt road that disappeared into the woods.

As soon as the first week of classes was over, Sigurd packed his camping gear and followed that road to its end, then took off cross country. He camped that night under a big spruce, making a bed of boughs. It became a weekly routine: he would take off on Friday afternoon and return Sunday night, sometimes even Monday morning. He waited all week for the opportunity to leave for the woods, according to early drafts of his memoir: "I had no professional pride in what I was supposed to do, no sense of mission. I would do whatever was required of me, but that was all. . . . In town I had a job to do, but out there was where I really lived."[3]

It was a renewal of his Daniel Boone days. He read books by Jack London, Rex Beach, Enos Mills, Ernest Thompson Seton, and, especially, James Oliver Curwood and patterned himself after the protagonists. He bought a rifle to hunt deer, and he also hunted rabbits and grouse and ducks. Once the weather was cold he would hang his kills high in the bare-branched trees so that wherever he hiked he had a supply of food waiting for him. He learned to track animals, and one day happened upon a pack of wolves feeding on a deer carcass. His first encounter with predation horrified him, as it would most people in a culture that portrayed wolves as bloodthirsty monsters. It would be ten years before his negative attitude about wolves and other predators changed.

His coworkers, he recalled later, were amazed that he could take off into the woods for a weekend with only tea, sugar, flour, and bacon for supplies. If they really were as surprised as he said, perhaps part of the reason had to do with his youthful looks. He appeared several years younger than his actual age of twenty-one; in fact, on the day he arrived at Nashwauk's high school for his first faculty meeting, he charged up the front steps two at a time past a teacher, who mistook him for a student and reprimanded him.

Such youthfulness would naturally make it more difficult to achieve the respect of fellow teachers and superiors, and Sigurd does not seem to have made the effort. In an early draft of *Open Horizons* he recalls how his days at school "seemed interminable"; he wanted to be outdoors. "I remember golden days in the fall when the skies were blue and the leaves drifting down when it seemed impossible to stay on," he wrote. And he apparently made his feelings known to those around him: "I developed a reputation as a sort of crackpot, never content without a pack on my back."[4]

By themselves, these statements would require cautious interpretation, for Sigurd Olson tended to dramatize, but the journal he kept regularly in the 1930s and 1940s makes clear the essential truth of his recollection: he hated to be indoors for long periods. Out in the wild he found peace and contentment that eluded him everywhere else. And if his obsession seemed strange to other teachers, it also did not make him attractive to the young women of Nashwauk. Despite his good looks and bachelor status, he was considered a poor choice as a potential date because he wanted to spend his Friday and Saturday nights outdoors rather than dancing or going to the movie theater. Not that he would have said yes: Sigurd intended to marry Elizabeth Uhrenholdt. But by the end of his first year at Nashwauk his obsession with the wilderness became an issue with her, too, and once again he almost lost her.

In his wanderings northwest of Nashwauk he had run across a miner named Al Kennedy, who lived in a cabin on McCarty Lake. Olson would recall in his memoirs that Kennedy had served time in prison for murder but was pardoned by President Theodore Roosevelt because of evidence suggesting self-defense. Kennedy invited

Sigurd to visit any time and offered free use of another cabin he owned on a lake named after him. This squat little cabin on Kennedy Lake about ten miles northwest of town became Sigurd's base camp on weekends, and he and Al Kennedy became good friends. So good, in fact, that before the school year was over Kennedy invited Sigurd to come with him to the Flin Flon region of Manitoba for a year or two or three and pan for gold.

For a devotee of James Oliver Curwood, this was an offer hard to resist. The Flin Flon was part of the western Canada myth popularized by Curwood in such novels as *Steele of the Royal Mounted:*

> This was Le Pas—the wilderness! Beyond it, just over the frozen river which lay white and silent before him, stretched that endless desolation of romance and mystery which he had grown to love, a world of deep snows, of silent-tongued men, of hardship and battle for life where the law of nature was the survival of the fittest. . . . Never did Philip Steele's heart throb with the wild, free pulse of life and joy as in such moments as these, when his fortune, his clubs, and his friends were a thousand miles away, and he stood on the edge of the big northern Unknown.[5]

Sigurd badly wanted to go, but Elizabeth delivered an ultimatum: if he went to Manitoba she would not wait around for him to return.[6]

Elizabeth would say after Sigurd's death that she regretted making him choose between her and the Flin Flon because his dream of traveling through the Far North haunted him for decades. He turned down Kennedy's offer. He also told Elizabeth that if they were to marry she had to understand his deep need to spend a lot of time outdoors. Elizabeth's mother, Kristine Uhrenholdt, urged her not to rush into the marriage. "Sigurd belongs in school for a couple of years yet and not as the head of a family," she wrote on February 18, 1921. "And if your love is not so strong but that it grows cold in a couple of years then it is better that you never are married. Life is not *play*, my girl, *remember* that, and even in the heavens of the warmest and truest love can come dark clouds." It was a prescient warning. Nevertheless, Elizabeth and Sigurd began planning an August wedding.[7]

❖

Although Al Kennedy could not convince Olson to come with him to Manitoba, he did give Sigurd a tip that would change his life. The wild country north of Nashwauk, he said, was nowhere near as impressive as the forested lake land to the northeast along the Minnesota-Ontario border. There one could find real wilderness, with waterways leading all the way to Hudson Bay. Kennedy told Sigurd that once he saw this canoe country he would want to spend his life there. Other people in the Nashwauk area confirmed Kennedy's opinion and added anecdotes of their own about the border region's incomparable beauty. Olson decided he had to see for himself. When his first year as a teacher came to an end in June 1921, he and four friends took off for the canoe country. They planned to rent canoes in Winton, Minnesota, a once-booming logging town with central access to the wilderness, and then spend ten days traveling the international border until they reached the former fur trade outpost of Grand Portage at Lake Superior.

But Olson nearly died before his first canoe trip got under way. Arriving in Winton on Thursday, June 16, Sigurd and his friends were disappointed to discover there were no canoes available for rent until the next day. Meanwhile, they found a campsite about two miles away, where the waters of the Kawishiwi River plunged over a precipice into Fall Lake. It was sunny, buggy, and hot, so everyone went swimming above the falls. Sigurd got dangerously close, and the current pulled him toward the edge. He struggled desperately to escape, and had he not succeeded, he surely would have been smashed on the rocks at the bottom of the falls and killed.

The trip itself proved much safer, and Olson saw a cross section of the canoe country. There were lakes where the water, though clean, took on the color of weak tea, steeped in the nutrients leaching from tamaracks and spruce, and there were spring-fed lakes where the water was crystal clear. There were ill-defined shorelines of nearly impenetrable marshes and bogs, and—most of the time—wooded shores highlighted by rugged rock formations. Glacier-strewn boulders lay everywhere, some as big as a cabin. Sometimes pines grew right out of the top of these Pleistocene discards, their roots sprawled over the boulder's surface, digging into fissures. There were islands of all conceivable shapes and sizes, from weathered chunks of bare granite protruding out of the water—a favorite with gulls—to thickly forested behemoths that stretched for two miles.

It was not all pristine. For the first thirty miles that they paddled along the border, from the west end of the immense Basswood Lake to the glacial gash called Knife Lake, the shoreline had in recent years been clear-cut on the American side, stripped of two- and three-hundred-year-old red and white pine. Stumps, brush, and saplings remained, along with a few isolated stands of evergreens. The ancient pines continued to thrive on the Canadian shoreline of these same lakes, making it difficult to get lost: the trees marked north as clearly as did Polaris at night.

Beyond the cutover, however, the forest was beautiful on both sides of the border. In addition to the tall pines, there were miles of spruce and balsam fir, infusing the air with a sweet perfume. There were gnarled jack pines along the shores, with tightly curled cones waiting for a fire to release their seeds. There were the flat-needled white cedars, aromatic and mysterious. Stands of aspen and birch provided a lively leaf melody when a breeze stirred, and a visual contrast to the dark foliage of the evergreens. Sometimes in the evening, just before the sun dropped below the horizon, its rays reflected off the water and cast a shimmering golden light on the shoreline rocks and trees; the birches, in particular, were suffused, their glow containing a tinge of pink not seen on darker trunks.

And there was wildlife. In his short journal from the trip, Olson did not mention seeing any of the black bears that lived in the canoe country, but he and his friends heard wolves howl at night. They saw deer and moose, including one bull moose that charged them at the narrows leading into Birch Lake. There were chipmunks and red squirrels and Canada jays at the campsites, and ducks and loons on the lakes and overhead. Bald eagles and ospreys nested in tall pines, and great blue herons stalked fish in the shallows.

It was not all fun. Sigurd's journal mentions a couple of nights that were sleepless because of mosquitoes, two times when he and his friends spent hours searching for their next portage, and painful portaging because they had to use their paddles for yokes. But an entry written halfway through the trip while they were windbound on a rocky island in Sea Gull Lake shows that he was drawn to this land:

This is beautiful. Everything is as God made it, untouched by man. My dreams have come true. I've seen real wild country and have not been disappointed. Lib would love this and if possible we will spend a week or so on Brule Lake after we are married. I can't help but continuously think of when I get home and Lib waiting for her man.

The men did not go all the way to Lake Superior. They cut their projected route of over a hundred miles by about a third, apparently because Sigurd had made a promise to Elizabeth to meet her at a specified time and he was worried about being late. After traveling about forty miles along the border to Saganaga Lake, the party turned south toward Sawbill Lake. As it was they barely made it, and he had a long hike out of the woods to catch a train to Seeley. "Hate to go in a way but a promise is a promise," he wrote.

Al Kennedy had predicted that Sigurd Olson would fall in love with the canoe country, and he was right. As soon as Olson completed the trip he began planning his next one. He decided to introduce Elizabeth to the wilderness on their honeymoon.

❖

The wedding took place at the Uhrenholdt farm on August 8, 1921. Sigurd wore a dark three-piece suit and a corsage on his lapel, Elizabeth a calf-length white gown. L. J. Olson performed the ceremony in the Uhrenholdts' living room, which had windows overlooking the farm. Elizabeth would remember being distracted by the family's herd of cows walking back and forth in the distance.[8]

Sigurd and Elizabeth did not announce their honeymoon plans until the day of the wedding. Elizabeth's parents were horrified and tried to convince them to go to one of the nearby resorts instead. Elizabeth had never been on a canoe trip, and Sigurd had planned a three-week voyage. But Soren and Kristine could not change the newlyweds' minds. After spending several days in Nashwauk, where they made arrangements for a new apartment, Sigurd and Elizabeth took a train to Winton. They purchased their supplies from J. C. Russell's outfitting company, and Elizabeth dashed off a letter to her parents: "I mustn't write much, Sig is in a hurry to start so we can make camp tonight. . . . Remember I love you even though you don't hear for three weeks." Kristine Uhrenholdt wrote to another daughter, Johanne, "I am a bit anxious about how it will go for Elizabeth to sleep outside in a tent these cold nights."

They started along the same border route that Olson had traveled two months earlier, then eventually turned north and explored the Canadian portion of the canoe country. But Sigurd soon found that Elizabeth could not keep up with him. Well before he was ready to stop for the night, she would ask if their campsite was near; to keep her going, he would respond that it was around the next point. When they reached that spot, he would say that they would go on a little farther. By the third day of their trip Elizabeth was so tired and sore they had to lay over for a day.

"Sig was about scared to death for fear I was going to be really sick," she recalled. "I got more toast and tea—I got all the attention." After she recovered, they kept to a more realistic pace and stayed out for three weeks as planned, although not entirely without incident: at a portage leading out of Ottertrack Lake they both were frightened—especially Elizabeth—by a sign that said "Wild Man, last seen east just across the portage." They realized it could be a hoax, but nevertheless did not feel at ease until they were safely across and back in their canoe.

After the Olsons completed their trip, they stopped to look at the local high school, located three miles south of Winton in the city of Ely. Sigurd was beginning to think of ways to earn a living near the canoe country. Then they rode a bus to Nashwauk and got situated in a small upper flat near the high school.

❖

Once classes were under way, Sigurd resumed spending his weekends outdoors, leaving Elizabeth alone in their flat. One of the neighbors was so bothered by this that she called Elizabeth and said, "You ought to tame Sig." Yet Elizabeth, recalling this period of their marriage, always maintained that she accepted the arrangement, although she admitted to times when Sigurd's absence bothered her. The first such occasion was November 13, 1921, her twenty-fourth birthday, just three months after the wedding. Sigurd was out hunting deer and returned home hours late. Elizabeth felt very hurt until she heard his explanation: he had wounded a deer and felt that he had to track it until he found it and put it out of its misery.

Yet as far as Sigurd was concerned, he was not spending *enough* time outdoors. Ever since he had given up the idea of becoming a missionary he had been searching for something to fill his life, something that would give it meaning and engage his creative spirit. He was happiest when he was outdoors, and he felt frustrated with a job that kept him inside so much and seemed to lead nowhere. The answer, he thought, might lie in a career as a writer or in a natural resources–related field.

He had first thought of becoming a writer a year earlier, in the fall of 1920. On a cold, gray November day he was walking the four miles from the high school in Keewatin back to Nashwauk and wondering what to do with his life. The answer that came to him seemed clear at the time: he would travel the wilderness and write about his experiences. He felt so happy about his decision that when he arrived in Nashwauk and stopped at a restaurant for coffee a waitress took notice of his cheerful expression and joked about it. Soon he enrolled in a correspondence school writing course, but he found the books dull and the instructor critical. He continued on his own in the spring of 1921, recording some of his impressions from his trips in the woods, without putting much effort or time into it.

With the help of his older brother, he had gotten one article published in the summer of 1921. Kenneth, who had joined the *Milwaukee Journal* in 1919 as a copy editor, recently had become the resort editor, in charge of travel features. Knowing of his younger brother's interest in writing, Kenneth asked Sigurd to write a feature article about his recently completed first trip through the canoe country. The story, along with five photos, was published on July 31 under the lengthy title "Canoe Tourist Finds Joys of the Great Outdoors Through the Vast Watered Wilderness of the North." It started:

> When the Great Creator had almost finished our country He stopped in His labors and pondered. There was one thing lacking, a spot more beautiful than the rest, where His children could come and soothe their weary spirits far from the smoke of cities and the discordant glamour of industry, unsullied by the hand of man, for God saw all that was to happen. He saw the ravaging of our beautiful forests, the despoiling of our streams and lakes by the greedy, selfish, unthinking hands of those who know no beauty and see only in the wonders of nature the resources for filling their own already bursting coffers.

It was, as he freely admitted later in life, a poor piece of writing. Yet his byline was in print for the first time: "By Sigurd Olson"—there for the whole world to see. It would not have happened without his older brother, a fact that may have grated a bit, at least later in life, because in the final version of *Open Horizons* Sigurd dropped his brother's name from his anecdote about the event. He wrote instead that he received a letter from "the editor of the Milwaukee *Journal*" asking him to write the story. Nevertheless, when the story appeared eight days before his wedding, Sigurd excitedly pasted it on the wall of his bedroom, and during the 1921–22 school year he began to write more articles. None were published, and none survive, but Olson later recalled consciously imitating the style of James Oliver Curwood.

Writing satisfied Sigurd's needs in a way that teaching could not, but he was realistic enough to understand that one published article was no guarantee of a steady income. He came up with the idea of running a mink farm, which he thought would provide a reasonable income and more hours to write, as well as time outdoors. Elizabeth quickly dispelled the idea by pointing out that a successful mink farm would absorb virtually *all* of his time. So Sigurd came up with a different plan. This one did not address his goal of writing, but it did seem to answer his craving for more time outdoors: he would be a field geologist. To achieve this, he would go back to the University of Wisconsin and earn a master's degree in geology. Elizabeth agreed. Writing to her mother about it on December 13, 1921, she said, "I certainly realize that teaching isn't Sig's work. It isn't that he doesn't do it well, but that he hates it."

Sigurd returned to his alma mater in September 1922, but Elizabeth did not go with him. They needed an income to make his education affordable, and Elizabeth took a full-time teaching position at a grade school in Hayward, Wisconsin, ten miles south of the Uhrenholdt farm. Years later she would say with a laugh that Sigurd spent almost all of the money she earned traveling back and forth to see her on weekends.

❖

Wisconsin's graduate program in geology ranked among the nation's top five, along with those at Chicago, Columbia, Harvard, and Yale. In the specialty of hard rock geology no school was better. The program drew students from all over the United States and Canada. Despite his average undergraduate record, he had no problem being admitted; Wisconsin policy allowed anyone with a bachelor's degree from the university to enter graduate school there. Sigurd registered for six courses, four of them basic teacher training courses in the education and agronomy departments. Evidently he had not ruled out a return to teaching, even though he had quit his job with the intention of going into geology. His major courses were structural geology, taught by Charles Kenneth "C. K." Leith, and metamorphic geology, taught by Alexander Newton Winchell. Leith and Winchell were among the best-known names in the field, and the two men would leave a lasting impression on Sigurd Olson.[9]

C. K. Leith had made his reputation through survey work in northern Minnesota's iron ranges and through his work with geologist (and later University of Wisconsin president) Charles R. Van Hise in studying the world's oldest rock formations. Northern Minnesota is one of the few places in the world where 4 billion-year-old Precambrian rock lies at the surface. Leith and Van Hise worked to learn the structure and stratigraphy of these rock formations and compared their findings with those from other Precambrian sites around the world. In the process, they made the region north and west of Lake Superior the most important area for studying Precambrian formations.

Leith, a tall man with silver hair, thick black eyebrows, round wire-rimmed glasses, and an ever-present pipe, was the department chair, and he ran the program in authoritarian fashion. He was a tough teacher, too, having little patience for those who did not come to class prepared to be called upon. Yet Olson would recall him with fondness. They had in common a great love of wilderness travel. Leith not only had known the canoe country intimately, he had spent nearly a year exploring the Hudson Bay region, a place of Olson's dreams. Leith brought these experiences into his lectures with great enthusiasm, giving his geological interpretations such vividness that some students signed up for the course a second time as auditors, so they could hear him again.

"Through his eyes," Olson recalled in *Open Horizons,* "we saw the shaping of the earth over untold millions of years with nothing ever permanent or at rest. . . . Time, he told us, was the great illusion, and if we could see the earth with the perspective of eons instead of years, we would understand."

Alexander Winchell, a quiet, bespectacled man with a goatee and a mustache, was in many ways Leith's opposite. Son of famous Minnesota geologist Newton H. Winchell, he made important contributions to the field of optical mineralogy, and his textbook on the topic was considered one of the best. However, he also was considered uncreative, because his work consisted mainly of compilations of statistics. Students found him personally warm and helpful, but exceedingly dull as a teacher because he read his lectures aloud, and they were full of statistical information. Sigurd's one moment of enlightenment in the class came one day when he could stand it no longer. As he recalled in *Open Horizons:*

> "I've decided," I said, "to drop mineralogy. I like living things. All this is dead," and I pushed my tray of specimens to one side.
> "Listen," he said. "These crystals are alive, their atoms constantly moving, each one a world and a universe in itself. There is nothing dead except in your own mind."
> Shocked, I went back to work while his words pounded their way into my consciousness "crystals alive . . . moving . . . each one a world in itself"—and from that moment the science of mineralogy became a living thing; never again was I to look at a rock or a crystal without remembering.

Leith and Winchell gave Olson a deep appreciation for the earth as a living planet, with a fluidity and dynamism evident to those who could open their eyes to a perspective of time measured in billions of years. This way of thinking would become the bedrock of Olson's philosophy. But, despite Leith's engaging lectures, and despite the revelation brought on by Winchell's rebuke, Sigurd grew disenchanted with school. After one semester, he quit.

In *Open Horizons,* Olson says he left graduate school because he came to realize that "success" would mean working for mining companies, while to him geology "was a way of understanding the land itself, the key to values not to be processed or sold." Sigurd was in his sixties when he wrote that, but his 1921 article in the *Milwaukee Journal,* which began by condemning those who saw only commercial value in nature—"the resources for filling their already bursting coffers"—lends some contemporary support to the statement. But he had entered the program because he wanted to be a *field* geologist. Why did he not continue, and try his luck with the U.S. Geological Survey or one of its state counterparts?

One reason is that he was not happy at Madison. He missed Elizabeth, and he also missed the wilderness. During class field trips to sites in southwestern Wisconsin, he would separate from the group so he could sit on a scenic ridge somewhere and think. And yet he did register for a second semester of classes at the beginning of February 1923, just days before he withdrew from the university. It is possible that Olson would not have completed the program in any case, but it seems likely that he would have completed at least a second semester of course work but for one major factor: Elizabeth was pregnant. She would have found out sometime between mid-January and early February. Sigurd, then, quit school when he did not primarily because he had lost interest, but because he found out he was going to be a father. He needed to find a job and start earning money.

The timing proved fortunate. Just when Olson decided he had to look for work, the school superintendent for Ely, Minnesota, arrived in Madison hoping to fill some immediate openings. Three high school teachers had resigned because of problems with a group of unruly students, and the superintendent wanted tough young men to restore discipline. Sigurd was hired on the spot. He and Elizabeth had looked at the high school in Ely right after their honeymoon; now he would work there, and live right at the edge of the canoe country wilderness.[10]

How Sigurd's parents reacted to the news is unknown, but the Uhrenholdts were concerned. "We don't think so much about that quitting and moving around," Kristine wrote to Elizabeth's sister Johanne. "As they say a rolling stone gathers no moss. It would have been better if they had waited a year or two until Sig was a little more settled."

❖ Four ❖

Northwoods Guide

1923–1929

E ly had been carved out of the wilderness late in the 1880s after the discovery of a band of iron ore deposits that became known as the Vermilion Range. Built next to the Chandler Mine on the south side of Shagawa Lake and incorporated as a city in 1890, Ely grew rapidly during the next decade as four new mines opened and the logging industry moved in to clear the forest of white and red pine. Immigrants who worked shifts in the mines found themselves sleeping in shifts in crowded boardinghouses.[1]

For a long time it was a rough town. There were four churches but five brothels, and more than twenty saloons bearing such names as Bucket of Blood and First and Last Chance. In the spring, when two thousand lumberjacks left the woods to spend their wages, drunken men staggered about and passed out on the streets. Fistfights, stabbings, and murders were frequent and often unpunished. When the evangelist Billy Sunday visited the area early in the twentieth century, he is supposed to have declared, "The only difference between Ely and hell is that Ely has a railroad leading into it."

When the Olsons arrived in February 1923 the nation was in its third year of Prohibition, so Ely, which had grown into a city of five thousand, no longer had one tavern for every hundred people. It was a calmer place, with cement sidewalks and streetlights, a park and a community center, and the city was on the verge of building a million-dollar high school. But facilities still were not keeping up with population growth, which would peak at a little over 6,100 in 1930. Sigurd and Elizabeth moved into an ill-heated one-room structure that formerly had been a coal shed. It was so cold they wore their winter hats to bed. A few months later, they found a small house along Boundary Street on the south side of Ely. This part of town was largely undeveloped and muddy; Sigurd referred to their address as "Frog Street and Pickerel Avenue."

Olson quickly proved he could handle the ruffians at the high school. In his first biology class several of the students attempted to take advantage of their new teacher. Sigurd initially tried ignoring them. When that did not work, he grabbed one of the miscreants, hauled him out of his chair, and flung him out the door. Then Olson turned to the class and said sternly, "Next?" He had no more trouble.

By most accounts, Sigurd was a popular teacher. John Smrekar, who became one of Olson's most outspoken opponents on wilderness issues, described him as friendly and fair. This was a common refrain among other former students, although Esther Ahonen qualified it by saying some people thought Sigurd favored the girls when he gave out grades. Olson could be tough on students who misbehaved or skipped classes or slouched or failed to work hard, and some students did not like him because of it. But for the serious student who was having troubles, Olson often went out of his way to help.[2]

Simon Bourgin was one such student. A bookworm and a talented writer, Bourgin suffered through chemistry during his last semester in high school. He failed the course and would not have graduated, but Olson intervened and convinced the chemistry teacher to change the grade. Bourgin went on to become a respected international journalist. "Sig was one of the lodestones of my life," he said.

For Bourgin, Olson's importance as a teacher went far beyond changing a bad grade. Bourgin grew up in one of Ely's five Jewish families. It was a city of intense ethnic loyalties: there was a Finnish side of town and a Slovenian side of town, and the Jews often felt out of place and unwanted. They were scorned as "Christ killers" by a priest at St. Anthony's Catholic Church and daily subjected to more subtle forms of prejudice. Olson was kind to Bourgin, and the two found they had something in common that relatively few in the city shared: a love of reading and discussing ideas. "Sig was kind of an intellectual island up in Ely," Bourgin recalled. When Bourgin was a teenager he shared and discussed with Olson novels by such authors as Ernest Hemingway, Theodore Dreiser, and John Dos Passos. Olson was a careful, if selective, reader of serious nonfiction, but his reading of fiction until then had consisted almost entirely of pulp outdoor adventure novels. Bourgin widened his literary horizons.

In the classroom, Sigurd appears to have been a better than average lecturer, not exciting to all of his students but appealing to many, and making lasting impressions on a few. Ruth Rothman described him as soft-spoken but wonderful, a teacher who commanded students' attention. Bill Rom agreed. "He was a natural speaker," Rom said. "His lectures were very flowery—that's the only way I can describe them. He made them interesting." Eugene Laitala went even further: "I have never heard better organized and more inspiring lectures."

It was *outside* the classroom, in the biology laboratory or in the field, that students found Olson most memorable. Helen Denley Barnes, writing to Olson in 1970, said she had been thinking of her youth and "my mind went back to a vividly clear picture of you":

> The environment, a somewhat dingy basement biology classroom. The population, a group of moving pieces of protoplasm . . . and the teacher, handsome in a rugged way; a gold crown that shown brighter on rainy days; an outdoor tan that was so permanent even the long winter season did not fade it . . . and a smile—oh, that smile—your very joy of living seemed to emanate from the twinkle in your eyes. You perhaps thought you were teaching us biology and I am sure that is what you were being paid to do. But for me and many others, the textbook knowledge was the least of what you imprinted in our lives. For your love of life and your keen appreciation of the beauty of the world around us was so contagious that I think only a few of your students escaped knowing a richer and deeper life because of your influence.

Barnes described Olson at his best, when he was able to convey the sense of wonder he felt in experiencing nature and in knowing the intricacies of the natural processes so drily depicted in textbooks. There is no indication that Olson was versed in the day's theories of pedagogy or that, after much reading and thought, he consciously practiced a philosophy of teaching: he just believed that biology and geology could not be taught adequately without firsthand experience. "Slides, dissection, and books were vital," he wrote in *Open Horizons,*

> but only in reference to the living world; better to know a bird, flower, or a rock in its natural setting than to rely solely on routine

identification and description. This kind of teaching had as much to do with awareness and appreciation as the actual accumulation of knowledge.[3]

Every fall and spring Olson took his classes on field trips. They visited an abandoned gold mine, a quaking bog, and various ponds, creeks, and rock formations, each time absorbing lessons that went beyond the narrow focus of the class. These outdoor excursions were the highlight of many students' memories of Olson. "It was not so much Sig Olson's classroom technique that I remember, but the way he expressed his feeling for the land and the lake country on a field trip," said Clarence Ivonen:

> I remember Sig Olson explaining glacier markings on some rocky ridge near Ely. His hand rubbed the scratches on the rock surface lovingly as he explained how millions of years ago the ice age brought down a sheet of ice that covered the region, bringing with it boulders that ground the scratch marks on the rock we were sitting on. It was as if Sig Olson had a personal knowledge of all those aeons of time which developed the rocks and rills and lakes of his beloved lake country of northeastern Minnesota. To this day I never pass a rocky ridge anywhere that I don't look for glacier marks and recall Sig Olson's remarks.

❖

Seven months after the Olsons arrived in Ely, just before 1:00 A.M. on September 15, 1923, Elizabeth gave birth to a baby boy they named Sigurd Thorne. She went into labor after a day of paddling and portaging with her husband. The story often has been told that Sigurd earned the glares of the nursing staff when, a couple of hours after the birth, he hurried from the hospital to Shagawa Lake for the opening day of duck hunting season. Roland Erikson, a friend of Olson, went farther in a manuscript submitted to *North Country* magazine in 1951: "A son was born while Sig, with tears in his eyes, stood in a duck blind firing away to open the duck season." Neither version is accurate, as Sigurd himself made clear in a letter he wrote to Elizabeth's sister Johanne the morning of his son's birth: "Little Sig is over in the corner in his crib chuckling contentedly to himself. Guess he must be glad duck season starts tomorrow."[4]

It must have been a difficult time for Elizabeth. She was a new mother in a new town, and it is not likely that Sigurd was much help with the baby. And their first son was just two years old when, on December 23, 1925, Elizabeth gave birth to another, Robert Keith. For Elizabeth, the first few years in Ely meant the hard work of taking care of babies. But Elizabeth, like her father, easily made friends. Letters she wrote to her mother indicate that by the end of the decade she and Sigurd had a very busy social life—busy enough that Kristine Uhrenholdt worried Elizabeth might get worn out. "You are right, Momma," Elizabeth wrote in an undated letter from the period, "so many parties are very tiring, but it is just like a merry-go-round—how are we to stop, and where, and with whom?" She went on:

> People in our position can't very well choose and pick except very tactfully. This morning I was ironing and I thought, "It's going to be a nice quiet weekend . . ." I'd no sooner finished thinking than the phone rang and Dorothy had decided to have the usual crowd over for Sunday night dinner. We all contribute one dish so it isn't hard on the hostess. My part is to make rolls. Again the phone rang and Sig with three other men were asked to sing at a dance the Rebecca Lodge is giving and of course the wives must go too— impossible to refuse to entertain people. The phone rang again— would I help serve a little tea one of the women was having on Friday—"Certainly, I'd love to"—and the truth is I do enjoy helping anyone. This afternoon the phone rang again and Mrs. Sutherland (who has a beautiful home) asked if we'd come to a bridge party on Friday night. So what can one do?

Sigurd was not as outgoing as Elizabeth, but he nevertheless became active in the community. He organized two Boy Scout troops and served as scoutmaster of both, and he often helped the local Girl Scout council. He also taught English to immigrants. Of all his activities in the 1920s, however, the one with the greatest impact on his and Elizabeth's life unquestionably was his summertime work for Wilderness Outfitters.

It began in 1923. When the school term ended that June Sigurd had been on the payroll for just four months. He needed to work during the summer to supplement his income and to start saving for his and Elizabeth's first baby. Forty years later, when Sigurd recalled the events of that summer in *Open Horizons,* he added drama by saying he visited Wilderness Outfitters every day for a month, hoping for a chance to guide, and that every day he would go back to Elizabeth with the same news: no job. It appears, instead, that the company offered him a job well in advance of the end of the school year.[5]

A letter Elizabeth wrote to her mother that spring indicates that Sigurd was, in fact, seriously considering a number of options:

> There are a couple men up here who outfit the tourists for their camping trips, and they want Sig to guide for them this summer. The tourists are beginning to ask for young men of some education to whom they can talk and visit, instead of the old-timers. The men . . . said they could guarantee Sig at least $180 per month plus expenses. Of course we haven't even made up our minds about anything. He could possibly get a job in the mines for about $125 a month, but they are underground so we don't like that very much, or he could get a job with the Great Northern Power Company helping surveying. I haven't the faintest idea what we'll do yet.

Given the Olsons' need for an income, it seems unlikely that Sigurd would have turned down other job possibilities unless he was sure about the outfitting work. He may well have waited for what seemed to him a long time before he got to guide his first canoe party, but he was on the payroll all along.

Olson guided many parties that summer of 1923, and he learned, "by trial and error," as he put it, how to find his way through the poorly mapped maze of lakes and rivers that made up the canoe country. At first he copied the old-timers and did not use a tent for himself, sleeping instead on pine boughs under the canoe, with mosquito netting strung from the thwarts. Eventually, he not only slept in a tent, he also carried along a small down pillow. The other guides and even his customers teased him about this, but, he jokingly recalled, after a couple of nights out they would often try to get it away from him.

Trying to become an expert guide quickly, Olson undoubtedly focused on the basics: the major canoe routes, the best campsites, the best places to fish for walleyed pike and largemouth bass and lake trout. He became intimately familiar with the location of the international border, because he frequently had to check clients through Canadian customs on Basswood Lake and had to purchase an Ontario guide's license and learn the province's fishing regulations. He certainly knew that the Ontario portion of the canoe country was called Quetico Provincial Park, and that the Minnesota portion included Superior National Forest, which was divided into three sections. But it may have been a while before he learned the background behind the creation of these adjoining reserves.

The 1.2 million-acre Quetico, for example, was created as a pine reserve in 1909 and was declared a provincial park in 1913 to add protection for its wildlife, which was being decimated by trapping and hunting. On the American side of the border, Minnesota forestry commissioner Christopher C. Andrews convinced the U.S. government to set aside the first five hundred thousand acres in 1902. Seven years later President Theodore Roosevelt expanded the reserve to 1.4 million acres and created Superior National Forest.

Sigurd soon learned that a guide's work is never done; he rises before the members of his party do, getting coffee and breakfast ready, and goes to bed after them, staying up to check over the equipment and organize supplies for the next morning. In between, he takes the lead in paddling and portaging, sets up camp, gathers firewood, builds a fire, cooks, and washes dishes. It is tiring work, but rewarding when, as often happens, the guide builds a rapport with his party. Inevitably, however, living in close quarters for a couple of weeks without the comforts of home creates at least some moments of strain, sometimes between members of the party, and sometimes between one or more of them and the guide. A good guide knows how to manage conflict so that the trip ultimately is satisfying to the group.

Sigurd gained this knowledge the hard way. At first he tended to plan a grueling route of a hundred miles or more, then would keep to it no matter what. Perhaps he was trying to impress the customers and other guides with his prowess, or perhaps he thought his citified parties *wanted* a rugged workout. One time, however, after two days of battling stormy weather in an attempt to keep to the schedule—days in which tempers got shorter and shorter—Olson threw out his plans and led his party to a beautiful campsite where they happily stayed for a whole week. From then on he avoided trying to break distance records on his trips, and he grew much more sensitive to the needs of his customers.

Still, there were times when a customer completely exasperated him, and, initially at least, he was not above putting that person in his place. One such time occurred when he was guiding a party of three young men from Chicago.

"Two of them were all right and helped with the usual chores around camp," Olson later recalled, "but the third was absolutely obnoxious. If it rained he blamed me. If the wind blew against us it was the same. The food was always bad and everything was wrong and of course he decided I was too contemptible to live with."[6]

One evening, during a lull between rainstorms, Olson suggested that the trio take out the canoe for a leisurely paddle while he cooked supper. Before they left, the difficult client took off his soaked jeans—his only pair—and asked Olson to dry them over the fire. This gave Sigurd his opportunity. While the men were gone, he took the buttons off the jeans and hid the jeans in his pack. Then he built a drying rack over the fire, burned some spare cloth underneath it, and tossed the buttons on top of the remains. Finally, when he saw the men returning, he pretended to have fallen asleep.

When the owner of the jeans saw the burned cloth and the buttons, he shouted, "My pants! They're all burned up!" Olson jumped to his feet and rubbed his eyes, pretending to be startled. Then, seeing the charred remains, he apologized profusely. That evening he cut up an old tarpaulin and sewed a pair of pants that the hapless client had to wear in discomfort for the rest of the trip. When they reached the end of their journey, Olson pulled out the jeans and gave them back.

"He was so angry," Olson recalled, "he refused to take the word of the adding machine when I figured out his bill. He said he would figure it out himself, and came out with a figure that was higher than mine, but he paid just the same and stalked out of the warehouse. . . . It was a sad farewell for him, but his two pals laughed with me the way it had turned out."

Eventually, however, Sigurd learned to treat even the most boorish client with respect, and advised others to do the same: "You are not going to change him by anything that you do; just accept that, and put on your tin ears." The skills of diplomacy that Olson began to develop as a guide would aid him tremendously later in life as a leader of the wilderness preservation movement, helping him to defuse skeptical members of Congress and bureaucrats and to bring together warring factions of environmentalists.

Many of Olson's guiding skills came not from trial and error, but from teaming up with the older guides. Francis Santineau taught him to make a warming oven by filling a big pot with hot water and putting a covered pan on top. Joe Chosa showed him a more efficient method of paddling. Big Bill Wenstrom demonstrated how to throw a canoe onto his shoulders. Johnny Sansted taught him to drop fish fillets into a paper bag filled with flour and give a few shakes, rather than sprinkling each fillet separately by hand. "Each one had developed certain skills, the result of many years of living in the woods," Olson recalled in *Open Horizons*. "None could explain how or when he had acquired them, but whatever its explanation, it worked, and even as I did, they watched each other until inevitably a guide was a broad composite of the total experience of every man he had been with."[7]

The guides also gave Olson a romantic sense of the land's history. Older lumbermen such as "Canada" Jack Major, Captain Horn, and Gunder Graves still wore their pants stagged high as they did during the river drives and tilted their black hats in swaggering fashion. Olson would get together with them at J. C. Russell's outfitting company in Winton and listen to them talk about the days when the St. Croix Lumber Company mills were running to capacity, when Fall Lake and Hoist Bay of Basswood Lake were black with floating logs. "I could all but hear the thundering at the landings up the lake," Sigurd later recalled.[8]

Other guides were descendants of the fur-trapping voyageurs who had played an important role in the North American economy during the eighteenth and nineteenth centuries. Primarily of French, Ojibwe, and Scottish heritage, such men as Pierre La Ronge, Henry and Leo Chosa, and Jack Linklater loved to tell stories about the feats of their colorful ancestors. The voyageurs typically lived short, harsh lives, but, like the mountain men of the American West, they were easy to romanticize. Rarely taller than five feet five, they paddled and portaged from daybreak to dark along their assigned sections of a thirty-five-hundred-mile route from Montreal to Lake Athabasca in what is now northeastern Alberta. They fought the waves, storms, raging rivers, hostile tribes, and trappers from rival companies. They dressed in breechcloths and moccasins, with colorful sashes across their breasts holding pipe and tobacco, and wore red caps and feathers on their heads. The canoe country at the edge of Ely had formed the middle link of the voyageurs' highway and still showed signs of these men who sang songs as they paddled: crumbling outposts, rusted trade knives and other tools, and the curiously trimmed lob pines that served as route markers.

Olson guided numerous times with Pierre La Ronge, and they playfully acted the part of voyageurs. Pierre called Sigurd "François," and they spoke to each other in French-accented English. As Olson recounted in *Open Horizons*:

> "Pierre," I might say, "when you go for catch dose trout, use hangerworm or hoppergrass."
>
> "Oui, oui, François," he would reply in mock desperation, "dere ees no hangerworm or hoppergrass een dees countree. All we have eese copper spoon," and with a gesture of utter bafflement any Quebecer might envy, "What can poor Pierre do?" . . .
>
> A ridiculous performance, perhaps, but it provided many laughs, and talking like men from the villages along the St. Lawrence somehow colored our attitude toward the life we were leading and gave all events, including the weather, a humorous twist.[9]

Sometimes after dark, when they had completed their work, La Ronge would light a pipe and recite his favorite poem, "The Voyageur," by William Henry Drummond. "All would go well until he came to the last verse," Olson recalled; "then his eyes grew round and dark and his voice husky as he declaimed":

> So dat's de reason I drink tonight
> To de men of de Grand Nor'Wes',
> For hees heart was young, an' hees heart was light
>   So long as he's leevin' dere—
>   I'm proud of de sam' blood in my vein,
>   I'm a son of de Nort' Win' wance again—
>   So we'll fill her up till de bottle's drain,
>   An' drink to de Voyageur.[10]

On such occasions, Sigurd said, "ghosts of those days stalked the portages and phantom canoes moved down the lakes. On quiet nights it seemed we could hear the old *chansons* drifting across the water and hear their banter."

In learning about the voyageurs, Olson came to see history with a vividness and excitement that he had not encountered in his formal education, and he found that this background also increased his appreciation for the canoe country. Hired in large part because parties were beginning to request educated guides, Olson turned his canoe trips into more than just fishing expeditions; he used his background in geology to talk about the canoe country's Ice Age birth, his woods lore to describe the flora and fauna, and his newfound historical knowledge to show his clients such historic sites as Ojibwe villages and pictographs and fur company trading posts.

Olson greatly admired the older guides from whom he had learned so much; he sensed in them the same authenticity he had found among the farmers and woodsmen of the Namekagon Valley. When they were not guiding, most of them worked as lumberjacks or trappers or miners. They were low in social standing but seemed not to care; they shared an outwardly happy-go-lucky attitude toward life and a deep love of the land in which they lived and worked.

The other guides accepted Olson and grew to respect his outdoor skills, but Sigurd never completely fit in with them; his status as a teacher with a college degree made him different from the rest and erected a barrier that could be scaled but not removed. This background, however, as his bosses had hoped, added to his popularity among the many parties of college-educated businessmen from urban centers in the Upper Midwest, particularly Chicago and Minneapolis. Olson possessed the rugged physique and skills of a woodsman, the knowledge and speaking ability of a teacher, and the romantic outlook and zest for life ascribed to the voyageurs of old. He soon developed a repeating clientele, and his summers became a series of canoe trips, totaling more than a thousand miles of paddling by the time school started in the fall. He was seldom home during the summer, and he got so used to sleeping on the ground that when he returned home he would spend the first night or two on the floor.

❖

Many husbands and fathers in Ely spent a lot of their free time outdoors; to all outward appearances, Olson differed only in degree. But nobody—not even Elizabeth—realized *why* the outdoors was so important to him. Since 1919, when he had fought battles of faith on the rooftop of the YMCA in Madison, Sigurd had been obsessed with what he called his search for meaning. To lose belief in the dogma of his father's church was one thing, but to lose faith in the idea of a mission in life, of an individual calling to some noble purpose—this cut deeply into the psyche of the Reverend L. J. Olson's second son. "For years I went on getting more bitter and disillusioned all of the time," he recalled in his journal on January 14, 1930. His only hope for happiness was to recover a sense of mission. Before that could happen, however, he needed to regain his faith in a greater power. His experiences outdoors, and especially his guiding trips into the wilderness, provided the seeds of a new faith.[11]

The first clue came on a trip into the western portion of Quetico Provincial Park sometime during the early 1920s. Camped one evening on an island in Robinson Lake, Olson got into his canoe after dinner and paddled to the nearby eastern shore of the lake, where there was a peak with a gorgeous view of the wilderness to the west. Sigurd climbed to the top in time to watch the sunset, but the experience proved to be more than an aesthetic appreciation of a glowing red sky. Writing about it a decade later, he recalled that as the sun began to dip below the horizon,

> I was conscious of being alone, a bit of life on the edge of creation and the world itself moving perceptibly away from the sun. At that moment, so perfect was the illusion that I could actually feel and see the movement and then, more than any other time, did I realize my closeness with the rest of the universe, that perfect communion with the beginnings of all things, a oneness with creation. For a long time, I sat without moving, until it was dark and the western sky a soft diffusion of color.

Olson felt a sense of peace and contentment, and a belief that he had experienced contact with a supernatural power. "From that moment, I was a spiritualist," he said. And he began seeking these epiphanies, or "flashes of insight" as he came to call them, whenever he could find time alone outdoors. During canoe trips, after his clients had turned in for the night, Sigurd often would take the canoe out by himself, searching for another glimpse of the infinite. "Most of all would I find what I sought on brilliant starlit nights," he recalled:

> I would paddle out swiftly onto the open lake if the moon was shining down its path. It never failed to come to me when going down that brilliant shining highway into space. Most completely of all

would I be taken when lying on my back looking at the stars. The gentle motion of the canoe softly swaying, the sense of space and infinity given by the stars, gave me the sense of being suspended in the ether. My body had no weight, my soul was detached and I careened freely through a delightfulness of infinite distance. . . . Sometimes the night cry of the loon would enhance the illusion. For long periods I would lie, having lost track of time and location. A slap of a wavelet would jerk me back into the present and I would paddle back to the glowing coals of the deserted camp fire, trying to fathom the depths of the experience I had been through.

Olson's clients often were amused by his behavior and teased him about his "poetic leanings" (just as they teased him for bringing his pillow). He took it good-naturedly and laughed along with them, but he thought that at least a few of his customers seemed to understand. He also began to notice how they, too, often were transformed during the course of a canoe trip. Gradually, during the first few days of paddling and portaging, they would drop the formalities and hard shell of their business personas and expose their true selves. They laughed more and played practical jokes. They sang. They watched the sun set and the moon rise, and they listened to the roar of rapids and the soft sighs of wind in the pines. Olson was amazed one day to see a wealthy, workaholic executive spend more than an hour watching an anthill.

These observations and personal epiphanies convinced Olson that nature in general, and wilderness in particular, could play a crucial spiritual role for modern civilization. For him personally, it provided tantalizing moments of wholeness and peace, a sense that there *was* meaning to life, if only he could find it. This made his search all the more important to him, and all the more frustrating. "Days when I have seen my vision," he wrote, "are glorious beads on the chain of my life; the others are drab unbrightened stones." He sensed that if he remained a schoolteacher he never would find his mission, and therefore never find lasting inner peace, yet he groped for alternatives. Eventually—at least by the end of 1925—he came back to his old idea of becoming a writer.

He had done no writing of significance since his 1921 article for the *Milwaukee Journal*. He had not gotten published again, and there is no indication in his private papers that he even had submitted anything for potential publication. But one October day—apparently in 1925, although possibly a year earlier—an outdoor experience made him return to his writing. He was on his way to the north end of Low Lake, a few miles north of Ely, intending to hunt the mallards feeding in the rice beds. As he portaged into the south end of the lake, he was stopped by the sound of someone chopping wood.

The man wielding the ax was a trapper who lived by himself in a small cabin near the shore. He was laying in his winter's supply of firewood, and Sigurd, watching, was struck by two thoughts. First was a recognition of the sheer beauty of the shimmering bright blue water contrasting with the golden leaves of the aspen behind the trapper. Second was a sense that the trapper was a *part* of the beauty, his unhurried preparations for winter part of a timeless, natural human behavior. Years later, in a draft of *Open Horizons*, Olson recalled his conclusion: "I must live in a cabin like that, be the trapper, write of the life around me, never again listen to bells or schedules, never again have to live indoors."

Olson's vision seems to have been about escaping from the "bells and schedules" of teaching just as much as it was about writing. This time he followed through, as he had not after his similar vision five years earlier on the road from Keewatin to Nashwauk. Over the next several months, he wrote three animal stories: "The Vengeance of Papette," about a fierce, semiwild husky; "The Fugitive," about an old whitetail buck; and "Snow Wings," about a snowy owl. On April 1, 1926, he sent all three to an agent in New York, along with a money order for eight dollars and fifty cents to cover the cost of marketing. He used the name Sigurd Thorne, because he thought his mother-in-law's maiden name (which he also had given to his baby) sounded more attractive for a writer than Olson.

❖

While Sigurd was waiting for word from New York, he got caught up in the first conflict over the wilderness canoe country. The issue was roads. The Forest Service wanted them for moving people and equipment to stop forest fires, and local boosters wanted them for tourism. Two of the proposed roads were particularly troubling to conservationists. One, called the Fernberg Road, would extend east from Ely for about fifty miles to the Gunflint Trail, providing a scenic route to the communities along Lake Superior. The other, eventually called the Echo Trail, would start near Ely and head northwestward for more than forty miles to the village of Buyck. The agency proposed building several short spurs from the Echo Trail, to connect with Lac La Croix and Loon Lake on the international border, and also to Trout Lake.

The Forest Service's concern about fire prevention was legitimate. Rangers had to patrol the forest and haul fire-fighting equipment by canoe, a slow and inefficient method at best. It took a long day of paddling from Ely just to reach the nearest fire tower. But conservationists knew the roads would bisect major canoe routes and open vast sections of land to resort development. The Fernberg proposal, for example, would have cut in half the main section of today's Boundary Waters Canoe Area Wilderness. At the time, however, the national forest's boundary was to the south of the Fernberg; such major canoe country lakes as Basswood, Moose, Snowbank, and Knife were outside Superior National Forest and not protected by law from development. The only barrier was access.

Wilderness preservation—the idea of setting aside large portions of federal land from most kinds of resource extraction, development, and motorized transportation—was still in its infancy in 1926, discussed primarily in professional publications such as the *Journal of Forestry*. The popular press, when it covered conservation issues at all, emphasized wildlife protection. There was no conservation group devoted solely to wilderness preservation; the long-established organizations, such as the Sierra Club and the Audubon Association, had narrower missions and small membership rosters of less than seven thousand each. But a new, Midwest-based conservation group with a focus on wildlife issues was ready to turn its attention to the wilderness canoe country. The Izaak Walton League of America, in the four years since its founding in 1922, had attracted well over a hundred thousand members, many times the number of any other conservation group in the country.

The league's rapid growth was spurred by its dynamic founder and president, Will H. Dilg. A gaunt man with thin lips and a deeply receding hairline, the former Chicago advertising professional was a crusader without peer. The well-known wildlife defender William T. Hornaday described Dilg as "a conservation John the Baptist, preaching in the Wilderness"; others compared him to Saint Paul and Saint

Stephen. Dilg spoke to the average Midwestern male who looked nostalgically to simpler times and worried that the outdoor opportunities of their youth were disappearing in an urban America: "I am weary of civilization's madness," he said, "and I yearn for the harmonious gladness of the woods and of the streams. I am tired of your piles of buildings and I ache from your iron streets. I feel jailed in your greatest cities and I long for the unharnessed freedom of the big outside."[12]

Dilg ran the Izaak Walton League like the fast-growing fraternal service organizations of the time, such as the Lions and the Rotary, were run: he referred to league members as "brother sportsmen," and in his speeches and through the organization's magazine, *Outdoor America*, he created an atmosphere of male camaraderie. In fact, the group's executive secretary had formerly managed the Kiwanis national headquarters. Dilg also convinced some of America's busiest, most popular writers—including Zane Grey, Emerson Hough, Gene Stratton Porter, Henry Van Dyke, Irvin S. Cobb, and James Oliver Curwood—to contribute to the magazine. They often infused their articles not only with a sense of nostalgia, but also with a spiritual feeling for the outdoors. "There is no religion healthier for a man's spiritual and physical well-being than the pagan worship of the woodsman," wrote Cobb.

The nostalgia, the masculine fellowship, the nature worship— these were things with which Sigurd Olson readily identified, and undoubtedly he would have become a member in any case, but he had an added inducement: in the summer of 1924 he guided Will Dilg. Olson later recalled that one night on Ottertrack Lake, as the men sat around a fire, Dilg vowed that the league would devote itself to preserving the area. Olson joined the league and in 1926 participated in the group's first battle over the canoe country.

The Izaak Walton League was not the only organization to fight against the roads, but it provoked the most anger in the range towns of northeastern Minnesota. While some of its allies were willing to compromise by agreeing to some short, dead-end roads that would help in fire fighting, the league insisted on keeping the entire national forest as a wilderness. Furthermore, the league wanted the federal government to consolidate the three sections of Superior National Forest by purchasing all the private land in between these sections.

Local business leaders were aghast. They saw tourism as their only chance to develop a locally controlled industry. Their economy was dependent upon the whims of corporations controlled by outsiders who seemed to have little regard for their concerns. The major logging companies had cut and run, turning the city of Winton into a virtual ghost town, and the iron mining industry was notorious for eliminating jobs through technological advances and for declaring long-term layoffs with little advance warning. The industry also had smashed efforts to unionize by bringing in thousands of Slovenians and other East Europeans, setting off intense ethnic rivalries in the formerly Scandinavian-dominated range cities. Local governments had retaliated by forcing the mining companies to pay excessively heavy property taxes, but the state government had intervened in the early 1920s and limited this option. Meanwhile, the cities had taken out huge long-term loans to pay for often extravagant projects. Worrying about what would happen when the loans came due, now that they could not force the mining companies to carry the bill, local leaders logically saw tourism as a potentially important source of much-needed revenue.

The city of Ely was not as overextended as many of the range cities. Hibbing, for example, was three million dollars in debt by 1931, more than the city of Duluth, which had ten times the population. As chief beneficiary of the proposed roads and the major American gateway to the canoe country, however, Ely became the site of the most vitriolic debate, a role it would continue to play for decades. The *Ely Miner,* a weekly newspaper, served as the mouthpiece for the city's pro-development establishment, printing editorials, articles, and letters congruent with its agenda, and often refusing to publish opposing views. This made it harder for those who disagreed to gain legitimacy in the community, and easier for the business community to subject dissenters to intense social pressure.

The *Miner* and the business establishment it represented saw the Izaak Walton League's position on roads and consolidation as "foreign to the principles of Democracy and striking at the very root of Americanism." Local residents who opposed the Fernberg Road and the Echo Trail became the targets of mean-spirited gossip, heated criticism, the silent treatment, and other forms of abuse common in a divided community. Sigurd Olson opposed the roads in the face of a bitter climate in his adopted hometown.[13]

There is little information about Olson's role in the fight against roads, his first experience with a communication campaign. In *Open Horizons,* he recalled simply that he and other guides "wrote letters to those we had guided, appeared at meetings and hearings, tried to explain what wilderness meant to us, and often found ourselves alone, facing older and more experienced men who believed the road program was the most wonderful thing that could possibly happen."[14] If he was not out guiding at the time, he probably attended a special meeting of the Ely Commercial Club on June 16, 1926; canoe country guides packed the meeting and forced a twenty-one to seven vote against the proposed roads. The club's president was Superior National Forest supervisor A. L. Richey, a federal employee and a strong supporter of the roads. Six days later Richey called another meeting that was dominated by Ely businessmen and reversed the vote.

Olson was a founding member of the local Izaak Walton League chapter; as such, he was among the most uncompromising road opponents and therefore an enemy to local boosters. Even Elizabeth disagreed with his opposition to the Echo Trail. For Sigurd, it was the beginning of a lifelong battle with the leaders of his community. When Richey died of a heart attack at the end of the roads controversy, local people accused Olson and the other road opponents of causing his death by putting too much pressure on him. Olson's Izaak Walton League chapter ultimately died from attrition—the antagonism was too strong.

The conflict ended in a September 1926 compromise engineered by Aldo Leopold. Two years earlier, as an employee of the U.S. Forest Service in New Mexico, Leopold had convinced his agency to create its first large-scale wilderness preserve by setting aside five hundred and seventy-four thousand acres of the Gila National Forest. Since then he had moved to Madison, Wisconsin, and become assistant director of the service's Forest Products Laboratory. He had taken two canoe trips in the Quetico-Superior region and, as an active member of the Izaak Walton League, was familiar with the controversy.

Leopold convinced the league's national office that it was impractical to insist on preserving the entire American portion of the canoe country as wilderness when so much of the land was privately owned.

Better to compromise with the Forest Service and save at least some of it now, he said, than risk losing it all through obstinacy. League officials agreed, and on September 17, 1926, U.S. Secretary of Agriculture William M. Jardine issued the final policy statement. The Fernberg Road would be built, but only to the fire tower about twenty miles east of Ely. The Echo Trail also would be built, but not the spurs from that road to Lac La Croix, Loon Lake, and Trout Lake.

Jardine also created three wilderness areas within Superior National Forest: the Caribou Lake, the Little Indian Sioux, and the Superior. (Until 1964 the creation, alteration, and dissolution of wilderness areas was at the discretion of the Forest Service and the secretary of agriculture. The Wilderness Act, signed by President Lyndon Johnson in September 1964, removed this power from the executive branch and placed it in the hands of Congress.) Jardine warned that these new lines on the map would mean little unless the government could consolidate the national forest and buy all the private land within the wilderness areas. Committing himself to that goal, he broke precedent by requiring all future Superior National Forest management plans to receive the approval of the secretary of agriculture.

The Izaak Walton League declared the compromise a victory, but the fears Olson and some of the other guides and Minnesota Waltonians held at the time were realized. Thirty-three resorts eventually were built on formerly wild land made accessible by the Echo Trail and the Fernberg Road, considerably shrinking the wilderness on the American side of the Quetico-Superior. True, much of the area had been logged, but the trees were beginning to grow back; the roads, on the other hand, opened the canoe country to intensive resort development that destroyed the sense of isolation on many lakes, and isolation cannot be renewed through a planting program.

❖

When the Olsons moved to Ely in 1923, a new junior college had just been established. Ely Junior College had opened in the fall of 1922 with an enrollment of twelve, all freshmen. In 1923 it expanded to include sophomores. When the new million-dollar high school opened in the fall of 1924, the junior college took over the top two floors of the old high school building, where it had some room to grow (the bottom two floors were used by the city's seventh and eighth grades). In September 1926, as Jardine was preparing to decide the fate of the road proposals, Sigurd Olson became one of several high school teachers given the opportunity to split his duties and teach part time at the junior college next door. It was a move up for him; besides teaching biology in the high school, he taught animal biology and human physiology at Ely Junior College.

Sigurd's promotion brought the year to a strong close; the only note of personal failure was his inability to sell any of the three stories he had written early in the year. "The Fugitive" had been rejected by five magazines, "Snow Wings" by four, and "The Vengeance of Papette" by three. His reaction to these rejections is undocumented; what is clear is that he continued to work on them and other stories throughout the winter.

He also changed his tactics. The agent in New York had sent his stories to leading magazines, such as *Collier's* and *Harper's* and the *Saturday Evening Post.* Sigurd decided to work on his own and try the easier-to-break-into "pulps" rather than the "slicks." He wrote a simple account of fly-fishing for largemouth bass on a little-used lake. Naming the story for the term a friend of his used for dry flies, he called it "Fishin' Jewlery." (Spelling never was one of Sigurd's strong points.) He sent it to *Field and Stream,* one of the top three outdoors magazines, and waited. On May 9, 1927, the magazine's editor wrote back. He wanted Sigurd's article.[15]

Olson got twenty-five dollars for "Fishin' Jewelry"; he and Elizabeth cashed the check, went to town, and celebrated. Sigurd finally had broken into the world of magazine writing, and, as he later recalled, figured that "from now on *nobody* can turn me down."[16]

He was wrong, of course: rejection would come, again and again. But "Fishin' Jewelry" was a start, and in 1928 and 1929 Sigurd got three more articles published, including the four-times-rejected "Snow Wings," which was accepted by *Boys' Life.* Meanwhile, on January 1, 1929, the not-quite-thirty-year-old Olson entered his first major business transaction: he joined with two other men and purchased J. C. Russell's outfitting company. They named their new organization the Border Lakes Outfitting Company; in casual conversation, they called it "the Border Lakes."

Olson's partners were Walter F. "Wallie" Hansen and Mervin W. Peterson, known to most people as Pete. Hansen, the youngest, worked with the canoes and camping equipment, and Peterson, related to

Hansen and the oldest of the three, took care of the finances. Sigurd was the only one of the three who guided, but once the Border Lakes got under way his days as a full-time summer guide were over. He spent his time managing the company's day-to-day operations.

Olson saw the Border Lakes as an investment and as a source of income to supplement his teacher's salary, but it is clear that early on he also viewed it as a potential means to get out of the teaching profession entirely, so he could spend the fall and winter months writing. He wrote in his journal, "If my outfitting business would only get sufficiently on its feet so that I could devote six months of the year to writing at my own pace and speed, I really think I would accomplish something worth while."[17]

But as the 1920s came to a close, Olson also was wrestling with the idea of beginning another career that he saw as quite removed from his dream of writing, yet tied to his love of the outdoors. He was thinking of becoming a wildlife biologist. The idea had begun to take root in 1928, when he guided University of Illinois zoologist Alvin Cahn through the Quetico-Superior wilderness. "It was through him that I first caught the meaning of ecology as a concept," Sigurd recalled in a draft of *Open Horizons,* "and now as I look back one thing stands out, the discovery of the sense of interdependency of all living things."[18] For six weeks they traveled the canoe country, studying fish parasitology and conducting a bird survey. They became friends, and Cahn, seven years older than Sigurd and an enthusiastic man with a full beard and rugged good looks, took Sigurd on as a protégé. He began sending Olson books on history, world affairs, and literature, encouraging him to broaden his scope, and he also began trying to convince Olson to come to the University of Illinois and earn a graduate degree in ecology.

❖ Five ❖

The Reluctant Ecologist

1930–1932

Sigurd avidly read the books Alvin Cahn sent him, but he was not
eager to start graduate school. "I would much rather dream and
write . . . than pin myself down to the cut and dried realm of classification and analysis," he wrote on January 12, 1930. The admission did
not come easily. "My conscience bothers me when I think of the work
I might be doing along zoological lines," he wrote after receiving another letter from Cahn that same month. "I fear that I will never be
able to equal his scientific ardor."

Feeling guilty that he might be letting a potentially successful
career slip away while he chased an ephemeral dream, Olson turned
for support to books by Henry David Thoreau, John Burroughs, and
W. H. Hudson. This probably was not the first time he encountered
these authors, but when he read them in December 1929 and January
1930 he was moved to begin keeping a journal to record his thoughts
and observations.[1]

It was a period of deep introspection. He read Thoreau and Burroughs and Hudson not to think about nature, but to think about
himself. He looked for similarities between his life and theirs, and between his reactions to nature and civilization and theirs, apparently
in an effort to convince himself that if he was similar to them, his
destiny must be to follow the less-traveled road of the writer, not the
thoroughfare of a mainstream career.

He was convinced. The three natural philosophers, he wrote, "are
akin to me in every action, every thought." On January 16, 1930, after
reading a biography of Burroughs, he wrote about the similarity he

saw between the life of the popular turn-of-the-century nature writer and his own:

> He found the same inability to resign himself to business and the humdrum existence of commercial life. After teaching school for some ten years and nagged by an ambitious wife to try to put his good brain to some lucrative use, he tries anything that will give him a release but only to find that he cannot devote his mind to it. In the midst of figuring and worry he finds himself slipping away to do some scribbling as his friends call it. Many is the time he was discouraged and hopeless but there was always his outdoors to give him renewed strength and vision.

Olson believed that he, like Burroughs, was not understood by family and friends, that they mistook his philosophical bent, his inward probing and dreaming, "for pure laziness and inactivity." At times, rightly or wrongly, he felt under pressure from Elizabeth to try to advance in his career, and he commented vaguely on the "restraints of marriage and the civilized life." Hearing about the exploits of his older brother, Kenneth, who had left the newspaper business and was now an assistant professor in journalism at the University of Wisconsin, put more pressure on Sigurd. "Perhaps all I am is a dreamer," he wrote. "Perhaps all of my meditation is merely an excuse for lack of ambition. At times I accuse myself of mental laziness—I hate detail and routine and am only happy when I am alone with my thoughts."

Olson also found much in common with the literary naturalist W. H. Hudson. In mid-January 1930 Olson read Hudson's reminiscence *Far Away and Long Ago*, a book that he would treasure always. He wrote on January 20:

> His early struggles to find the truth, how like mine they are. His unwillingness to give up the joys of his youth. Have I not time and time again vindicated my own tenacious clinging to my boyhood by the same reasoning. . . . I no longer attribute my longing for the woods as a desire to get away from work and responsibility. I know that it comes from an inherent love of nature and a very necessary communion with the wild.

Olson wrote very little about Thoreau in his journal, but noted a similar fondness for solitude and simplicity and identified with

Thoreau's statement that "the mass of men lead lives of quiet desperation." Olson took comfort in knowing that Thoreau, as well as Hudson and Burroughs, had refused to surrender to societal definitions of male responsibility and acceptable career paths. He also believed that those who *did* surrender—the vast majority of people—were missing genuine fulfillment in their lives. "Many go through life without making an effort to unearth the hidden stores within them and die having lived sterile lives in their own arid deserts," he wrote on January 17, 1930. "Many go through stifled by the narrowness of their daily affairs, little dreaming that at their very doors for the asking is a wilderness to explore, the wilderness of their understanding."

Olson knew that the solitude and silence he found in the canoe country wilderness had provided ideal conditions to experience a sense of oneness and harmony with nature, and such experiences had always brought him greater self-knowledge and at least temporary peace of mind. His outdoor excursions had come to serve as a metaphor for his spiritual journey: by exploring the physical wilderness around him, Sigurd was coming to know the wilderness within. In January 1930 he wrote two key conclusions. First, writing was his greatest joy and had to be a central part of his life: "The more I think of the goal of my life, the more I am convinced that for me life holds one thing, and that is the expression of my views of life, existence as seen through my eyes." Second, any career that kept him indoors held no attraction: "Other occupations have one goal, an office, executive ability, organization. If that is the goal no profession has anything for me." Or, put another way: "I must have freedom above all else and writing is the only occupation that will give it to me."

But what type of writing? He was drawn to the nature essay, but there were two issues to consider. One of them was money. If he wanted to write full time he had to make enough money to provide for his family. With the stock market crash just three months earlier and the looming threat of bank failures, this was no small concern. Essays were hard to sell and did not pay well; fiction and nonfiction stories in the better magazines made more sense from a financial standpoint. "There is where the money lies," he wrote, "and it would be nice to indulge one's dream and get paid for it." But Sigurd was ambivalent about money. On January 16, after reading a how-to book about writing, he wrote that it depressed him. "What hurt me last night more than anything else was running into the sordidness of writing for money. If it is to be a sheer money making profession for me then I want nothing of it."

The second issue was originality. Olson worried that if he wrote essays he would be seen as an imitator of Burroughs and Thoreau. "I must find some other type of work that will stamp my writings with individuality," he wrote on January 16. Several days later, after reading *Far Away and Long Ago* for the first time, Olson brightened. He felt closer to W. H. Hudson than to any of the other literary naturalists, for Hudson's primary response to nature, like Olson's, was visceral, an intense intermingling of wonder and joy. In *Far Away and Long Ago*, Hudson wrote how he "rejoiced in colours, scents, sounds, in taste and touch: the blue of the sky, the verdure of earth, the sparkle of sunlight on water." Olson, who sometimes stood on hilltops, waved his hat in the wind, and "shouted to the skies that I was alive," readily identified with such sentiments. "How well do I recognize the same in my own reactions," he wrote in his journal on January 20.

Perhaps most important, Hudson wrote about experiencing moments of an almost overpowering awe, what he called "animism" or "this sense of the supernatural in natural things." At times, during Hudson's childhood in Argentina, his encounters with nature brought such a surge of emotions that he became frightened. "The sight of a magnificent sunset was sometimes almost more than I could endure," he recalled, "and made me wish to hide myself away." He especially felt it in a grove of white acacia trees near his home:

> I used to steal out of the house alone when the moon was at its full to stand, silent and motionless, near some group of large trees, gazing at the dusky green foliage silvered by the beams; and at such times the sense of mystery would grow until a sensation of delight would change to fear, and the fear increase until it was no longer to be borne, and I would hastily escape to recover the sense of reality and safety indoors, where there was light and company. Yet on the very next night I would steal out again and go to the spot where the effect was strongest.[3]

This sense of the supernatural in nature, which Hudson retained as an adult, was the feeling Olson had experienced so many times, the "flash of insight" that he sought again and again in his outdoor

73

excursions. After reading *Far Away and Long Ago*, Olson concluded that Hudson was one of a mere handful of nature writers who had both experienced such moments of epiphany and written about them. Sigurd wrote in his journal:

> There are few who see what I see, very few. Even the great writers of nature, many of them have failed. Occasionally there crops out an inkling of it but none of the clearness of perception and depth of feeling that I know. Why I should have it I cannot know, perhaps it is an inherited instinct from some far ancestral mystic. Surely none of my family have it; if they do it is hidden and unrecognizable. In me has been concentrated the natural mysticism of centuries of my race. I have been given the seeing eye. It is my mission to give my vision to the race in return for the beauty that has been shown me.

The hubris that permeates this passage is easily misunderstood, and it would be wrong to assume that Olson felt an arrogant confidence in his writing ability. His egoism focused on his role as a messenger, not on the medium through which he spread his message. He believed he had found in the wilderness glimmers of hope and truth that he had lost in his drift from the Baptist faith, and he felt it was his duty—even his destiny—to share his findings with others. He wrote about it many times in his journal, but expressed it best in 1942:

> There is something of the crusader in me, the evangelist. I cannot rest unless it comes out, and I will never be happy unless I give myself wholly to the task at hand. . . . I feel that I have a message, something to contribute, something real and vital that many are missing.[4]

There is a sense here of evangelical fervor, a sense of duty, a sense of altruism, and a sense of ambition. Sigurd Olson may not have become the Baptist missionary his father would have preferred, but certainly he felt he had a calling, and a calling to do something great. His major struggle, which he well recognized in January 1930, was to find the best way to achieve that mission while at the same time reconciling it with social expectations, the demands of marriage and fatherhood, and his need for regular contact with nature.

Olson hoped and dreamed that he could accomplish his mission through writing, and early in 1930, after reading the great literary naturalists and beginning the habit of writing every day himself, he was optimistic—almost euphoric, in fact: he called this period his "rejuvenation of 1930." He remarked that writing was a psychological purging:

> I am not happiest when I am writing but I am perhaps happiest just after I am through. It is like physical pain, really enjoyable in a sense because of the relief after it is over. So with writing, not so pleasant at the time although one must admit that there is some pleasure to putting down thoughts on paper, but satisfaction afterward that counts most.

Olson's happiness depended in part upon regular attention to his writing, but finding uninterrupted blocks of time was difficult. He would write in his classroom for half an hour or an hour in the morning until the students began to shuffle in ("I must begin now to think of the scorpionidae and the myriapodia, king crabs and whatnot," he wrote on January 22 as class time approached. "Back to earth. Goodbye to dreams for another day"), but this was not enough time to accomplish much. He also wrote at home in the evenings, but was frustrated by ringing telephones, knocks at the door, "and the hundred and one things that make for interruptions of one's thoughts." And his young business, the Border Lakes Outfitting Company, which he hoped would do well enough so he could quit teaching and write full time most of the year, was at the moment taking time *away* from his writing. In March he had to begin spending most evenings writing letters to customers and getting everything organized for the summer season. "I haven't time to do anything or think of anything but my business and how that irks me," he wrote on April 2, 1930. "How I hate it. I never was meant to make money in that way. It is all sordid for me and I can never throw myself into it."

But having little time for writing was just part of the problem, for Olson's happiness also depended upon the recognition that comes with publication. And when *Harper's* and the *Atlantic Monthly* both rejected his winter's output, a fictional adventure story about loggers, he was more than unhappy. "I feel that my writing is more or less an illusion," he wrote on April 2, "that there is no use in my going on and that I might as well give it up."

Once again, Sigurd began to think about going to graduate school in ecology, which would get him out of what he called "the stultifying atmosphere of this school system." Surely, he wrote, "my soul will shrivel from the dryness within these walls." But was this a good reason to uproot his family and start a master's degree program at the age of thirty-one? He wrote on April 7:

> Some days it looks like a fascinating outlet, but then again it gives me the sensation of going into a dungeon . . . from which there is no escaping and which will only prolong the day when I will be able to do what I want. . . . I do not want to meddle with too much of science at the sacrifice of my soul. I must retain my original freshness of perception.

Indecisiveness continued to gnaw at Olson throughout the year. In the fall he found some real writing success: four feature articles published in leading outdoor magazines. But the pleasure this brought him, along with any accompanying confidence, apparently disappeared when he received a critical evaluation from New York literary agent Thomas Uzzell. Sigurd had sent Uzzell his twice-rejected and twice-revised logging adventure story, hoping the agent would be able to tell him what to do to break into the decent-paying magazines. Uzzell's September 25 response was blunt:

> When a man who has had some success with action stories or with the sport and outdoor magazines generally, develops an ambition for sales to better markets, he breaks out in a number of different ways. He knows that his handling of his material for the other markets isn't right for his new purpose but he usually does not know what to do about it. Apparently your solution has been to recognize the unsuitability of the action story motivation for the better markets and to leave out the motivation altogether!

It got worse. "There is no character interest here," Uzzell wrote. "Your boys merely recklessly throw themselves into danger and get out by sheer good luck." Even when Uzzell showed some restraint, the comment stung: "I suspect that you are not yet an entirely self-conscious artist in any of your fiction." He had just one compliment. He told Olson that the manuscript "is most striking evidence of your ability to write effectively of the life and activity of the region." Olson's immediate reaction to the letter is not known, but two weeks after receiving it he began checking on graduate school fellowships. At the advice of University of Minnesota ecologist Ralph King, whom he had recently guided, Olson made his first contact with Aldo Leopold, who was working for the U.S. Forest Products Laboratory in Madison, Wisconsin. King had told Olson that at least one fellowship was available through the Sporting Arms and Ammunitions Manufacturers' Institute. Leopold conducted the group's annual game survey and was likely to know about the fellowship.

He did. Leopold told Olson on October 20 that there were two open fellowships: one was for the study of pheasants and other upland game birds in Michigan, while the other was for the study of the scaled quail in New Mexico. He told Olson how to apply for each. "I am anxious to have a personal interview with you," Leopold added. "If you ever get near Madison, drop in. Also keep me informed as to your progress in getting places." On November 11 Leopold wrote about a prairie chicken research assistantship in Kansas and advised Olson to go to a school "where *game management* is the objective of research rather than game zoology."

Olson also wrote to Alvin Cahn at the University of Illinois, where game management was *not* the objective of research. Cahn excitedly wrote back that Olson had stirred the interest of his colleague Victor E. Shelford, the nation's leading animal ecologist: "I had a nice talk with Shelford this week about you, and he is thoroughly delighted with the prospect of having a graduate student interested in vertebrate ecology—a very rare combination. I am the first vertebrate ecologist he had, and there have been none since I went through the mill."

Olson was not yet ready to commit himself to attending graduate school, but he took another step in that direction late in November after reading a how-to book by his literary agent. Uzzell's book scared Olson into thinking that a writing career was impossible, and on December 4 he wrote in his journal that Elizabeth seconded the opinion. He was not sure he really wanted to go back to school, but he knew he needed a change of careers: "Every day is torture—I come to work down and out, spend the day and go home at 4 still too distraught to do anything. I say and I cry out to the four winds—life is too short for that sort of existence." And so, early in December, Sigurd Olson began to test the dark waters of scholarly research, gathering information for a possible master's thesis on the predatory mammals of Superior National Forest.

❖

The timing was ideal. Over the past seven years biologists and conservationists had been starting to question the wisdom of predator control, especially as practiced by the federal government's Bureau of the Biological Survey. Established in 1905, the bureau started out as an information clearinghouse, keeping track of the various state bounty programs and publishing pamphlets that described how to kill predators. In 1915 Congress responded to pressure from the Western livestock industry and gave the bureau $125,000 to establish its own predator control program. By the early 1920s government agents were killing tens of thousands of carnivores every year.[5]

Wolves, the most despised, suffered the heaviest losses. For more than two thousand years they had been used as symbolic representations of evil in Bible stories and folklore and popular fiction. To the average American in the early twentieth century, wolves were murderers that killed defenseless animals for fun. It made sense to get rid of them. The Bureau of the Biological Survey wiped out whole breeding populations. Agents spent months at a time tracking down and killing the last individual animals, invariably labeled "outlaws" by ranchers. By the mid-1920s only a few breeding packs were left in the West, and only where there was no ranching. In 1928 the government could find and kill just eleven wolves.

As the wolves and other predators disappeared, a number of scientists—some of them within the bureau itself—began to question the program. At the 1923 annual meeting of the American Society of Mammalogists, some biologists compared the poisoning campaign to the use of poison gas in World War I. Within the agency, some of those who opposed wholesale extermination of predators began deriding the exterminators, calling them "gopher chokers."

The Bureau of the Biological Survey and its supporters did not take opposition lightly; bureau chief Paul Redington announced in 1928 that "We face the opposition . . . of those who want to see the mountain lion, the wolf, the coyote, and the bobcat perpetuated as part of the wildlife of the country."[6] The agency suppressed dissent within its ranks and in 1930 asked Congress for $10 million to wage a final ten-year war against predators. That May the Society of Mammalogists held a symposium on the issue at its annual meeting, where a number of scientists pointed out that the government was on the verge of exterminating species with no solid proof of significant destructive behavior and in the face of some evidence that predators may help ranchers and farmers by keeping rodent populations in check. The study of animal populations and ecological relationships was in its infancy, and many biologists felt that it was foolish to exterminate species of predators when so little was known about them.

The argument between biologists who favored continuing the poisoning campaigns and those who opposed the idea became public in 1930, as newspapers and magazines covered the issue in the context of the huge appropriation being considered by Congress. The leading outdoor magazines especially paid attention; *Outdoor Life* led the way with feature articles in June, September, November, and December.

Sigurd Olson was among those who had entered the public debate, and not on the side of the predators. As he was beginning his research in December 1930, the current issue of *Sports Afield* came out with his article "The Poison Trail," an account of a winter trip he took through the canoe country with government trappers to pick up poisoned predators, especially timber wolves. They traveled for a hundred miles through what Olson described as "one of the finest big game areas on the continent and incidentally one of the most harassed by the killing packs." By the time they returned to town they had picked up the bodies of four wolves, four coyotes, and ten foxes.

Olson showed no warm feelings toward wolves, calling them "grey marauders" and killers. "Such jaws and teeth," he wrote, "it was little wonder that they could ham-string moose or deer and drag them down." When one of his companions mentioned that the crust on the snow would make it easy for the wolves to catch deer, Olson replied, "Yes, and I wouldn't be surprised if they've started their murdering already." Olson described the grim reaction of his group after they found and examined a wolf-killed deer carcass: "What we most feared, had happened. Only the fat of the entrails had been eaten. They were already killing for fun."

This was not the first time Olson had shown hostility toward predators in a published article. In his article "Snow Wings," published in the March 1928 *Boys' Life*, he called the snowy owl the "most feared of all the winged marauders of the North" and said that "the swish of his great feathered pinions had become an omen synonymous with tragedy." In the same article he called pine martens "killers" and described the scream they make after killing a rodent as "a snarling screech so venomous and filled with hatred that all the evil in the race of killers might have for that one instant been concentrated in the body of one."

Olson originally wrote "Snow Wings" in 1926 and "The Poison Trail" in 1928, and it is unclear when *Sports Afield* bought the latter. Conceivably, then, "The Poison Trail" might not have reflected Olson's actual feelings about predators in December 1930. The notes he kept as he began his research that month, however, largely support the view expressed in his published articles. On December 6, for example, he described the timber wolf as "the greatest destroyer of big game in this area," and he reiterated his belief that wolves "will kill for just the joy of killing" and that "a great deal of unnecessary killing goes on." He questioned the value of trapping and poisoning, but only because the American portion of the canoe country "is fed by bands drifting down from the Ontario Wilds," and so "for every wolf trapped there might come down dozens in a night from the north."

Olson did contradict one opinion stated in "The Poison Trail." In the article, he indicated that wolves hamstring their prey; this was a widespread popular belief that added to the wolf's reputation for cruelty. On December 6, he wrote that of the deer carcasses he had examined so far, none had shown any signs of injured hamstrings. He also recalled the one time he had actually seen a wolf kill a deer. On that occasion—along the Basswood River one June day several years earlier—he watched as a wolf caught a fawn by the nose and threw it, breaking the fawn's neck. The wolf had not touched the hamstrings.[7]

Sigurd spent much of his free time in December trailing wolves and deer, examining carcasses, and talking to local game wardens and trappers. He asked them to record when and where they spotted wolves or deer carcasses; to estimate how much of each carcass had been eaten at the time they found it; to measure the tracks of the largest wolves; to record dates and locations of mating sites and dens; and to estimate the number of wolves per township within Superior National Forest.

Population estimates were bound to be little more than educated guesses, of course, and Olson received estimates yielding totals for Superior National Forest that varied from 228 to 350 wolves. After World War II, researchers would develop better, if still imperfect, techniques for studying wolves: they would conduct aerial surveys and play tape-recorded howls to locate and count the animals, and would place radio collars or identification tags on captured wolves so that researchers could study individual animals after releasing them. But when Olson conducted his research in 1930, counting wolves was pure guesswork, and studying their habits meant observing them, examining the carcasses of trapped wolves and their prey, and gathering anecdotes from reputable woodsmen.[8]

As he began his research, Olson also jotted down some information on other predators, such as foxes, lynx, weasels, and mink, but it is clear that he was most interested in wolves, and secondarily in coyotes. Even so, he was worried about returning to school and remarked that while a master's thesis on the wolf might be "all right in its way," it still "bores me terribly—all of it."

On Christmas Eve Alvin Cahn wrote to Sigurd, encouraging him on: "I happen to be on the inside of a lot of things that are going on, and by next year this entire subject of predatory mammal control is going to be right up on top and receive a good and thorough airing! As I see it, here is an opportunity of a life-time to hit the nail on the head while it is hot—and it will be hot within a year, I can assure you." Sigurd's initial reaction to the letter is unknown. Before he could respond, he came down with a serious illness.

He had caught a cold before Christmas. So had the boys. Sigurd Jr. and Bob, now seven and five, both developed croup. Family tradition would have had them traveling down to the Uhrenholdt farm at Seeley, Wisconsin, for Christmas, but the boys were too ill. Elizabeth could not bear the thought of not going home. The farm and her parents and her happy childhood memories were a vital part of her, and she clung to them as Sigurd clung to his need of the outdoors. It was a sore point with Soren and Kristine, who believed their daughter ought to establish her own holiday traditions. Still, Elizabeth called them to see if she and Sigurd could come sometime after Christmas, leaving the boys with friends in Ely. Soren, initially adamantly against the idea, relented after Elizabeth started crying over the phone.

Sigurd's cold was getting worse, but he did not protest Elizabeth's plans. He could be very self-centered when it came to doing the things that were most important to him, but he also was a very compliant husband who let Elizabeth take charge of most family matters and almost always accepted whatever she wanted or decided. Several days after Christmas he drove Elizabeth the two hundred miles to the farm in their unheated car, and almost immediately he developed pneumonia.

Breathing became a chore as his lungs filled with fluid, and it soon was obvious that local medical care would be inadequate. Frantic, Elizabeth called one of Sigurd's summertime canoe trip clients, Charles Bacon, a highly regarded doctor at Chicago's Presbyterian Hospital. Bacon, who was very fond of Sigurd, rushed north to Seeley with drugs and medical equipment. By the time he got there Olson was fighting for each breath, and Bacon told Elizabeth that Sigurd might not make it past midnight. If he did, Bacon added, there was hope.

Olson spent days under an oxygen mask, sedated with morphine. A friend from Ely brought the children to stay with a family in Hayward while their father slowly recovered. Later, in April, Sigurd would recall the period almost with nostalgia:

> Those nights when all was peace and quiet, when all my worries were gone and I seemed to be drifting off into space, the gurgling of the oxygen tanks and their likeness to rapids in the dusk, how can I ever forget it. It was the closest I ever came to sheer beauty and peace. And more, death will never again be a fearsome thing, or the hereafter—it is all so natural and so welcome when the time has come.

Maybe it was his closeness to death, maybe it was the letter from Alvin Cahn, maybe it was all the time he had to think while he recovered from pneumonia, but in February 1931 Sigurd Olson made up his mind and applied to graduate school. "After all," he wrote in his journal a few weeks later, "I believe this is the saner thing for if I was to give up everything for writing I am afraid there would be nothing but failure ahead. This way if I go ahead and get some more scientific work out of the way I can still write occasionally and have that satisfaction and make a good living too." Following up on Aldo Leopold's tip, he applied to the University of Michigan, which awarded the pheasant fellowship; he also applied to Michigan State College and to the University of Illinois.

Cahn wrote back on March 12 that all of the zoology department faculty members at Illinois had given Sigurd a high rating and that he was first on the list of forty applicants for an assistantship. Soon afterward, Leopold and Ralph King broached the possibility of trying to get Sigurd a three-year fellowship to study moose, which would open the way to a doctoral degree. The funding was uncertain, however, and Leopold thought that Michigan "is a better place to make a start" in any case. When the University of Michigan and Michigan State College awarded their respective fellowships to others, Sigurd accepted the offer from Illinois. "Personally," Cahn wrote on May 11, "I think it is a rather good year to come here, from the point of view of your health."

Elizabeth was willing to go along with her husband's plan, undoubtedly hoping it would lead to a new career and a better attitude. Her sister Johanne, apparently reflecting comments she had received in a letter from Elizabeth, wrote to Soren and Kristine Uhrenholdt about Sigurd's decision: "Sig has been growing more and more irritable and dissatisfied and I think that he really needs a change. He is too young to settle down for year after year in the same routine, particularly with his disposition. And nothing will help to get him really well again so fast as a new interest will do."[9]

❖

Although the formal, scientific use of the term *ecology* was sixty-five years old in 1931, as a field it was still very young, with much disagreement over its proper scope and fundamental principles. It attracted students of natural history, biology, physiology, botany, and other disciplines and was for the most part divided into two almost entirely independent camps: plant ecology and animal ecology.[10]

The plant ecologists, having gotten a head start in research, dominated in theory-building, and since the turn of the century the theory-building had been dominated by a Nebraska-born American named Frederic Clements. More than anything else, Clements is known for promoting the idea of ecological succession among plant communities. He argued that a given area's vegetation progresses through a series of identifiable stages (which he called a *sere*) to a final climax stage. While soil conditions determined the mix of vegetation in early stages, climate ultimately determined the species that constituted an area's climax community. Because lasting climatic change takes place only over very long periods of time, Clements's climax communities existed in relative equilibrium. Fires, plows, insects, and axes could disrupt a sere or a climax community, but the process leading to the climax stage would then start once again.

Clements also recognized interrelationships between plants and animals. In 1916 he introduced the concept of *biome*, which he defined as "an organic unit comprising all the species of plants and animals at home in a particular habitat." While he argued that plants, not animals, wielded the most influence in a community, his concept of the biome opened the door to a working relationship between plant and animal ecologists. One of the first people to step through that door, and certainly the most influential among Americans before World War II, was Victor E. Shelford.

Trained at the University of Chicago under Henry Chandler Cowles, America's first professional ecologist, Shelford earned his doctoral degree in 1907 after completing a dissertation on tiger beetles. Six years later he published a pathbreaking book, *Animal Communities in Temperate America*. The book was the first to discuss what he called "food relations" and eventually would be called food webs; it also anticipated the concept of niche, a function of population dynamics and food supply. *Animal Communities* established Shelford as a leading ecologist, and in 1915 he became the founding president of the Ecological Society of America.

Shelford adapted Clements's concept of succession to animal ecology, arguing that animal communities progress toward a climax equilibrium in which predator/prey population fluctuations and other food supplies reach a balance. But Shelford did not approve of the artificial separation of animal and plant ecology. To him, ecology meant "the science of communities," and he maintained that the biome was the "natural ecological unit." He was distressed at the lack of botanical knowledge among animal biologists, and he chastised botanists for failing to recognize the influence of animals on plant communities.

In the 1920s Shelford began a long and often difficult collaboration with Frederic Clements in an attempt to create a unified theoretical approach that they called bioecology. Shelford was a thoroughly practical man, but Clements was dogmatic and at times defensive, and only strong determination on the part of both men gave the project any chance of success. Their partnership from 1927 through the 1930s was the most exciting in the field. When Sigurd Olson entered the University of Illinois in the fall of 1931 and was assigned Victor Shelford as his major professor, he unwittingly was about to benefit from the ongoing exchange of ideas between America's two leading ecologists.

And he hated it. He got along well with Shelford, but he hated laboratory work and memorizing Latin names and the jargon of scientific ecology. "I hate the very sound of the word Ecology," he wrote on December 14. "When I get through with it here, I am through. I will bury it away someplace and never again as long as I live ever touch it."

To make matters worse, the Olsons lost nearly all of their savings shortly after arriving, when banks in Ely and Urbana failed. Sigurd's assistantship covered tuition and provided a small salary, enough to get by, but they had to live in a cheap house right next to a railroad. Three times each night the house shook as the Panama Limited roared past on its way south from Chicago. Elizabeth and the boys had given up friends and the comforts of home to put Sigurd through graduate school, and Elizabeth, who also was grieving the death of her mother, was getting tired of her husband's complaining and his long search for fulfillment. The day after Christmas Sigurd wrote that she had reproached him and asked why he could never be happy. He did not know the answer. "How I have thought and explored the innermost reaches of my nature and found nothing but confusion," he wrote. "For ten years that has been going on and still I am at sea."[11]

During the last week of 1931, while he was staying with relatives in Ann Arbor, Sigurd visited the University of Michigan School of Forestry and Conservation. This was the program Leopold had recommended, where game management rather than ecological theory was the focus. Olson thought that perhaps he was simply at the wrong school, but he found the atmosphere in Ann Arbor just as stifling as that in Champaign. Just one professor seemed to feel as he did about nature. "The others," he wrote, "were so bound up in their own petty affairs that they hardly had time to talk or visit and [placed] far too much [value] upon their dignity to ever smile or get enthusiastic. These men have lived too much indoors. . . . How few are the men who love the game for its own sake."[12]

Once again he turned to Thoreau for encouragement, and also to Ralph Waldo Emerson. Writing in Ann Arbor on December 29, he listed his favorite excerpts. From Emerson he had gathered the following advice: "A man is relieved and gay only when he has put his heart into his work and done his best"; "Only true happiness can come from and through yourself"; "Be yourself, there is no other quite like you. Only through the development of your own genius will you acquire self reliance." In Thoreau he found what he took as confirmation: "A man should greet each dawn joyfully and always consider the nights too long an absenting from one's work."

Olson would repeat this passage from Thoreau many times in the years ahead. But what work could he find that would make him greet the dawn with joy? On New Year's Eve he again felt sure he knew, having reached the same conclusion he had come to a number of other times but found hard to follow. He had spent the day in the Detroit Museum of Art and again confronted the fact that it was the aesthetics of nature, not the science, that absorbed him. "What has kept me in the woods all of these years is the love of beauty," he wrote:

> If I was watching a beaver it was not the beaver and its habits as much as it was the light on the pool, the dark mystery of the forest around the pool, the symmetry of the dam. If I was trailing a deer, it was not so much the habits of the deer as it was the vistas I gained along the ridges and through the trees. If it was ducks, it was more than anything else the view of a flock against the sunset or dawn in the rice rather than the birds themselves. In other words it was the scene as a whole which drew me and that I mistook for a keen interest in natural history for lack of a better explanation.

Olson concluded once again that what he wanted more than anything was "to paint either in word or color the pictures that have been before me." And so, during his second and final semester at Illinois, he spent as much free time as possible working on his writing. (He briefly considered trying to make it as an artist but decided that at thirty-two he was too old to start.) At the same time, despite his boredom with school, he worked hard enough to earn a total of eleven A's and one B. He did a number of field studies, writing papers on plant and animal succession and invasion in several different types of ecological communities, including a prairie, a beech-maple forest, a lake, and, notably, the Indiana Dunes area along Lake Michigan. The dunes were the site of Shelford's doctoral research, and in the 1950s Olson would become active in efforts to protect them from economic development.

Along the way, Olson not only learned the ecological concepts advanced by Shelford and Clements but also absorbed their key assumptions, the most important of which was an organismic perspective. Shelford and Clements argued that a biotic community was a complex organism in which the whole was greater than the sum of the parts. This idea, which Clements had taken from the nineteenth-century evolutionary theorist Herbert Spencer, logically led to a belief that nature did not lend itself to the reductive methodology commonly used in modern science. This train of thought meshed well with Olson's romantic inclination and with the profound and completely immeasurable wilderness epiphanies that had given him momentary feelings of oneness with the entire universe. He would have an organismic ecological perspective the rest of his days.

The science of ecology, on the other hand, began turning away from an organismic perspective even before Shelford and Clements completed their collaboration with the publication of *Bio-Ecology* in 1939. British ecologist Arthur Tansley attacked the concept in 1935, saying that these "wholes . . . are *in analysis* nothing but the synthesized actions of the components in associations."[13] Tansley advocated a reductionist approach that focused on the study of energy relationships within an *ecosystem*, a term he created to emphasize the integrated and systemic—but not holistic—relationships among organisms. This approach, which focused on energy transfers and cycles of such nutrients as nitrogen and phosphorus, came to dominate the field by the 1940s, while the organismic perspective became the idea of ecology that dominated among conservation group leaders and ultimately lodged in the public mind.

The organismic approach to ecology that Olson learned at the University of Illinois led to a complete reversal of his attitude toward predators. If the "whole" of a biotic community is greater than the sum of its parts, then all of the parts become valuable. As Aldo Leopold would write in 1941, as part of an essay that became "The Round River":

If the land mechanism as a whole is good, then every part of it is good, whether we understand it or not. If the biota, in the course of aeons, has built something we like but do not understand, then who but a fool would discard seemingly useless parts? To keep every cog and wheel is the first precaution of intelligent tinkering.[14]

Victor Shelford had reached this conclusion, but without Leopold's eloquence, before the end of World War I. In 1917 he became the chair of the Ecological Society of America's Committee on Preservation of Natural Conditions, which over the next four years selected six hundred natural areas in North America for preservation as "living museums." During the 1920s the committee publicly lobbied for a number of wildlands, and Shelford also advocated an end to the indiscriminate poisoning of predators. By the time Olson entered the University of Illinois, Shelford was leading the Ecological Society of America in an acrimonious battle against the Bureau of Biological Survey. Under his tutelage, and that of Shelford protégé Alvin Cahn, Olson joined the ranks of wolf advocates.

Olson's master's thesis, "The Life History of the Timber Wolf and the Coyote: A Study in Predatory Animal Control," relied on the material he had gathered late in 1930, before his bout with pneumonia. At that time, he had taken a generally dim view of wolves. The thesis showed the enthusiasm of a convert from the very first paragraph:

During the past quarter of a century the American people have heard much in regard to the conservation of animal life, but to the majority of them, the word conservation has meant and still means, the saving of our herbivores at the expense of other forms of life. The predators, those animals which live upon the herbivores, have not come under the plan of conservation as outlined, and in most areas, an attempt has been made to eliminate them entirely, disregarding the effect these animals have upon the balance of life in the communities in which they live. . . .

The public, always gullible, has accepted the most exaggerated reports as to the activities of these animals. If a government ranger or hunter makes a report that timber wolves kill a deer a week, it is accepted as fact and immediately any program which will tend to eliminate the terrible menace to wild life is heartily endorsed. If a statement comes out that a mountain lion has killed an elk, or coyote a sheep, it is without further evidence concluded that all

mountain lions are elk killers, and all coyotes live upon are sheep. . . .
We are all familiar with similar instances and because there has
been no attempt to disprove these theories, no money expended in
honest scientific endeavor to find out what is the truth, the campaigns of extermination have been going on unchecked.

Olson's thesis attacked the stereotypes he had advanced in "The
Poison Trail," particularly the notion that wolves kill for the pure joy
of killing and subsequently waste much of what they kill. He did
not discount the possibility that wolves take pleasure in the hunt—
although he argued that "their depredations have been grossly over-
estimated"—but rather than turn the issue into a moral one, he said
that wolves have an instinctive desire for the chase no different from
that of hunting dogs. As to their wasting food, he pointed out that
an untouched deer carcass is not sufficient evidence for the claim
that wolves waste food; his own field research as well as the information given him by Ely-area game wardens and trappers showed that
wolves often returned to a kill days or even weeks later, indicating
that the carcasses were treated as stored food. "The fact that a pack
of timber wolves will kill several deer in a night, leaving them where
they fell without touching their carcasses is a storage act pure and
simple," he wrote, "and not done for the joy of killing as many would
make believe."

Olson did not completely overthrow the stereotypes. For example,
in a paragraph in which he mentioned in passing another reason why
wolves might not return to their kill—that they had grown suspicious of carcasses after being subjected to years of trapping and poisoning campaigns—he demonstrated that even when he was defending the wolf he could fall into his earlier habits of description: "The
wolves, passing by one of their own kills a day later, are again the
shrewd, crafty killers, suspicious of everything." Overall, however, his
thesis was testimony to his conversion to the organismic perspective
of ecology and a newfound fondness for predators. He concluded
with a call—radical for its time—to designate the canoe country's Superior National Forest as a carnivore sanctuary.

Olson eventually published parts of his wolf research in *Ecology*
and *Scientific Monthly*,[15] and his work continued to be cited decades
later—despite technological advances that greatly improved the study

of wolves—simply because it broke ground in university research. "Sig Olson's was the first scientific study of the wolf anywhere in the world," said L. David Mech, who sixty years later was one of the world's top authorities on wolves. "Although it did not lead to any major insight into the life of the wolf, it was a milestone in first treating the wolf as a worthy subject for scientific research."[16]

At the time, however, Olson was thinking less of his contribution to wolf knowledge than of his return to wolf country. On April 20, 1932, a month before his second and final semester of graduate school was over, and exactly six weeks before his thesis was approved, Olson sat in Shelford's economic ecology class, hating every minute of it. "I am reaching a point," he wrote in his class notebook, "where the farcical nature of what I am doing is beginning to impress me. This is not what I want. I am going away never to come back."

Six

A Need for Recognition

1932–1935

In June 1932 the Olsons returned to northern Minnesota. The house they had rented on White Street had long since been rented to others, so they located temporary quarters in Winton, in an old cottage that had neither electricity nor running water. By fall they had found a square, two-story frame house for rent on one of Ely's nicest streets. Broad and shaded by beautiful maples, Harvey Street ran west to east, parallel to the city's main street two blocks to the north. Ely's central school complex—grade school, high school, junior college—faced Harvey Street one block to the east of the Olsons, and one block to their west was the Presbyterian church where the Olsons worshiped.

At a time when almost one person out of every four was unemployed and the country was nearly in a panic over the economy, Sigurd was moving up. With his master's degree in hand, he was among Ely's most educated citizens, and in the fall he was assigned for the first time to teach mostly at the junior college. His high school teaching load was reduced to one course, down two classes from his previous load. "That will raise my self esteem somewhat," he wrote on September 16.

By and large, the Olsons led a very conventional life. Sigurd resumed his work with the Boy Scouts at the district level and gradually became involved to varying degrees in a number of local organizations, including the American Legion, the Rotary Club, the Masons, the Ely Commercial Club, and the St. Louis County Club. He sometimes sang with local quartets and the Presbyterian church choir. Elizabeth had a large circle of friends and took charge of the family's social calendar. Sigurd Jr., who turned nine in September 1932, and Robert, who turned seven that December, remember their early childhood with much fondness. Robert recalled:

> My father loved horseplay and laughter. In a moment he could be like a kid, rolling around on the floor, laughing fit to split. He used to tell us "moose stories" at bedtime, raw material made up on the spur of the moment like "the moose with the rubber horns" or the adventures and misadventures of Roscoe and Boscoe, the two little chipmunks, which sent us giggling and screeching with laughter under the covers at last.

"Dad never read us books as far as I can remember; he made up his own stories," Sigurd Jr. said. I can remember lying up on the bed, my brother and I, just shrieking with laughter, not just us kids but dad as well."

Their father also entertained them, along with their friends, by making a silly face that he called "the look of eagles." "It would send us kids into *hysterics*," said Sigurd Jr. And the elder Sigurd loved to sing, getting the whole family involved. Robert recalled:

> To live was to sing. As a family we sang in the living room at night, around the campfire, on long drives to the cities, laughing at mother who joined in but could never carry a tune. Our program was catch-as-catch-can, mainly the old folk songs, cowboy ballads, work songs, spirituals, "Frankie and Johnny," "The Streets of Laredo," World War I songs like "Tipperary" and "There's a Long Long Trail," old favorites like "Home on the Range" and "The Red River Valley."[1]

If Sigurd could not remember some of the words, he would fill in with syllables: da, da, da. Elizabeth recalled a time when Robert made his parents laugh by saying, "Sing, daddy—but none of that 'da da' stuff."

Of course, there were many family excursions outdoors. Day trips in the summer might mean paddling a canoe along the sparkling, island-filled Burntside Lake northwest of Ely, or the darker, mysterious Kawishiwi River to the east. Fall meant exploring the mallard-filled wild rice marshes of Garden and Basswood Lakes or gathering pine knots to add color to the fireplace flames in the long months ahead. Winter included many cross-country skiing excursions along a ridge south of town that Sigurd called "the skyline trail," from which they enjoyed a magnificent view of the sunset. Spring meant watching the ice break up, gathering pussy willows, and listening to the rollicking calls of the loons as they returned from the Gulf states.

Sigurd and Elizabeth took the boys cross-country skiing almost as soon as they could walk, and in canoes from the time they were babies. "That was just part of everyday living," said Sigurd Jr. Gradually the boys learned the techniques of skiing and canoeing and of other outdoor activites; occasionally their father would give them some advice, but mostly they learned through imitation. Sigurd Jr. remembered that "Dad looked so natural in the canoe all the time that I thought, 'That's the way I'm going to be.' And just by watching him I learned to do it."

In much the same way, the boys learned the ways of nature. Their father did not lecture to them as they hiked through the woods; he would simply point things out in an interesting way. "He was a born teacher when it came right down to it," said Sigurd Jr.:

> You learned as he made observations on things. If you asked questions then he'd tell you, but he wouldn't say, "Now here's something" and then give you a lecture on it. It would be like this: "Oh, look at that piece of shale. This was probably lake bottom here at one time. See how it's layered here? See how it's broken here? Well, that probably got disrupted and something pushed it up there, a harder rock." That kind of thing. And that's the way we'd learn.

Looking back on his childhood sixty years later, what most impressed Sigurd Jr. was how his father made almost everything fun: "We didn't have to have major adventures to make a trip memorable. There always seemed to be things along the way that you could see—small things, mostly—but in seeing them and talking about them they became mini adventures." The elder Sigurd *did* have a temper, and he would not tolerate shoddy work, but both sons remember idolizing him during their early childhood.

The only unconventional aspects of the Olson family were, in Robert's words, his father's "insatiable appetite for ramming around the woods, and this inextinguishable urge, the need to write."

The appetite for the woods was obvious to everyone. Sigurd could never get enough of the outdoors and often was away from home.

"Dad used to take off on a Friday night and go trout fishing or something like that with one of his pals," recalled Robert. "He'd spend the whole weekend in the woods. I remember his coming home at ten-thirty, eleven o'clock some nights after trout fishing. It used to worry Mother sick. He'd just come home when he felt like it. Then he'd go deer hunting in the fall—that was maybe for a week—and a lot of duck hunting."

Sigurd Jr. pointed out that "Dad of course had his school work to keep up with." But, he added, "when he could, which was fairly often, particularly during duck season, he'd go hunting, and be gone Saturday and Sunday, or go on a fishing trip and be gone overnight. He'd take off at least once during the fall and go pheasant hunting in western Minnesota."

None of the family resented this. Elizabeth always maintained that she both expected and accepted her husband's excursions. Robert qualified her account, but just a little:

> I think she would have *liked* to have had him around more. Undoubtedly there would have been a *preference* for something more conventional. But you get used to a lot of different things. I accepted the fact that Dad was gone weekends out in the woods. That's the way it was. I didn't think anything of it and my mother so far as I know never said anything to me. The rambling around was fun—he'd come home with fish and ducks and he'd have family feeds, neighbors and friends getting together for fall duck feeds. That was all good, healthy stuff.

Sigurd Jr. also accepted it: "I can never remember resenting the fact that we didn't go along. I can remember *wanting* to go along."

Less obvious to the children in the early 1930s was their father's "inextinguishable urge" to write. It had not yet become disruptive of family life. Nor did they realize how unhappy he was in his career; he worked hard to keep his feelings hidden. "Each morning," he wrote in his journal on December 15, 1932, "I come to work heavy of heart, each noon go home with a forced smile and at night look forward only to sleep and forgetfulness. I try to hide my despondency from Elizabeth . . . and of course the boys never catch on. If they only knew, life around home would take on a blueish tint."

Elizabeth, of course, was highly aware of Sigurd's desire to write, and she knew he hated his job, but she had no inkling of the under-lying psychological needs that he expressed in his journals. On February 6, 1933, for example, he again wrote of his desire to quit teaching, and he discussed the main alternatives, writing or ecology. Ultimately, it came down to this:

> What I want is to be able to do something different so that my friends can point me out as one who has ability of a sort and can make his way by his brains alone. I cannot stand mediocrity—I must know that I am being appreciated. Ego, my vanity must be satisfied.

Teaching did not satisfy Sigurd's need for recognition; the need was far too great. A journal entry from November 11, 1933, is a case in point:

> Sigurd Ferdinand Olson, the name at least has a lilt to it and a swing. Ferdinand at second glance has a note of Spanish romance and so for that matter has Sigurd. My ideal is to make that name, above all else, something to conjure with. Sig Olson is common, Sig is bad but Sigurd Ferdinand is something different again. It needs the Ferdinand to take it out of the realm of mediocrity, and to give it euphony. . . . As I develop, it will become increasingly well known and respected.

Sigurd often played with his name, writing it different ways down a sheet of paper: Sig Olson, Sigurd Olson, Sigurd F. Olson, Sigurd Ferdinand Olson. He also experimented with his mother-in-law's maiden name of Thorn, which he thought had a nice ring to it. Unwittingly misspelling it by adding a final e (just as he and Elizabeth did when they made it Sigurd Jr.'s middle name), Olson sometimes sent out freelance articles under the byline Sigurd Thorne or, less frequently, Sigurd Thorne Olson. This was all part of a concern for image that was a symptom of both his desire for greatness and his fear of mediocrity.

Writing provided an opportunity to find a kind of recognition that extended beyond what Olson could get in Ely. It also addressed his unusually strong urge to lose himself in *creative* work. But he did not yet have much confidence, and he often felt frustrated in his ability to express what he felt. "Only one who has experienced what I have, the longing for creation, can understand how terrible it is to find oneself inadequate," he wrote on October 19, 1933.

On an autumn excursion, Sigurd had witnessed a stirring sunset from the shore of a river. The heavy mist over the water, the sun casting a deep golden glow on the aspens and birches, the boulders silhouetted against the glowing sky, the gurgling of rapids—it was all too much beauty for him to capture, he wrote the next day:

> It was almost more than I could bear. It hurt me. I wanted to run away and sob. It hurts me today. Why should it—it should make me happy. Is it because I am over sensitive or that I realize that I can never attain or hold such beauty? But I must if I am not to go insane. I must capture some of that somehow—create something durable.[2]

All of this must be taken into consideration in order to understand Olson's reaction to an offer from Aldo Leopold that arrived in the mail early in November 1933. Leopold, having accepted an appointment in July from the University of Wisconsin at Madison, had just become the country's first titled professor of game management, and he wanted Olson to become his first doctoral student.

"I have no funds as yet," Leopold wrote, "but if I had an extra strong man lined up and a definite amount to shoot at, it might help me to get them. . . . What would be the minimum stipend necessary to attract you?"[3]

After all that Olson had been through at the University of Illinois, it would not have been surprising if he had rejected the offer quickly. But he did not. Instead, he agonized over it: "Do I want to do that sort of thing again, and tie up another three years of my life, hunting the unattainable?" he wrote in his journal.[4]

Sigurd told Elizabeth that this was his last big opportunity, that to turn Leopold down "would forever damn me in his eyes and in the eyes of all those who are interested in game." Elizabeth responded that she wanted him to do whatever would make him happy. "Perhaps in the end it will mean travel and fame and a chance to do a tremendous amount of good," Olson wrote in his journal. "Then too I believe Lib would be quite proud of me, as she would realize that I was doing something worthwhile. No longer would it be the treadmill of getting nowhere."

Sigurd may have been thinking of the success enjoyed by his older brother, Kenneth, who had left the University of Wisconsin to become a tenured professor in journalism at the University of Minnesota. And yet:

> The only thing that will give me real joy is the painting of word pictures, moods, and emotions. To describe a hillside covered with snow so that my reader could feel what I feel, there is something worth while. . . . If I accept Leopold's offer, there it will be again, research and more research.[5]

Sigurd's November 17 response to Leopold was ambivalent. While he showed interest in the offer, he seemed to go out of his way to make it easy for Leopold to find someone else. "I am afraid that I will have to ask too much to put me in the running," Olson wrote. "I am 34 years of age, have a family of two growing boys to support, insurance, and other incidentals which would make it impossible for me, in view of the fact that my annual outlay has been keyed up to a certain figure, to accept a stipend as low as I could were I single and on my own." He told Leopold how much his combined income from teaching and from the Border Lakes Outfitting Company amounted to each year and said perhaps he could work something out if he would be able to continue as manager of the Border Lakes, "but that naturally would take me out of the field of research during the summer months." Olson must have thought that Leopold would reject these terms.

But Leopold did not. "I am glad you wrote me frankly concerning the difficulties of our working together," he replied on November 23. "Assuming that an arrangement could be made which would not call for your services during the active outfitting season, between what dates would you have to absent yourself for company work at Ely?" Leopold also asked if Olson would be interested in studying white-tailed deer in Wisconsin, or in studying the state's marshlands.

Whatever doubts Sigurd had, he moved fast, writing back on November 27 to say that if he could manage the Border Lakes during the peak tourist season, from June 1 to September 15, he could probably accept Leopold's offer; he added that either research topic would be interesting, but hinted that the marshland survey was closer to his heart, because "ducks have become more or less of a religion with me."

On December 5 Leopold sent Olson a telegram saying he had found four hundred dollars for a two-month survey of Wisconsin marshes, starting immediately. Leopold believed that the temporary job would lead to longer-term employment as a waterfowl specialist. Sigurd would be able to do his doctoral research while receiving a monthly salary that exceeded what he made as a teacher. Olson hurriedly sent Leopold a telegram in reply: "Am requesting board for leave of absence. Will let you know as soon as I know. Give latest date."

But Leopold had to renege. "I am extremely sorry to have caused you all this disturbance," he wrote on December 7, "but I was entirely unaware that you still held your teaching position." The marshland research job was a civil works position with a prerequisite of unemployment. "I had hoped to get by on your outfitting business by simply regarding it as an investment rather than a salary," Leopold said, but he could not get around Olson's teaching position.

Leopold was not finished, however. He had found another game management position at roughly the same salary, with no restrictions on current employment. The work would involve studying tax-defaulted, vacated farms for possible development as gameland.

But Olson had lost heart. It was embarrassing to request a leave of absence only to lose the position he had hoped to take. And Leopold should have known better; Olson's letter of November 17 had made it clear he was employed. Sigurd turned down the new offer, and in his journal once again confessed that life as an ecologist was not the life for him anyway: "I can see myself back in a room at night, trying to get some small comfort out of pounding off some little article. . . . The secret of my discontent with all scientific research is that at heart I am not a scientist, although I am rated as one. . . . It bores me to death and always will."[6]

❖

Being pursued by Aldo Leopold, even if nothing came of it, must have felt good to a man who believed he was not getting enough recognition. But Olson received public attention and praise beyond Ely that same fall of 1933, when he traveled to Minneapolis and testified at his first public hearing on the management of the Quetico-Superior canoe country.

The October hearing at the Curtis Hotel was held by the International Joint Commission, which under a 1909 treaty between the United States and Canada was responsible for studying and resolving questions about the use of international waters. At issue was an immense waterpower development plan proposed by Edward W. Backus, a Minnesota lumberman whose holdings on both sides of the border in the canoe country made him the continent's fourth-largest newsprint manufacturer. Backus, who already had built dams that controlled water levels on the border lakes Namakan and Kabetogama, proposed building nine storage dams that would generate twenty thousand horsepower for his power dams between Rainy Lake and Lake Winnipeg. He wanted the cost to be borne by power users and by the governments of Canada and the United States.[7]

Under Backus's plan, several thousand miles of canoe country shoreline would have been flooded, wiping out rapids, waterfalls, islands. Little Vermilion Lake's water level would have been increased by eighty feet, Loon Lake's by thirty-three feet, Saganaga and Crooked lakes' by fifteen feet. Lac la Croix, part of the U.S. government's initial reservation of land in 1905 because of its beauty, would have been raised fifteen feet. Nearly all of its three hundred islands would have disappeared, and the virgin pine along its shores would have been inundated.

The International Joint Commission had begun studying the proposal in 1925. At its initial hearing that year in International Falls, Minnesota, a city heavily dependent on Backus for its economic well-being, Backus was the only witness who supported the plan. This undoubtedly reflected his reputation among local citizens for dishonest and ruthless behavior. He had, for example, once attempted to cheat a widow with ten children out of the income she got from leasing her riverfront property to him. One of her children had died, and she asked him if he would pay his rent in advance so she could pay for the funeral. Backus agreed, but the receipt she thought she was signing actually gave him the right to use her property for free from that time on. She sued, and Backus lost in appeals court.

Despite the forty-four to one outpouring of testimony against the waterpower proposal, the commission had decided to pursue a feasibility study. Seven years passed before the study was completed. Meanwhile, American conservationists had tried to make things more difficult for Backus by asking the U.S. Congress to pass a bill forbidding any alteration of water levels on federal land in the area. They also had asked for a ban on shoreline logging. When President Herbert Hoover (a former national officer of the Izaak Walton League of America) signed the resulting bill into law as the Shipstead-Nolan Act on July 10, 1930, it was the first time the U.S. government had enacted a law meant to preserve wilderness.

The engineers working for the International Joint Commission had released their report in April 1932 without a formal recommendation, but they had outlined a proposal that supported Backus in almost every way. Conservationists had taken comfort in the dissent of one of the engineers and gained hope when Backus ran into deep financial difficulties that forced his companies into receivership, but the receivers had continued to press forward with a modified version of his proposal. When the commission held its final hearings during October 1933 in the cities of Winnipeg and Minneapolis, it still was anyone's guess what the decision would be.

The *Minneapolis Star* portrayed the hearing in its city as a mostly tedious affair: "All through the three days of testimony in Minneapolis—much of it inexpert, irrelevant and tiresomely personal, never have the commissioners betrayed impatience or blatant lack of interest. Never has a witness, no matter how verbose, been hurried."[8] Sigurd Olson, who represented Ely area outfitters and resort owners at the hearing, may have been one of the verbose witnesses to whom the reporter referred. According to his own recollection late in life, as well as Elizabeth's, he spoke on the stand for forty-five minutes instead of the allotted ten. He said that C. A. McGrath, the Canadian chairman of the commission, kept him on the stand visiting about canoe routes.

The day after he testified, Sigurd wrote in his journal nothing about how long he had spoken and nothing about McGrath, but it was clear that something important had transpired. "I went down to the hearing with little knowledge of what I wanted to say and up to the time I took the stand, I knew nothing," he wrote. He did not even remember what it was that he *did* say. He only recalled this: that of all the people who testified that day, he was the only one to receive applause. Mulling this over, Olson decided that "somehow I have the power of conveying my enthusiasm to others, particularly men. I can make them see and feel what I see and feel of the out of doors."[9]

Sigurd saw this revelation as having direct bearing on his dream of writing, but his testimony also marked the beginning of a new phase in his role as a wilderness activist. In the past, his conservation work had been almost exclusively at the local level, mostly speaking to Ely civic groups about the necessity of preserving the canoe country wilderness. He had, for example, convinced the Ely Commercial Club in March 1933 to oppose a Minnesota Power and Light dam on state land at the outlet of Gabbro Lake (located just inside the southern border of today's Boundary Waters Canoe Area Wilderness). The project was stopped later in the year when the Minnesota Legislature passed a law similar to the federal Shipstead-Nolan Act. Olson's testimony in Minneapolis gained him attention at the state level of the Izaak Walton League. Even more important, he was commended by a man who was emerging as a national leader in wilderness preservation: Ernest C. Oberholtzer, soon after the International Joint Commission hearing, placed Olson on his select mailing list of conservation correspondents.

Oberholtzer, known to his friends as "Ober," has been described as "an elf"—not just because he stood five feet six inches tall, weighed 130 pounds, and had protruding ears, but also because he had a lively spirit. He was a great storyteller who loved to entertain guests at his rustic island home on Rainy Lake, along the Minnesota-Ontario border northwest of Sigurd Olson's home in Ely.[10]

Oberholtzer first saw the canoe country in the summer of 1908, right after he graduated from Harvard University with a degree in landscape architecture. Soon he was exploring the far north in Canada with Billy Magee, an Ojibwe guide who became a close friend. They found old Hudson's Bay Company outposts and traveled through land that no white man had seen in well over a century. By 1912 Oberholtzer began to confine his wilderness travels to the Rainy Lake watershed, which included Quetico Provincial Park and Superior National Forest. More interested in learning Ojibwe culture and history from Billy Magee and his people than in holding a steady job, Oberholtzer settled on Rainy Lake and lived a quiet, simple life.

Quiet and simple, that is, until he heard about Backus's water-power plans. Oberholtzer was one of the people who testified against the proposal at the original International Joint Commission hearing in International Falls in 1925. After the hearing, he and Sewell T.

Tyng, a neighbor's son-in-law who happened to be a Wall Street lawyer, put together a brief that they filed with the commission. This brief, in turn, attracted the attention of a group of Minneapolis men who also opposed the waterpower plans. At forty-one, Oberholtzer was older than most of these men, as well as less gainfully employed, and they pushed and prodded until he agreed to work for them and lead the effort to stop Backus.

Actually, however, their intentions went way beyond stopping Backus. Oberholtzer developed a plan to seek a treaty between the United States and Canada that would establish a land management program for the entire fourteen thousand square miles of the Rainy Lake watershed. He wanted most of the watershed to be preserved as wilderness, which in turn would be surrounded by a buffer zone of government-owned land that would be leased to private camps; beyond the buffer zone would be the homes and highways and cities. The two countries would jointly manage the watershed, with an eye toward maximizing fish and wildlife populations and practicing modern forestry. Logging would be allowed, except near the shorelines of lakes and streams, where it would be visible to passing canoeists.

By the end of 1927, Oberholtzer had received support for his plan from the U.S. Forest Service, the U.S. secretary of agriculture, and the Izaak Walton League. He and his friends from Minneapolis then created the Quetico-Superior Council as an organization associated with the Izaak Walton League but with the express purpose of seeking the international treaty. Oberholtzer became its president.

Sigurd Olson probably first heard of Oberholtzer in January 1928, when the Izaak Walton League's magazine, *Outdoor America*, published the Oberholtzer speech that led to the establishment of the Quetico-Superior Council. Olson apparently wrote to Oberholtzer for the first time on December 26, 1930, saying that an international reserve "is the only solution to the problem." A year later, while he was on Christmas vacation from the University of Illinois, Sigurd made his first donation to the Quetico-Superior Council, a check for twenty-five dollars. But the two men did not meet until at least the fall of 1932, when Olson's Border Lakes outfitted Oberholtzer and several others who were traveling along the international boundary to gather information that might help in building arguments against

Backus's dams. After Sigurd's testimony in October 1933, they began to visit each other every now and then, and to work together on conservation matters.

Most of the surviving correspondence consists of carbon copies of Oberholtzer's conservation letters, which he sent to a number of people; Oberholtzer made enough copies that those who received the last one sometimes found the type on the green onionskin paper difficult to read. There is no personal correspondence between the two men, nothing that might indicate a genuine friendship.

It seems more likely that their relationship was that of mentor and pupil. Oberholtzer was fifteen years older than Olson and had a far superior liberal education. Despite the rustic simplicity of his home on Rainy Lake, Oberholtzer was sophisticated to a degree that Olson undoubtedly admired and possibly envied. Oberholtzer counted among his friends a number of East Coast intellectuals, including Samuel Eliot Morison, Van Wyck Brooks, Conrad Aiken, and Max Perkins. He knew millionaires and had ties to the White House through his friendship with the mercurial Interior Secretary Harold Ickes.

Not only that, Oberholtzer had explored the far north, which Olson had longed to see for himself, and wrote articles that spoke a language with which Sigurd could identify. "Men want the simplicity, the healing peace, the imaginative stimulus of the wilderness," wrote Oberholtzer, who added in another article that "while some attempt has been made to guard and restore a small part of the material resources [of the Quetico-Superior], scarcely anything has been done until lately even to recognize—much less protect—those far more unique and precious factors involved in the spiritual resources."[11]

Elizabeth Olson recalled a number of occasions when she and Sigurd visited with "Ober" at his Rainy Lake home; if it was summer, they usually would sample some of Oberholtzer's homemade ice cream. Certainly during these visits, or perhaps other times when Sigurd came alone, Sigurd and Oberholtzer would have discussed their common interests in the canoe country's history. (Oberholtzer undoubtedly showed his passion for Ojibwe culture, while Olson displayed *his* primary interest in the legendary exploits of the voyageurs.) And at times they must have talked about the *meaning* of wilderness as they each saw it, and the attendant problems and opportunities for preserving wildlands.

After October 1933 Oberholtzer began to bring Olson into active involvement with the Quetico-Superior Council; Sigurd's affiliation with the organization would bring him national recognition as a conservationist. The first fruits of his wider participation came in April and May of 1934, with the publication of Sigurd's first magazine articles focusing on conservation.

Both articles—the first in *Minnesota Waltonian*, the second in *Minnesota Conservationist*—took issue with federal management of Superior National Forest. The *Waltonian* article examined what had happened in the forest since the secretary of agriculture created three wilderness areas in September 1926. The secretary's decision had been part of a compromise with the Izaak Walton League under which the U.S. Forest Service was allowed to build three roads into the heart of the canoe country to respond more quickly to forest fires. Olson, who had opposed the compromise, said in the article that a number of people already had built branches off these roads to private lakeshore properties. Olson argued that such a result was inevitable:

> The last few years . . . have shown us that these so-called fire protection roads have slowly graduated from that lowly status to well graded, and smoothly surfaced highways over which automobiles can travel with safety and comfort. . . . Such is the inevitable evolution of a fire protection trail in the Superior. What is more, as soon as these trails have assumed the character of fairly well-travelled roads, private individuals invariably construct, oftentimes with the aid of the counties, lateral branches into private holdings of lake shore property or timber. When this begins to happen, the country immediately adjacent to any main trail becomes a network and the former wilderness is a thing of the past.[12]

Olson argued that it was time to hold the line in Superior National Forest and to allow no more roads. He said the Forest Service should prevent fires by the same means as Ontario's Department of Lands and Forests in Quetico Provincial Park: seaplane. Even with the roads, he pointed out, Forest Service firefighters usually had to paddle and portage far into the wilderness to reach a fire, while a seaplane could quickly reach the vast majority of blazes.

"Roads or Planes in the Superior" was a strong opinion piece that treated the Forest Service with a reasonable degree of fairness. The article in *Minnesota Conservationist*, however, which attacked both road building and the agency's logging policy in the area, strayed beyond bounds. Sigurd implied, without showing evidence, that more roads were planned, and his list of unsound developments within Superior National Forest included a logging railroad, timber-cutting operations, and a waterpower project that had occurred outside of the forest's boundaries. Olson also argued that regional forester Earl W. Tinker, whose recent management experience had been in Colorado, could not tell that the Superior required different management strategies than the western forests. Olson ended the article with a stirring statement that showed his ability to use the rhythm of language for emotional effect:

> To cut up the Superior with innumerable roads, within which will ultimately be found highly managed plots of timber, to settle in its midst working communities, to make of it in other words a highly specialized timber production plant, will be a tragedy to all lovers of the wilderness, a tragedy whose full significance will not be appreciated until the last wild place is gone forever.[13]

Tinker cried foul in a half-page response that the magazine boxed off and placed in the middle of Olson's article. "Mr. Olson shows a rather astonishing lack of information to the facts," he wrote. Tinker defended his personal record, which had included a stint as Superior National Forest supervisor before he went to Colorado, and pointed out Olson's errors and false implications. He said that if Olson had come to the forest headquarters in Duluth he could have examined the road plan map and avoided spreading false information. "There has been and is no change in the policy laid down in the plan for the Superior which was approved by the Forester and which has been agreed to by the Quetico-Superior Council," wrote Tinker.

These first two conservation articles showed Sigurd's dedication to wilderness preservation, but they also displayed flaws that made the leadership of the Quetico-Superior Council somewhat leery of him for quite a few years. The thirty-five-year-old teacher from Ely who was beginning to expand his role as a conservationist sometimes made careless statements and used inflammatory language. He had not yet learned to apply to the political wilderness the lessons he had learned as a guide—lessons in cultivating at least the respect, if not the friendship, of even the most difficult people.

Like his fire-and-brimstone-preaching father, Sigurd tended to think in terms of absolutes, and he saw wilderness issues in black and white. The earliest piece of conservation writing in his collected papers is a speech he apparently gave before Izaak Walton League members in Ely in 1929. At issue was a timber sale of fifty-six thousand acres at the southern edge of the canoe country. "The old battle has begun once more," Olson's speech notes declare:

> Shall industry or the wilderness survive. . . . Are we going to sacrifice it to the ogre of commercialism? . . . The Forest Service claims that it can improve certain areas, that by cleaning up some places that the looks of the country will be improved. Whoever heard of improving on Nature? A dead stem in place is beautiful, so is a windfall-tangled shoreline.

Olson's idea of wilderness management was more restrictive than Oberholtzer's view, which was endorsed by the Forest Service. Oberholtzer, along with the Quetico-Superior Council and other leading conservationists such as Aldo Leopold, believed that logging should proceed in the Quetico-Superior as long as the shorelines were protected so canoeists could not see the cuttings. Sigurd, however, told Oberholtzer in one of his first letters, "You can't touch that country without taking something away from it that can never be replaced." On May 5, 1931, jotting down notes for a speech, Olson wrote, "We are slowly coming to realize that there is more value to a tree than just the monetary, that there is an esthetic value, an intangible something hard to explain but there just the same." And in an undated draft of a speech written in about 1934, he predicted that "the day is not far distant when the shadow of the logger's axe will no longer hang over the most picturesque areas of the north, when the people will demand that it be left inviolate."

Before Sigurd could fully act as a representative of the Quetico-Superior Council—or of any other conservation group—he would have to learn to sometimes subordinate his personal views for the sake of the larger organization and its goals. With the Quetico-Superior Council, that meant not pressing for an end to logging within the canoe country wilderness, at least not until after the major goal of an international treaty had been accomplished.

Gaining favor with Ernest Oberholtzer and the Quetico-Superior Council certainly was in Olson's interest if he hoped to become widely known as a conservationist, although there is nothing in his papers that indicates he realized this fact. Oberholtzer and his group were going places. The fight against Backus ended with a disappointing technical victory in April 1934, when the International Joint Commission ended nine years of speculation by deciding to neither approve nor reject Backus's proposal. But the battle had generated publicity in such national publications as the *New York Times* and the *New Republic*. And the publicity, combined with the persuasive skills of Interior Secretary Harold Ickes, led President Roosevelt to sign an executive order on June 30, 1934, creating the President's Committee for the Quetico-Superior.

The President's Committee made Oberholtzer's dream of an international treaty the official goal of the White House. Oberholtzer and two Quetico-Superior Council officers were members, along with two others representing the federal agriculture and interior departments. In July of 1934, the Department of the Interior chose as its representative someone who would play a major national role in wilderness preservation: Bob Marshall, the thirty-three-year-old director of the U.S. Office of Indian Affairs' Forestry Division.[14]

Born to wealth—his father was a prominent constitutional lawyer in New York City—Bob Marshall had grown interested in wild places during childhood vacations at the family's retreat in the Adirondacks. He earned his Ph.D. in plant pathology from Johns Hopkins University in 1930. That same year, *Scientific Monthly* published his first widely read, and ultimately most important, defense of wilderness. "The Problem of the Wilderness" declared that wilderness is important to human physical and psychic health. "As long as we prize individuality and competence," Marshall wrote, "it is imperative to provide the opportunity for complete self-sufficiency."[15]

Implicitly referring to the theories of Sigmund Freud, which had gained cultural currency during the 1920s, Marshall said that wilderness is a "psychic necessity," because it provides surroundings conducive to reflection and the opportunity for people to act out their suppressed desires for adventure. Wilderness could provide Henry

James's "moral equivalent of war," said Marshall, who quoted Bertrand Russell's statement that "many men would cease to desire war if they had opportunities to risk their lives in Alpine climbing."

Marshall also described the aesthetic qualities of wilderness, its "dynamic beauty" that, unlike a classical symphony or a famous painting, constantly changes.

Conceding that the majority might well prefer roads to places of great beauty, Marshall, a Jew whose family had championed civil rights, argued that wilderness is a kind of minority right, that "there is a point where an increase in the joy of the many [by building more roads, for example] causes a decrease in the joy of the few out of all proportion to the gain of the former."

Marshall ended his article with a plea for lovers of wilderness to unite: "There is just one hope of repulsing the tyrannical ambition of civilization to conquer every niche on the whole earth. That hope is the organization of spirited people who will fight for the freedom of the wilderness."

The article launched Marshall on his way to a reputation as "the most efficient weapon of preservation in existence."[16] Sigurd Olson probably did not read it, at least not at the time. He seems to have first heard of Marshall after the formation of the President's Quetico-Superior Committee in the summer of 1934. On December 10, 1934, he read an excerpt from a talk Marshall had recently given, in which Marshall had said, "The wilderness is a world so delicate that the slightest introduction of artificiality ruins it irreparably." This was almost exactly what Sigurd had said a few days earlier in a speech in Duluth, and he sensed that he had found a soulmate. He wrote to Oberholtzer: "There is a man after my own heart. I wish we had a thousand like him and our battle could be won."[17]

Bob Marshall and Sigurd Olson would become good friends. They came from tremendously different backgrounds—a wealthy Jewish intellectual atheist who grew up in New York City and the middle-class son of a Baptist minister who was raised in rural Wisconsin—but they were close in age (Sigurd was two years older than Bob) and, most importantly, they shared an exuberant, joyous passion for the outdoors. Sigurd's early fondness for trying to paddle as far as he could in a day was matched and surpassed by Bob Marshall's obsession with record-breaking mountain climbs and hikes. He once climbed fourteen Adirondack peaks in one day, and he made one-day hikes of more than thirty miles in thirty-five different states.

Like Sigurd, Bob Marshall was at heart a romantic who contrasted the freedom and beauty of wilderness to "the strangling clutch of a mechanistic civilization." And Marshall also was essentially conservative, even though politically he was a socialist who advocated nationalizing the country's private forest lands. A homely man who was slightly taller and heavier than Sigurd, Marshall did not drink, preferred to win people with politeness and humor rather than try to force his opinion down their throats, and disapproved of what he called "smutty talk." (One time, a bunch of yellow jackets got into his pants and as they stung him he ran around yelling, "Oh dear, oh dear!" This disgusted one of the foresters accompanying him, who shouted, "If you have to cuss for God's sake cuss like a man!")[18]

By the time Marshall came to know Ernest Oberholtzer in the summer of 1934, he had decided to create the national organization he had called for in his *Scientific Monthly* article. With the support and help of Oberholtzer, Leopold, and five other men, Marshall published a pamphlet on January 1, 1935, announcing that "for the purpose of fighting off invasion of the wilderness and of stimulating . . . an appreciation of its multiform emotional, intellectual, and scientific values, we are forming an organization to be known as the WILDERNESS SOCIETY."

The pamphlet was not widely distributed; the initial intent was to build a small organization of dyed-in-the-wool activists. Sigurd Olson heard of the group from Oberholtzer, and on April 15, 1935, he applied for a charter membership: "Please enroll me as a member who has never learned to compromise when the question of wilderness has come up." The group's secretary, Robert Sterling Yard, responded on April 19, "I shall make you known to fellow members by that designation and foresee that you will be popular." Yard was right, although he certainly did not know just *how* right he was. Olson one day would become the Wilderness Society's president.

❖ Seven ❖

Storms of Life

1934-1938

Aldo Leopold was a persistent man. Although he stopped trying to bring Olson to Madison as a doctoral student after December 1933, he continued to push Sigurd toward a job in the game management field. During the next two years he gave Olson's name to government officials seeking to hire someone with Sigurd's background, and he sent job announcements to Sigurd.

And why not? Aldo Leopold also was a logical man, and it seemed logical to him that someone who had invested his time and meager life savings during the Depression to get a master's degree in ecology would want to find a job in the field. But Leopold's help, while it was not unappreciated, increased the tension in the Olson household during 1934 and 1935.

Sigurd received three job offers: from the National Park Service, from the U.S. Forest Service, and from the new U.S. Soil Erosion Service.

The Park Service and Forest Service jobs were one-year positions, both in the East, that could have opened the door to something permanent. One involved supervising Civilian Conservation Corps workers in Maine's Acadia National Park; the other entailed supervising wildlife research in White Mountain National Forest in New Hampshire.

Sigurd's reasons for rejecting these two jobs are not clear. When he turned down the Park Service job on June 6, 1934, he said that he had arranged for someone to take his place for the summer as manager of the Border Lakes Outfitting Company, but that the replacement had backed out at the last minute. This is almost exactly the same reason he gave the Forest Service the following May. Perhaps he had bad luck two summers in a row, but he may simply have been giving a plausible excuse to save face.

Elizabeth Olson recalled her husband's turning down the White Mountain National Forest position after a family meeting during which Sigurd Jr. started crying when the boys were asked how they felt about moving. Robert Olson, recalling the same incident, described it as an example of how his father could be compliant to the wishes of family members.

Sigurd's journals make no mention of the Park Service job or of the family meeting, but they make clear that his decision about the White Mountain position was not hasty. He spent the better part of a month thinking about it and talking it over with Elizabeth and with friends. And the same was true of the job with the Soil Erosion Service, which he was offered in the fall of 1934. He would have been in charge of wildlife management on one hundred and fifty thousand acres near La Crosse, Wisconsin. This job was the hardest of the three for him to reject. Not only was it permanent, but the pay was 20 percent higher than his combined income from the junior college and the Border Lakes.

He agonized over the decision. Years later, in early drafts of *Open Horizons,* Sigurd recalled how he took the telegram offering the Soil Erosion Service job and went out to one of his favorite duck blinds, located on the Stoney River. He wrote that he paced in front of his blind at sunset, wondering what to do. He remembered looking at his sleeping bag rolled out under a spruce, at his canoe cached in a willow thicket, and at a bare patch of ground darkened by ashes of campfires past. Then he heard a flock of mallards crossing high above, looked up, and saw them silhouetted against the orange glow of the sunset. After the mallards had passed, he walked to the fire spot, took the telegram from his pocket, tore it, and used it to start the fire.

The anecdote may well be a romanticized memory, but the letter he wrote on October 12, 1934, rejecting the job lends support. Olson wrote that the previous two weeks had "been a torture" to him because he had to decide whether or not he really could stand to move away "from my beloved border country." He said that people might think he was crazy, but "I do not believe that I could ever forget the many years in this wilderness region or the many places I have learned to love, no matter how engrossing the work itself would be. Knowing that, there was only one thing to do, stay on here and forget the outside."[1]

Olson's love of the canoe country was not the sole reason for rejecting the three job offers that came his way in 1934 and 1935, but it clearly was one of the most important. Another was his suspicion that he would not be happy in the careers they offered, even though they would get him outdoors. About the White Mountain National Forest position, for example, he wrote in his journal: "I pictured myself in New Hampshire, roaming around making observations—statistics, helpers, thirty to forty of them making observations for me. What do I know about game management, what do I know or care."[2] And yet he wrote in his letter rejecting the job that "the work at White Mountain was the type of thing I had long been wanting to do and my refusal was extremely disappointing to me."

The contradiction in these two statements may again indicate an attempt on Sigurd's part to save face when turning down the job, but it also reflects his inability to make major career decisions, an inability that frustrated both him and Elizabeth. "It is hard to come to any conclusion," he wrote in his journal on September 28, 1934, debating the Soil Erosion Service job:

> It is such a momentous step, one that cannot be passed over lightly. What will it lead into, where will it put me. Will it, as Elizabeth says, give me work which I like to do. That is by far the most important consideration. Can I lose myself in this work, wrap my entire being up in it . . . or will it be just another job again.

The children were for the most part unaware that they might leave Ely, except for the one family meeting when Sigurd Jr. cried over the idea of moving. For Elizabeth, however, it meant constant uncertainty, never knowing if her family would be staying in Ely or going somewhere else. Sigurd realized that it was hard on her. He wrote in his journal on June 28, 1934, "Lib is so miserable the way things are and I don't blame her. . . . If I was not so selfish I would make her believe that I am all set and want nothing more than I have." But this was impossible for him.

Perhaps it was especially for Elizabeth's sake that the Olsons bought and moved into a new home in August 1934. A two-story cream-colored frame house on top of a hill just south of Ely, it was modest but pleasant, and its location at the edge of the country, next to wide-open fields and a wooded ravine, foretold innumerable family cross-country skiing trips in the years ahead. The home on Greenvalley Road (really a dead-end alley) would be Sigurd and Elizabeth's last. (Eventually, their property and the surrounding area would be incorporated into Ely, and their address would become 106 East Wilson Street.) Their buying it at a time when Sigurd seriously was considering job possibilities elsewhere seems to present another example of his inability to make up his mind, and perhaps of an attempt to provide the family and especially Elizabeth with a modicum of stability.

At the root of Sigurd's indecisiveness was his unquenchable desire to succeed as a writer and his deep fear of the financial risk that seemed unavoidable if he was to achieve his dream. He had to quit teaching to give himself the time, energy, and focus necessary for writing success, and he knew it. "As long as I have to face another winter of teaching and forget the writing I must do," he wrote on August 14, 1934, "then I will be in agony."

School that fall of 1934 started out better than the thirty-five-year-old Olson had expected, because for the first time he taught solely at the junior college. "It is not half bad and the kids love me," he wrote on September 9. But twelve days later he received the Soil Erosion Service job offer and entered another period of turmoil. Then, early in November and less than a month after rejecting the La Crosse job, Sigurd traveled to Minneapolis for a job interview at the University of Minnesota. The details have long since been forgotten by family members, but the trip was an eye-opener to him at the time.

"I went down to the city to settle an important question," he wrote upon his return on November 5:

whether or not I could stand to leave this country. . . . As I stood on Hennepin Ave. and watched the great crowds, masses of people rushing from store to store, from work to work, milling and jostling one another, pushing, and hurrying . . . I could not help but see how much fuller a life a man can live up here and how much those people—who after all are my audience—need someone to give them the fresh primitive perceptions.

The evening he returned home, Olson read an essay on poets that divided them into three types: those who merely repeat and have nothing original to say; those who create but use their talent to make jingles and short-lived, entertaining rhymes; and those who interpret the life about them and are obsessed with sharing their vision. Entertainers die, the article said, but true poets never die. Sigurd recognized himself as a true poet, and he knew he had to get back to his writing and not pin his hopes on other careers:

> Soil erosion, game management, zoology and all the rest are of no value in themselves except inasmuch as they can give me a livelihood while I am doing the other. The only thing that will make me happy then is to realize my dream, to keep working along the lines of my ambitions, using all other avenues merely as a crutch to further my true ends.

Sigurd was ready to try an experiment, hoping to find out if there really was a writer inside him waiting to break out. He needed a significant block of time and a place where he could work undisturbed. He thought he should build a writing shack near home, but apparently was not ready to commit himself financially to that extent. So, as the first snows of winter drifted over the north country, frosting the pines and sculpting the fields, Sigurd Olson hatched a plan. During the year-end holiday season he would rent, for a couple of days, a cabin ten miles south of town on Bear Island Lake, where he could write philosophical essays in peace.

He went on New Year's Day 1935, carrying a Corona typewriter and a copy of Thoreau's *Walden*. The whole family came along to send him off, snowshoeing across Bear Island Lake, their laughter rising up into the cold bright sky. Then they said their good-byes and left Sigurd in his long-coveted peace. After they left, and after he had taken time to absorb his surroundings, Sigurd put a sheet of paper in the Corona and typed: "Here I am all alone in a cabin in the north far away from town, warm and comfortable with no one to disturb me whatever. This is what I have longed for for years."[3]

He had prepared for the trip by thinking about the kind of writing he must do and had reached a firm conclusion: "No one has as yet developed a philosophy of the wilderness. That is up to me. . . . My work must be strong and hard and masculine, the love of men for the wild, its truth, its unvarnished joy, its compensations, the feeling of being alone." But the experiment was doomed by its very nature. Trying to write in a rented cabin put a kind of pressure on Sigurd that he did not experience at home; he felt the unblinking eyes of friends and family bearing down on him. "What do Laura and Oliver expect?" he wrote. "What does Esther expect, Dr. Cahn, Ben Mizzen and the rest? What do they expect from me, the embodiment of the north country?" He had no answer.

Initially, he worked at the typewriter. As he grew frustrated he switched to writing by hand, which still felt more natural to him. Nothing helped. He started two essays about wilderness, stopping the first after a paragraph and the second after two pages. Other than that, he mostly recorded random thoughts and observations and the sickening feeling growing inside him. "I am out here to write and find absolutely nothing to write about," he scribbled.

On the second day, he wrote that he had not given himself enough time. "How in creation can I find out what I want by forcing myself?" he asked. Still, he continued to pressure himself: "What on earth is the matter with me? . . . Either find out that I have something or else decide that I have nothing at all and that my whole dream is poppycock." Ultimately, however, he was willing to settle for anything: "If I can write one good paragraph while I am here it will be enough. . . . Elizabeth is waiting for you, watching, hoping you will do something."

But not even one good paragraph would come. Sigurd went home on January 3, sad and empty-handed. "It is quite hopeless to try and do what Thoreau did, quite hopeless to try and do what Burroughs did," he wrote in his journal. "I have not got it within me—I have the feelings perhaps but not the ability to put them down. All I can write about is natural history—the wolf situation, the duck situation, the habits of the deer, the habits of the beaver, semi scientific stuff."

The lesson he took from the Bear Island Lake retreat was this: "Think of the terrible mistake of thinking that I might make a living writing."

But then inspiration hit. In February, Sigurd completed a draft of his first wilderness essay written in the first-person narrative style that would become his hallmark. He wrote about a canoe trip he had taken several years earlier to Saganaga Lake, located on the international boundary several days east of Ely by canoe. Saganaga was special to Olson; when he made his first canoe trip through the area in 1921 it was the first lake he entered that was completely untouched by the devastation of tall-pine logging. More than a dozen glacier-carved, island-strewn miles long from its southwestern to northeastern ends, with scattered bays large and small, Saganaga Lake had given Sigurd many memorable experiences over the years.

About 1930, however, the Gunflint Trail, a rough road wandering northwest out of Grand Marais on the Lake Superior shore, was extended to Saganaga, and a resort called Gunflint Lodge was erected. When Sigurd heard about it he was horrified; eventually he went back to see it for himself. This somber reunion was the subject of the essay he wrote in February 1935.

The essay began with Olson's crossing the portage into the southwestern end of Saganaga, and he built suspense into the story simply by following a chronological time line. At first, he wrote, he saw no change; he pitched his tent on a favorite point and started his cooking fire with tinder he had left a couple of years before. After dinner he paddled the last several miles to his half-dreaded destination in the southeastern corner of the lake, still seeing nothing out of order as dusk descended and the shores behind him grew black with shadow.

Coming around a final point in the darkness, he saw it: a big lodge with light streaming from its windows, through which he could see the shapes of couples dancing. Instead of the chorus of frogs he had heard on the other side of the point, he heard bits of popular music and a saxophone. Eventually some people got into a motorboat, and Sigurd listened as they roared past, watched their headlight bounce across the water and strike the shore, felt the swell of their wake as it reached his canoe.

Surprisingly, given Olson's emerging reputation as a hard-line wilderness preservationist (in just two months he would ask the Wilderness Society to enlist him as one who never compromised on wilderness issues), the essay's conclusion was ambivalent. He wrote that as he returned to his campsite he knew that "something intangible and precious had gone forever," yet he wondered what that really meant. Had Saganaga Lake changed? Or was the real change in him? The penultimate paragraph is one of acceptance:

Then a great peace came over me, a peace not unmixed with sadness, and I seemed to hear the pines and the wind and the rocky shores say to me, "You, my son, lover of the wild, are part of us. We who have been here always, understand your need of sunlight and shadow, peace and quiet, wind and storm. Long after you are gone shall we be here, and on these time-worn shores shall waves still beat. . . . The glow of sunset shall we know and dawn, and once again shall reign the silence of the ages. Be not distraught, my son, by sounds that now seem strange and new, for they are also life. What matters now if noise and laughter shatter for a moment the quiet we have always known, and which will come again. We who have seen the great ice come and go, we who have watched the passing of tribes long dead, the migration of the caribou, the march of countless seasons, know no time. . . . This is but a moment, oh lover of the wild places of the earth. For us there is no change.

The final paragraph, less accepting, is more ambivalent:

I turned once again toward the brilliance of the shore I had left. Faintly, as a caress of the night wind, came the strains of music across the water. Dipping my paddle once more, the canoe slipped quietly into the darkness of the islands. In the north toward Cache Bay, the sky was bright with the shifting lights of the Aurora, the ghost dance of the past, and though I believed the pines and the wind and the rocky shores, I knew for me it was farewell to the Saganaga I had known.

Sigurd was excited about "Farewell to Saganaga," although he wrote in his journal on February 19 that Elizabeth thought it was "far too emotional." He had experienced the sensation mentioned by Burroughs and Thoreau, the feeling that his essay had almost written itself. He put it in a manila envelope and sent it off to the *Atlantic Monthly*, hoping for his first big break. On March 9, still waiting for a response, he wrote that he wanted eventually to write a book of essays along the lines of "Farewell to Saganaga."

On March 11 a rejection from the *Atlantic* shattered his reverie. "Today I am sick at heart and tired and almost bitter," he wrote. "Another winter gone with nothing accomplished. . . . 'Farewell to Saganaga' may mean farewell to all of my dreams, farewell to all that I thought worthwhile." But he could not bear the thought of quitting: "I cannot give in, I must go on or die. This cannot be the end—

there must be some way out—Oh Lord help me do what I want to do or it will be the end of everything for me."

Olson's bleak mood coincidentally resonated with the nation's distress over the economy, and somehow both individual and national suffering seemed to be captured in a discouragingly symbolic way by news reports of dust storms in the Great Plains. An early spring, hot and dry, had brought the storms to Kansas, Oklahoma, and Texas in February. Five days before Sigurd received the *Atlantic*'s rejection letter, topsoil from the West had been carried by winds all the way to Washington, D.C., where Secretary of Agriculture Hugh Bennett used the drama of a dust storm that darkened the Senate hearing room to convince Congress to give the Soil Erosion Service permanent status under a new name, the Soil Conservation Service. Four days after Sigurd received the *Atlantic* letter, Kansas was blacked out by dust storms. "Lady Godiva could ride thru streets without even the horse seeing her," said one news report.

Then, on April 14, 1935, the worst storms shrieked out of the plains of eastern Colorado and western Kansas, making it impossible to drive and forcing dust through even the tiniest cracks of well-constructed buildings. Cattle, horses, hogs, and other domestic and wild animals suffocated as the dust filled their lungs. The day came to be called Black Sunday. Now, besides coping with the Depression, Americans were facing the fact that they were wasting the topsoil that made possible the nation's reputation as a land of plenty.

The next day—the day a reporter in Denver coined the term Dust Bowl—Sigurd, thinking about the storms, typed a one-page essay about the prairie. It would not have been surprising, given his bout with despair after the *Atlantic*'s rejection, had he composed a dark essay that reflected his recent mood and the state of the nation. But the temperament that made him susceptible to anxiety and self-torture also made him unusually sensitive to the beauty and possibilities of life, and his essay was joyous, with a theme of renewal.

Like "Farewell to Saganaga," it was a first-person narrative, in which Sigurd recounted a trip he had made in 1934 to Blomkest, Minnesota, a country town eighty miles west of Minneapolis where his father was finishing his last year of active ministry. It was Easter, and Sigurd, coming down from a cold and snow-covered north to the vibrant colors and sounds of spring emerging on the prairie outside his father's church, could not help but see similarities between the lessons of nature and those of Christianity:

> This was Easter morning on the prairie, sunlight, the glint of water lying in the hollows, meadowlarks, the gurgle of mourning doves, cock pheasants stalking over the plowed fields, the song of the frogs as a minor undertone to all of the rest, over all an impression of bursting life, light and song. One can understand somewhat the appeal of the prairie after walking over its open stretches, seeing its colors and hearing its songs; forget somewhat the sinister threat of dust storms, starving cattle, drought, dying trees, prelude to the desert. This morning the prairie was itself, Easter with its promise of joy and resurrection.

Sigurd was not yet ready to expand "Easter on the Prairie" and send it to an uncertain fate, but his message of resilience and hope, while it spoke to a larger audience in a time of trouble, also served as a reminder to himself. Once again he had learned two key lessons. First, the sense of oneness with the earth that he craved and often experienced was essential to his *own* resilience and hope; it was, to extend his analogy, the counterpart of the Christian experience of being saved. And if sin consists not merely of individual moral transgressions, but also of an underlying separation from God or nature, then at-one-ment with the earth is an atonement, a reconciliation that makes healing possible:

> How often hasn't that truth burst upon me that the main source of leisure and happiness to me is in the daily and continual observation of little things, wind and sun, lighting, leaves, smells, movement, the very act of breathing. Here is a cult and a substantiation of my belief that in nature is the cure all. Here is my religion and here what I must try to bring out in all of my writing.

In another journal entry he added, "There is only one thing that is worthwhile, and that is the spiritual."[4]

But at-one-ment, to be more than a brief flash of insight and peace, to bring lasting reconciliation, requires surrendering to the still, small voice within, the spark of divinity that gives purpose to life. This was the second lesson Sigurd had encountered again. He could never truly be at harmony with himself or the world, no matter how many wilderness epiphanies he experienced, if he did not follow his inner calling as a writer. "It will not make much difference if I don't write anything worthwhile from a financial standpoint," he wrote in his journal. "I must write to keep my sanity. Writing is the insulin of a disease of long standing. I must take my regular dose or go under."[5]

❖

The fall of 1935 started much the same as any other for Sigurd; he kept trying to think of careers that would be fulfilling and leave time for writing. One idea expressed in his journal was to take over the Uhrenholdt farm for his elderly father-in-law. A few days later, recalling the reception he had gotten the year before at the International Joint Commission hearing in Minneapolis, he wrote about trying to make a go of the lecture circuit. Later on he brought up his oft-mentioned idea of taking a leave of absence from the junior college, using the money from the Border Lakes for subsistence, and really giving his dream of writing a chance. At times he lay awake most of the night, trying to figure out a solution. But as Christmas approached, Sigurd, having finished one freelance article and begun working on another, felt rejuvenated. "I have it in me," he wrote. "This time I will win out."[6]

Then tragedy struck. Julius Santo, dean of the junior college, became gravely ill. He was a good friend of Sigurd's, probably the closest of his outdoors "pals," as Sigurd called them. The dean had been featured in four of the five fishing and hunting stories Olson had sold to leading outdoor magazines, beginning with "Duck Heaven" in the October 1930 issue of *Outdoor Life*. They had shared many campfires at favorite spots like a point on the Stoney River and the mouth of the Range River on Low Lake.

Santo had a romantic past that Sigurd loved; after the world war he had prospected for gold in Mexico and eventually hooked up with the revolutionary leader Francisco "Pancho" Villa. He worked for Villa for half a year, then resigned in disgust because, as Sigurd recalled, "the army never fought on feast days or when it rained." Somehow this would-be revolutionary ended up in northern Minnesota and became dean of Ely Junior College when it opened in 1922. Now, in mid-January 1936, he lay dying, suffering searing pain in his legs and chest and breathing with great difficulty.[7]

Sigurd was the only visitor he wanted. "There is my hunting pal, a hunting pal no more," Olson wrote on January 16. Sigurd spent many hours with Santo, but the death watch was hard. "I can hardly sleep for I always see before me those desperate eyes, pleading for help and grasping so pitifully at every straw of hope," he wrote on the 20th. Less than a week later it was over. Sigurd was with him at the end. The dean told Olson he was about to die and Sigurd protested, but Santo insisted that he knew. Then, sentimentally, Sigurd told Santo to prepare a campsite, cut the firewood, and set out the decoys, and one day he would join him. The dean smiled and nodded but did not speak. "The end came very swiftly," Sigurd wrote in his journal, "one convulsive jerk and he fell over into my arms."[8]

The funeral was held on January 28. Sigurd wrote:

> When I saw this morning the old pair of boots that have tramped with me so far, when I saw the old rifle, and the duck hunting paraphernalia, it was hard to bear. I loved him. . . . I will never find another pal to take his place. . . . There is a bond, stronger than almost anything else, between the men who have sat across camp fires in the wilds. No matter what else they may be, the comradeship there is stronger than death. How can I ever go to the old point on Low Lake or up to the Stoney again?

Nine days later, the same Sigurd Olson who had spent much of the previous few months trying to figure out how to escape from Ely Junior College applied for the position of dean. "Don't care greatly whether I get it or not but as a matter of pride I felt I had to apply," he wrote in his journal.

He got it, and felt miserable when he heard the news. "They have made me Dean and I am taking my old pal's place," he wrote on Valentine's Day:

> I sometimes feel these days as though the net has wound itself more and more closely around me. Now there will be no escape and what was hard before becomes doubly impossible now. My leave of absence is out of the question under the new setup. . . . So many have congratulated me and so wholeheartedly that there is no question in my mind but that they are really happy about it. It is one of the compensations of living in a small town and is recognition which usually does not come unless one dies. . . . What I wish I could do is go into this thing joyfully and make Elizabeth happy

just this once. Instead I have her worried to death and as miserable as she ever was, knowing that I am still unhappy. Why cannot I resign myself to the inevitable and forget the dream that has been hounding me so long? Why don't I realize that I cannot make my living writing and that what I must do is only use it as a side line? . . . The maddening part of it all is that everyone thinks I have the ideal setup and am the happiest man in the world. Irony.

At first it was not so bad. Olson was writing regularly, had an article titled "The Romance of Portages" published in the April *Minnesota Conservationist*, and he confessed at one point that he was "happier this spring than ever before."[9] In March he received recognition of sorts when Victor Shelford, who had been his professor and adviser at the University of Illinois, asked him to chair a committee of the Ecological Society of America. The committee's task was to promote the introduction of wolves to the newly established Isle Royale National Park in Lake Superior, not far from Olson's home. With Shelford's advice, he also was working on a scholarly journal article based on his master's thesis.

Then, at the end of May, Olson received an intriguing request from Bob Marshall, director of the U.S. Office of Indian Affairs' Forestry Division and Wilderness Society founder. They had met for the first time the previous summer when Marshall visited northern Minnesota and had hit it off right away. Now Marshall wanted Olson to spend most of his summer visiting four Indian reservations in Minnesota and Wisconsin in order to recommend how the government and the Indians could work together to increase tribal income through recreational development. "I feel that your experience in Lake States recreation and your viewpoints tie up more closely with the manner in which I feel that our recreational resources should be developed than any one whom I know, and that is why I am anxious for you to undertake this study," Marshall wrote.[10]

On June 17, 1936, Olson took off for the Grand Portage Reservation on the Minnesota shore of Lake Superior, which Marshall predicted would become the major point of entry to Isle Royale. While he was staying at the reservation, he took a brief trip to Isle Royale to gain some firsthand information for his committee work with the Ecological Society of America. From Grand Portage, Olson traveled west to the Red Lake Reservation, four hundred thousand acres in north central Minnesota surrounding the two huge and shallow Red Lakes; then to northeastern Wisconsin and the Menominee Indian Reservation, through which the wild Wolf River flowed; and finally to the small Lac du Flambeau Reservation in north central Wisconsin, near Minocqua. He spent ten days to two weeks at each reservation, meeting with tribal leaders and government officials and scouting the land.

The exploring was fun, although in Minnesota it was a terrible year for tent caterpillars: cars skidded on the caterpillar-carpeted highways, and trains sometimes could not climb the grade. Sigurd at times found the woods near Grand Portage almost impassible because of the caterpillars' thick, cottony webs. Everywhere he went the furry creatures, deep blue with gold flecks, dropped on his head like a light rain, and he could hear them chewing en masse on the foliage all around him.

Marshall gave Olson specific objectives and even some preliminary conclusions, including a goal of developing recreation in such a way "as to conflict as little as possible with the surrounding primitive values."[11] Sigurd's reports contained nothing surprising, but they were thorough, and were greatly appreciated. "To say I was delighted with your four reports is to express it very mildly indeed," Marshall wrote on August 27. He said that the Office of Indian Affairs had already modified its programs at the four reservations. The most notable change was at Red Lake, where logging operations were being postponed south of Red Lake Village because Olson had said the recreation plan should be given a decent chance: "It may be," Olson had written, "that this small area will return far more as a resort development than from its timber stand."[12]

Soon after Sigurd completed his reports, he had to begin turning his attention back to Ely Junior College, and in the fall of 1936 the full weight of his new position as dean descended upon him. It was not long before he was complaining that he had no time to write, and by December he was wishing he could quit. "Bob and Junior and Elizabeth do not know the torment in my soul," he wrote in his office on the 12th, "do not realize what lies in back of my days over here." During the holidays he completed an article about the "priceless spiritual heritage" of wilderness areas; ironically, *Nature Magazine* rejected the article because it had just accepted a similar one by Bob Marshall.

Soon after the new year, Olson became preoccupied with canoe country wilderness issues and had less time for either introspection or writing. Just after Christmas President Roosevelt had given Quetico-Superior wilderness supporters a big boost by adding 1.3 million acres to Superior National Forest. The executive order was similar to a number he had written with the intention of bringing relief to poor counties by taking over tax-default lands. In this case, it made Superior the largest national forest, with a total of 3.5 million acres.

Most of the added land came from the cutover region along the international border north of Ely from the western end of Basswood Lake east to Saganaga and north of the Kawishiwi River. The major canoe routes on the American side of the Quetico-Superior wound through this area, so the executive order gave conservationists hope that the Superior Wilderness Area would be extended across the new federal lands.

Basswood Lake posed an immense problem, however. It was an ideal starting place for wilderness trips because it was centrally located and shaped like a funnel, with a relatively small southern entry broadening out in the north to provide access to major canoe routes on both sides of the border. But half a dozen resorts already had been constructed on its shores, and it was the year-round home of several families.[13]

Much of the tourist traffic came across the so-called Four Mile Portage, which connected Basswood Lake with Fall Lake and the village of Winton. The portage had been built in 1901 as a logging railroad, but the rails were pulled in 1920 after the tall pine had been stripped from the region along the American side of the border. Meanwhile, shortly before World War I, three Native American families headed by brothers with the last name of Chosa had moved from Michigan and taken up residence on Basswood Lake, where they worked as commercial fishermen. When the loggers pulled the rails, Henry Chosa bought land from the lumber company on both ends of the Four Mile Portage and began using the grade to haul fishermen by truck, for a fee, back and forth between Fall and Basswood Lakes.

In the 1920s other people began building resorts on Basswood and took clients across the portage themselves. Chosa fought them in court, saying they had to pay him because he owned both ends of the portage. He won, and since then resort owners had been paying him fifty cents for every client taken over the road.

But Henry Chosa developed a new plan in the 1930s. The Fernberg Road had been built to the south of Basswood Lake, one of two key roads approved as part of the 1926 decision by the secretary of agriculture to establish three wilderness areas within Superior National Forest. This made it feasible to build a road directly to Basswood by means of a spur from the Fernberg Road to the Four Mile Portage. Believing that direct access would bring extra income to his tourist business at the north end of the portage, Chosa wanted the road, and so did several resort owners and newer residents. The major resort owners opposed the idea because, despite paying Chosa, they made a significant portion of their income from the Four Mile Portage. They also knew that a road would encourage more people to build resorts, eroding their current near-monopoly.

In 1935 Chosa and several others who owned land along the Four Mile Portage erected barricades in several locations and threatened to charge a toll of a dollar per person at each barricade. The intent was to force the main resort owners to agree to a road, and Chosa and his allies applied to the town board for a right-of-way. The issue went to court once again, and in 1936 the court ruled in Chosa's favor.

Early in 1937 the town board received another request for a right-of-way, and conservationists were deeply worried. If a road went to Basswood, there would be no hope of extending the Superior Wilderness Area to include this key lake. But the heavy toll charges ultimately would force the major resort owners to support the road, unless some other answer could be found.

Sigurd Olson was the first conservationist to hear of the new right-of-way application, and he immediately wired Ernest Oberholtzer, who presented the issue to the President's Quetico-Superior Committee at its next meeting. Regional forester Earl Tinker, often at loggerheads with Olson about wilderness, surprised Oberholtzer at the meeting by saying that the Fernberg Road never should have been built. Bob Marshall, attending his last meeting as a member of the committee because he was about to leave the Interior Department for a new position as director of recreation and lands for the U.S. Forest Service, was so upset that he offered to buy the necessary land himself if government money was not available.

While the President's Committee was discussing alternatives, Olson went into action at the local level. On March 9, 1937, he arranged a dinner meeting at Ely's Forest Hotel to organize a new chapter of the Izaak Walton League. In his introductory remarks, he criticized community leaders who had attacked the Quetico-Superior program and its supporters:

> This town has gone on record time and again as being opposed to this ideal [of the international treaty proposed by the President's Quetico-Superior Committee] and there are certain individuals here who, knowing nothing about the entire plan, have accused the leaders of this movement of materialism and of trying to benefit financially in everything they did. . . .
>
> We have something here which other communities have lost long ago and furthermore what we have is of statewide and national significance. This country does not belong to Ely, it belongs to the entire middle west. This being the case, however, Ely will benefit just insofar as she preserves what she has, and will lose insofar as she permits the country to deteriorate. . . .
>
> This group has been called together to form a body which might take action. It doesn't have to be a large group, but it does have to be composed of men who are conservation minded, men who can act together on certain definite objectives and who will not quarrel when projects come up that might mean the desecration of our country. We want unity, and coherent action. The reason the old club broke up was that a certain element came in who were across the line, who were more interested in selfish views than in conservation. They did not see eye to eye with the conservation ideal, but instead made it difficult to put across any ideas without nullifying their meaning.

That night, Sigurd became president of the new Jack Linklater Chapter of the Izaak Walton League, named for Olson's old guiding friend, who recently had drowned on Basswood Lake. Ernest Oberholtzer admired Sigurd's work and enthusiasm: "You have been a bright star of hope at Ely," he wrote. "It's almost a miracle that there really could be someone in that location, who really cares for the preservation of the border wilderness and who really knows what it's about."[14] A number of people in Ely, however, did not expect this sort of thing from a junior college dean. They expected the dean to be civic-minded, which to them meant chamber-of-commerce-minded. Some people had resented his activism from the beginning, but now that he had a position of respect and authority in the community it seemed worse. He was beginning to make enemies, and, just as he said in his speech, they would accuse him of supporting wilderness regulations for his own materialistic ends.

The problem, at its root, was the Border Lakes Outfitting Company. While his earnings from the company—based on his one-third share in the profits as well as his salary as manager—fluctuated from year to year, in a good year they amounted to a little over half of what he made as dean and provided more than a third of his total income for the year. In 1935, for example, he earned $700 from the Border Lakes and $1,935 as a teacher. In 1936 the Border Lakes did much better and he earned $1,500, along with $2,470 as dean of the junior college. Altogether, he made enough by 1938 to let Elizabeth hire a maid to do the cooking and cleaning, to buy an Oldsmobile sedan (albeit a demonstrator model at used-car prices), and to make major home improvements. In the middle of the Depression this stirred at least a little resentment; some of the less fortunate in Ely referred to the area where the Olsons lived as "snob hill."

The charges of materialism also were directed at Olson's connection with one of his partners, M. W. "Pete" Peterson. In 1926, three years before Border Lakes was founded, Peterson built one of the first resorts on Basswood Lake. Peterson's Fishing Camp was by no means a family resort, but unlike many older resorts of the time it *did* have electricity (consisting of a generator run by a Studebaker automobile engine).

While Peterson's Fishing Camp was a separate business in which Olson had no investment, it formed a working relationship with Border Lakes Outfitting. For a fee, the resort hauled Border Lakes customers over the Four Mile Portage with its Model A truck and provided launch tows on Basswood to jumping-off places on the international border. The resort also provided the towing service when canoe parties returned to the northern reaches of Basswood, and many Border Lakes customers spent the first and last nights of their vacations at the resort. In return, Peterson directed resort customers to the Border Lakes if they decided to take a canoe trip, and also paid Border Lakes 10 percent of the towing revenue. In practice, however, Peterson's Fishing Camp received most of the financial benefits of the relationship, because few resort customers took canoe trips. This was a sore point for Olson. While there is evidence that he tried to increase his share of towing revenue to 25 percent, there is no evidence that he succeeded.[15]

Peterson was the resort owner who challenged Henry Chosa in court in 1936 over the issue of charging tolls on the Four Mile Portage, and there is no question that his resort, as well as the Border Lakes, stood to lose money if a road to Basswood were constructed. It is not surprising, then, that people who favored the road would see Olson's wilderness activism, including his founding of the new Izaak Walton League chapter, as convenient posturing rather than an idealistic stand.

Some, in fact, saw Sigurd as a hypocrite. Here he was, in the spring of 1937, advocating that Basswood Lake be made part of the Superior Wilderness Area, saying that the lake was threatened by development, when his outfitting company had made good money over the past eight years by using Basswood Lake and the Four Mile Portage as the major jumping-off place for canoe trips. The Border Lakes' ties to Peterson's Fishing Camp had helped it grow quickly to rival Wilderness Outfitters, the oldest and largest tripping company in Ely. The competition led Wilderness Outfitters to erect its own Basswood Lake resort in 1930. Built in a rare stand of virgin pine, Basswood Lodge became one of the canoe country's most popular resorts and, with more than twenty buildings, one of the largest.

The Border Lakes Outfitting Company also was the only Ely-area business to advertise regularly in the three leading national outdoor magazines: *Outdoor Life, Field and Stream,* and *Sports Afield.* And Sigurd wrote freelance articles at various times for each of these publications. His closest association was with the Minneapolis-based *Sports Afield,* the nation's oldest outdoor magazine. He had become good friends with its managing editor, Robert C. Mueller, in the late 1920s when he guided Mueller on a canoe trip through the Quetico-Superior. Mueller took an interest in Olson's writing career, and in

1929 he began publishing Sigurd's articles. Most of them were hunting and fishing stories with such titles as "Confessions of a Duck Hunter," "Spring Fever," and "The Blue-Bills Are Coming." They were action-filled and written with lighthearted masculine humor, as in this excerpt from "Stag Pants Galahads," published in November 1930:

> Long before daylight, I heard a whisper, "pile out you swamp angels, it's almost time." It was the dean, as I might have guessed. He never could sleep worth a damn the night before. I looked at my watch. It was only four-thirty and wouldn't be light for another two hours.
>
> "Start the fire," I mumbled, "and when it's nice and warm, call me." A disgusted snort was my only answer.

Sports Afield also bought four pieces of fiction that, Sigurd confessed decades later in *Open Horizons,* probably saw the light of day only because of Mueller's friendship. One of these was the dog story "Papette," published in two parts in January and February 1932. As in all of Olson's fiction, the prose imitated the melodramatic style of popular pulp adventure writers:

> Mortally wounded now, choking with her own blood, Grey Neck turned and with a last desperate effort, hurled herself at the enemy. Over and over they rolled upon the snow, spattering it with red wherever they touched. At last the wolf felt her strength ebbing and tearing herself away, she ran weakly over the snow, dripping blood at every step. Papette hesitated in surprise, then bore down upon her, caught once more the pearl grey throat and this time did not relinquish 'til every vestige of life had fled. Slowly she released her hold and gazed at the still grey form beside her.

While the quality varied, Olson was good enough and apparently popular enough to get thirteen articles published in *Sports Afield* during the 1930s, a decade in which the magazine's circulation grew from seventy thousand to more than two hundred and fifty thousand. Looking back on this period many years later, Mueller thanked Sigurd for contributing to the magazine's success: "Through the medium of your stories and articles, you played a formidable role in helping to build *Sports Afield* in the old days. Your help and encouragement and Pete's [M. W. Peterson] at Winton and later did much,

much to prepare me for what little role I played in building *Sports Afield* in the early years."[16]

But if Olson helped Mueller and *Sports Afield*, the reverse also held true, and not simply because Olson gained recognition as an outdoor writer. Mueller personally directed outfitting business Olson's way. Also, by publishing Olson's thirteen stories during the 1930s and ten stories by a Border Lakes guide named Emil Anderson, Mueller gave Olson's company publicity that reinforced its advertising. Sigurd understood the benefit of this relationship and more than once wrote about it in his journal, as in the following from a December 1933 entry:

> If I make enough of a name for myself and write the sort of thing I wish, the things that will appeal, think of the free advertising we will get. . . . After all every article that comes out is an advertisement and I know how much that is worth. . . . At least it is one of the compensations and one not to be ignored and you should be able to make a grand independent living from it. It is something that will mean cash.[17]

By the time he wrote that, Sigurd already was beginning to worry about bringing too many people to the wilderness. A few months later, for example, in a talk he gave to the Arrowhead Association, a regional chamber of commerce in northeastern Minnesota to which he belonged, he pointed out that the canoe country was within easy access of the large Midwestern cities. But then came a warning:

> Here is one danger point: we as an association are attempting to attract the millions from the Middle West. And here comes the problem of trying to develop the country from the standpoint of securing its highest public use and still retaining its wilderness character. It is self-evident that crowds of tourists can rob a country of its charm as easily as excessive road building or power development.[18]

There is no doubt that Olson's wilderness activism was driven by a genuine, heartfelt, nonmaterialistic ideology rather than by financial considerations; there is simply too much evidence in his letters and journal entries of the period for us to come to any other conclusion. But he also wanted to make as much money as possible from the Border Lakes Outfitting Company, perhaps in part to keep up the lifestyle to which he and Elizabeth were growing accustomed, but mostly so he could afford to quit the junior college and write full time during the fall and winter months. (He was willing to sacrifice his social standing, but not basic financial security for his family, to achieve his dream.) And Sigurd's desire to become a successful writer was so strong that it created the potential for him to develop a blind spot when it came to the Border Lakes Outfitting Company. At the very least, he did not seem to recognize his own small role in the slow diminishment of wilderness solitude and silence brought about by a steady increase in canoe country tourism.

Ely's business leaders undoubtedly recognized Olson's beneficial relationship with *Sports Afield* and appreciated the publicity his articles gave to their area. They had no idea that his interest in making money from the Border Lakes was less to add to his salary as dean than to replace that salary so he could quit and write. Their problem with him, in the spring of 1937—a problem that would be repeated with varying formulations in the years ahead—was this: why was it acceptable for Sigurd Olson to make money by bringing in to Basswood Lake as many tourists as he could, but wrong for them to help their other tourist businesses by building a road to the lake? They could not see the difference, and they sensed hypocrisy.

The furor over the proposed road to Basswood Lake ended without Bob Marshall's having to follow up on his promise to open his wallet. He did, however, help work out a plan in which Peterson and the other major resort owners opposing the road cooperated with the Forest Service to secure rights-of-way around the properties of Henry Chosa and his allies, and the same resort owners contributed toward building a new Four Mile Portage wholly on state and federal land. This eliminated the toll charge and kept the resort owners united against the proposed spur from the Fernberg Road. "Thank God for Bob Marshall and the position he now holds," Sigurd wrote on June 23, 1937.

That summer, Olson canoed through the Quetico-Superior with Marshall. The trip lasted just five days, but they saw the country in Bob Marshall fashion, "in big chunks," as Sigurd put it.[19] The trip cemented their friendship, and before it was over Marshall promised to see if he could find Sigurd a wildlife management or research position in the Forest Service. That fall, Sigurd wondered what he would do if Marshall found him something. He thought he would reject it, as he had turned down the positions found for him by Aldo Leopold. This time, however, he did not have to decide. On January 28, 1938, Bob Marshall wrote to say that the Forest Service was in such serious financial straits because of the Depression that he had not found anything for Sigurd.

Since 1933 Aldo Leopold had tried and failed several times to get Olson to change his career. Leopold finally had given up. Sigurd had never on his own initiative applied for any permanent position in which he could use the knowledge he gained in his graduate work at the University of Illinois. Now Bob Marshall had tried to help Olson but could not find anything. He, too, had given up, and never again would Sigurd seriously consider a professional career in ecology. It was the end of one part of his search.

❖ Eight ❖

The Hidden Life of a Dean

1936–1940

Sigurd Olson was the kind of dean who is accessible to students, a welcome quality at any college but a critical one in a small school such as Ely Junior College, where the annual enrollment was around one hundred and fifty. And he prodded good students to see beyond the two-year degree. Before he became dean, perhaps three or four students finishing their second year at the junior college would go on to the state university or a liberal arts college to complete a bachelor's degree; not long after he took over, the number continuing their education grew to fifty per year. The junior college's yearbook in 1940 paid him tribute on its opening page:

> Because he understands our problems,
> Because he is a vital part of our college,
> Because he is well liked by everyone,
> We, the students of Ely Junior College,
> Dedicate THE VOYAGEUR 1940 to our Dean.

"Sig looked out for students," recalled Bill Rom, who attended the school in the 1930s and ultimately became a highly successful outfitter in Ely:

> I had a desire to go into forestry or some natural history field, and there were a couple of other students in my class too who wanted to do the same, and he got all three of us a job in the summertime on portage crews, building fire trails and portages all over the Kawishiwi District of the Superior National Forest. I worked there three years and I worked there one year as a fire tower man, all because of Sig's help. And this enabled me to go on to college at the University

133

of Minnesota, and I graduated in 1940 in wildlife management. If it weren't for Sig, I don't think I would have ever gotten beyond junior college, because this was right in the middle of the Depression, you know, and nobody had much money.[1]

The faculty also appreciated him. "There was a splendid esprit de corps in that small college and without Sig I don't think we might have had that," said George Gould, who taught botany and zoology at the school from 1936 to 1942:

> The Depression kept us poor, but World War II had not yet torn up our values and traditions. Sig was a gentle, erudite man, yet a strong leader. Ely Junior College turned out an amazing number of professionals for the size of the school. It was a close-knit faculty—the Oliver Halls, Paul Kramers, Jesse Mikelsons, Mary Helen Krafts, just to name a few. On balmy autumn afternoons, we would picnic at a lake, and when snow lay on the ground there was merry conversation in Mary Helen's classroom, over a box of Stover's chocolates.

Olson also helped build a sense of community at the junior college by starting a school newspaper and an annual yearbook, and—his earliest innovation—by starting a school tradition of Friday-morning assemblies. Every week the whole school would gather for skits and musical performances put on by students and teachers, for announcements and sometimes a brief talk by the dean (Sigurd's standard first talk of the year was about proper study habits), and always for group singing. At first they used mimeographed song sheets, but later they turned to a book of songs called "America Sings," which was full of patriotic songs and other standards such as "Grandfather's Clock" and "Sweet Evalina."

George Gould recalled that the faculty and many of the students thought the assemblies were "terribly boring," but nobody said a word because "we wouldn't hurt Sig's feelings for anything. Sig loved to sing—*oh*, he loved to sing, and he had a nice baritone."

To the teachers and students who knew him, it comes as a shock to hear that he hated his job. The only sore spot of which faculty were aware was his difficult relationship with school superintendent Stanley Adkins, an arrogant, domineering man who seemed to worry much more about the state of the buildings and grounds than about the education within. ("He would have made a better head custodian,

I sometimes think, than a superintendent," said George Gould.) Students were not aware of even that, and no one suspected any deeper problems.

It was, after all, a prestigious position, being dean in a small town. The dean socialized with civic leaders, was active in community organizations, spoke at civic banquets—in short, led a busy, fruitful life that brought local recognition, respect, even admiration. But while Sigurd longed for respect and admiration, he wanted it on a much larger scale than what a small town could give, and he did not enjoy the social and civic responsibilities:

> I have always hated club work, the 4-H idea, forestry club, scouts, etc., all good organizations and with worthy ideals, but dead to me personally. I have worked with them, hating every minute spent because there was no escape, suffering nostalgia, tortures of the mind, going through with it, speaking at banquets, get togethers. . . . In a few weeks will come the scout drive and I will have to give enthusiastic speeches to my committees, despising myself for doing it.[2]

Ironically, because he was effective at these things people kept asking him to do more:

> Now they want me to take over the Superintendency of the Sunday School. That is the last straw. Then they want me to reorganize the League, another straw, then leading the singing in church gatherings, the assemblies at school, taking an active part in a hundred things that go against me. It seems that the very things I am good at are the things I despise myself for doing.[3]

And it was not just the social activities of a dean that bothered him. He felt that nearly everything he did in the office was busy work, a waste of time. This frequently made it hard for him to face another day. "This morning," begins a typical journal entry, "a pit in the center of my stomach, more like vomiting than going to breakfast, forcing down the food, trying to smile and be cheerful, gritting my teeth and going off to work. It cannot last without something breaking."[4] And as the years dragged on, he even found it hard at times to focus on the students:

> I am paying no attention to the students as far as their vocational guidance is concerned. Day after day I merely tolerate them, smile

as I come in, pose and pose all day long, trying to make them feel that I am busy. Nothing is more damning to a man's soul than to put in day after day of what he considers sheer idleness, even though he might spend the day on busy work, chasing here and there, doing any one of the thousands of little things that most people would think of as work. That to me, however, is violating one of the first essentials of happiness, that is putting in your day doing something useful and to you constructive.[5]

The fact that he did not get along with Adkins and had to deal with a school board that sometimes argued that the junior college was a waste of money—the "petty political bickering of an ignorant school board," as he put it[6]—certainly did not help, but it was not the main problem. The main problem was his burning desire to *be* somebody, to make a name for himself. Out of this desire arose the uncommon unhappiness that he expressed in his journal. And behind this desire was a sense that he would not feel fully alive until he was making a mark in the world. "I am continually feeling that what I am doing has no basis, no solidity," he wrote, "that I am on the bench watching a show but not a part of it, that I am perched as it were on a limb ready to fly, that there is no permanence—no foundation."[7]

Sigurd described himself as being part of "shadow America"—one of the multitudes who, in Thoreau's words, lead lives of quiet desperation. At parties, he would laugh at jokes and pretend to have a good time while actually he was counting the minutes, imagining that his real life—his destiny as a writer—was passing him by. Even visiting with friends on Sunday afternoons at times was a chore for him, and when he and Elizabeth would go to the homes of friends for an evening of cards, he would sit in a corner and read. "There is nothing that interests me outside of my own selfish ideal," he confessed in his journal.[8]

And always, in the background, were the self-destructive comparisons with his older brother. In 1937 Kenneth Olson became dean of Northwestern University's Medill School of Journalism. Under his leadership over the next twenty years, the annual enrollment would grow from one hundred to five hundred, and the program would develop into one of the most prestigious in the country. Kenneth Olson was a national figure in his field—an "incisive, soft-speaking, most kindly journalist-scholar," according to the *Christian Science Monitor*—and would soon appear in *Who's Who in America*. "Ken and his new job," Sigurd wrote when he heard the news in May 1937, "makes me feel like a piker."[9]

Four months later, Sigurd made a decision he had put off for years. He had long wanted a studio where he could get away and write undisturbed. For a long time he thought he would find the answer in an abandoned cabin somewhere, and he scoured the countryside. For a brief month or two in 1930 he had one at Grassy Lake; what became of it is no longer known. In January 1935 he had tried to work in isolation in a cabin at Bear Island Lake, but he had felt so much pressure to perform in the two days he had allotted that the experiment had been a miserable failure. He also had thought of building a studio near home, but had never been willing to spend the money. In September of 1937, realizing that as dean he found it harder than ever to find undisturbed blocks of time, and possibly spurred by his brother's prominent new job, Sigurd spent the money to take apart a single-car garage in front of his house and turn it into a writing studio.

"The shack," as he called it, was ready by October 1. It was nothing to look at from the outside, a drab, rectangular, olive frame with brick-red shingles on the roof and a pair of windows on every side. The door was on the long side facing the house, which was about twenty yards to the north.

The interior had pine siding and a wood floor, but the emphasis was on function, not beauty. The single shelf running along each wall right above the windows was simply a long board, propped up in places with two-by-fours. There was a woodstove for heat and a large wooden desk along the windows facing the house, with a light hanging from the ceiling above. Eventually the shack would fill up with two more desks and several tall file cabinets, but at first it must have seemed spacious.

The renovation cost one hundred and fifty dollars, or two-thirds of Sigurd's average monthly pay. This was three times what he had expected, and Elizabeth told him he would have to earn the money back by selling stories. But Sigurd was not worried; three articles in the outdoor magazines would take care of the money, and he believed that his new surroundings would help him pound them out in no time. No more trying to write in the dining room or an upstairs bedroom, suffering every time the phone rang or the kids got loud. "Now it will make no difference how many are in the house, what company we have or how many guests," he wrote. "Nothing will bother me out here. . . . I am going to work as steadily as I can, every week four or possibly five nights, Saturdays occasionally, but never Sundays. Sundays belong to my family."

As soon as he could move his typewriter into the shack, Olson began a heavy writing schedule. On weekday afternoons he would shut himself in the shack as soon as he got home from the junior college, emerging for supper but returning as soon as the last cup of coffee was finished. Once the weather turned cold he delayed writing until after supper, waiting for the woodstove to heat the shack, but then he would go out and type away for hours.

In the eighteen-month period from October 1937 to March 1939 Olson wrote nineteen articles. Seven of them were accepted. But the successes did not come easily, nor did they convince Sigurd that he could support his family by writing and outfitting. It took an average of three submissions for each of the seven published articles to find a home, and he still found himself confined to the outdoor magazines, which paid only fifty or sixty dollars an article. *Field and Stream* bought "Fireside Pictures," "Mallards Are Different," and "What! No Bass?" *Sports Afield* bought "The Immortals of Argo," "The Mallards of Back Bay," and "Wilderness Areas." Only one of the seven went to a different type of magazine, and that one—which we will come back to—brought him no money at all.

As for the other twelve, he submitted them to magazines forty-six times during this period. He worked furiously, searching for what he called his "medium," a writing format that would bring him not just satisfaction and recognition but also enough money to let him quit the junior college. He needed to break into the higher-paying national magazines, such as the *Saturday Evening Post.* "If I could only sell one story or article to the *Post,* I would no longer fear," he wrote in his journal on December 9, 1937. "One good check and it would all be settled." He mailed articles to the *Post* five times during this year-and-a-half period; he also submitted five times to *Scribner's,* four times to *Atlantic Monthly,* four times to *Collier's,* and three times each to *Good Housekeeping* and *Country Gentleman.* Some of the articles were northwoods fiction, but most were essays, including revised versions of "Easter on the Prairie" and "Farewell to Saganaga."

All were rejected. In fact, he received about ten times as many rejections as letters of acceptance. It was terribly painful. Out in the writing shack he had finally experienced a satisfying sense of productivity, but it seemed to be going nowhere. "By the looks of things, the world will not discover me until I am dead," he wrote to Don Hough, a friend and a successful freelance writer who wrote for the *Post*. "Perhaps the world is better off at that."[10]

Sigurd tried to get help from Thomas Uzzell, the New York agent he had worked with early in the 1930s; Uzzell said Olson's fiction had improved but was not yet good enough to get into the better national magazines. Olson could not bring his characters to life, the dialogue was horrible, and there was not enough drama in his plots.

Olson's story "Beaver Time" displayed all of these faults. During 1938 and 1939 it was rejected by the *Post*, *Country Gentleman*, *The American*, *Liberty*, and *Esquire*. Alternately titled "Outlaw Beaver" and "Song of the Bush" over the course of its revisions, it told the story of Johnny Chabot, a French-Canadian guide determined to continue his family's tradition of trapping beaver in an area that had become part of Quetico Provincial Park. Chabot resented government regulations that made it illegal to trap along the waterways he considered his own. The other protagonists were a schoolteacher named Marie, who had hired Chabot to take her on a canoe trip so she could write a story about beaver; an Ontario game warden named Jim Dowling; and an old trapper and trading post entrepreneur named Pierre LaRonge.

In the story, Dowling is out to catch a pilot who has been illegally transporting beaver pelts out of the park. Chabot, meanwhile, has gone trapping to get pelts for the pilot. Marie wants to help her guide avoid arrest and enlists the aide of LaRonge, who tells her that the pilot plans to steal Chabot's pelts and possibly kill the guide. In the end, LaRonge and Marie find Chabot and help him trick the pilot, setting up an arrest by Dowling. An excerpt from the story in which LaRonge tells Marie about the pilot's intention to steal from Chabot shows Olson's weak ability to write dialogue and develop character:

To her dismay, the old Frenchman laughed loud and long. "Dat ees not de worse, Marie," he answered, "de plane she's hi-jack every trappaire in de bush, steal hees fur, leave heem in de woods. Mebbe dey get home, mebbe not."

"Pierre," she gasped, "are you sure—do you mean that he'll be double-crossed, that they'll take his hides—kill him for that bunch of fur?"

"Dat ees true, Marie," he answered, "eet ees all very very funny," and he laughed until the tears rolled down his wrinkled cheeks.

In desperation, she shook him, pleaded with him, begged him to be serious.

"Marie," he said at last, "you do not understand. De odder night in my cabin on Lac Milione, de pilot he was drunk and tell Pierre which place he lan' wid your Johnee. Dat much I know."

"If they take his fur," she answered, "he'll not be done, you know that, Pierre."

"Dat ees just de point," the old woodsman crowed in her ear. "Ole Pierre, he's been what you call double cross, eh, Marie, and Johnee, an' de odder boys. Dat mak eet so very funnee."

"Well, I don't see anything so very funny about it," she snapped impatiently. "We've got to do something and in a hurry. Tomorrow night the moon will be full and he'll be coming down. What are we goin' to do, Pierre?"[11]

Thomas Uzzell, writing to Olson about the story on April 27, 1938, was, as usual, critical. "The man-to-man conflict," he said, "is not brought out with sufficient drama, the complication is not sufficiently striking, there isn't enough character interest. Pierre, for example, is a type rather than a person; Marie and Donny are shadows. Even Johnny Chabot is more of a type than an individual."

Olson did not rely solely on Uzzell for help with his fiction. He frequently turned to Elizabeth and the two boys, then in their teens, asking their advice on his stories. Robert best remembered "Beauchard's Beaver," a story about a French family that had trapped along a northwoods stream for several generations and the beaver colony that they saved from fire, predators, and starvation. "He worked on it and worked on it," recalled Robert, "and the whole family got involved, we all had to discuss it—he'd read it to us, so we couldn't back off being involved. And then he sent it off, and it came back rejected—once, twice, thrice."

Asking his family's advice did not mean he wanted to hear the truth. If they criticized what he wrote, he tended to get irritable and to storm back to the shack. Elizabeth, in particular, bore the brunt of this, because he often had her mark up his drafts with a pencil. While she never edited any of his work extensively, she frequently made good suggestions. Sigurd tended to see the narrative forest, while Elizabeth saw the trees. She would point out if he was repeating himself, or if he was assuming too much knowledge of natural history on the part of his readers, or if some of his details seemed to contradict other parts of the same narrative. He would get angry, but often enough he would end up incorporating some of the suggestions into his next draft.

As the rejections mounted, the frustrations that Sigurd for years had poured out in his journal and to Elizabeth began to spill over into everyday home life. "I can remember the terrible apprehension when Dad got a reply from a magazine, over whether it was going to be accepted or not," recalled Robert:

> All those rejections were accompanied by withdrawal, depression, tension. The house—I mean, you might as well pull down the shades like a funeral when he got a rejection. It was grim; it was funereal, and we just scattered to the corners. Who *needs* this? Who needs this sort of thing? And it went on, year after year. His writing and the success of his writing was a major factor in the family happiness. He didn't just go out and pound out a story and send it in— no, the whole family was involved.

Robert said he hated to be the one who had to go out to the shack to tell his father it was time for dinner, for that meant facing a sharp reply and an angry, irritated glare. (One time, Sigurd threw his glasses across the desk when Elizabeth's sister Johanne called him in to dinner. Afterward, he felt terrible about it.) But mostly, recalled Robert, the father who once had made up silly bedtime stories for his sons grew more and more distant as they entered their teenage years in the late 1930s: "He was aloof and we didn't want to get on the wrong side of him. He was a bomb waiting to go off. He wasn't rough or violent, and I don't recall that he *ever* took off after either of us. He just *suffered* us, just was not approachable."

Sigurd Jr., looking back more than fifty years to the same period, could not remember being exposed to the kind of anguish expressed in his father's journal. But he did not reject his brother's account, and a couple of journal entries from the period indicate that he was at least somewhat aware of his father's change in personality. On March 9, 1939, for example, the elder Olson wrote, "Junior said last night, 'Dad, remember when we used to sing all the cowboy songs?' It struck me hard, that accusation, for that was what it was—Why don't we sing anymore? Always, I say, 'Wait until things iron out, wait until I quit and begin writing'—wait, wait, and the days go by. Soon they will be gone and I will have to sing alone."

It was hard on everyone. How was Elizabeth supposed to understand it? How could she understand why her husband wanted to throw away a good job in the middle of the Depression to take up a career as a freelance writer when he was receiving ten rejections for every acceptance, and when his annual income from the articles he sold amounted to maybe one of his paychecks as dean? Years after his death she would admit that she never did truly know her husband. She said she told him that his unhappiness at the junior college was "silly," because everyone there liked him so much.

Sometimes Elizabeth lashed back. In his journal entry of January 13, 1938, Sigurd quoted her as saying, "For fifteen years we have never known what we wanted to do, never known where we should live or when we might quit." On another occasion she told him that the boys were worried about him and that his moping was not fair to them. And on February 19, 1939, after yet another rejection letter, she asked him, "Are you *still* going to keep on with your writing?" Sigurd wrote that he answered, desperately, "I will write until the day I die."

Sigurd felt guilty about his unhappiness and what it was doing at home; he sometimes wrote in his journal that he envied the people he knew in town whose aspirations did not go beyond Ely and who were content in their simple lives. He knew he was a good teacher and dean; perhaps, he wrote, he should let the rest go and try to enjoy these things. But he questioned his ability to do it: "Could I forget my wanting to write?"

At times he felt as though he *was* beginning to forget his dream, that he was getting too comfortable and was giving in to mediocrity. In January 1938, after *Collier's* had rejected an essay, he wrote of his fear:

I know my dream, know what I want to do, but it will die and I will continue doing the thing that is easy, live comfortably and after a time give up entirely. Then the ghost of what once was me, the bright flame of the personality that was Sig Olson—adventurer, woodsman, explorer, author, lecturer, idealist, man of the wilderness—will stroll through my rooms as a ghost, looking disdainfully at the comforts I have gained. Then when I am alone and it reproaches me, I will know the meaning of the words, "He sold his birthright for a mess of pottage," for that is exactly what I have done. That is exactly what all men do who give up their dreams. A man who loses his dream is old, one who has it is perennially young. I see it now as I have always seen it, but now it is stark reality.[12]

Olson's journal contains many entries between 1930 and 1941 in which he expresses feelings of melancholy, irritability, and hopelessness. On a dozen or so occasions during these years, his journal also contains references to, or signs of, suicidal thoughts. On October 10, 1939, for example, he said he wanted "to get rid of this deadly weight, the sickness inside of me, the suicidal frame of mind with which I greet every day." A year later, on October 31, 1940, he wrote, "I am suicidally sick and the only way I can pull myself out of the morass is to keep on writing." And on April 3, 1941, he wrote, "Another birthday in the offing and if anything more tortured and distraught than at any other time in my life. I have felt suicidal before but never quite like this."

One does not lightly dismiss such statements, but using them to describe Olson's inner state also poses significant problems. One is that Sigurd had a chronic tendency to overdramatize matters, in both his published and his unpublished writings. Another is that there is no pattern to these journal entries, just a few scattered over more than a decade; this presents difficult problems of context. The day after the April 3 entry, for example, he wrote:

Today is April the 4th and as usual I am calm and thoughtful and perhaps reflectful of the past and future. . . . I am a peculiar hodge-podge of desires and I wonder if the day will ever come when it will be different with me. For twenty years I have done something that never did particularly appeal. Nevertheless I have been fairly happy and have gotten considerable out of life.

Professional psychologists do not diagnose depressive illnesses without confirming the daily existence of several key symptoms over a span of at least two weeks.[13] In Olson's case, the only contemporary evidence is from his journal, and he rarely wrote more than five entries in any two-week period. Nor is there any clear-cut daily or seasonal pattern to the dark moods he described. At best, then, any conclusion must be tentative. We do know that one of Sigurd's uncles in Sweden spent a lifetime in and out of hospitals, undergoing treatment for mental illness. We know that his father, L. J. Olson, suffered from insomnia, which can be a symptom of depression. In addition, Sigurd's brother Leonard suffered a nervous breakdown in 1952, at the age of forty-nine.

This family history lends strength to the argument that Sigurd suffered from some form of mental illness. But *what* form and *how* ill are much more difficult to say with certainty. Sigurd controlled his inner feelings well enough that few people were aware of his unhappiness. According to his sons, he never withdrew from his interests or extracurricular activities. He had an engaging personality. Friends who knew him then say he loved jokes and laughed easily, loved music and singing. At the same time, Sigurd was obsessed with fulfilling what he believed to be his destiny, and he struggled to satisfy a deep need for approval and recognition. An insatiable need is the mark of a neurotic, and the evidence is strong that Olson, at the very least, suffered from a neurosis. However, while it is possible that he suffered from clinical depression, or from some other more severe form of mental illness, to make such a claim with certainty is to speculate beyond the evidence.

Sigurd's problems were not the only cause of the tension in the Olson household at the end of the 1930s. The Depression had sapped the life out of the Uhrenholdt farm in northern Wisconsin, and by the fall of 1938 foreclosure was a real threat. To make matters worse, Soren Uhrenholdt, at the age of eighty-one, was in poor health. At Thanksgiving Soren's children and their families gathered in Seeley as they always did, but with the realization that this might be the last time they saw Soren or the farm.

After the meal, according to Olson's subsequent recollection, Soren cleared his throat to indicate that he had something to say. "You know that I will not be with you long," he said, "that the day will come when you will wonder what to do with the old place. When that time comes, I hope that some one of the family will make this their home, that strangers will never come here to live. Here, like the trees, you have your roots. Here is where you are always home."[14]

Mostly, Soren wanted to talk about the pines that he had nurtured over the decades, even through bad times, when neighboring farmers had sold their timber for quick cash. Some had thought he was merely being shrewd, holding out for top prices, but on this bittersweet day he said he hoped his children would not give in and cut them down. "When they are gone," he said, "you too will be gone and this old place will become just another of the rented farms of Wisconsin."

When Soren sat down there was an embarrassed silence. Elizabeth and her sister Christine wept quietly, but nobody said a word. After a few moments normal conversation resumed, and no one spoke of Soren's wish. The old man got up and left the room to take a nap.

Afterward, Sigurd felt horrible. He felt he should have said something to reassure the man who had been like a father to him. "I failed them all," he wrote in his journal.[15] But he did not know what to say. To most of the family, the farm was a white elephant. The sons were finding it impossible to keep their own farms out of the red, let alone take over the responsibility of another one. They had no education, no options, and eventually would quit farming and leave the state. To most of the children, the logical course of action was to sell the timber *and* the farm.

Soon, however, three of the children—Elizabeth, her older sister Johanne, and Jens, the firstborn child who more than any of the others helped carve the farm out of the Wisconsin Cutover—came up with a plan. Together, they and their spouses would buy the homestead; Johanne and her husband would come there to live and take care of Soren. They could not afford to keep the entire farm—three pieces were carved off to be sold—but they were able to save the heart of it, the home and Soren's beloved pines nearby. And ultimately, after Soren's death—he surprised everyone and lived another nine years— these three families presented ninety-seven acres to the State of Wisconsin as the Uhrenholdt Memorial Forest.

Taking up the shared financial burden of the Uhrenholdt farm was not easy for the Olsons. Earlier in 1938 they had added a garage to the west side of their house, put in new windows and weather stripping, installed a new water heater, bought a rug, chair, and bed—and then had bought that Oldsmobile sedan. The total cost of the purchases and remodeling almost equaled a year of Sigurd's pay as dean. They also had recently hired a maid to do the cooking and cleaning.

Soon after the Olsons began making their portion of the Uhrenholdt farm payments, they were confronted with another financial problem: Sigurd's parents could not survive on their meager pension. In 1939 Sigurd and his brothers began to make monthly contributions. The unexpected financial responsibilities for the farm and for Sigurd's parents, combined with monthly payments for the car and remodeled house, made it even harder for him to consider quitting his job to take a chance on making a living writing. "If it wasn't for my debts," he wrote in February 1939, "it would be different. They chain me to the earth, shackle me so effectively. There is no hope."[16]

It would be wrong to suggest that the Olson household was constantly miserable. Many days were filled with the normal routines and behaviors and emotions of any typical household, and there were times of genuine happiness. Usually these revolved around the outdoors. After the Olsons moved to the house on Greenvalley Road in 1934, Sigurd Jr. was old enough to hunt duck and grouse, and he accompanied his father every fall. Later, Robert joined the duck and grouse hunts, and when the boys entered high school they also hunted deer each fall. In the winter they often went cross-country skiing before and after school and on weekends. Spring and summer were the busiest seasons for fishing and for exploring nearby lakes and streams in the canoe. Travel away from home mostly meant visiting relatives in Wisconsin and Minnesota, except for a family vacation to Yellowstone in 1935.

They also gained a new member of the family, in a manner of speaking. Andrew Curtis Uhrenholdt, son of Jens, named after his uncle who died in the world war, lived with the Olsons for two school years beginning in 1938, when he came to Ely to attend the junior college. Tall, quiet, and good-natured, Curtis, as he was called, loved the outdoors and fit right in with the family. "He was more like a brother than a cousin," recalled Sigurd Jr. Surprisingly, the only family canoe trips the Olsons took during the 1930s were during the two summers Curtis lived with them. They all felt a sense of loss when he graduated from the junior college in 1940 and joined the navy. By that time, of course, the world was at war again, but the United States did not seem likely to enter soon, and nobody thought twice when Curtis was assigned to the USS *Arizona* in Pearl Harbor, Hawaii.

❖

Of the seven published articles that Sigurd Olson wrote during the first eighteen months after building his writing shack in October 1937, the most important was the one for which he received no pay. He called it "Why Wilderness?" and early in 1938 he sent it to *American Forests* magazine. It already had been rejected by the *Saturday Evening Post, Atlantic Monthly, Scribner's, Cosmopolitan, Forum,* and *Esquire,* and had been among the also-rans in a *Reader's Digest* writing contest.

Why he chose *American Forests* for his seventh try, as opposed to, say, the Wilderness Society's magazine, *Living Wilderness,* is unclear. The magazine was published by the American Forestry Association, which was funded largely by lumber companies, and its editor was Ovid Butler, a man who would oppose the Wilderness Act and was once called "the slickest, slipperiest weasel that ever paraded as a ground squirrel." Its last in-depth article on wilderness preservation, twelve years earlier—a response to Aldo Leopold's classic "The Last Stand of the Wilderness"—had been decidedly negative.[17]

But Ovid Butler liked Olson's article. "I am much taken by your manuscript 'Why Wilderness,'" he wrote on February 23, "and would like to retain it for publication in *American Forests* provided you are willing to contribute it to the wilderness cause."

"Why Wilderness?," published in September 1938, was not Olson's first article promoting the wilderness idea, but it was his first to appear in a national conservation magazine, and it was among the early articles helping to shape debate about the meaning of wilderness. Bob Marshall wrote to Sigurd full of excitement about it. "I really think it's as good an article on the wilderness as I have ever read," he wrote on November 12. "It certainly explains better than anything I know what the wilderness does to people psychologically."

The ideas expressed in the article were not especially original. Olson wrote that as wilderness was becoming increasingly rare, it no longer should be feared, but treasured. He discussed the psychological benefits of wilderness—how it helps people find perspective and peace in their lives, how it binds travelers together in a kind of comradeship unknown in everyday life, how it provides an opportunity to experience danger, struggle, and accomplishment. Sigurd undoubtedly was showing his debt to Marshall when he wrote that only two experiences can satisfy the demand for adventure and comradeship, "the way of wilderness or the way of war."

Sigurd himself had expressed most of these ideas in earlier articles. "Reflections of a Guide," published in the June 1928 issue of *Field and Stream*, touched on the benefits of wilderness, as did "The Romance of Portages," published in the April 1936 issue of *Minnesota Conservationist*, and "Wilderness Areas," which appeared in *Sports Afield* in August 1938, just one month before "Why Wilderness?" was published. Sigurd was especially proud of "Search for the Wild," a two-part article that appeared in *Sports Afield* in May and June 1932, because it was his first and, until September 1938, his only published article entirely devoted to his beliefs about wilderness.

"Why Wilderness?," however, contained much better prose than the others, and this is what Bob Marshall liked best. "One thing that distinguishes it especially is its beautiful writing," he wrote. "Unfortunately, many wilderness articles—including some of my own—fail lamentably in this respect." Olson took a concept such as the psychological effect of wilderness and turned it into a lyrical passage meant as much for the ear as for the eye:

> I have seen staid educators, dignified surgeons, congressmen and admirals tie up their heads in gaudy bandannas, go shirtless to bring on the tan of the northern sun, and wear bowie knives in their belts. I have seen them glory in the muck of portages, fight the crashing combers on stormy lakes with the abandon of boys on their first adventure. I have heard them laugh as they haven't laughed for years and bellow old songs in the teeth of a gale.

There were rough spots, places where the sentence construction was a bit awkward or the punctuation questionable, but Sigurd was beginning to find his writer's voice, and a number of passages showed hints of the unpretentious yet lyrical and romantic style for which he would become known. Bob Marshall singled out the closing paragraph as one of his favorites:

> Why wilderness? Ask the men who have known it and who have made it part of their lives. They might not be able to explain, but

your very question will kindle a light in eyes that have reflected the camp fires of a continent, eyes that have known the glory of dawns and sunsets and nights under the stars. Wilderness to them is real and this they do know: when pressure becomes more than they can stand, somewhere back of beyond, where roads and steel and towns are still forgotten, they will find release.

The only part of the article that Marshall found difficult to accept was a section describing a theory that was emerging as a central tenet in Olson's defense of wilderness. Olson wrote:

When we recall that many of us are hardly a generation removed from the soil, and that a scant few thousand years ago our ancestors roamed and hunted the fastnesses of Europe, it is not strange that the smell of woodsmoke and the lure of the primitive is with us yet.

Racial memory is a tenacious thing, and for some it is always easy to slip back into the deep grooves of the past. What we feel most deeply are those things which as a race we have been doing the longest, and the hunger men feel for the wilds and a roving life is natural evidence of the need of repeating a plan of existence that for untold centuries was common practice.

In his letter praising the article, Marshall asked Olson to explain what he meant in greater detail. Olson's response made it clear that he believed this primitive attachment to nature has a biological origin. His response also demonstrates that Olson used the term *racial* not as an exclusive reference to those who shared his white, Nordic heritage, but in the inclusive sense of the phrase "the human race":

I am confident that a way of life can become deeply implanted in the racial genetic set up. . . . If temperatures, pressures, climatic and nutritional influences may in the long run affect the genes of a species, surely, there should be some background to the idea that a race might actually pass on a deeply rooted feeling for a certain way of life.

I do not believe for an instant that a father can pass on [genetically] a required skill . . . but I do believe that man as an animal race has ingrained in his chromosomes a need of freedom, physical struggle, primitive living, which a few thousand years of living in towns has not begun to root out. Our genetical research has been entirely along lines of the physical. Nothing has been done to speak of along lines of emotion and feeling for things. That is still wilderness as far as geneticists are concerned.[18]

Olson had first written about racial memory in his 1928 article "Reflections of a Guide." He had not yet, according to all available evidence, read in any depth the writings of Emerson or Thoreau, of Burroughs or W. H. Hudson. The journal that he began keeping two years later, in January 1930, indicates that he had just started paying serious attention to these writers, so it is unlikely that he got the idea from any of them, even though all but Burroughs describe the same basic idea at one time or another.

Perhaps Sigurd got the idea from his school days, when he first came across the romantics and primitivists, writers such as Wordsworth and Coleridge and Whitman and Ibsen who reacted against the excessive rationality, industrialization, and urbanization of the world around them. It is also possible that he was influenced during his travels in the mid-1920s with fellow guide Jack Linklater. Part Cree Indian and part Scot, Linklater sometimes would stop suddenly on the trail or at a campsite and listen to what he claimed was the sound of Indian music or voices, despite the fact that he and Olson were far from other people. Olson was convinced that Linklater really heard something, and that he heard it because, as an Indian, he had maintained his culture's close ties to nature.

The most plausible explanation for Olson's belief in racial memory, as well as for other beliefs that will be described later on, is that the original *feeling* was native to Olson, not derived from another source. It was something he felt in his bones, and he experienced it most vividly during his wilderness epiphanies. Olson was indebted to Emerson, Thoreau, Burroughs, and other writers not primarily because they taught him new ways to think about the relationship between nature and civilization, but because they confirmed what he already sensed, and helped him put his feelings into words.

Olson would give far more emphasis to the idea of racial memory than any other leading wilderness movement thinker; he would mention it time and again in his writings and speeches. The theory provided a biological basis for Olson's justification of wilderness preservation on spiritual grounds. "Because man's subconscious is steeped in the primitive," he said, "looking to the wilderness actually means a coming home to him," and the impact of traveling into it is so strong that "reactions are automatically set in motion that bring in their train an uplift of the spirit." Wilderness visitors may experience "burning instants of truth when everything stands clear," or may realize life's purpose "after long periods of waiting."[19]

Bob Marshall, too much a rationalist despite his strong romantic streak, could not quite accept this fundamental piece of Olson's emerging wilderness doctrine. Eventually, however, Sigurd would find support in the writings of a prominent figure in the young field of psychology: Carl Jung. As early as 1911, Jung had described a theory similar to Olson's "racial memory." He wrote, "Just as our bodies still retain vestiges of obsolete functions in many of our organs, so our minds, which have apparently outgrown these archaic impulses, still bear the mark of the evolutionary stage we have traversed, and re-echo the dim bygone in dreams and fantasies." Jung argued that these impulses were manifested in a "collective unconscious," a common, inherited psyche that predisposes people to produce similar, archetypal ideas. He wrote that when people separate themselves from this instinctual nature, "they then experience the full impact of unconscious forces." To put it in Sigurd Olson's words, denying our instinctual need for close ties to nature "results inevitably in frayed nerves, loss of enthusiasm and appetite for present modes of existence." The key difference between Jung and Olson was that Jung believed we come into contact with the collective unconscious in our dreams, while Olson thought we could find it in the wilderness.[20]

❖

The month that "Why Wilderness?" was published, Sigurd thought his devotion to the cause was about to get him fired. He had been very active with the Minnesota Division of the Izaak Walton League, which vocally supported the Quetico-Superior program. The division urged federal acquisition of all remaining pieces of private land scattered throughout the three wilderness areas in Superior National Forest, and the word spreading throughout the small towns near the canoe country was that the Izaak Walton League wanted to turn much of Superior National Forest into a national park. This would place an immediate ban on logging, mineral exploration, hunting, and trapping in the area, and the rumor made many area residents both worried and angry.

Olson, who was vice president of the Minnesota Division's Arrowhead District, which encompassed the northeastern part of the state, wrote to all Arrowhead chapter presidents on May 12, 1938, and called the rumors "dangerous propaganda." He also got his Jack Linklater Chapter in Ely to approve a resolution supporting the Quetico-Superior program and wrote a letter to the *Ely Miner*, the city's weekly newspaper, accusing Quetico-Superior program opponents of intentionally misrepresenting the facts to divide public opinion.

The *Miner* printed Olson's letter and a response from the executive director of the Timber Producers Association in Duluth:

> Following the example of his patron saint and mentor, Ernest Oberholtzer, Mr. Olson accuses those who oppose them of "misrepresenting facts." To those of us who know what it is all about there is no need to resort to such tactics. . . .
>
> I'm not angry at Mr. Olson for accusing me of deliberate misrepresentation. I'm only sorry for him, because I know that when he gets a little older and has had a little practical experience he will learn that when you find a reformer you will usually find a man who is looking after his own interests, and he will find that his hero has made a satisfactory business out of this border racket for more than twenty-five years.[21]

Over the the next year and a half pressure from the business community continued to grow. For the second time, Sigurd's Izaak Walton League chapter in Ely died of attrition, and by September 1938 he knew that some people wanted to pressure the school board to fire him. "Elizabeth thinks I am through and perhaps I am but what of it," he wrote in his journal. He recognized the irony in his situation: the people who were trying to pressure him had no idea that he did not want to be dean anyway. "I have been camping here," he wrote, "soldiering on the job, ready to fly on a moment's notice, reckless in a sense because I have never cared much what might happen, a recklessness misconstrued by others—brave, not afraid of losing his job, principles, etc."[22]

Olson was correct when he argued that Quetico-Superior program opponents were misrepresenting the facts; none of the leaders of the league or the Quetico-Superior Council were currently pressing for national park status. But it was hard to convince area residents of this, because throughout the 1920s the Park Service had successfully taken land from the Forest Service in a number of locations, including the Olympics and the Sierras of Washington and California, and in 1934 the agency *had* recommended park status for a large portion of Superior National Forest. Ely residents also knew that Olson at one time had advocated park status. In 1929, for example, he said in a speech, "The only force in the United States that can put the Superior National where it belongs as a national park and forever inviolate is the Izaak Walton League." It is not surprising that many believed the rumors.

The Quetico-Superior Council worried about the negative publicity, because the group was trying to build faith in northern Minnesota that its program would be good for the economy. With the possible exception of Oberholtzer, none of its leaders could even remotely be considered fanatics or radicals. The key figures were Frank Hubachek and Charles Kelly, the senior partners in a Chicago law firm, and Frederick Winston, a Minneapolis lawyer who had met Kelly in law school at the University of Minnesota. All three were lifelong Republicans who believed in government interference only when it was absolutely necessary to protect the public interest. [23]

Frank Hubachek was the one who would grow closest to Olson. Five years older than Sigurd, "Hub" first explored the canoe country in 1919, after completing his wartime service in the French ambulance corps. He came to know the boundary waters better than anyone on the council except Oberholtzer. Hubachek was lean and rugged, with a deeply receding hairline. Always one to say exactly what he thought needed saying, Hubachek often was warm and generous, but he could be surly, and to those who ended up on the wrong side of the Chicago loan office that he owned in addition to his law firm, he could be ruthless. But Hubachek pulled Ely's Wilderness Outfitters out of insolvency early in the Depression, and, beginning in 1937, when he bought a stand of virgin white pine on Basswood Lake to save it from logging, he spent tens of thousands of dollars a year hiring unemployed loggers in the Ely area to maintain the stand and hundreds of other acres that he gradually bought along the lake. His attitude toward the canoe country and its citizens is summed up in a comment he made to Olson in December 1939:

Each of us can fight for what he personally wants but each of us ought to be keenly mindful that the objective he wants is going to mean suffering and trouble to those interested in other and inconsistent objectives. Don't forget Lake County, struggling decently and gallantly to keep going. Don't forget the Finn settler with his forty acres of pulpwood. Neither can you forget the thousands whose entire living is dependent on the tourists who in turn are drawn by the wilderness magnet. And of course we can't forget our children and their children, who are certainly entitled to the physical and spiritual benefits of solitude and you can't get that out of tin cans or with the smell of gasoline in your nostrils or within earshot of a railroad whistle.[24]

Hubachek and Olson would get into many arguments over the years, yet no matter how angry they got they always would find a way to stay friends.

Hubachek's law partner, Charles Kelly, had never taken a canoe trip, nor would he. The love of his life was a dairy farm in western Wisconsin that he owned. A big man with a thin smile, Kelly seemed to work more hours than the day was long. He was an effective manager who enjoyed managing, and Hubachek recruited him to the wilderness cause. He not only served on the executive committee of the Quetico-Superior Council but also was appointed to the President's Quetico-Superior Committee and for many years would act as its chair. Kelly was Olson's age, but cut from quite different cloth; he was very reserved, even secretive, and tended to see problems in any straightforward strategy proposed by wilderness advocates. He and Sigurd would work together for decades but would not become close.

Fred Winston, who chaired the executive committee of the Quetico-Superior Council, was the oldest and wealthiest of the group. The son of a pioneer Minneapolis railroad builder, he was born in 1892, seven years before Olson. He was quiet, dignified, and considerate; like Kelly, he had many contacts that proved useful in aiding the Quetico-Superior program. An avid fisherman but not a canoeist, Winston nevertheless devoted long hours to the cause in the council's small, shared office on the top floor of the Flour Exchange building in Minneapolis. He would grow quite fond of Sigurd, but would have less contact with Olson than either Hubachek or Kelly did.

Hubachek, Kelly, and Winston were mum about the possibility of mineral exploration in the canoe country (they did not want to see it happen but did not want to call attention to it because mineral rights on most of the federal land were privately owned), but they did not want to ban logging. Their goal was to create an international land management program that would attempt to balance all uses over the entire fourteen thousand square miles of the Rainy Lake watershed.

Gaining the support and trust of northeastern Minnesotans was difficult under the best of circumstances; the mining industry and state government had helped create a climate of distrust toward outsiders. The national park rumors made it that much harder for the Quetico-Superior Council, and their worries grew even stronger in 1939, after the Forest Service reclassified the three Superior National Forest wilderness areas as "roadless areas." The decision seemed perfectly logical to the Quetico-Superior Council; the agency wanted to make clear that logging was acceptable in these areas, and this was in keeping with the Quetico-Superior program. Furthermore, the Superior Wilderness Area had been extended over the new federal land surrounding Basswood Lake, where there were half a dozen resorts on private land. Even Bob Marshall thought the label "wilderness area" had to go—he called it hypocritical. But the leaders of the Minnesota Division of the Izaak Walton League did not like the new designation and made plans to propose a resolution at the group's annual meeting in December calling for full wilderness status for the roadless areas. Logging would be banned, just as it was in the seventy-two other wilderness areas established by the Forest Service within the previous fifteen years.[25]

This put the Quetico-Superior Council in a bind. Oberholtzer agreed with the idea of wilderness status, seeing it as part of the overall mosaic envisioned in his large-scale land management program. But he thought that the timing was bad and that the most pressing problem was federal acquisition of the private lands scattered throughout the roadless areas. Hubachek, Kelly, and Winston, on the other hand, were adamant that logging be allowed except near shorelines. They did not want the Minnesota members of the Izaak Walton League to bring the issue up at their convention because if the resolution passed, the Quetico-Superior Council would have to either abandon what several of its leaders saw as an essential part of its program or fight the league. Kelly, for one, said he would quit if the council backed down.

During the first week in November 1939 Hubachek talked to Bob Marshall, who in September had gotten the Forest Service to adopt new regulations that gave greater protection to all wilderness areas. Marshall thought he might be able to get a pledge from his agency not to log in the roadless areas for ten years, which would buy some time and allow conservationists to focus on land acquisition.

Less than a week later, before he could carry out his plan, Marshall was found dead of a heart attack on a train bound from Washington to New York. It was two months before his thirty-ninth birthday. "It was a terrible shock," Olson wrote on November 20. "He was a great chap and a wonderful friend." Oberholtzer wrote to Olson, "The loss of Bob Marshall is not only a great personal loss to all of us who knew him but a serious blow, I'm afraid, to the Quetico-Superior program. There was no other man within the Forest Service so well qualified to work out the problems of the Superior Wilderness."[26]

Marshall's death made it all the more imperative to keep the Minnesota Division of the Izaak Walton League from pressing forward with a resolution for giving wilderness status to the roadless areas, and the Quetico-Superior Council called on Sigurd Olson to stop them. Sigurd, however, was inclined to support the league. "More than anything else in the world, I would like to see what is left of the canoe country given the protection of Wilderness Area status," he wrote on November 20. After Fred Winston told Olson that if he backed the proposal he would "break faith with the Council," Olson wrote to Hubachek in frustration that he was "between the devil and the deep blue sea."[27]

Hubachek responded with a long, thoughtful and typically frank letter. "Any man who fancies himself to have a godlike ability to discern the true and best course in a situation of this kind is simply a damn fool," he said. "I wish someone—maybe it is you—had the gift of thought and tongue to bring these foolishly warring elements together." Oberholtzer also encouraged Olson, writing that "I think you are the best possible person" to keep the Minnesota members of the Izaak Walton League from causing a schism. But Oberholtzer was worried about Sigurd. He wrote to Fred Winston, "I like him very much but have been disappointed at times in his ability to handle difficult situations publicly with competence."[28]

It was the council's first real test of Olson, and this time, at least, their concerns were unnecessary. At the Curtis Hotel in Minneapolis on December 14, Sigurd convinced the Minnesota Division of the Izaak Walton League that the time was not right to press for wilderness status in the canoe country. The man who had enrolled in the Wilderness Society in 1935 as someone "who has never learned to compromise" had learned a closely related lesson: sometimes it is necessary to avoid conservation battles that can yield short-term victories in order to make and sustain long-term gains. A relieved Fred Winston wrote to Charles Kelly that "everything is O.K. now for which our thanks are due our tried and true friend Sig Olson." Back in Ely, Sigurd wrote in his journal, "I have demonstrated once more that I have something, that I can talk. . . . When I go away and am lauded as a speaker, I begin to bloom and feel that at last I am on the peak."[29]

Nine

The War Years

1940–1946

S igurd Olson never was particularly interested in the goings-on of the world. He was not especially well read in history or economics or philosophy or any other branch of the humanities. He tended to vote for Republicans but was not a party loyalist like his friends on the Quetico-Superior Council. He wrote in his journal that when he read the *Reader's Digest* he skipped the political articles and turned to the fiction and personal experience stories.

Sigurd was driven by his passion for the outdoors, his obsession with writing, and his personal search for meaning, and rarely did his journal stray from these overriding interests. All through the trauma of the 1930s, not a word appeared in his journal about the Depression, about the millions out of work, about the riots and strikes, or about the wheelchair-bound president who told Americans that the only thing they had to fear was fear itself. Not a word appeared about the New Deal and its alphabet soup of government programs and agencies: the AAA, CCC, FERA, FDIC, HOLC, NRA, NLRB, TVA, WPA. Certainly Olson knew about these things and probably occasionally talked about them with family and friends, but by all accounts he showed little interest in the politics of the larger world.

Bit by bit, however, the world intruded upon him. Global economic misery might have been possible to ignore, but not a second world war. In September 1938, as Sigurd was enjoying the publication of his article "Why Wilderness?" in *American Forests* magazine, one hundred and forty thousand brown-shirted workers paraded into Zeppelin Field in Nuremberg, Germany, where one hundred and thirty antiaircraft searchlights threw beams of light twenty thousand feet into the sky. "Sieg Heil! Sieg Heil! Sieg Heil!" they roared, and Americans listening to their radios half a world away heard live for the first time the harsh voice of Adolf Hitler, sometimes calm and measured, often angry and explosive.

A year later, in September 1939, Germany invaded Poland. Before the month was over, Russia also invaded Poland and signed a pact with Hitler. That fall Russia claimed the Baltic states and invaded Finland. Another global war was under way.

It was the plight of the Finns, so close to the roots of his own ancestry, that caused Olson to write about world events in his journal for the first time. "All that is worthwhile now is keeping the Russian hordes from overrunning the beautiful civilizations of the north, Sweden, Finland and Norway," he wrote on February 23, 1940. "They are the bulwark of civilization":

All other activity, writing, painting of pictures, scribbling, worrying about my job, the house or vacations or the Border Lakes, all of it seems puerile compared to the odds they are fighting against. . . . Writing of funny little stories, or even serious little stories telling of a man's love of the earth and the wilderness, seem foolish when men are dying and suffering, giving their all, when women and children are being bombed. The only important thing at all is the maintenance of the kind of civilization that we think is worthwhile.

The next four months were marked by one sobering headline after another. Finland surrendered to Russia. The Netherlands, Belgium, and Norway surrendered to Germany. Italy entered the war. Then, on June 14, 1940, came the event that made the war seem real to many Americans for the first time—the Germans captured Paris, and newspapers carried wirephotos of Nazi troops marching in the Place de la Concorde. England was next in line, and its new prime minister, Winston Churchill, rose in the House of Commons and said, "Let us therefore brace ourselves to our duties, and so bear ourselves that if the British Empire and its Commonwealth last for a thousand years, men will still say, 'This was their finest hour.'"

After the fall of Paris, opinion polls showed that the vast majority of Americans favored selling airplanes to the Allies, but few believed yet that the United States should get more deeply involved. Most people continued to go about their daily business, aware that an ominous cloud hung over the future but hoping the rain would miss them.

❖

In the months after the fall of Paris, Olson did not mention the war again in his journal. He turned back to his main preoccupation: what to do about his writing. Since the publication of "Why Wilderness?" he had experienced nothing but frustration. He had temporarily put aside any notion of fiction to write several new essays and rewrite several old ones. Reactions at home were great; several friends had cried when they read a story about his childhood that he called "Grandmother's Trout." But he needed professional advice, and he had decided that a woman would understand his writing better than a man, so he had replaced Thomas Uzzell with another New York literary agent, Jane Hardy.

"You write charmingly," Hardy had responded after reading "Grandmother's Trout," "but you will never sell until you learn to put your perfectly lovely writing around a real plot." She had wanted him to turn his story into fiction. Instead, Olson had sent his material to yet another New York agent, Ann Elmo of the AFG Literary Agency. "They are all exceedingly well handled," Elmo had replied, "but . . . there is practically no market for this type of thing. I do think it would be advisable for you to incorporate these experiences in fiction."[1]

So Sigurd had gone back to fiction. But after Elmo had seen his new version of "Grandmother's Trout" in fiction form, she had said the essay was much better. His freelance-writing friend Don Hough also had read some of Sigurd's short story attempts and had told him he was "a million miles from fiction," and even Elizabeth had said she did not think Sigurd could write fiction at all.[2]

In the summer of 1940, Sigurd was scratching his head trying to figure a way out of his problem. He found it relatively easy to sell fishing and hunting stories, but they paid a paltry amount and gave him relatively little satisfaction. He loved to write thoughtful nature essays and seemed to write them better than anything else, but he found it impossible to sell them. Fiction seemed to be the only medium in which he could make enough money to quit the junior college, but he was horrible at it, mostly because he could not bring his characters to life. And the reason for that, he confessed, was that he wanted to write about his *own* way of looking at the world, not that of others, even others of his own creation.

"People do not interest me," he wrote. "I do not understand or care to understand others. I am so egotistical that I care only for my own reactions. I am a harp on whose sensitive strings the winds of the world blow, and my task is to set to music the strains I alone can hear."[3]

At the beginning of September 1940, Kenneth Olson, visiting his younger brother in Ely, had a journalist's answer for Sigurd's problem; he recommended trying for a syndicated newspaper column. Sigurd pounced on the idea. "After fifteen years of searching for my medium, I feel at last that it is close," he wrote on September 2. He immediately set to work producing short interpretive outdoor sketches of roughly five hundred to seven hundred and fifty words each. He wrote about little things that meant much to him, such as the movement of a canoe, the memories associated with duck decoys, the sound of wings over a marsh. His column, he wrote, "will be of a philosophical turn, a reflective turn, my personal reactions to the world I live in, each event, each happening an adventure of the spirit."[4] Within two months he wrote sixty of them, sent them to Kenneth at Northwestern University, and continued to write more while he waited for his brother's reaction. It would take five months for Kenneth to respond.

❖

Meanwhile, a new problem for canoe country wilderness supporters was beginning to develop in 1940. Two Ely businessmen bought shoreline property on Crooked Lake in the heart of the Superior Roadless Area next to the international border and began building resorts. One of them was at Curtain Falls, one of the area's most famous scenic attractions. Technological advances had increased the safety and reliability of seaplanes and made possible the development of a whole new kind of tourism: fly-in fishing. While the problem was not yet a big one, Olson predicted it soon would pose a major headache and said it pointed out the urgency of getting the U.S. government to buy the tracts of private land within the three roadless areas before too many other fly-in resorts were built.

It would take eight long years and an act of Congress before the U.S. government would start consolidating the roadless areas, however, and in 1940, when just four pilots in the Ely area were advertising fishing trips, Olson was not able to convince even Ernest Oberholtzer that the airplanes posed a serious threat.

Oberholtzer *was* concerned about a different problem: protecting some of Quetico Provincial Park's key lakes from shoreline logging. Lumberjacks operating in the southwestern portion of the park were observing restrictions on cutting near the shorelines of lakes along the international boundary but were under no obligation to preserve the shores of interior lakes. The President's Quetico-Superior Committee arranged several meetings with Canadian authorities beginning in January 1941 to discuss the issue. Olson was one of the American representatives, and, using a map, he showed the Canadians the lakes most important to canoeists.[5]

At the time of the first meeting, Olson feared that even the ancient stands of virgin white pine on the Ontario shores of Basswood Lake might be cut, but Frank A. MacDougall, the new deputy minister of Ontario's Department of Lands and Forests, reassured him and the other Americans. MacDougall formerly had served as superintendent of Ontario's Algonquin Provincial Park, where he had established shoreline logging reservations, so he was sympathetic to the council's concerns. Within a year, MacDougall established shoreline reservations for the interior lakes and in 1943 banned logging altogether from roughly half of the park, a five-hundred-thousand-acre section adjoining the border. The U.S. Forest Service, meanwhile, acted on the urging of conservationists and, in 1941, created its own two hundred and fifty-thousand-acre "no-cut zone" in the Superior Roadless Area on the American side of the border.

One of Olson's conservation activities during this period was not unambiguously beneficial to the canoe country wilderness. In 1940 he began a four-year, highly successful program to introduce a new species of fish—the smallmouth bass—to the Quetico-Superior. The results possibly proved to be more than he had bargained for.

The new executive director of the Izaak Walton League, Kenneth Reid, came up with the idea late in 1939 after taking his first canoe trip in the area. An avid fisherman with a soft spot for smallmouth bass, Reid was surprised not to encounter any during his trip. Afterward, Reid mentioned his surprise to C. F. "Cap" Culler, a regional supervisor of fish culture in the U.S. Fish and Wildlife Service and a national officer in the league. Culler thought the idea of introducing the species to the canoe country ecosystem made sense—it had been introduced successfully earlier in the century to the nearby Lake of the Woods region. He promised to arrange for the fish, and Reid wrote to Olson to ask if he would stock them.

Sigurd thought it was a great idea. "I agree with you that this little experiment might really mean something to this country in the future," he wrote to Reid on September 28, 1939. He told Reid he already had applied for permits to stock smallmouth bass in Burntside and Basswood Lakes, and also intended to stock Knife Lake. "If they take here the way they did in the Lake of the Woods country, we will really have something to be proud of. From Basswood and Knife the bass will spread to all of the border lakes, both American and Canadian and it might be that eventually the entire Quetico-Superior will be stocked. That is something worth working toward."

Sigurd released the first smallmouth shipments in Basswood and Knife Lakes during 1940, and his prediction of success would prove correct. In 1943 *Outdoor America* would show a photo of him holding a two-and-a-half-pound smallmouth from Basswood Lake. The "final proof," he called it.

The main reason for introducing smallmouth bass to the canoe country was to give fishermen one more exciting species to catch. In other words, it was a strategy for promoting tourism. Basswood Lake already was the source of national attention in the outdoor magazines for its record-breaking northern pike; eventually it would be praised in the same publications as one of the nation's best lakes for smallmouth bass.

The problem was that while nearly all canoeists also did some fishing, few of those who came to the Quetico-Superior for the primary purpose of fishing took canoe trips. Instead, they stayed at resorts and traveled by motorboats, motorized canoes, and seaplanes. Olson was aware enough of the power of publicity to understand that his *Sports Afield* articles served as advertising for his outfitting company. It is hard to imagine that he did not realize that introducing smallmouth bass to the canoe country would encourage more wilderness traffic of a kind that he increasingly found intolerable. He already had expressed worries about attracting too many canoeists to the area, let alone people in motorboats and seaplanes. Nevertheless, Olson helped stock the smallmouth bass until at least September 1950.

There is also the question of whether Olson's training in animal ecology should have made him think twice about introducing a new species into an ecosystem. In this case, possibly not. By the 1940s ecologists were well aware of the dangers of introducing an exotic species into an ecosystem. While the smallmouth bass was new to the canoe country, however, it may not have been seen as a true exotic, because it was native to much of Minnesota. Still, just two years after Olson's last documented bass stocking, he supported a law preventing anglers from carrying live minnows into Canada. "I agree," he wrote on October 4, 1952, "that the importation of minnows across the line into Canadian waters is a biological hazard. . . . Being familiar with Canadian biologists and fisheries men, my feeling is that this regulation was invoked solely for the purpose of protecting Canadian waters from undesirable fish."

It is possible, of course, that Sigurd thought of imported minnows as undesirable and smallmouth bass as desirable. But perhaps by 1952 he also had changed his mind about the wisdom of the smallmouth bass program. Letters and other documents from the time contain no answers to this puzzle, but it would not be the last contradiction in Olson's life.[6]

❖

Kenneth Olson wrote to Sigurd in February 1941 after what to the younger of the two deans seemed an interminably long time. Kenneth was full of praise for the written sketches that Sigurd hoped to turn into a syndicated newspaper column. "I think they are so damned good that I can't find anything to criticize," he wrote. "I tried rewriting a couple at first but my efforts fell flat compared to yours. You have an ability to paint word pictures and a feeling for this out of doors that I cannot touch."[7]

In February 1941, Olson sent twenty of his columns to Basil Walters, editor of the *Minneapolis Star Journal*. Walters loved them. "Man, you can write," he exclaimed. "This stuff simply yells for outlet in my opinion."[8] He thought Olson's columns had too much of a Minnesota flavor to have a good chance of being syndicated nationally, but he wanted to help attract attention to Olson's writing and said he would publish the essays for a couple of months as Sunday features, paying Olson five dollars an article for one-time publication rights. The *Star Journal* began running Sigurd's columns on the front page of its Sunday magazine on March 23.

Meanwhile, Olson wrote a query to Paul Meyers, manager of the North American Sportsman's Bureau in Chicago, which published several outdoor columns and an annual *Sportsman's Guide and Directory*. Sigurd had written a handful of articles for Meyers since 1937, and had served on the bureau's advisory board along with such well-known outdoor writers as Ozark Ripley, Robert Page Lincoln, and Harold Hollis.

Meyers responded on March 17 that he would like to see Olson's columns, but he also spelled out the serious difficulties in trying to syndicate outdoor writing. Meyers said newspaper editors liked to use local writers who wrote about local topics and people. "That, Sig, brings fan mail and fan mail is the thing the publisher feels justifies today's most valuable cost of white space," he wrote.

Second, he continued, while newspaper circulation was at an all-time high because of the escalating war in Europe, war news meant less space and little need for features. "I have had a dozen newspaper publishers tell me that if we had a scoop on the second coming of Christ they wouldn't know where to put it," Meyers wrote.

Finally, he said, newspaper readership studies regularly rated outdoor columns low in importance. That made it harder to sell an outdoor feature. "The reason for it may be that so far no one has been found who could write an outdoor column that is DIFFERENT," he wrote.

Sigurd felt sure his essays *were* different, and on March 20 he sent Meyers a sample of twenty, featuring such titles as "Black Dirt," "The Worth of a Tree," "Moonlight Escapade," "Rose Quartz," and "Robinson Peak." Olson wrote:

> I have no illusions about the difficulties that will be encountered, but I also am confident that once they begin to run, they will go to town and the papers will be asking you for it instead of you trying to sell them. . . . I think the world is ripe for a return to the philosophy of Burroughs and Thoreau. At least a dash of this type of thinking would be a welcome change, an antidote perhaps for the news of war and propaganda.

The essay titled "Interval" probably shows Thoreau's influence better than any other Olson essay from this period. It also shows his goal of writing nature essays that often used elements of natural history and often depicted outdoor recreation, but that went beyond such standard formats to include personal reflection about relationships between humans and nature. "Interval," which Sigurd wrote in January 1941, was about a recent late-afternoon walk along the Moose Lake Road northeast of Ely. Logging trucks had roared by for more than an hour, forcing him into the deep snow on the side of the road. He feared he might not find a moment's peace to enjoy the winter woods around him. Eventually the trucks stopped coming, and Sigurd stepped back onto the road. He walked quietly, watching and listening. Then he stopped:

> I had not long to wait, for over the darkening hills came the note of a great horned owl, hoo – hoooo – hoo – hooooooooo—and an answering note much deeper and more resonant than the first: hoo – hooooo – hoo – hoooooooooooo. Back and forth went the booming, haunting calls of Bufo virginianus and with them went the fear of death to the cowering snowshoe hares in the alder swamps, to the budding partridge in the groves of aspen, to countless waiting birds and animals for miles around. That call was the most feared hunting call in the wild. It came again and again, and, for the moment, I was far from the road, and trucks and civilization itself were forgotten. As I listened, a swift vision came to me of big timber and miles of wilderness, lonely valleys bathed in moonlight, rivers and lakeshores where there were still no sounds but those of the wild.
>
> Then I was conscious of a sound as of a great wind coming out of the north, as though a storm was breaking over the country that might tear every tree from its roots, and, at that moment, the calling of the horned owls stopped. The sound of the storm increased until it seemed as though it would engulf me and every living thing on earth. Blinding lights burst over the hill behind me, and a hurricane of shrieking metal roared out of the night. Desperately, I sprang for the side of the road as an empty truck sped by. The interval was over.

In this essay, the personal reflection is implicit rather than explicit. Olson is saying that the logging truck replaced nature's peace with anxiety and a sense of dislocation. Perhaps he even meant for readers to look more deeply and see the logging truck as a symbol of techno-logical progress. The imagery is much like that used by Melville and Twain, who understood that American desires for wealth and power—symbolized by technological progress—were clashing with a senti-mental attachment to the rural landscape and the happy, healthy so-ciety it symbolized. Olson certainly had read Thoreau's variation on this theme in *Walden*, where technological progress is symbolized by "the iron horse," the train, which makes the countryside "echo with his snort like thunder." But Thoreau could appreciate the promise of progress as well as show its cost. Olson's "Interval," on the other hand, sees only the cost. Sixteen years later, in an essay called "The Whistle," Olson would start with a similar situation but would use the symbol of a train to reach a more optimistic conclusion that rec-onciled wilderness and civilization.[9]

Meyers liked Olson's essays and agreed that they were quite differ-ent from what he called the "now I sit me down and bait my hook" type of outdoor column, but he was a little concerned that they were too philosophical. He sent samples to a number of outdoor editors, and their responses trickled in throughout April 1941. Meyers told Sigurd that Gordon MacQuarrie, a reporter at the *Milwaukee Journal* who was one of the country's most respected outdoor writers, had high praise for the column. A newspaper editor in Racine, Wisconsin, wrote that Olson "put a lifetime in five hundred words, very philo-sophical and different." But an editor in Minneapolis said the col-umns were not "fishy and hunty enough," and Buell Patterson, the editor at Meyers's syndicate, also questioned the heavy dose of con-templative writing.[10]

Meyers, however, was ready to radically change the bureau's "Amer-ica Out of Doors" column. Up to twenty outdoor writers had shared the column, which was published in dozens of papers throughout the Great Lakes region and some states to the south, and Meyers thought it would be more successful if it could be built around one writer whose name would become familiar to readers. Meyers did not want to make the change until he found just the right person. He thought Sigurd might be that person, and he made plans to visit Ely early in May 1941 to make an offer.

Waiting for Meyers to arrive, Sigurd worried that he would be forced to drop his interpretive style. He decided he would rather give up his dream of syndication. "If I change," he wrote on April 29, "I will sell my soul and make myself unhappy. I know nothing about gadgets and how to do things, where to go, and the details of fishing equipment, that means nothing to me. . . . That would be plain work." But Meyers did not want Olson to change his approach, and he convinced Sigurd to sign a five-year contract with a clause allowing Sigurd to drop out if his income the second year did not exceed $3,600. Olson also agreed to a six-month probationary period, during which he would receive no income.

In the summer of 1941 Olson wrote about a hundred columns, making a total of two hundred and fifty since he had started working on the idea a year earlier, and for which he had received no pay. He alternated between happiness and gloom. On one hand, the steady writing had improved his ability to come up with ideas and his ability to express them, and he dreamed of resigning as dean should the column take hold. But on the other hand, Paul Meyers sometimes took weeks to respond to the columns Sigurd sent, and Sigurd had no idea if Meyers was putting forth much effort to make the column succeed. Kenneth told Sigurd he hoped Meyers was not taking him for a ride.

Sigurd worried too. If Kenneth was right, he wrote in his journal, "then the bottom is out of everything. Nothing else counts and I will be completely sunk, no hope whatever. I cannot approach other writing with hope anymore."[11]

But the column was selling. "The Sig Olson column is stirring up more enthusiasm than the old 'America Out of Doors' column did," Meyers reported on September 19. He was phasing Olson into the column gradually, so that by January he would be the sole author, producing four columns a week. Two of the papers that subscribed to "America Out of Doors" were already publishing just Olson's columns. All signs looked good for the end of the probationary period on December 16, and Meyers said Olson would be paid as expected.

Steady writing and dreams of success kept Sigurd happier than he had been in years. So happy, in fact, that at times he worried it might not last: "What I am afraid of now is that the world will blow up just as I am getting it organized to suit me. A life of preparation and getting ready and then everything lost just as victory is in my grasp."[12]

❖

December 7, 1941, started out as a typical winter Sunday. Sigurd and Elizabeth and Robert, who was just shy of his sixteenth birthday, spent the afternoon skating on One Pine Lake south of Ely, and eighteen-year-old Sigurd Jr. went skating with a group of friends on Fall Lake not far from the Border Lakes Outfitting Company warehouse. But it turned into the day Sigurd had feared, the day the world blew up—for him and for millions of others. Robert recalled it fifty years later:

> It was a grey day, as I remember, cold and rather bleak, with the dark pines frowning along the lakeshore, a landscape in black and white, like an old woodcut. But we had a fire and were having fun. Then we were standing around the car listening to the radio. The announcer was speaking excitedly about the Japanese attacking a United States base at Pearl Harbor. . . . My parents were suddenly quiet and grim. We packed up and went home, the fun gone from the day.[13]

Sigurd Jr. and eight or ten friends had come in out of the cold and were having cocoa and cookies at a friend's house in Winton, talking and laughing, when they heard the news over the radio. "Boy, you talk about a change!" he recalled five decades later. "Everybody knew that their lives had changed right at that point. One of the guys, who was about three years older than the rest of us, took off and the next morning he went down to Duluth and signed up for the navy."

The most immediate concern was for news of Curtis Uhrenholdt, the nephew and cousin who had lived with the Olsons for two years while he went to the junior college. Days passed before they finally heard: he was one of the thousand-plus men who died when the USS *Arizona* exploded and sent a fireball so high that it shook the Japanese bombers thousands of feet overhead. "I can still hear my mother's cry," said Robert.

In the weeks and months afterward, it became ever more clear that a whole way of life had ended on one Sunday in December. The nation, heavily opposed to joining the war in the fall of 1941, now thought of little else. Even the junior college in the isolated little city of Ely, Minnesota, soon was caught up in it. All students began taking an extra physical education course, and the engineering, shop, physics, and chemistry classes were redesigned to emphasize skills

needed for the war effort. The college also enlisted volunteers as aux-
iliary air wardens and organized a reserve officer training program.
Olson led war bond rallies in the auditorium.

Enlistments and the draft took a heavy toll on Ely Junior College.
It started soon after Pearl Harbor, with some of the older students
quitting to join the armed forces. By 1943 enrollment would be so
low—just thirty students, one-fifth of the normal enrollment and
nearly all women—that the less sympathetic members of the school
board once again would talk about closing the junior college. And
not only students left: three months after Pearl Harbor, George
Gould, the college's zoology and botany teacher, joined the navy;
Dean Sigurd Olson had to take over his classes. Two other teachers
later joined the military, as did Sigurd's secretary; he absorbed the
secretary's workload, doing all the record keeping, transcripts, reports, and correspondence.[14]

Sigurd himself tried to enlist. He still felt bad about missing the
action in the first world war, so in November 1942 he applied for a
commission in the Marine Corps. Five friends wrote letters on his
behalf, extolling his courage, honesty, physical condition, and leadership ability. Frank Hubachek, who wrote one of the letters, was not
altogether happy about the prospect of Olson leaving for the Marines:
"It is going to be a bad day for the wilderness if you leave Ely," he
wrote on November 10. "Our enemies are always watchful for such an
opportunity and I have no doubt that they will move in when your
eye is elsewhere." But the Marines said that the forty-three-year-old
dean was too old.

That same fall Sigurd Jr. enlisted in the army, and in March 1943 he
left home for training with the 86th Infantry. He became a platoon
leader in the ski troops of the Tenth Mountain Division and in 1944
fought in the northern Apennines in Italy. The division opened the
way through the Alps for the Allied forces. His unit suffered a casu-
alty rate of 75 percent; he was one of the lucky ones.

Robert enlisted as soon as he turned eighteen at the end of 1943; he
joined the Army Air Corps and experienced his father's World War I
fate—the war ended before he was sent overseas.

The elder Sigurd wrote in his journal that he sometimes felt cheated
at missing the action once again, and showed at times his tendency
to romanticize the adventure and comradeship and glory of war. At

other times he found himself counseling young men leaving the junior college for the military, and with them he neither romanticized what lay ahead nor appealed to nationalistic propaganda. He invariably told them that he hoped they would not hate the individuals they had to fight, that Japanese and Germans and Americans were all the same underneath, that all people are related just as all life is related. To his son Sigurd Jr., newly married and about to go to Europe, he wrote the following:

> Sig, this is for you. When the time comes for you to do your shooting or whatever it is that you are called to do, remember this: killing in the army is an impersonal thing. This civilization of ours has a malignant cancer growing away inside it, a cancer that is as much living tissue as the rest of the body but something that has to be cut out immediately if the body is to survive. . . . Your job is to help cut out the infection and if cutting out the infection means destroying those responsible for it then you should have no more compunction about it than if you were a surgeon cutting out live tissue during an operation. In other words do not let this war become personal to you. It is a cold, deadly, impersonal business all the way through. In order that men may live happily in the future, live in peace without fear or want, such cancerous growths as Hitler's and Hirohito's philosophy must be destroyed. For beliefs can be as malignant as disease and the only way to destroy the cause is to do away with those who foster and support such beliefs. This is a war against a false philosophy of life, in fact it is a crusade against evil and your generation has been called to fight and cleanse the earth once again. Mankind it seems always has to fight for liberty and the right to happiness.[15]

The war also brought about the slow and painful demise of "America Out of Doors." After Pearl Harbor the nation's industry diverted raw materials to national defense; the accompanying sharp decreases in production of domestic goods meant an equally sharp drop in advertising. Newspapers began cutting their features, and syndicated columns were among the first to go. In the spring of 1942 rumors of government-mandated cuts in pulpwood production created a newsprint scare, and a number of papers canceled Sigurd's column. He agreed to accept just twenty-five dollars a month from the syndicate, less than a sixth of what his contract had promised.

In the summer of 1942 Paul Meyers joined the army, leaving the syndicate to William B. Otto. The newsprint scare became reality at the end of the year, when the war production board ordered publishers to reduce their use of paper by 10 percent; further reductions of up to 45 percent were predicted. Just nine papers were still printing "America Out of Doors" by September. Otto offered the consolation that the papers canceling "invariably praised the service highly, and almost without exception stated that they intended to take it up again later if it is still available."[16]

Late in 1942 Sigurd decided to try to market his essays in book form, under the title *Hours Afield*. He picked one hundred of his favorite columns, twenty-five for each of the seasons, and in January 1943 sent a sample of forty to the Macmillan Publishing Company. Macmillan turned it down, and three other publishers did the same during the next year. Essays were difficult enough to sell in good times, they said, and none was willing to take the chance in a wartime market, especially when their use of paper was restricted.

By March 1944 only four newspapers were publishing "America Out of Doors." "The paper situation is so serious that it would be quite out of the question to try to put on any new accounts now," Otto wrote to Olson on March 2. "Publishers are scratching their heads to figure out how they are going to get by." He asked Sigurd what they should do.

Olson, normally a prompt respondent, took more than two weeks to reply. "Somehow I hate to write this letter as it means the end of a dream that someday America Out of Doors would really go to town," he wrote on March 18. "That perhaps is why I have delayed writing you as long as this. It seemed I just could not bring myself to it." He told Otto to end the column. A year later, in his journal, Sigurd recalled sadly that "America Out of Doors" was "the closest I ever came to really arriving."[17]

In February 1943, stress began to take a physical toll on Olson: he developed an ulcer. A year later, shortly before Sigurd told William Otto to stop running "America Out of Doors," Elizabeth wrote to her sister Johanne about it: "Sig has ulcers so badly that I doubt he can go on with school next year. He has tried hard to hide it—feels humiliated for some reason. He's in serious condition and I think the only thing that can help him will be a year without school work."[18]

❖

Ulcers would remain a recurring part of Sigurd's life, but he soon got the break from his work that Elizabeth said he needed. The war that claimed Olson's nephew and scattered his children and sapped the life out of his most successful writing venture also, in the end, provided Sigurd with one of the greatest adventures of his life. On July 5, 1945, two months after the Allied forces achieved victory in Europe, he set sail from New York City on the *Princess Elizabeth*, bound for a shattered continent as a civilian employee of the U.S. Army.

The offer came out of the blue. As soon as it was clear that Germany was about to surrender, the army began making plans to bring home three million Americans. Realizing that it would take months to get them all back, the army planned a variety of activities—including college course work—to keep the soldiers reasonably content and active while they waited. The army recruited college faculty from the United States to spend a few months in Europe teaching the GIs. Kenneth Olson was selected for an administrative position at the army's university in Shrivenham, England, far to the west of London near Swindon, and he was put in charge of finding faculty members. So it was that Sigurd got a call in May 1945 and, after getting approval for a leave of absence from Ely Junior College (which surprised both him and Elizabeth), found himself on a steam liner just a few weeks later.

Shrivenham American University was located on the grounds of an old manor that had been used by the British Royal Air Force for wartime training. Massive beeches with shiny gray trunks and immense oaks with outstretched gnarled branches surrounded the ivy-covered manor, and they in turn were surrounded by a broad lawn. Sigurd stayed in a small room in one of the makeshift barracks. A German prisoner of war cleaned Olson's room and placed fresh flowers on his table every morning.[19]

Classes started on August 1, with Sigurd teaching zoology and geology to the soldiers, many of whom were officers used to giving orders rather than taking them. He was nervous at first, but he wrote that he found the soldiers more attentive and hardworking than most students he had taught back home. German POWs were available for classroom-related work; one, an artist, made a number of sketches for Olson, drawings of protozoa and crustaceans and millipedes and frogs. He often took his geology classes on field trips, combing the countryside and finding pieces of flint and chert.

There was plenty of time for Sigurd to explore on his own or travel with his brother and other faculty members. He often walked or rode a bicycle along the quiet roads outside Shrivenham. Fifteen miles to the south, beyond the rolling pastureland of the downs where the skylarks sang, was a range of hills with a two-thousand-year-old road built by the Romans. On top of the ridge was a fort where King Alfred had fought the Danes in the ninth century, and beyond were ceremonial places of the Druids. In mid-July Sigurd traveled to Stonehenge, timing his visit so he could sit in the midst of the circle of stones under the light of a full moon.

There was lots more: Picadilly Circus, Stratford-on-Avon, Salisbury Cathedral, Windsor Castle. He saw Winchester Cathedral and the grave of Izaak Walton and the country churchyard where Thomas Gray wrote his "Elegy." One of his most memorable experiences came in October 1945, when he was a dinner guest at Oxford University and got to visit with the renowned ecologist Charles Elton. They spent much of the evening talking about wilderness, but Sigurd was flattered to hear that Elton and several other Oxford faculty members had read his wolf research with great interest.

The most important event during Olson's time in England occurred on September 15, when he traveled to Bingham's Melcome, far to the south of Shrivenham near Dorchester. He had been invited to spend the night at the manor by its owner, Ellinor Grogan. Lady Grogan, as Sigurd called her, was seventy-nine years old and the last of a family line that had occupied the manor for seven hundred years.

Bingham's Melcome was a gray stone house surrounded by gardens of purple asters and daisies and golden glow. Beyond the flower gardens were hedges, and beyond them a bowling green with a view of rolling hills that went on for miles and miles. There was a library full of rare books and tapestries and rugs, a dining room with an inlaid table that had washed up on the beach when the Spanish Armada was destroyed in 1588. Every room contained landscape paintings by famous artists and portraits of descendants and others with ties to the manor. Lord Byron, Lord Tennyson, Percy Bysshe Shelley, and T. E. Lawrence were among the many notable people who had stayed there. Sigurd was impressed, but no less so than he was with Ellinor Grogan. That night, sitting in his bedroom, he wrote to Elizabeth about the manor, and especially about Lady Grogan:

> She is very old and very beautiful, possibly eighty years, but with the alivest and most wonderful mind of anyone I have ever met. She is real aristocracy and speaks of lords and dukes and kings and bishops as commonly as we speak of people we know. . . . I helped her fill lavender bags and she gave one for you for your birthday with a little note to go with it. So you have something no one in Ely will ever get, a lavender bag made by British royalty and a personal note from Lady Grogan.[20]

But Ellinor Grogan also was impressed with Sigurd Olson. Early in the evening Sigurd had pulled from the shelf a copy of W. H. Hudson's *Green Mansions* and told Grogan that Hudson was one of his favorite authors. It was the beginning of a lively discussion, for Grogan had known Hudson well and he had done much of his later writing in the manor. She showed Olson the desk Hudson had worked at, let him read letters Hudson had written to her, took Sigurd outside to show him where Hudson had loved to stand and look out over the hills. Sigurd told her all about his feelings for nature and his dream of writing. When Sigurd left the next day she told him, "Very seldom do I run into anyone who has the deep feeling about things that I have. It seems as though I have known you always." They visited a number of times while Sigurd was in England, and she encouraged him to follow his dream. Years later he would say he owed her "an enormous debt," because her faith helped keep him from giving up on his writing.[21]

He needed that faith just then. He found a lot of time to write while he was in England, but he was running into the old problems with yet another agent, Anita Diamant of the Writer's Workshop Inc. in New York. He had started sending her essays during the first half of the year while he was still in Minnesota. He probably sent them too soon, because her initial reaction was that they were "rather discursive and even verbose at times," while later on she said they were "beautifully done." But even after she liked them she said the market for such writing was "extremely limited" and said she wished he would try writing fiction.[22]

So, during that summer and fall of 1945, Sigurd wrote nine short stories. He did not situate them in the British countryside that was all around him, but in the north woods of his memory, with titles such as "The Gilmore Party," "Bush Fever," and "Ordeal by Portage." Diamant responded by describing her own ordeal: "It's difficult to get through them and we found ourselves exerting effort to keep on with the story in each case. . . . If you really want to sell stories, Mr. Olson, you simply must accelerate the action."[23]

Despite the frustration he felt when he received such criticism, it is clear from his letters that while Sigurd was still worried about his ability to write, he also was having the time of his life in England. His being away from home may have been good for his marriage, too, for he seemed much more appreciative of Elizabeth. He wrote her many letters—often enclosing dried flowers or evergreen twigs or other little things he found on his walks—and often expressed his love. "All my life is wrapped up in you and around you," he wrote in one letter. "Never make any mistake about that. I may seem hard to live with and sometimes you think I don't love you, BUT I DO with all my soul and all my heart and nothing will ever change that."[24]

Elizabeth, too, found that she deeply missed her husband. She told him that something vital was missing with him gone, and that she read and reread his letters until she knew them by heart. "I don't deserve it, I know," Sigurd wrote, "and if I have made you love me, it is probably just an accident that I was so lucky."[25]

Shrivenham American University was scheduled to close in time to get the last of the soldiers and the faculty home for good by Christmas of 1945. At the end of November Elizabeth wrote saying she bet that Sigurd was feeling sad about it: "As a sentimentalist at heart you'll be unhappy and sick at heart."[26] She looked forward to having Sigurd home, and not just because she missed him. The past several months had been difficult for her both physically and emotionally, because both her father and Sigurd's mother had fallen very ill. She had been shuttling back and forth between Seeley, Wisconsin, and Willmar, Minnesota, helping with the care of Soren Uhrenholdt and Ida May Olson. (Sigurd's parents had moved to Willmar, a city west of Minneapolis, when L. J. Olson retired in 1935.) Sigurd was on leave from the junior college until the fall of 1946, and Elizabeth looked forward to having him ease her burden.

Kenneth Olson returned home for Christmas, but Sigurd did not. Early in December he was offered the chance to spend several months touring the European mainland with the Lecture Bureau of the U.S. Army's Information and Education Division, and he cheerfully accepted. On December 18, 1945, three days after the end of classes at Shrivenham, Sigurd climbed aboard a beat-up military landing craft at Southampton and sailed across the English Channel to France. He spent Christmas in Paris. Elizabeth was angry, but never said a thing in her letters. Eventually, by the end of January, her father's health took a turn for the better, and so did she.

From January through June of 1946 Sigurd visited concentrations of American troops in France, Germany, Austria, and Italy. He was part of a panel that spoke to soldiers about the facts and fallacies of sex, and he also regularly (and ironically, considering his years of frustration) gave a talk called "How Do I Want to Live?" In France, he was attached to the American Embassy and lectured at the Sorbonne and at the University of Alsace-Lorraine, speaking about conservation and wilderness preservation in the United States.

There was much to enjoy: skiing in the Bavarian Alps, canoeing on the river Ell in France and the Main in Germany, hiking in the Black Forest. In May he was able to break away for a short trip to Denmark and Sweden. But what he would remember the most was the horror and destruction. He had seen the devastation in London but was not prepared for what he found on the mainland, and especially in Germany. "Every major city was in ruins," he wrote a year later, "all the railroads, all the rolling stock, all the bridges, only the small villages seemingly intact." And the cities were full of people without hope, stunned, apathetic, never smiling, wandering the streets with vacant expressions. During his travels through war-torn Europe he saw women and children searching garbage cans for food, people begging on the streets, and black marketeers. At Easter he watched as repatriated Germans arrived by train in cattle cars and stood on the platform with fear in their eyes and no place to go.[27]

Many of the Germans resented the Americans. In Berlin, where many women were working in the piles of rubble from bombed-out buildings, his landlord asked, "How long will you Americans stay? You have no right to take our homes." After an army officer had made a mess of the house with a party, the landlord called the Americans pigs. "There were many stories of Americans being beat up," Sigurd recalled a year later, "and it was uncomfortable being anywhere except behind American barbed wire after dark."

His most gruesome assignment was to tour twenty-two concentration camps in Germany, beginning with Dachau on March 8. At Dachau, he was struck by the contrast between the pretty village with window boxes full of bright geraniums and the camp nearby with the huge smokestack for the human incinerators. But the worst was Belsen. He saw the lampshades and other decorations made of human skin by the wife of the commandant. He saw one of the torture chambers, with clubs lying on the floor and the walls still covered with pieces of brain and hair. "Someday when I get home," he wrote, "I want to bury my head in my pillow and just weep." Every now and then for the rest of his life he would have nightmares.[28]

Sigurd also talked to many Jews who had been prisoners in the camps and went through the files of the war crimes investigators, looking at countless photos of tortured and mutilated human beings. "I wondered how anyone could so debase themselves as to glory in such depravity in the name of patriotism," he wrote later.[29]

All of this was in preparation for the Nuremberg trials. Sigurd was assigned to attend as an observer for the U.S. State Department and the Supreme Headquarters of the Army of Occupation. His letters to Elizabeth indicate that he spent three days at the trials, from March 20 through March 22, 1946. He stayed with a group of Russian observers and found himself—the son of a temperance-preaching Swedish Baptist minister—trying to keep up with his vodka-drinking associates. They went on toast after toast, until Sigurd could take no more and resorted to surreptitiously pouring his drinks into a potted plant next to his chair.

Nuremberg's Zeppelin Field, where Hitler had staged his Nazi rallies, was largely intact, but the central city was devastated. "Due to the rubble there is a continual film of white dust over everything," Sigurd wrote to Elizabeth. "Even the air feels dusty and after an hour you feel coated with it inside and out. Everyone looks grimy and miserable. It is even reflected in the troops."[30]

Olson had excellent seats at the trial each day, and he wrote home about the expressions and mannerisms of Field Marshal Hermann Göring, Nazi Party deputy Rudolf Hess, and foreign minister Joachim von Ribbentrop. What most surprised him was how normal they appeared to be. He wrote on March 20, "I sat and looked at them, realizing that before me were the greatest criminals in human history, and I couldn't help but feel they should look like monsters. Instead they looked like a typical group of American businessmen, like any Rotary Club picked at random on a Wednesday night."

As his time in Europe drew to an end, Sigurd's thoughts sometimes turned to his unhappy occupation in Ely and his dream of quitting to write full time. His confidence, damaged by Anita Diamant's broadsides, was boosted by Ellinor Grogan, with whom he stayed in contact, and at the beginning of April a chance encounter on a train between Frankfurt and Berlin greatly inspired him. A Russian who had been talking to Olson gave him an English translation of an essay on the origin and development of ethics, written by the Russian Prince Pyotr Alekseyevich Kropotkin. One passage especially struck Sigurd, and he wrote it down twice in his pocket notebook:

> When the poet has found the proper expression for his sense of communion with the Cosmos and his unity with his fellow man, he becomes capable of inspiring millions of men with his high enthusiasm. He makes them feel what is best in them and awakens their desire to become better still. He produces in them those very ecstasies which were formerly considered as belonging exclusively to the preserve of religion.

It was a clarion call, and Sigurd took it to heart: "In other words, this is what you want to do, not adventure stories or hunting or fishing or conservation—but stories that are the expression of my own sense of communion with the cosmos and man—I want to inspire. . . . My job is to find proper expression—medium for my feeling. . . . Go into the wild and come out with a message."[31]

Sigurd returned to the United States at the end of June 1946, almost exactly a year after he had left. Earlier, in a letter to Elizabeth, he reflected on what the year had meant to him:

> One thing I have found out is that there is beauty wherever one goes, if one knows where to look, that people can be kindly and thoughtful and lovable in all climes and under all conditions, that America is a young country with much to learn but as a young country it has a tremendous power and potential that older coun-

tries oftentimes lack, that culturally I mean . . . a feeling for the aesthetic things and the enjoyment of little things is oftentimes lost in
our terrible speed and rush, but that there are whirlpools in America, sort of backwashes where the swirl and flow has had time to settle down and where people have time to think and enjoy. Such a
backwash is in our own Ely, I have discovered, and in all places out
of the flow.[32]

❖ Ten ❖

A Professional Conservationist
1946–1949

Sigurd Olson may have written fondly about living in a small city "out of the flow" of high-pressured modern society, but he was referring only to the proper setting from which he could regularly launch himself into the major currents of American life. As much as his firsthand experience of war-torn Europe had increased his appreciation of the physical comforts of life in Ely, it had diminished neither his need nor his desire to achieve recognition beyond what any small town could provide. Quite the contrary. For nearly a year Olson had been treated as a man of rank and privilege, meeting with the dons at Oxford, lecturing at the Sorbonne, and staying at picturesque country estates. The thought of resuming what he viewed as the petty realities of his job as dean was almost unbearable, and Sigurd's mood turned bleak almost immediately upon his return home from Europe at the end of June 1946. His son Robert, who lived in Ely for a short time after the war, recalled:

> For reasons we could not fathom he was angry and almost catatonic. He would hardly speak and went for long, desperately silent hikes. No joyous return to the north country. Not brimming with tales of new adventures. Mother complained that he showed *no* affection whatsoever.

It would have been a logical time for Olson to tell the school board that he had no intention of returning to the junior college. The board would have named the acting dean, Donald Stubbins, the new dean, so the college would not have suffered, even though the fall semester was just two months away. Sigurd's children were adults, so he did

181

not need to think about supporting them. (In fact, he and Elizabeth recently had become grandparents: Sigurd Jr.'s wife, Esther, gave birth on May 14, 1946, to a son they named Gregory Thorne Olson.)

But it had become clear that Ely Junior College was about to be swamped by a wave of veterans. Figures from the college newspaper later would show that enrollment had returned to the prewar level of about one hundred and fifty, and roughly ninety of the students were former soldiers. Some of them had specifically asked if Olson would be the dean; they had known him since they were children and he had been their Boy Scout leader. "I feel duty bound to stay with it another year and do not feel I can let them down at this time," Olson wrote to a friend on August 22.[1]

The decision took a terrible toll on him. Elizabeth Olson recalled it as "a most miserable year," and, ironically, the veterans for whom Sigurd had returned to the college added to his difficulties. Elizabeth said there was a subtle tension between those who had held different ranks in the armed services. "The lieutenant was a little better than the sergeant," as she put it, and at times former officers tried to advise Olson how to run the school.

The veterans took over, in a sense. Five or six hours a day a group of them could be found gambling in the attic lounge of the junior college, playing "hi-lo jack" and "smear." This was hard for the son of a Baptist minister to take, but Sigurd did not know what to do. One day he finally lost his temper and broke up the game, shouting, "This is a school, not a casino!"[2] But the gambling soon resumed, and Olson did not interfere again. On December 2, 1946, he wrote in his journal, "Whatever happens, this is the last year and I wish it could end NOW."

It was a sad holiday season for the Olsons. Elizabeth's eighty-nine-year-old father, Soren Uhrenholdt, died six days before Christmas, and Sigurd's mother, Ida May Olson, died on January 15 at the age of seventy-five. When Sigurd turned to his journal on January 23, 1947, death was on his mind. "The hopelessness comes from the thought that life is over," he wrote. "I look forward to years of no accomplishment, no one great dream to realize." The forty-seven-year-old dean was suffering physically from stress; his eyes had become painfully sensitive to light, and periodically they would twitch. He speculated that he had twenty years left of life. "Only twenty years—is it that I feel the long hand of death reaching through the mists? Am I dying now?"[3]

Olson turned to books for support. Among them was *Peace of Mind,* a book of Freudian pop psychology by Rabbi Joshua Loth Liebman. Published in the fall of 1946, *Peace of Mind* had shot to the top of the *New York Times* best-seller list, where it would remain for nearly five years, a record surpassed only by Norman Vincent Peale's *The Power of Positive Thinking.* (Liebman, however, committed suicide in 1948.)[4]

To find peace of mind and to build a healthy society, Liebman said, Americans must combine the fruits of modern psychology with "the accumulated spiritual wisdom and ethical precepts dating from the time of the earliest Prophets." Liebman argued that traditional ideas about God and religion had created a repressive culture. Rather than view themselves as subjects of a feudal God, Americans needed to claim their destiny as co-creators with God. "The religion of the future," Liebman wrote, "for the first time, may become a partnership religion in which men will not only *say,* but will *feel,* that they are indispensable to God."

Liebman confirmed what Olson had come to believe. Ever since that spring morning in 1919 at the University of Wisconsin when he climbed down from the roof of the YMCA building and resigned his presidency of the evangelistic Student Volunteers, Sigurd had been engaged in a search for spiritual meaning. He nominally had remained a Baptist because he did not want to upset his parents by switching faiths, but he had been relieved to find no Baptist church in Ely when he and Elizabeth moved there in 1923. They initially attended a Methodist church, but eventually joined friends and social acquaintances at the Presbyterian church. Sigurd loved the traditional Christian hymns and for a time sang with the church choir, but organized religion did not have a high priority in his life.[5]

He did not, for example, feel guilty about occasionally missing Sunday services to go fishing or hunting or cross-country skiing or canoeing. Nor did he feel bound by Christian dogma. As early as 1933, after reading the philosopher Benedict Spinoza, Olson wrote in agreement that "Our salvation now is [in] calm thought and contemplation rather than [in religious] authority." He may have returned to the fold at least briefly in the mid-1930s, for a 1936 letter from his mother says that "Dad was overjoyed to hear that you have surrendered your life to Christ." But even if Ida May had correctly understood her second son, his prodigal return to an evangelical Christianity must have been no more than a brief affair. Nothing in his own journals or letters supports his mother's statement. Instead, he had exposed himself to a number of different religious faiths, through the parties he guided in the wilderness, through friends in the conservation movement, and through reading such books as *The Perennial Philosophy* by Aldous Huxley, Lin Yutang's translation of Confucius, and Ralph Waldo Trine's best-selling book from the 1890s, *In Tune with the Infinite*.[6]

Huxley and Trine, in particular, tried to convince their readers that the same spiritual truths underlie all religions. Huxley took a scholarly approach, filling his 1945 book *The Perennial Philosophy* with quotes from the great thinkers and mystics of all of the world's major faiths. His sources included the sixteenth-century Spanish mystic and founder of the barefoot Carmelites St. John of the Cross; the fourteenth-century German philosopher Meister Eckhart; the sixth-century B.C. Chinese philosopher and founder of Taoism Lao-tzu; and the ninth-century Indian philosopher Shankara. Huxley argued that organized religions tended to develop problems when they focused solely on one aspect of God: as personal and transcendent, for example, while downplaying or ignoring his immanent and suprapersonal nature. The real God is *all* of these, he said.

Trine, on the other hand, was more interested in healing troubled readers than in scholarly analysis, and Olson was excited enough by *In Tune with the Infinite* to buy copies for his mother and younger brother. "There is a golden thread that runs through every religion in the world," Trine wrote. He predicted that people the world over eventually would recognize this golden thread:

> When we make it the paramount fact in our lives we will find that minor differences, narrow prejudices, and all these laughable absurdities will so fall away by virtue of their very insignificance, that a Jew can worship equally as well in a Catholic cathedral, a Catholic in a Jewish synagogue, a Buddhist in a Christian church, a Christian in a Buddhist temple. Or all can worship equally well about their own hearth-stones, or out on the hillside, or while pursuing the avocations of every-day life. For true worship, only God and the human soul are necessary. It does not depend upon times, or sea-

sons, or occasions. Anywhere and at any time God and man in the bush may meet.[7]

It is hard to imagine Ida May Olson agreeing with Trine that the doctrine of her faith was a "narrow prejudice," but for Sigurd, who had found a more fulfilling experience of a sacred reality in the wilderness than in church, books such as *In Tune with the Infinite* served as important confirmations of his own intuitive understanding. And on January 13, 1947, in the midst of his unhappiness about work, his sorrow over the death of his father-in-law, and his concern for his dying mother, he outlined in detail for the first time his beliefs about God, beliefs that would prove central to his wilderness philosophy.

Olson wrote the three-page journal entry in response to John Burroughs's essays about God and religion. Sigurd had just read the essays for the first time in many years, probably seeking to ease his grief and inner turmoil. But he apparently had forgotten just how strongly Burroughs attacked religion. Like Olson, Burroughs had grown up with an intensely religious father whose God resembled the angry and vengeful lord of Jonathan Edwards. Chauncy Burroughs, like L. J. Olson, was both a grim man and a fundamentalist Baptist; when John defied his edict against Santa Claus and hung a stocking one Christmas Eve, Chauncy filled it with horse manure.[8]

John Burroughs suffered a gut-wrenching crisis of faith at the age of nineteen (very much like Sigurd's experience at the age of twenty) and fell away from organized religion. The naturalist eventually ridiculed what he called "theological pap" and praised scientific reason: "The atmosphere of our time is fast being cleared of the fumes and deadly gases that arose during the carboniferous age of theology." He argued that there is no evident purpose or design manifest in nature, only the laws of matter, force, and biology. To Burroughs, evolution's most important result was the human development of moral consciousness.

Olson could agree that, as he put it in his journal, "heaven and hell are out of the picture," but he found Burroughs's overall perspective unsatisfying. Whether or not there was a personal God—and Olson's unpublished writings indicate he never reached a final conclusion on the matter—Olson believed the Christian axiom that God is love, "the great power which surges through all of humanity." Burroughs described the evolution of moral consciousness with the same detachment that one might use in explaining the evolution of the human appendix. Olson described the same process from a liberal Christian perspective in which any act of love is an act of co-creation with a God who is an integral part of the evolutionary process:

> Man is a biological accident, is therefore humble, realiz[es] that . . . he [must] live as Christ would have him live, that he himself does not count except as he gives [to] and loves others. . . . The spirit of man is the flowering of nature, greater than any other phenomenon, greater than the whirling spheres, greater than space, infinity.

Sigurd Olson had long been disturbed by the modern tendency to dismiss as fantasy any claims to truth not based on rational, scientific analysis. In an unpublished essay he wrote during the 1930s, he said, "Our enemies have debunked and analyzed and have tried to strip our souls of the last thread of connection with the infinite." He described the wilderness epiphanies in which he had experienced a sense of connectedness with the universe and wrote that those who do not "permit themselves to submit" can never understand the spiritual feelings that bring inner peace. "It is as difficult for them to understand," he added, "as for a man who has never seen the wilderness, to know the joys of exploration and discovery. For them, never having probed the depths of their own sensibilities, there is no wilderness, nothing new, for they have never glimpsed the land beyond the rim."[9]

When he wrote that essay, Olson saw himself as being in "the forefront of the battle to retain a few last entrenchments of the spirit." Science and technology were destroying the religious truths that had provided spiritual sustenance, the truths that had given meaning, and offering nothing in their place. Olson believed that wilderness could help people find meaning and purpose. In wilderness they could rediscover the timeless, creative force of the universe, regain a sense of being part of that force, and, in this glimpse of "the land beyond the rim," come to a new understanding of God and of themselves.

Olson's journal entry of January 13, 1947, was a reaffirmation of his mission "to give men a picture of God as he really is." He was driven, as he later put it, to help "keep the flame alive, give people something to hold to, something to fight for that is bigger than politics, bigger than the problems the world is constantly facing, something in the way of a philosophical concept that lies at the root of any happiness the race can find."[10]

And his *own* happiness required that he embrace his mission. For more than twenty-five years he had lived a life that had left him unsatisfied at best and that too often had caused him anguish. True enough, there had been moments of joy and adventure and friendship, and he had found moments of deep meaning in the wilds near his home, but all the while he felt that his real life was passing him by. "All I have ever wanted is to sit down and write," he wrote in his journal on January 10, 1947. "I must make good my dreams, the things I have denied. . . . If I do not, then I die, then all has been for naught."

His mother's death five days later may have strengthened Sigurd's resolve, for on January 30 he wrote in his journal that he intended to resign from the junior college:

I think it had to come to some sort of a pass such as this to force the issue. Now I know that nothing is worthwhile sacrificing my peace of mind for, a job, prestige, nothing. That if I continue I will be lost forever. It has come to the parting of the ways and I am taking the hard way, something I should have done ages ago. . . . Well, I am ready now and I shall sink or swim by my own efforts.

Olson made his new beginning official in mid-April, when the snow was starting to melt and migrating ducks were landing on newly opened stretches of the Kawishiwi River, where Sigurd often skied. On the evening of Monday, April 14, 1947, ten days past his forty-eighth birthday, Sigurd Olson gave his resignation to the Ely school board. "I cannot believe it," he wrote in his journal. "It does not seem possible. But now that it is done, I must begin to work out my salvation. I must write as I have never written before. I must remake my life. I must make good for Elizabeth's sake. We must have fun. . . . I am going to be a different man, a different person entirely."

Sigurd's decision was big news in Ely. The next issue of the *Ely Miner* proclaimed in large bold letters at the top of the front page, "Dean Olson Resigns." (Sigurd wrote in his journal, "I look at that

and ask myself . . . if I have done something terrible.") Olson viewed
his decision as the beginning of a new life for himself, but some saw
it as the end of an era for Ely Junior College. George Gould, who had
taught botany and zoology there from 1936 until the war called him
away in 1942, wrote to a friend that it would be extremely difficult to
find someone to fill Olson's shoes:

> As I see it, the college might as well be closed, for it was he who
> breathed life and inspiration into the institution. They'll never find
> anyone who will be interested as Sig was in the woes of each and
> every little backwoods lad, nor will they find another dean who
> will patiently plot each student's career as if it were his own son's.
> There'll never be anyone that they might procure from outside who
> will have the real "feel" of the local situation; who will understand
> the problems of Range youth, particularly the more isolated parts
> of the Range, like Sig does.[11]

❖

Olson began his new career with a new literary agent, Lurton Blassingame, who, like Olson's earlier agents, was based in New York. For
extra criticism, Sigurd also sent his writing to Frederic Litten, a colleague of his brother Kenneth at Northwestern University. Realizing
that fiction was his weakest medium, yet fearing that his survival as
a freelance writer depended on his ability to sell fiction, Olson set to
work rewriting the adventure stories he had sent to Anita Diamant in
1945 and 1946. By August each of five short stories had been rejected,
and he was wallowing in negative comments.

"The writing is not adequate," wrote Litten. "The cliche and the
trite (word and phrase) are too often found. Errors of technique
harm the effect; the transitions are abrupt." Blassingame chimed in,
saying that Sigurd's stories were wordy and sentimental, and that he
made punctuation errors and "other mistakes that irritate editors."[12]

The criticism deeply hurt Olson. "Evidently it means that I cannot
write that sort of thing," he wrote in his journal. He must have expressed the same idea to Litten, because on October 3 the journalism
professor pleaded with Sigurd to keep trying: "Sig, send me your fiction. I recognize the talent and it will one day be acknowledged by
all. . . . You are destined to go far—please believe this." But Sigurd
would try writing short stories only a few more times. "Short stories I
do not know," he repeated in an undated journal entry. His greatest

happiness had always come from writing the sketches that appeared in his "America Out of Doors" syndicated newspaper column, and from the longer essays he had written back in the 1930s, such as "Grandmother's Trout" and "Farewell to Saganaga." "This is the sort of thing you quit to do," he reminded himself; "this is the stuff that the world might be waiting for. . . . You have suffered, you have suffered greatly for this ideal. Only by writing what you feel you must can your sacrifice be warranted."[13]

Olson's "search for medium," as he had called it—his struggle to find the best way to reach out to the public—was over. Unresolved, however, was the unpleasant problem of earning enough money to support himself and Elizabeth. His final year's salary as dean had been $4,200, and his one-third share of the Border Lakes Outfitting Company profits had amounted to $1,200. He intended to remain part owner of the Border Lakes, but that still left a shortfall of $4,200, unless he was willing to sacrifice some measure of his standard of living. His journal gives every indication that he *was* willing to live with a smaller income, but does not specify a bottom line. Let us assume that he was willing to cut his total income by 25 percent, to $4,050. Subtracting $1,200 in expected income from the outfitting business would leave a shortfall of $2,850; in other words, that is the amount he needed to earn through writing.

This was nearly impossible. If he could have written fiction of good enough quality to break into such top national magazines as the *Saturday Evening Post*, he might have been able to do it, but he knew his fiction was horrible. He realized that his happiness depended upon writing essays, and that his writing skills were best suited to this format, but essays were extremely difficult to sell. His one hope for a dependable writing income was his old standby, the outdoor magazines. He could sell a fishing or hunting story for a hundred dollars, maybe a hundred and fifty if he was lucky. But to make almost three thousand dollars he would have to sell twenty to thirty articles a year, and he had never before sold more than six articles in a twelve-month period.[14]

❖

All of this must have been going through Olson's head during the fall of 1947 and undoubtedly provides at least part of the explanation for a major change in plans that occurred by the end of the year. For instead of spending the winter quietly working in his writing shack, Olson accepted a paying job as a conservationist and began crisscrossing the continent as the leading public spokesman for a Quetico-Superior movement that was in desperate straits.

As Olson had predicted in 1940, fly-in fishing had grown to pose a serious threat to the wilderness character of the canoe country. Seaplanes not only made it possible to drop sportsmen into remote lakes deep in the wilderness for a few hours of fishing, they also made it profitable to build resorts on isolated tracts of private land on lakes within the roadless areas of Superior National Forest. By 1944, nine Ely-area resorts advertised fly-in fishing trips. After the war, as pilots returned home and aircraft industries retooled excess factory machinery, wilderness flying became a booming business. When Olson returned to Ely from Europe at the end of June 1946, nearly twenty fly-in resorts were operating or being built. And there was room for many more within the one hundred and thirty-five thousand acres of private land scattered among the roadless areas.

Ironically, the very existence of the roadless areas increased the value of these resorts; surrounded by a million acres of federally protected wilderness, the resorts operated, in effect, their own private preserves. As Olson had written on April 24, 1945, in a letter to Izaak Walton League executive director Ken Reid, it was "a God-given setup for someone who wants to make a killing."

The problem extended into Canada, even though Quetico Provincial Park had no private inholdings and no road access. In 1946 Canada had built a small customs office on Basswood Lake and government officials had begun soliciting pilots to fly into Quetico Provincial Park. The province also was preparing to lease land in the park for cabins and resorts.

For American conservationists, the timing could not have been worse. The President's Quetico-Superior Committee and the Quetico-Superior Council had been inactive since the start of World War II. Ernest Oberholtzer had forcefully carried the cause on his own, but in ways that had perplexed his friends. "Ober would stir up trouble that did more harm to what we were trying to do than otherwise," Charles Kelly later recalled.[15]

Oberholtzer had needlessly antagonized Minnesota officials during the war years by vehemently and unfairly attacking the state's proposal to build a road along Lake Superior through Grand Portage village. Largely because of the dispute, Minnesota refused to discuss the possibility of exchanging land with the federal government to expand Superior National Forest or to eliminate the one hundred and thirteen thousand acres of state property within the roadless areas. This effectively kept the wilderness smaller on the American side than Oberholtzer had hoped.

Ontario officials, too, had come to see Oberholtzer as extremely unrealistic. His proposed treaty for zoning the entire Rainy Lake watershed required much more of the Canadians than it did of Americans, because most of the watershed was in Ontario. Oberholtzer had not built public support for the treaty in Canada, and his stubborn refusal to budge on the details of his proposal made it impossible to gain support from the Ontario government. There was no hope that Canada's federal government would ratify a Quetico-Superior treaty without the assent of Ontario, because the nation had a long tradition of strongly asserted provincial rights.

The province found it difficult even to justify maintaining the wilderness character of the small part of the Rainy Lake watershed known as Quetico Provincial Park. The Quetico's inaccessibility had long made it the destination of choice for wilderness enthusiasts entering the canoe country on the American side, but this very fact made quite a few Canadians angry. Provincial records showed that from 1935 to 1943 an annual average of more than thirteen hundred Americans visited the park, compared to just *three* Canadians. Businessmen from the small cities near the Quetico complained that Minnesota resort owners received all of the financial benefit of the park, while Canadians paid all of the expenses. When they saw the fly-in resort boom in the Superior Roadless Areas, they demanded a piece of the action, and their government responded with its plan to lease portions of the park.

Ontario's actions deeply shook the Quetico-Superior Council's leaders. In a letter to Oberholtzer on August 8, 1946, Frank Hubachek said that if Ontario enacted its plans the following summer, "that fact in itself will doom our efforts, except for some miracle which reasonable men cannot expect to happen." Hubachek said that neither he nor Charles Kelly could in good conscience continue obtaining donations toward the program if there were no hope of success. "If we cannot get the Canadians to reverse their present policy for at least twelve months from this fall," he continued, "I will have to leave the arena because the cause is lost. . . . It is bitter to see twenty-one years lost in this manner." Kelly agreed with Hubachek and wrote that if there was no progress within five months, "it is my present intention to resign and to accept the defeat of our program as an accomplished fact."[16]

That fall the American conservationists won the reprieve that Hubachek and Kelly said was absolutely necessary. Ontario promised to hold off all development within Quetico Park for a year—later extended to two years—to give the United States a chance to address the problems presented by seaplanes and roadless area inholdings. But little further progress was made during the following twelve months. Success required simultaneous publicity campaigns in two countries and the coordinated efforts of the Quetico-Superior Council, the President's Quetico-Superior Committee, the Izaak Walton League and the Wilderness Society. Oberholtzer, who was sixty-three, no longer was capable of carrying the full load of such a massive operation. The council needed a new public spokesperson, and late in 1947 the group turned to Sigurd Olson.

Frank Hubachek, who knew Olson the best, wrote to Sigurd on November 5, saying that he was "extremely anxious" to talk to Sigurd about the struggling Quetico-Superior program. "There is no central focal point," he wrote. "We are not going ahead as fast as we should." Hubachek followed up his letter with a personal visit and convinced Olson to attend the President's Quetico-Superior Committee meeting in Chicago on November 24. Charles Kelly extended the job offer during the meeting: Olson, should he accept, would become the Izaak Walton League's wilderness ecologist, and adviser to the President's Committee and the Wilderness Society. Kelly and Fred Winston would be responsible for obtaining donations to pay Olson's still-to-be-determined salary.

The offer did not come as a surprise to Olson; in fact, the same proposal had been made in August 1946. Olson had responded by saying he felt "duty bound" to serve at least one more year as dean of Ely Junior College in order to help the soldiers returning from overseas. If the offer was no surprise, however, the arrangement was cer-

Sigurd Olson with his older brother, Kenneth, and their parents, L. J. and Ida May Olson, ca. 1900

Left to right: Sigurd Olson and his brothers, Leonard and Kenneth, ca. 1908

All photographs except where noted are courtesy of the Olson family collection.

In the Students Army
Training Corps,
University of Wisconsin,
Madison, Autumn 1918

At Picnic Point, Madison, with
Elizabeth Uhrenholdt, 1919

With Al Kennedy (*right*) near Nashwauk, Minnesota, 1920

After a successful deer
hunt, early 1920s

Honeymoon photo, August 1921

Elizabeth and Sigurd Olson, mid-1920s (Photo by Glenn Powers)

Traveling with game warden Urho Salminen (*right*) in 1927 to gather information for an article on predator control. "The Poison Trail" was published by *Sports Afield* in December 1930.

With Border Lakes Outfitting Company partner Wallie Hansen (*left*), 1929

Left to right: Sigurd Jr., Elizabeth, and Robert K. Olson, ca. 1930

Bob Marshall (*left*) and Sigurd Olson, 1937 (Photo courtesy the Wilderness Society)

Leading an Ely Junior College field trip, 1937 (Photo by Milt Stenlund)

A winter hike, 1941

A string of bass, ca. 1942, two years after Olson had helped to introduce the smallmouth bass to the Quetico-Superior canoe country

Sigurd and Elizabeth on a canoe trip in honor of their twenty-fifth wedding anniversary, August 1946

Supreme Court Justice William O. Douglas (*third from left*) joins Sigurd (*left*) in singing Olson's "C&O Canal Song" on March 29, 1954, following a hike designed to draw public attention to efforts to preserve the historic and scenic canal near Washington, D.C. (Photo by Abbie Rows, courtesy U.S. National Park Service)

At a Cree village along the Churchill River, 1955

The Voyageurs at Cumberland House, August 12, 1955, at the end of their first Churchill River expedition. *Left to right:* Eric Morse, Elliott Rodger, Denis Coolican, Anthony Lovink, Omond Solandt, Olson

Olson in September 1960

National Park Service Advisory Board, March 25, 1963. *Front row, left to right:*
Dr. Stanley A. Cain, Harold P. Fabian, Interior Secretary Stewart Udall, Marian S.
Dryfoos, Dr. Edward B. Danson Jr., Earl H. Reed. *Back row, left to right:* Daniel B.
Beard, National Park Service director Conrad L. Wirth, Frank E. Masland Jr.,
Dr. Robert G. Sproul, Sigurd Olson, Dr. Robert L. Stearns. (Photo courtesy U.S.
National Park Service)

At a celebration of the fur trade era,
Crane Lake, Minnesota, 1966

Meeting President Lyndon B. Johnson at a White House reception, March 29, 1968.
Vice president Hubert H. Humphrey is partly visible to the right.

A book signing in the Twin Cities, January 21, 1973. (Photo by Craig Borck, courtesy *St. Paul Pioneer Press*)

tainly unusual, proposing that two men from one conservation group, the Quetico-Superior Council, raise the money to pay the salary of a man employed by another conservation group, the Izaak Walton League. Olson may never have known the reason, but it was because the ever-so-cautious Charles Kelly was worried that Olson might damage the reputation of the council. When the group first considered hiring Olson in the summer of 1946, Kelly described his fears to Fred Winston. "I have never wanted Sig for our program because he is a little too fanatic," he wrote. Kelly thought Olson was "a little intolerant of other people's ideas and values" and doubted that he would be tactful enough for "the hard-boiled people we have to deal with."[17]

Kelly's comments are ironic, given that the guiding force and most visible person behind the Quetico-Superior program, Ernest Oberholtzer, had developed exactly the reputation that Kelly associated with Olson. But Kelly had at least one legitimate reason to worry more about the man from Ely. On various occasions Olson publicly had stated his belief that both logging and motorboating should be banned in the canoe country. Even Oberholtzer, who sympathized with Olson, had not gone so far in public statements; such a position simply was not part of the Quetico-Superior program. Kelly feared that people suspicious of the council's intentions would misinterpret Olson's hiring as proof that a ban on logging and motorboating in the roadless areas was the group's secret goal, and he worried that such a rumor would cripple the entire program.

Kelly recognized Olson's ability to inspire others, however, and he wanted to channel this talent to good advantage, so he devised the unusual arrangement with the Izaak Walton League. "If he goes to the League we would get much of the benefit of his help that we would get if he were director of our own group," Kelly wrote in August 1946, "and we would avoid some of the difficulties."[18]

Olson did not immediately accept the job offer at the meeting in Chicago. He had, after all, resigned from the junior college determined to devote full time to his writing. He returned to Ely to think it over. He borrowed Kelly's correspondence files of the previous two years and studied them to gain new insights into canoe country problems. It did not take him long to decide to postpone his career as a freelance writer. "I must go into the fight with everything I've got and stay with it until we are through," he wrote to Kelly on December 3. As to salary, Olson was both idealistic enough and hard-pressed enough to tell Kelly that "whatever can be worked out will be satisfactory with me. . . . The important factor right now is to get to work and get things underway."[19]

❖

Sigurd and Elizabeth Olson moved to Chicago in mid-January 1948 for a five-month stay while Sigurd got his work under way. Kenneth Olson found them an apartment near Lake Michigan, which they sublet from the nationally syndicated columnist Sydney Harris. On January 12, Olson reported to the law offices of Hubachek and Kelly to begin his work as "a freelance canoeman trying to get the rest of the world excited about saving what to me is the finest recreational resource on the continent, our wilderness canoe country."[20] His salary of seven hundred dollars per month was about two hundred dollars more than he had made as dean, but out of that came his traveling expenses, which in the months ahead often would absorb more than half of his paycheck.

Olson's major tasks for the winter and spring were to combine personal lobbying with mass media publicity to get through Congress a bill that would allow the U.S. Forest Service to purchase private inholdings in the Superior Roadless Areas. This would be a precedent-setting bill, for the Forest Service did not have authority anywhere in the country to buy land for recreational purposes. It also was a vital first step in addressing the airplane problem, because it would be impossible to ban air transportation to fly-in resorts without any means for providing compensation to the resort owners. Despite support from Minnesota's congressional delegation and from some local government leaders, the bill had been stalled since its introduction in the House and Senate early in 1947.[21]

The issue was compensation. The three counties containing Superior National Forest land currently received 25 percent of the forest's annual gross revenue, which came almost entirely from timber sales. Logging income fluctuated from year to year, however, and Forest Service restrictions on logging, beginning with shoreline reservations in the 1930s and continuing with the establishment of a no-logging zone across a third of the roadless area acreage in the early 1940s, decreased the potential forest revenue. The counties saw the proposed acquisition bill as a chance to increase and stabilize their income and demanded that the bill direct the federal government to pay annually either 1 percent of the fair market value of each acre of national forest land or a flat rate of twelve cents per acre. Either method would immediately double the fifty-six thousand dollars the counties were currently receiving.

Similar compensation clauses had been introduced in Congress a number of times during the previous twenty years, and none of them had ever gotten out of committee. When Sigurd Olson started his new career, the Superior National Forest acquisition bill seemed headed for the same fate. Members of Congress argued that a 1 percent rate or a flat fee would be too expensive because every county in the nation would demand similar treatment and the country could not afford it.

Olson shuttled from Chicago to Washington to Duluth in attempts to reach a compromise, and also wrote articles promoting the bill for the *Christian Science Monitor* and such national conservation and outdoor magazines as *Sports Afield, Outdoor America, The Living Wilderness, Nature Magazine,* and *American Forests.* By early May, John Blatnik, the Democratic representative from northeastern Minnesota who had introduced the acquisition bill in the House, reported that Congress was willing to accept an annual federal payment to the counties of three-fourths of 1 percent of the fair market value of national forest land. This would provide far more income than the counties currently received, and only about fifteen thousand dollars less than their original demand.

But the good news quickly turned bad. The county commissioners agreed to accept the rate only if the bill provided for a minimum valuation that would give them the extra fifteen thousand dollars. Conservationists were nearly out of hope because Blatnik had stated that he would continue to support the bill only if the counties were satisfied. They also were running out of time, because if the acquisition bill did not pass Congress by summer, Ontario was expected to go ahead with its development plans for Quetico Provincial Park.

With perfect timing, *Sports Afield* published an editorial by Olson in its May issue. "Quetico-Superior Challenge" was meant to shock its readers and stir them to action. First came the shock:

The brutal fact is that the immense populations of the Midwest, not to mention the millions from other states beyond, are in immediate danger of being robbed of one of the finest recreational opportunities on the continent today, the privilege of breaking away from civilization and cruising by canoe through the primitive lakes of the Minnesota-Ontario border.

After describing the physical, historical, and intangible qualities that made the region unique, and explaining the threat from airplanes and private inholdings, Olson ended with a call for action, asking readers to "talk and write and plead through every medium" to build national support for the acquisition bill. "If we fail to get immediate action," Olson warned, "the development of airplane fishing camps will spell the doom of our cherished canoe country within a year."

To put pressure on Congress, Charles Kelly sent copies of "Quetico-Superior Challenge" to all newspapers in Minnesota, Wisconsin, Michigan, Illinois, Indiana, Missouri, and Ohio. Olson sent nearly a thousand additional copies to members of the Outdoor Writers Association of America. Editorials in favor of the acquisition bill soon began appearing. In mid-May, Olson managed to get the county commissioners to meet in Duluth one more time. He brought along a number of county residents who were angry that the commissioners might spoil this chance to improve local revenues, and he also brought the state's conservation commissioner, Chester Wilson, who told the commissioners that if they did not accept the compromise payment rate they could expect lower state appropriations in the future. The commissioners voted in favor of the lower rate.

Freed from all stumbling blocks, the acquisition bill sailed through during the final days of the 80th Congress. On June 8, the day after Representative Blatnik put Olson's "Quetico-Superior Challenge" in the *Congressional Record*, the bill passed the full House. A day later, it cleared the Senate, where the bill's major sponsor was Minnesota Senator Edward J. Thye. President Harry Truman signed the Thye-Blatnik bill into law on June 23, 1948. Blatnik thanked Olson for his "invaluable work" in getting the bill passed. "The publicity which you gave this through your excellent magazine and newspaper articles certainly brought results," he wrote, "for so many Congressmen told me of receiving letters and wires from interested organizations and individuals." Fred Winston of the Quetico-Superior Council wrote to Olson, "It was a piece of good fortune when you came to work for the Quetico-Superior. I feel better about the whole situation since you have been on the job."[22]

Despite its precedents—authorizing the Forest Service to buy land for recreation and setting a national standard for federal payments to counties—the Thye-Blatnik Act had its faults. By forbidding condemnation of developed tracts smaller than five hundred acres but allowing condemnation of sites with no development at the time of the bill's passage, the act ensured the monopolies of fly-in resort owners and thereby increased their profits and property values. This, in turn, ensured that the five hundred thousand dollars authorized under the act for roadless area acquisition would not be nearly enough.

But for the second time—the first was when shoreline logging was banned in 1930—Congress had taken steps to preserve wilderness. And for the second time, the wilderness area responsible for stirring Congress to action was the Quetico-Superior canoe country. During a spring in which Wilderness Society cofounder Aldo Leopold died while fighting a Wisconsin grass fire and Izaak Walton League executive director Ken Reid suffered the first of two strokes that would disable him, the victory was good news indeed. The Wilderness Society praised the act as a "worthy precedent" and added, "It may well be that an important part of this significance will be in the fact that airplane threats to this unique primitive area so definitely inspired the Congress of the United States that wilderness preservation was thus so strongly affirmed as national policy."[23]

❖

As the acquisition bill moved toward President Truman's desk, Olson began directing his time and energy to resolving the airplane problem. By the summer of 1948, Ely had become the busiest freshwater seaplane community in the country. At least twenty-five planes were based there, and more flew in from other Minnesota cities. Dozens of planes traveled to the most popular lakes every day. Canoeists reported that pilots sometimes landed nearby, taxied over, and offered rides at $2.50 per person. Pilots also had cached motorboats on lakes deep within the wilderness on both sides of the border and had set up a number of permanent camps, making it increasingly difficult for canoeists to find an open campsite.

The coalition of conservationists for whom Olson worked debated several remedies that might put an end to commercial flights in the Superior Roadless Areas. They ultimately settled on a strategy of convincing President Truman to use his authority under the 1926 Air Commerce Act to create an airspace reservation over the canoe country. The executive order would forbid flying over the area at an altitude below four thousand feet, and would prohibit landings. So far, however, all airspace reservations had been created out of concerns for public safety or national defense. None had been proposed, much less created, for the purpose of preserving wilderness. Olson's job was to lead a publicity and lobbying campaign that would make it impossible for Truman to say no.[24]

Olson was involved in all aspects of the campaign. He drafted the Forest Service's official request for the airspace reservation and became a familiar figure in Washington, D.C., at the U.S. Department of Agriculture, in the Congressional Office Building, and at the White House. He wrote half a dozen articles for such publications as *Sports Afield*, *American Forests*, and *Nature Magazine*, and he edited a pamphlet for the President's Quetico-Superior Committee that was distributed to Superior National Forest visitors and to libraries across the Midwest. He spoke to local and national civic and conservation organizations to enlist support, and he testified at public hearings. He also kept Canadian officials informed about the status of the airspace reservation request, and he painstakingly began building a favorable public climate in that country for achieving the main goals of the Quetico-Superior program.[25]

One of Olson's most important public relations successes began with a meeting in Philadelphia during March 1948, when he and Frank Hubachek got *Saturday Evening Post* management to commit the publication to a story about the canoe country and the airplane issue. In June, as the Thye-Blatnik bill awaited President Truman's signature, Sigurd and his older son took *Post* reporter Harold Martin and photographer Frank Ross on a ten-day canoe trip through the Superior Roadless Areas and into Quetico Provincial Park. The wildness of the Quetico must have contrasted even more than usual with the fly-in resorts on the American side: the park was officially closed because dry weather had created a high risk of forest fires, and Olson had received a special permit to enter. There were no other people in the entire park.

Martin, who had traveled all over the world on assignments for the *Post*, clearly was impressed. "Of all the stories I've been on, none has ever been more delightful or more fun," he wrote to Hubachek on July 7. He said he especially would remember "the grand association with Sig and his son, which meant as much to me as did the pleasure of being in the wilderness itself. I could not have gone in with a better guide."[26]

In fact, Martin apparently was so disarmed by Olson that he ignored a cardinal rule about letting one's sources exert control over a story. Olson later said he wrote the first draft himself, and the final version of "Embattled Wilderness," which appeared in the *Post* on September 25, 1948, supports the claim. Throughout the story are phrases and sentences that strongly resemble Olson's writing style and vocabulary. The article says, for example, that the airplane "destroys for the man in the canoe the intangible, almost indescribable quality of the wilderness, a quality compounded of silence and solitude and a brooding sense of peace that sinks into the spirit."[27]

Despite his years of dreaming that one day he would be published by the *Post*, Olson could not afford to mention his partial authorship to friends for quite some time, because the article's impact depended upon the credibility of *Post* reporting. "Embattled Wilderness" helped set the stage for coverage of the issue in major Midwestern newspapers and in such national papers as the *New York Times* and the *Washington Post*. Charles Kelly ordered eight thousand reprints, a number of which were given to key legislators and White House staff as a potent indicator of national interest.

But convincing President Truman to establish a precedent for airspace reservations required more than a show of national support. Conservationists could not expect the president to sign an executive order if there was any opposition from Minnesota's senators or the local congressional representative, John Blatnik. And support for the Thye-Blatnik Act did not guarantee support for the ban on wilderness flying. As Blatnik said in a letter to Olson on April 19, 1949, "Sig, this air travel ban is becoming a controversial issue. . . . Any complete air ban on air travel is out of the question, since the interests of the resort owners and other local groups are involved."

Blatnik's nervousness was perfectly understandable. His district included Olson's home town of Ely, where tension already had built to the point of physical threats. Just a month before Blatnik wrote to Olson, airplane supporters had attempted to intimidate a local canoe outfitter who had voted against a pro-airplane resolution passed by the chamber of commerce. Later that evening, as he opened the door of his house to let out a guest, someone threw a cherry bomb or its equivalent at their feet. In the months to come, Frank Hubachek would report receiving death threats and threats of arson, and the owner of Ely radio station WXLT would sell the station, explaining that he had received threats after broadcasting a story about the crash of an airplane that had been hauling dozens of fish over the legal limit.[28]

Most local residents deplored the bully tactics, but they understood the frustrations and resentments that led some to adopt them. Northeastern Minnesotans lived in the poorest part of the state; most of the land had fallen tax delinquent during the Depression. They were tired of having to adapt to the whims of mining companies that had no stake in their communities. The one industry local citizens had come to feel they could control themselves was tourism, so it was not surprising that a proposal to ban wilderness flights would meet with bitter opposition. But conservationists and the Forest Service made matters worse by not consulting or even informing local officials and the community about the airspace reservation request until after the fact. This confirmed the worst feelings of distrust among area residents and made it more difficult for those who sympathized with the conservationists to voice their opinions. The biggest challenge facing conservationists, therefore, was not to get national public opinion behind them, but to generate significant local support for the airplane ban in the midst of a climate of bitterness and distrust. Only then could they hope to get the key Minnesota congressmen to write letters to President Truman asking him to sign the executive order.[29]

To that end, Sigurd Olson wrote, directed, and starred in a thirty-minute color documentary film called "Wilderness Canoe Country." Produced by the President's Quetico-Superior Committee, filmed by outdoor lecturer and photographer Grant Halladay, and narrated by well-known broadcaster Paul Harvey, the film built more vital support for the airplane ban in northeastern Minnesota than all of the speeches, articles, and other conservationist propaganda put together. It also attracted the attention and support of groups, private individuals, and government officials throughout the United States and Canada.[30]

"Wilderness Canoe Country" was the first-person narrative of a middle-aged father taking his son on a canoe trip into the Quetico-Superior. Near the beginning, the film showed the pair—played by Olson and his son Robert—sitting at a campfire along the Basswood River. Narrator Paul Harvey spoke for the father, extolling the canoe country's virtues, while the film switched to scenes of "plunging rivers still wild and free." Harvey told of the earlier fights by conservationists to save the wilderness from roads and dams, and of the Quetico-Superior program, which called for an international wilderness and for careful zoning of fifteen thousand square miles of Ontario and Minnesota. But now a new threat had developed, Harvey warned, "greater than any developments yet proposed: invasion by air."

The film cut to the next morning, showing the father and son as they traveled past Basswood Falls, where French voyageurs occasionally had capsized and drowned. Later, the two men gazed at Ojibwe pictographs at the eastern end of Crooked Lake. As they paddled out of the narrows and saw the vast expanse of the lake, the distant drone of a seaplane broke the silence. The sound became a deafening roar as the plane approached and then landed nearby in a wild spray of water. Harvey, reading Olson's words with his trademark staccato, exclaimed, "Twenty minutes from town! With no portaging, no paddling, no fighting the wind, no overnight camps. Crooked Lake—a place to catch a limit of fish . . . just a colored panorama from the air."

Later, the father and son reached Curtain Falls, a beautiful landmark that had become the site of a fly-in resort. "There at last was the proof!" declared Harvey. "Where once a timbered shore, now boathouses, docks, and cabins, even a plane moored alongside! It was out of place, almost unreal in that setting."

The father and son turned their canoe north toward Quetico Provincial Park, where they knew they could get away from the planes. "Canoes are a part of the legend of wilderness travel," Harvey reminded, "part of the silence and the ancient scene. A hundred canoes could have been on the lakes nearby and we wouldn't have known they were there, but one plane and the feeling of isolation is destroyed." Harvey concluded by saying that if planes were not banned and an international wilderness created, "the wilderness canoe country will live only in our memories."

The President's Quetico-Superior Committee held an invitation-only preview for the news media in Chicago before the film's public release in February 1949. Sigurd's brother Kenneth, dean of Northwestern University's Medill School of Journalism, helped with the arrangements and attended the event. Reporters from the *Christian Science Monitor*, Associated Press, United Press International, NBC, and the leading outdoor magazines were among those present. In Washington, showings were arranged for congressional and White House staff. Detroit TV station WXYZ broadcast "Wilderness Canoe Country," and twenty-eight copies of the film eventually were sold or loaned to such organizations as the Sierra Club, the Wilderness Society, the American Forestry Association, the Minnesota Conservation Commission, the University of Minnesota Extension Service, the Minneapolis Public Library, and the U.S. Forest Service. "Wilderness Canoe Country" also was distributed north of the border by Cinema Canada.

Most important, however, were the showings to civic groups in northeastern Minnesota. Sometimes a Forest Service official or Olson himself would show the film, but the vast majority of the time the person in charge was Frank Robertson, who was a friend of Olson and a former state president of the Izaak Walton League. Robertson took the film to garden clubs, church groups, chambers of commerce, scout troops, ethnic lodges—wherever he could get his foot in the door. He eventually showed "Wilderness Canoe Country" more than eight hundred times, wearing out his first copy after five hundred showings. And the payoff was immediate: by the end of May 1949 seventy-five organizations in northeastern Minnesota had declared their support for the airplane ban, and just ten had opposed it.

These public statements generated by Olson's film successfully countered the claims of pilots and fly-in resort owners that local opinion was united against the airplane ban. Senator Edward Thye endorsed the airspace reservation in May 1949, and freshman Senator Hubert Humphrey wrote to President Truman in favor of the executive order in July, using a draft written for him by Olson. Blatnik, however, tried to avoid taking a position; he faced reelection in 1950 and knew that the issue had created bitter feelings in his district. But because he did not publicly *oppose* the airplane ban, he did not hurt the conservationists' chances of convincing President Truman to sign the executive order.

Truman took the proposal to his Key West retreat in mid-December. On December 17, after discussing the issue with his staff while lounging in his swimming trunks on Truman Beach, the president walked up to his study in the Little White House and signed the executive order. White House staff member Russell Andrews later told Olson that, just before signing, Truman joked, "This is a battle between the beaver and the airplane boys. Let's give it to the beaver."[31]

❖

Sigurd Olson's wilderness activism had caused him some trouble in Ely over the years, but his leading role in the wilderness campaigns of 1948 and 1949 made him a lightning rod for local hostility. The first sign of this intensified opposition appeared in a letter to the editor of the *Ely Miner* published on June 17, 1948. The letter, written by Basswood Lake resident Leo Chosa, was a 750-word personal attack on Olson's character, accusing him of "double-edged, two-faced propaganda" and "base trickery." Chosa—who in 1921 had towed Sigurd and his young friends across Fall Lake to launch Olson's first canoe trip—called Olson a stooge of the logging industry whose real goal in removing roadless area resorts was to make it easier for the pulpwood companies to move in. "Surely no man could be so gullible and naive," Chosa concluded, "as to imagine that the big companies will pass up a chance to grab a million cords of pulpwood so a few farmer boys can paddle Sig's canoes in a primitive setting."

After President Truman signed the executive order banning wilderness flights, Chosa expanded on this theme in a pamphlet called *Isolate and Exploit*, which was published by the Ely Chamber of Commerce. Chosa referred to Olson as one of the "glib-talking stooges [who] have bustled about the country, far from the scene of exploitation, to distract the attention of public spirited men and women." Banning the plane was essential to the government's purpose, he claimed, because the ban eliminated 98 percent of the area's use, and because "the airplane is the eyes of the public": if nobody could fly over the area, the big logging companies could destroy the forest unnoticed. The Chamber of Commerce printed seventy-five thousand copies of the eight-page booklet in March 1950 and distributed them at Midwest sport shows and fly-in resorts.

Olson's Ely opponents also convinced *Minneapolis Star* outdoor writer Jack Connor to accuse Sigurd of flying in the equipment and personnel for the filming of "Wilderness Canoe Country." He presented no opportunity for rebuttal and did not name the Ely guide who provided the false information.[32]

While the Olsons' true friends in Ely were not swayed by the misinformation, many people were. Soon after the first attack by Leo Chosa, Sigurd noticed acquaintances crossing the street to avoid him. As the rumors intensified and opposition to the airspace reservation proposal grew more vocal and more bitter, some people treated Olson as a traitor. "Your name has been mud around here for some time past but that is mild to what the dear citizens of Ely think of you now," a friend wrote to Sigurd on March 26, 1949. Many years later, Bill Rom recalled, "Some of the young fellows around town threatened Sig and they even came out and announced that he should leave town."

It was a painful experience. "It is easy to carry on this sort of cold warfare when away from this town," Sigurd wrote to Hubachek on July 12, 1948, "but to live here and face it every minute is another matter." The following April, Olson wrote to another friend, "I've been accused of so many things the past year that I'm glad my dear mother is gone or she'd really be worried."[33]

But the attacks on Olson were not entirely without foundation. It was common knowledge around Ely, for example, that when Sigurd was dean of the junior college he sometimes had taken weekend escapes deep into the canoe country, paying a pilot to fly him in. On at least one occasion the pilot let Olson fly the plane himself for a while. And Sigurd had viewed these excursions as giving him some fresh insights about the canoe country, and even an abstract sense of oneness with the land. On September 3, 1940, when he was beginning to write short sketches to submit to a newspaper syndicate, he wrote in one journal-entry draft:

> I am beginning to feel at home in the air, can now enjoy the view, recognize landmarks. Before it all seemed a jumble, it was difficult

to know where we were. Now I am feeling at home in the air, know where to go, feel that the country is more mine than ever, I am a part of it. . . . The map has now become more a part of me than ever and I am at home. This is good to know, will do away with the feeling that plane travel is unnatural, gives one the feeling of oneness that must belong to the birds where a continent is home. One loses the sense of smallness, of the possibility of being tied and therefore lost. Now I am big in my understanding, my feeling for the land.[34]

On the same day, however, he wrote another draft of a manuscript on wilderness flying, and this version presented a much different perspective. In flying in, he wrote,

I had failed to work for the joy of knowing wilderness. Last time [reaching his campsite], this was the climax of five full days of woods travel, many portages, many tribulations, miles of bucking the wind. Now I knew. It had come too easy, there must be effort in order to achieve real satisfaction. . . . I had been in the wilderness but . . . was not really of it. It had slipped by me and I had lost the meaning, the real value of it.

Five months before he wrote these two perspectives on flying, Olson had written to Ernest Oberholtzer that airplanes destroyed wilderness solitude and ought to be banned from the canoe country. Apparently, he had conflicting feelings that took some time to sort out. Even as late as November 1943 he was able to write a draft of an "America Out of Doors" column in which he described his attempt at piloting a plane, and, while the article did not definitively state that he was flying over the wilderness, it clearly implied that this was the case. After that column, he never again wrote anything privately or publicly that indicated he harbored any positive feelings toward wilderness flying, and in September 1945 *Sports Afield* published his article "Flying In," which gave the issue its first national exposure and placed Olson squarely in the camp of airplane opponents.[35]

Criticism of Olson by other Ely residents during the airplane conflict also was based on the fact that the Border Lakes Outfitting Company began flying fishermen into the canoe country during 1948, while Sigurd was lobbying on behalf of the airspace reservation. Although Olson no longer was actively involved with the company, he remained an owner, and so the company's flying left Olson open to charges of hypocrisy. As soon as he heard about the Border Lakes activities in the spring of 1949, he tried to convince his partner and company manager M. W. Peterson to stop. Peterson initially balked, but by June 1 Olson got the Border Lakes and Ely's two other major canoe outfitting companies to sign an agreement that they would no longer fly parties into the roadless areas.[36]

Olson also caused some of his own trouble by making a poor decision as the leader of a nationally publicized canoe trip in August 1948. The trip was part of an annual "Trail Riders" series of expeditions sponsored by the American Forestry Association. Two days before the party of thirty-one was to begin its trip, Olson received a call from the organization's headquarters in Washington, D.C., asking him to change the route to one that was a hundred miles longer. Worried about imposing so much extra hauling on the large number of women and elderly people in the group, Sigurd asked the Forest Service to fly in some of their gear and leave it along the route. Olson's opponents eventually found out what he had done and publicized it. To make matters more embarrassing, they pointed out that a Forest Service airplane rescued one of the group's members who had twisted her ankle on a portage. The victim? Elizabeth Olson.

Despite the accusations of hypocrisy, despite the charges of misleading the public while secretly working for the timber industry, and despite the resulting ostracism in his hometown, Sigurd Olson's new career as a professional conservationist energized him. He had spent most of two years away from home, traveling a regular circuit between Chicago, Washington, and Toronto. He took pleasure in the friendships he was building with members of Congress, top federal land management agency personnel, and the leaders of national conservation groups. He enjoyed seeing his articles and speeches and the documentary film produce tangible results.

After the end of 1947, when he accepted his new role as the spearhead of the movement to preserve and protect the Quetico-Superior wilderness, Sigurd Olson rarely kept a journal. Undoubtedly part of the reason was simply the increased demands on his time. As he wrote to his family on his fiftieth birthday, April 4, 1949, "What a whirlwind this past year has been. Instead of slacking off as people should do when they reach this ripe old age, my pace has been speeded up double, triple and sometimes quadruple." But there is another explanation for the demise of Olson's journal: for the first time in his life he felt happy with the scope of his work. And in a brief entry on that birthday he displayed a newfound feeling of hope:

> I have made the break and new horizons have opened up—a fuller life—more realization—more and bigger objectives.
>
> I have found fame and friends and encouragement. When I write now it will be with a new and bigger audience. No short stories of adventure or love—it will be books of my feelings and probings on life and nature and mankind.

❖ Eleven ❖

Widening Horizons

1950–1954

During the first few months of 1950, in the wake of the successful campaign to create an airspace reservation over the Superior Roadless Areas, Sigurd Olson received a number of tangible signs of his rising status in the national conservation movement. There were invitations to speak before the Sierra Club and the American Wildlife Institute, and requests to investigate the management of a primitive area in California and to testify at a Department of the Interior hearing in Washington, D.C. He also was inducted into the capital's prestigious Cosmos Club, where he could share a drink or a meal with Nobel Prize and Pulitzer Prize winners or any of the other thirteen hundred distinguished members, as well as stay overnight in its bedrooms. But the most intriguing development was the courtship of the National Parks Association.

The NPA, founded in 1919 by National Park Service director Steve Mather as a friendly ally of the service, had a little over three thousand members in 1950. The group had not attained the widespread support Mather had envisioned and continually struggled to make ends meet. Nor had it grown into Mather's idea of a Park Service friend; instead, the NPA often had attacked park management and had befriended the Park Service's territorial and budgetary enemy, the U.S. Forest Service. Mather withdrew his support early on, chagrined at the beast he had created.

By the late 1940s, the NPA had lost much of its spark, hampered by a board of trustees grown old, conservative, and too attached to notions of genteel politics to be much of a thorn in anyone's side. This was highly frustrating to the NPA's executive director, Devereux

Butcher, who also edited the group's publication, *National Parks Magazine*. Butcher, a short, wiry, intense man, was totally devoted to his purist's vision of national park management and did not like having to tone down his rhetoric and therefore limit, in his view, the effectiveness of the organization. When William Wharton, who had served as the NPA's president since 1935, began talking about stepping down in favor of someone younger, Butcher promoted Sigurd Olson as a successor.

Butcher had discovered Olson in the early 1940s, when he found a copy of Olson's 1938 *American Forests* article, "Why Wilderness?" In 1944 he asked Sigurd to write a similar article for *National Parks Magazine,* and the result, published in January 1946, was Olson's strongest statement yet on behalf of undisturbed nature:

> Wilderness to the people of America is a spiritual necessity, an antidote to the high pressure of modern life, a means of regaining serenity and equilibrium. . . . I have found that people go to the wilderness for many things, but the most important of these is perspective. They may think they go for the fishing or the scenery or companionship, but in reality it is something far deeper. They go to the wilderness for the good of their souls.

Butcher called Olson's article "one of the finest statements of the kind ever written";[1] he had the NPA reprint five thousand copies and began sending it to all new members. He sensed a kindred spirit, someone who would tirelessly defend the national parks, and Sigurd's work on behalf of the Quetico-Superior in 1948 and 1949 convinced Butcher that Olson would be a strong leader for the NPA. Late in November 1949 he asked if Olson would be interested.

Sigurd was *very* interested, but, while his Quetico-Superior work had allowed him to demonstrate the skills that sparked the NPA's offer, the offer in turn made clear some real limitations in Olson's current job setup. Charles Kelly did not want Sigurd to do any conservation work that might in any way cause problems for the Quetico-Superior program, and by nature Kelly was extremely cautious. In this case, Kelly reminded Olson that Quetico-Superior proponents had for years been accused of seeking national park status for Superior National Forest. He worried that if Olson became president of the National Parks Association the old rumors would be resurrected and might wreck any chances for the international treaty that was the Quetico-Superior program's goal.

The most Kelly would agree to at the time was to allow Sigurd to be elected to the NPA's board of trustees and to the group's executive committee, with the understanding that the presidency might be acceptable within a couple of years. So Olson became an NPA trustee on May 19, 1950. A year later, under pressure again to accept the presidency, Olson agreed to become the group's vice president.

Olson really had little choice in holding the NPA at bay. Like most conservation groups, the NPA did not pay its president, and Sigurd must have thought about the financial ramifications of reaching a breaking point with Charles Kelly. At the same time, it is unlikely that money played the central role in Olson's decision to accede to Kelly's wishes, because Sigurd genuinely loved his work on behalf of the canoe country wilderness and believed that the next couple of years were critical to the prospects of an international treaty governing management of the Quetico-Superior. It was this wilderness outside his backyard, therefore, that occupied most of his time from 1950 through 1953.

Olson's major task was to build a network of support in Ontario, for there was no hope of a treaty without the assent of the provincial government. Sigurd had begun this phase of his work in 1948, while he also was lobbying for the Thye-Blatnik Act to give the U.S. Forest Service authority to buy private inholdings within the Superior Roadless Areas. Kelly and Frank Hubachek had provided Sigurd with his major Canadian contacts: Clifford Sifton, whose family owned the *Toronto Globe and Mail* and the *Winnipeg Free Press*, as well as smaller newspapers and radio stations; Harold Walker, a prominent Toronto lawyer; and James Cowan, a Toronto public relations executive. All agreed that it was essential to create a Canadian Quetico-Superior committee to build support for the program from within Ontario and counteract charges that the proposed treaty was little more than a trick to create a playground for wealthy Americans.

Walker and Cowan began putting together a list of prominent Canadians as potential committee members and with Olson's help arranged a luncheon in March 1949 to launch the organization. Walker's friend Vincent Massey, chancellor of the University of Toronto, surprised those attending by reading a letter from General

Dwight D. Eisenhower, who was nearly as popular in Canada as he was in the United States. In the letter, which was the result of behind-the-scenes spadework by Ernest Oberholtzer, Eisenhower said, "As one American citizen who has long been interested in the proposal . . . I cannot let pass this opportunity to assure you of my personal enthusiasm for the project—although my duties have not and will not permit me any active participation."[2]

The new Canadian Quetico-Superior Committee quickly began trying to build provincial government support. In July 1949 the committee invited Ontario's new premier, Leslie M. Frost, to attend a meeting at the home of committee member Donald Hogarth, who was president of Steep Rock Mines in Atikokan, just north of Quetico Provincial Park. Sigurd Olson, the sole American at the meeting, showed his film, "Wilderness Canoe Country." Frost was sympathetic and, meeting again with Olson and Harold Walker the following day, made it clear that he was willing to at least see a draft of the treaty when it was ready.

In the months ahead, Oberholtzer wrote a new version of the treaty proposal, and in 1950 Olson began showing it to White House officials, to Harold Walker, and to journalist Donald O'Hearn, a friend of Premier Frost whom Olson enlisted as executive secretary of the Canadian Quetico-Superior Committee. A number of changes were recommended, especially by O'Hearn and Walker, who knew that Oberholtzer's vision was not politically viable in Ontario. There was no way the province would agree to dominion regulation of nine thousand square miles of its territory, especially when the treaty called for similar regulation of just five thousand square miles in Minnesota.

Olson agreed. He had traveled northwestern Ontario, had seen the unpaved streets of the towns, and had been heckled by chamber of commerce members when he spoke of the proposed treaty. The residents of these towns wanted to participate fully in postwar prosperity. They were determined to develop their natural resources and demanded a highway to connect them to Port Arthur and Fort Frances. Oberholtzer's treaty seemed to restrict them to perpetual frontier status.

Late in 1950, Olson wrote a new draft that narrowed the focus of wilderness preservation to the region's interior, and especially to

Quetico Provincial Park and the Superior Roadless Areas. To most people, the term Quetico-Superior had come to mean this core area of a little over three thousand square miles, rather than the nearly fifteen thousand square miles defined by Oberholtzer. Since 1927, when Oberholtzer had first proposed an International Peace Memorial Forest and generated support from the American and Canadian Legions, logging camps and mines and roads and towns had in many places intruded upon the wilderness of his memory. Olson wrote the new treaty draft to better reflect political reality. In doing so, however, he permanently damaged his friendship with Oberholtzer, who wrote to him on January 4, 1951:

> That proposal . . . violates the whole Q.S. program as fostered these many years. It also entirely misinterprets the action of the various Legion bodies in both countries from the beginning until now. . . . It would take too long now to go over again all the developments and documents of the past twenty-five years bearing upon these points. I have already repeated them to the point of boredom. . . . Personally I am ready to give anything that I have left to avert a settlement in the border region that runs counter to the well-established understanding of the Quetico-Superior program.

Hubachek and Kelly, on the other hand, agreed with Olson and eventually convinced Oberholtzer to accept a change in language that still gave special recognition to the wilderness of Quetico Park and the Superior Roadless Areas while retaining the original goal of a more extensive peace memorial forest. They could not, however, convince Oberholtzer that they had to accept the Port Arthur-to-Fort Frances highway, which would cut right through the heart of the watershed, in order to build enough support for the treaty in northwestern Ontario. Oberholtzer did not publicly break with his friends, but it hurt him to see his lifelong dream slowly whittled away, and he nursed a growing distance between himself and Olson.

Traveling through northwestern Ontario in 1950, Sigurd made some headway in convincing local residents that the Americans were not trying to force them to accept a program they could not support. But he came to realize that rewriting the treaty and supporting the highway would not be enough in the long run. Every year there were new applications for building cabins and resorts in Quetico Park. For the time being, the government routinely denied permission, but for how long? Conservationists had done almost nothing to build support for the broad idea of wilderness preservation in Canada, let alone the specific wilderness of the Quetico-Superior. Indeed, Oberholtzer had given so little regard to Canadians over the years that he had created quite a bit of resentment. Olson knew that a long-term program of positive, Canadian-driven publicity was essential to wilderness preservation, treaty or no treaty.

To that end, Olson arranged a July 1950 Quetico Park canoe trip with three members of the Toronto Anglers' and Hunters' Association, including the group's secretary, John Mitchele. Olson hoped to get them excited enough about wilderness preservation in general, and Quetico Park and the international treaty in particular, that they would start building grassroots support through their organization.

Mitchele took Olson's idea one step further: he invited an Ontario journalist named Fred Bodsworth. At the time, Bodsworth, who eventually became one of Canada's best known nature writers, was just beginning to break into the magazine market, and he hoped to write about the trip for *Maclean's*, which was then Canada's equivalent of the *Saturday Evening Post.* Bodsworth recalled years later that "*Maclean's* approved the idea, gave me some expense money, and I went along and spent two weeks paddling bow in a canoe and talking with Sig in the stern."[3]

The experience, he said, changed his life. Bodsworth, who had grown up along the shore of Lake Erie in a small Canadian fishing port, had never taken a wilderness trip before. Nor had he met anyone like Sigurd Olson:

> He had the scientific underpinnings, he could talk about lichens and forest succession and the mineralogy of rocks, but he also had another entirely different functional level of bush lore expertise. He could look at a lake and know right where to go to get a couple of fast lake trout for supper while the rest of us pitched tents. He could find his way across an invisible portage that had not been used for a couple of years, find the salt or tea in a food pack amid a muddle of a hundred other little packets, and knew exactly how much wood it would take to bake a bannock. In that two weeks Sig Olson assumed for me a kind of mythic godlike caliber that mellowed a little as my experience broadened but never entirely left me.

The resulting article gave Quetico Park exactly the kind of Canadian publicity Olson hoped for. "The Fight to Keep the Wilderness Wild," published in *Maclean's* on May 15, 1951, told of the pressures that threatened the park, from road developments to the "covetous glances" of resort planners. Bodsworth also spoke of the battles waged over the years by conservationists on both sides of the border, and of the proposed treaty. He did not say anything that had not been said by American conservationists in American publications, but he wrote from a Canadian perspective and for a Canadian audience. He mentioned Olson just once in the article and identified him not specifically as an American, but as an Izaak Walton League ecologist, in order to minimize the gut-level hostility many Canadians felt whenever Americans tried to influence Canadian policies. He also let Olson edit a draft of the article, but told Sigurd not to write his comments on the manuscript so Bodsworth could send it on to *Maclean's:* "I wouldn't let them see it with another man's handwriting on it, for then they would suspect that other parties were interested in it for publicity reasons and maybe take a dim view of the whole business."[4]

Sigurd, of course, *was* interested in the article for publicity reasons, but he saw the canoe trip with Bodsworth as just the beginning. On July 29, 1950, just after the trip was over and long before Bodsworth's article was completed and published, Olson wrote to Kelly his vision of what could be called "canoe public relations," although Sigurd himself would not have thought of using such explicit terminology. "I feel that this first all-Canadian trip will be the forerunner of many others which will bring to the attention of Canadians the real values of the Quetico," Olson wrote.

The first indication that Olson was right came soon after Bodsworth's article appeared. Eric Morse, national director of the Association of Canadian Clubs, contacted Bodsworth and asked how to get in touch with Sigurd Olson. Morse had recently taken a small group of prominent Canadians and foreign diplomats on a weeklong canoe trip along the Gatineau River near Ottawa. The diplomats had never canoed before, but had been coaxed into the trip after being teased during a dinner party about trying to understand the real Canada from the cocktail circuit. The canoe trip was such a success that the men vowed to try it again in 1952. Morse, in charge of planning, read about the Quetico in Bodsworth's article and decided that was where his group would go.

Late in 1951 and early in 1952, Olson and Morse were in contact by mail, planning a two-week trip for August around a central portion of Quetico Park known as Hunter's Island. For Olson, it was an opportunity to introduce some influential VIPs to the wonders of the canoe country and to the hopes conservationists held for its preservation. Olson did not canoe with the group but met the men on August 18 at Horse Portage, a mile-long hike into Basswood Lake, their final destination. He was to take them by motor launch to the Basswood home of F. B. Hubachek. Forty years later, Omond Solandt recalled the experience:

> Our first meeting with Sig was very auspicious. We arrived at the portage landing after a tough day paddling in rain against a head wind and were not looking forward to walking a mile uphill with canoes and packs. Sig and Joe Kerntz, a very experienced local guide who was Brookes' [Hubachek's] manager awaited us. After a warm but brief welcome they shouldered our two canoes and set off at a brisk pace.
>
> When we got to the end of the portage we found Hub's Tub, a commodious work boat, waiting to whisk us down Basswood Lake to Brookes' establishment while we drank cold beer. When we arrived we had showers and then a huge dinner of steak and apple pie followed by a sauna and bed. No wonder we thought well of Sig, Brookes, Joe and all their friends![5]

A year later, Olson joined the group for the first time on another two-week trip through Quetico Park. Sigurd thought their average daily distance of twenty-one miles was too much for full enjoyment, but the dawn-to-dusk regime of paddling and portaging also forged lasting friendships. They worked well together, establishing routines that took advantage of each person's talents, and they gave each other the space and freedom to fully enjoy their time away from high-pressure jobs. They joked together and sang songs, took predawn plunges in misty bays before drinking their morning coffee, and fell asleep at night listening to the loons. There was a wild, windy day when they virtually sailed down white-capped Sturgeon Lake, using their paddles not to go forward but to keep from tipping, and a repeat the next day when they had to use their bodies as shields to keep the canoes from smashing on the rocks as they approached their campsite. And, of course, they got lost. Omond Solandt recalled:

> Sig was in country that he vowed was familiar to him so he took over the task of guiding us to a wonderful campsite he knew. After far too much paddling we realized that we were lost. Sig stoutly denied this charge and assured us that he was just searching for his grandmother's grave which he yearned to revisit! Such slips were rare and only served to further endear him to us.[6]

Before the men returned home they planned a trip for 1954: they would follow the 266-mile section of the historic voyageurs' trail that formed the international boundary from Grand Portage to Fort Frances. The expedition ended up receiving extensive media coverage in Canada, and from then on Olson and his companions were known as "the Voyageurs."[7]

The makeup of the group guaranteed media interest in their annual expeditions. In addition to Olson and Eric Morse, the Voyageurs included Omond Solandt, a doctor who planned Canada's national defense research; Major General Elliot Rodger, vice chief of general staff of the Canadian Army; Denis Coolican, president of the Canadian Bank Note Company; Blair Fraser, an editor and writer with *Maclean's* magazine and a broadcaster with a large Canadian following; Antonius "Tony" Lovink, the Netherlands ambassador to Canada; John Endemann, a South African diplomat; and Tyler Thompson, U.S. minister to Canada. Age, in addition to prominence, sparked the interest of reporters. These were not young men fresh out of college; none of them was under forty when he first joined the Voyageurs, and several of them were in their fifties when they started taking rugged canoe trips through the Canadian bush.

Olson made seven expeditions with the Voyageurs, beginning with the Quetico Park trip in 1953 and ending with a grueling four-hundred-mile journey down the Hayes River to Hudson Bay in 1964, when he was sixty-five years old. In between were two voyages along the Churchill River, a trip across northern Saskatchewan from Reindeer Lake to Lake Athabasca, and a subarctic journey along the Camsell River and Great Bear Lake to the Mackenzie River, the Mississippi of the north. The group changed a little from trip to trip; typically, six

of the Voyageurs went along. Olson, Morse, Solandt, Rodger, Coolican, Lovink, and Fraser made the most trips and formed the group's
core. Olson, the oldest and most experienced, was the unanimous
choice of the others to be the leader, with the final say whenever the
travelers faced a difficult decision. Using a title from the fur trade, the
Voyageurs called him "the Bourgeois." Years later, Omond Solandt
described Olson as a strong leader who knew how to delegate:

> In looking back on our trips together I realize that part of the magic
> of his leadership was a gift for encouraging each Voyageur to do his
> thing and to defer to him in his chosen area. For example, Sig did
> not monopolize the role of naturalist. Eric knew more than Sig
> about flowers and history and Elliot was an expert on birds, espe-
> cially waterfowl, and was also greatly interested in animal tracks. He
> had a habit of wandering off after the work was done to scout the
> neighborhood and often came back with antlers or other trophies
> of the chase. He was also unmatched as an assistant to the cook.
>
> I established a modest reputation of keeping track of where we
> were. Once, after the cocktail hour, Sig decided that he would honor
> me by appointing me cartographer to the expedition. He had trou-
> ble finding the right word and finally decided that the closest he
> could come was pornographer. So from then on map reading be-
> came pornography![8]

Beginning with the 1954 trip that gave the group its name, all of
the Voyageurs' expeditions were along historic routes of fur traders
and explorers. As they paddled, the group often sang the traditional
chansons of the original voyageurs: "En roulant ma boule," "La belle
Lizette," "La claire fontaine." In the evenings, Eric Morse would read
selections from the diaries of such men as David Thompson, Peter
Pond, and Alexander Mackenzie, who had traveled the same waterways and stayed at the same campsites a hundred and fifty or more
years before. The times were quite different, of course—on the Churchill River they encountered Cree Indians who could not fathom why
anyone would want to travel the river without an outboard motor—
but many sites remained unchanged.

The historical connections enriched the journeys for all of the
white-collar Voyageurs and played a major role in Canadian media
publicity, for in the 1950s the country was embracing its geographi-
cally rooted cultural history. When the Voyageurs completed their

first Churchill River journey in August 1955 and stepped out of their canoes at The Pas, Manitoba, far from the urban centers of Canada, they were greeted by television crews and newspaper reporters. They could count on regular coverage of their journeys by major newspapers in Winnipeg and Toronto and Ottawa, and also—not surprisingly, given Blair Fraser's connection—were featured in *Maclean's*. In Ottawa, where several of the Voyageurs lived, the *Evening Journal* not only routinely printed Denis Coolican's diaries of the trips but also published them in pamphlet form.

Sigurd Olson did not foresee all of this in 1952 and 1953, when he first met and traveled with the Voyageurs and became their Bourgeois. Nor did he realize what the Voyageurs might mean to wilderness preservation across Canada. Their importance—including his own role—would begin to be clear by the 1960s. But in 1953, after his first two-week canoe trip with the group, two thoughts were uppermost in his mind. First, he sensed that he was forming what would become the most satisfying friendships of his life. Second, he knew he had gotten the Voyageurs interested in helping to preserve the Quetico-Superior wilderness. As he wrote to the Izaak Walton League's Ken Reid on November 15, 1953, "That little nucleus in Ottawa will be our main anchor to windward when the treaty comes up."

As it turned out, Olson's "little nucleus in Ottawa" provided much more immediate help than he envisioned. President Truman's executive order creating an airspace reservation over the Superior Roadless Areas had not put an end to the issue. As soon as the order took effect, Ely pilots and resort owners violated the law to force a court battle. The trial began in Duluth, Minnesota, on July 29, 1952, before District Judge Gunnar H. Nordbye. Olson was among those testifying for the U.S. government; each time he tried to answer a question the defense attorney sprang to his feet and objected.[9]

The judge gave comfort to the pilots when he casually remarked that he took fly-in fishing trips into Canada, but his ruling on September 26 supported the conservationists and gave wilderness preservation its first judicial backing as a legitimate function of the federal government. Because the defendants intended to appeal, Nordbye issued an injunction that allowed some flying during the appeal process, but only for the purpose of maintaining the property of three resorts deep in the canoe country.

On May 4, 1953, shortly before the new fishing season opened, a *Duluth Herald* gossip columnist reported being told by the executive director of the Ely Chamber of Commerce that "ban or no ban, they're going to fly in guests the same as last year." By mid-June, despite an appeals court ruling in favor of the U.S. government, the owners of the three interior resorts were flying in guests on a daily basis. By late June the government had done nothing, and the resort owners grew increasingly bold. On June 30 the *Duluth Herald* reported that the Ely Chamber of Commerce was sponsoring a Fourth of July drawing for a free plane trip to one of the resorts.

That same day, three FBI agents arrived in Ely. They were soon joined by two U.S. marshals, three Minnesota game wardens, and three Forest Service rangers. On July 2 the U.S. marshals flew to the resorts, seized the planes, arrested the pilots, and handed subpoenas to the resort owners. Over the next several days Forest Service officials flew stranded resort guests back to Ely, where FBI agents questioned them and game wardens checked their fishing licenses. The *New York Times* ran stories three days in a row, with such headlines as "Campers Stranded as U.S. Seizes Planes Violating Ban in Minnesota" and "Two Hundred in Woods Face Rough Trip Home." Judge Nordbye later levied fines totaling three thousand dollars.

The government's action put a temporary end to the flying, and in October the U.S. Supreme Court ended the resort owners' hopes of overturning the executive order when it refused to review the lower courts' decision. But two of the resort owners soon found a way to obey U.S. law while still using airplanes to reach their property. Both of the resorts were on Crooked Lake, which straddled the international border. They planned to use the twin facts of geography and political jurisdiction to continue their flying in 1954.

In December 1953 one of the resort owners requested a special customs agent for Crooked Lake, saying he would pay all expenses. He and the other owner planned to fly above the airspace reservation, land and clear customs on the Canadian side of Basswood Lake, fly to the Canadian side of Crooked Lake in Quetico Park, take passengers and supplies by motorboat across the border to their nearby resorts, and clear U.S. Customs through their special agent. Olson had foreseen this possibility as early as 1949, but short of an airspace reservation over Quetico Park there seemed little that could be done.

Two of Olson's Voyageurs, however, had a connection. Eric Morse and Tony Lovink were good friends of John Baldwin, chairman of Canada's Air Transport Board, which issued permits to U.S. pilots asking to fly into Quetico Park. They helped Olson establish contact, and early in April 1954 he flew to Ottawa for a meeting. During their two-hour meeting, Baldwin decided to have his agency forward any Quetico flying applications to Olson, who, on behalf of the President's Quetico-Superior Committee, could write letters asking the board to deny permits. "The only hitch in the wonderful plan," Olson wrote in an April 6 memo, "is the fact that I am required to send a copy of my letter to the applicant."

Back home in Ely on April 7, Sigurd had second thoughts. "It will be an intolerable situation for me here," he wrote to Hubachek. Olson asked the Air Transport Board to mail the applications to him in care of the President's Quetico-Superior Committee in Chicago rather than to his home in Ely and said that the letter requesting denial of the permits would be signed by committee chairman Charles Kelly, rather than by Olson.

It is unclear how many applications Olson screened during the summer of 1954; his papers indicate at least five, including an application by a Duluth company working for the Crooked Lake resort owners. All were denied, but, since the requests for denial were signed by Kelly, Olson was spared from disclosing his personal role to his neighbors in Ely. After the tourist season ended in the fall of 1954, his services were not needed; in April 1955, before the first requests for summer flying were received, Ontario established an airspace reservation over Quetico Park.

❖

While much of Sigurd Olson's time in the early 1950s was devoted to Quetico-Superior affairs, he kept his promise to the National Parks Association. In May 1953, despite the unfolding drama of illegal flying that would lead to the U.S. government's pre-Independence Day raid in the canoe country, Sigurd Olson flew to Washington to attend the National Parks Association annual meeting and become its president. Charles Kelly still was not comfortable with the idea, but he and Hubachek nevertheless donated money to the NPA to establish a travel fund for Olson.

Sigurd took charge of the NPA four months after Dwight Eisenhower replaced Harry Truman in the White House. Because Eisenhower had earlier helped the Quetico-Superior program with his letter to Vincent Massey, the outlook for the canoe country was hopeful. Besides, Kelly and Hubachek were staunch Republican supporters. Olson also maintained personal ties to the White House. While Russ Andrews, the Truman White House staff member who had worked with Olson on the airspace reservation, was gone, Sigurd had a new contact in one of President Eisenhower's economic advisers, Gabriel Hauge. Olson knew Hauge's father, a Minnesotan. Before the end of 1953 Olson would get a chance to meet with Eisenhower in the White House and discuss the Quetico-Superior program. Eisenhower even would see Olson's film, "Wilderness Canoe Country."

As president of the NPA, however, Olson was directly involved with conservation issues on a national scale, and outside of the canoe country the Eisenhower administration seemed anything but promising. Eisenhower's GOP platform promised "restoration of the traditional public land policy," which in the Republican stronghold of the American West meant opening federal lands to resource development or selling them to the states and private citizens. Eisenhower appointed a Chevrolet dealer from Oregon, Douglas McKay, secretary of the interior. McKay began a two-year purge of seven thousand Interior Department personnel and opened most national wildlife refuges to gas and oil leasing. His critics called him "Giveaway McKay"; he called his critics "punks."[10]

The national park system already had been under attack for some time; during World War II, Grand Canyon, Yosemite, and Shenandoah National Parks had been opened for mining to fill military contracts, and a tunnel was built underneath Rocky Mountain National Park. Loggers had tried to gain access to Olympic National Park. But the pressure increased after the war, as the nation's booming economy built demand for minerals, lumber, and other resources. In the West, ranchers tried to abolish Wyoming's Jackson Hole National Monument, and the federal government proposed dams for a number of rivers, threatening pristine lands in several national parks and forests. One of these, a proposed project for the Upper Colorado River, became the major national conservation issue during the first few years of Olson's NPA presidency.

Early in 1953, preparing for an unsympathetic administration,

Olson already had played a key role in the ongoing struggle against development interests. The Park Service during the war had acquired a strip of land along the Pacific Ocean near Washington's Olympic National Park. It had never been annexed to the park, and state officials and loggers wanted the more than forty-six thousand acres to be transferred to Olympic National Forest so logging could begin. Eisenhower's election made the transfer a distinct possibility, and the National Parks Association and other conservationists urged the Truman administration to annex the strip to Olympic Park before leaving office.[11]

In December 1952 President Truman announced he would do so, but after an uproar in the West as well as pressure from the National Chamber of Commerce, he seemed to distance himself. With just two weeks left in office, he still had not signed the executive order. In fact, the draft of the proclamation was nowhere to be found. Early in January, Olson went to the White House and asked his friend Russ Andrews to track down the document. It took a day of phone calls, but Andrews finally located it at the bottom of a pile of folders in the Interior Department. He had it delivered to the White House and took it to President Truman, who signed it.

But the parks in 1953 suffered as much from fiscal neglect as from outside threats. During World War II federal funding for the parks had dropped to 20 percent of prewar spending. Funding had increased after the war, but by 1953 was still below 1940 levels, despite the fact that the number of park visitors had more than doubled. Roads were crumbling, buildings were deteriorating, water and sewage systems were failing. Park rangers were grossly underpaid, heavily overworked, and often lived in wretched tar-paper shacks built by the Civilian Conservation Corps during the Depression and meant to last just five years.

Bernard DeVoto, a conservationist and historian of the American West who also was an outspoken *Harper's Magazine* columnist, wrote in the October 1953 issue that the situation was hopeless unless Congress was willing to make available huge emergency appropriations. He estimated a quarter of a billion dollars was necessary. He assumed Congress would not comply:

> Therefore only one course seems possible. The national park system must be temporarily reduced to a size for which Congress is

willing to pay. Let us, as a beginning, close Yellowstone, Yosemite, Rocky Mountain, and Grand Canyon National Parks—close and seal them, assign the Army to patrol them, and so hold them secure until they can be reopened. . . . If [their] staffs—and their respective budgets—were distributed among other areas, perhaps the Service could meet the demands now put on it. If not, additional areas could be temporarily closed and sealed, held in trust for a more enlightened future.[12]

Although De Voto's article created a stir—and led to increased donations to the National Parks Association—emergency appropriations were not immediately forthcoming from Congress. The parks, of course, remained open.[13]

As president of the NPA, Sigurd Olson assumed the job of being a prominent, vocal supporter of the national park system, which in 1953 included twenty-eight national parks, five national historical parks, eighty-five national monuments, and more than eight hundred areas in other classifications, mostly national capital parks. He also was to preside at meetings, enforce the NPA's bylaws, nominate all standing committees, and supervise the staff. This meant regular visits to Washington, where he would stay at the Cosmos Club and walk a block to a three-floor building on P Street Northwest shared by the NPA and the Wilderness Society.

It also meant traveling to other parts of the country, especially at first, when he felt he needed to see a number of parks and monuments himself to better understand the problems. But combining his NPA work with his Quetico-Superior duties made for a grueling schedule. In May 1953 he made trips to Chicago, Toronto, Ottawa, Washington, D.C., Milwaukee, and Rochester, New York. In June he traveled to Grand Rapids, Michigan, for the annual convention of the Izaak Walton League (he continued to serve as wilderness ecologist), and to Grand Portage, Minnesota, to help Park Service officials in an unsuccessful attempt to negotiate an agreement with the tribal council permitting national monument status for Grand Portage National Historic Site.

His schedule got busier during the summer. On July 3, Sigurd—with Elizabeth, this time—left Ely for a month-long swing through the West. They attended the annual meeting of the Wilderness Society in Augusta, Idaho (where Sigurd took a short postmeeting pack trip into the Bob Marshall wilderness), and visited a number of national parks and monuments, including Glacier, Yellowstone, Grand Teton, Craters of the Moon, and Olympic. On the way back to Ely Sigurd attended the Outdoor Writers Association of America annual meeting in Missoula, Montana, to speak about the Quetico-Superior program. Sigurd was home barely a week, then took off again, this time for his first canoe trip with the Voyageurs. That lasted from August 8 to August 24. Then, after a week at home, he took another canoe trip with Elizabeth and Grace Lee Nute, a historian who wanted to see the Quetico for her Minnesota Historical Society series of books on the area's history.

When Sigurd first drafted his schedule on April 28, he left one item for September: "Cleaning up debris of summer." But it was a sign of what lay ahead of him for almost twenty years, month in and month out. His summer schedules included far more business-and-pleasure trips to scenic areas than his winter schedules, and far fewer all-business trips to Washington, but he often left himself little time to relax. And in the summer of 1953 he encountered an extra source of stress: his eighty-four-year-old father, L. J. Olson, died on May 29 after nearly three weeks at Rice Hospital in Willmar, Minnesota. Sigurd was traveling almost the entire time, working on Quetico-Superior matters and being sworn in as president of the NPA. As soon as he got home he and Elizabeth rushed down to Willmar, where they stayed until after the funeral.

High stress would remain a constant in Olson's life. The ulcers that first plagued him in the early 1940s while he was dean of Ely Junior College continued to flare up throughout the next several decades. Once, during a trip to St. Paul, he visited a faith healer: she put her hands on his stomach and he swore he could feel the warmth radiating from them. The pain temporarily disappeared. Eventually, he became such a good consumer of antacids that he was given a supply of note pads bearing the Riopan trademark.

Sigurd also suffered from insomnia, especially on the road, and took aspirin or sleeping pills to help him rest. None of his health problems, however, bothered him as much as his facial tic. What had started as an involuntary twitch of his eyes during his last year at the junior college gradually came to affect his entire face. When his stress level declined, such as after a good night's sleep, he could control it for a short time, but the twitching soon would resume. He was embarrassed by it, and felt even worse because of Elizabeth's reaction. She was horrified and tried to get him to stop it, believing that he could if he tried hard enough. When he traveled he sometimes wrote to her about it, hoping to please her. "For your birthday I am telling myself as one present I am going to show you I can control [it]," he wrote in November 1949. In February 1952 he wrote: "I am terribly sorry for some of the memories I left with you of me but do not worry too much about me while I am out. Yesterday I do not think I made a twitch. If I can control it here, or if it controls itself, then I know it will gradually disappear." When it became clear that will-power alone would not do the trick, Sigurd's doctor prescribed medication. It was only partially successful, but Elizabeth made sure her husband took it every day for the rest of his life.[14]

❖

In the months after his tour through the western parks, Olson became involved in two important conservation issues that demonstrated both the pleasures and the difficulties of his role as president of the National Parks Association. One was a new fight over a proposed highway along the Chesapeake and Ohio Canal in Maryland, and the other was a long-running battle to prevent a major Colorado River water project from ruining a wild portion of Dinosaur National Monument.

Olson's involvement in the Chesapeake and Ohio Canal issue began a few weeks after January 3, 1954, when the *Washington Post* editorialized in favor of the plan to build a highway along the historic canal and towpath. The existing highway between Cumberland, Maryland, and Washington, D.C., traveled up and down many ridges, and the newspaper joined those who called for a flat route that would be safer in the winter. U.S. Supreme Court Justice William O. Douglas, who had made public his attachment to nature in his 1950 book *Of Men and Mountains*, responded with a letter to the editor in which he described the Chesapeake and Ohio Canal as "a place of retreat, a long stretch of quiet and peace at the Capitol's back door—a wilderness area where man can be alone with his thoughts, a sanctuary where he can commune with God and nature, a place not yet marred by the roar of wheels and the sound of horns." Douglas challenged the editorial's author to join him on a hike along the entire 185-mile stretch and predicted the hike would change his opinion of the proposed highway.[15]

Post editors Robert Estabrook and Merlo Pusey both accepted the challenge, and, along with Douglas, invited nearly three dozen others along, including Sigurd Olson and other representatives of major conservation groups. The thirty-seven hikers got under way in a snowstorm on March 20, 1954. It was a difficult trip, and only nine managed to make it on foot the entire distance from Cumberland to Washington.

Sigurd, to his embarrassment, was not among those who earned the label "the Immortal Nine." After about a hundred and fifty miles his left ankle swelled badly, and he could not put on his boot. He spent the second to last day of the expedition riding a horse at the front of the group, next to another rider dressed in a Confederate officer's uniform and carrying a Confederate flag. Two other riders followed. When some horses in a field next to the canal galloped toward the riders, Sigurd's horse was crowded by the others right off the bank. He was thrown and bruised his left calf so badly that by evening he could not step on the leg. Even so, he completed the final eighteen miles the next day on foot, his left leg painfully stiffening every time he rested.

Despite his injuries, Sigurd enjoyed the trip immensely. "It was a wonderful experience all the way through, even though I had a little tough luck," he wrote to his family on March 28, the day after the hike ended. The hike had received tremendous publicity, with daily coverage by the three television networks as well as the *Washington Post* and other newspapers. Reporters and photographers from *Life* and *Time* magazines also covered the expedition. Fifty thousand people gathered at Georgetown to greet the hikers at the end of the trip. Olson recounted how he became the "poet laureate" of the group, every day composing several verses of a humorous theme sung to the tune of the *Old Canal Song*. The first verse:

> Oh the Old Potomac's rising
> And the whiskey's runnin' short
> And we hardly think we'll get a drink
> 'Til we get to Williamsport
> 'TIL WE GET TO WILLIAMSPORT

Every night around the campfire the group would sing the song, which reached a total of thirty-two verses. "NBC is having them run off," Olson wrote, "and *Life* and *Time* and the newspapers all wanted copies so they will appear in a number of places. The Justice was so tickled with them he was singing them all the time."[16]

After the hike, Douglas established the C & O Canal Committee, with Olson and six others—including Estabrook, who reversed the *Post*'s stand—serving as members. Meeting in the justice's chambers, the group hammered out a report that Douglas submitted to Interior Secretary Douglas McKay on April 22. The committee stopped the road and continued to meet over the years to achieve official park status for the area. In January 1961 the Chesapeake and Ohio Canal was designated a national monument.

Olson and Douglas became good friends. They hiked the canal again on a reunion journey and in 1958 hiked in Olympic National Park to protest salvage logging. They also canoed together in the Quetico-Superior. When Douglas celebrated his twentieth anniversary as a member of the Supreme Court in April 1959, Olson was one of forty-two invited guests on a list that included Lyndon Johnson, Clark Clifford, Abe Fortas, and one other conservationist—Harvey Broome, a founder of the Wilderness Society and a member of the C & O Canal Committee.

The canal hike represented the most pleasurable aspects of presiding over the National Parks Association. Olson was able to spend time outdoors with an interesting group of people, making new contacts and friends and at the same time helping to achieve a worthwhile goal. It was a type of conservation work at which this former canoe country guide excelled, and the little ways in which he made such trips enjoyable for others—the song he composed, for example—made him both popular and subtly influential. He also was able to act with a great deal of autonomy: he did not have to rely on NPA staff, and his hands were not tied by the board of trustees.

The advantages of this freedom are especially clear in comparison to Olson's experience in the fight to prevent construction of a dam near Echo Park in the center of Dinosaur National Monument. Stopping the dam, which was part of a massive proposal called the Colorado River Storage Project, became the most important conservation cause of the decade. It posed a clear test of the inviolability of the national park system, and wilderness activists believed that if the park system failed the test, the chances of establishing a national wilderness preservation system were remote.

On March 20, 1954, the day Olson and Douglas and thirty-five others tramped out of Cumberland, Maryland, in the middle of a snowstorm, President Eisenhower approved Interior Secretary McKay's recommendation to include the Echo Park dam in the overall project. Olson visited the White House shortly after to point out the significance of the issue, especially in light of Eisenhower's State of the Union message on January 7, in which he had pledged to "protect and improve" the national parks and monuments. He came away convinced that the White House staff did not understand why the issue was controversial and that "little actually simmers through the lace curtains surrounding the chief."[17]

Eisenhower's announcement sent the controversy, which had been flashing hot and cold since the 1940s, into its final phase, and the nation's major conservation groups, as well as many minor ones, worked together in unprecedented fashion. The Sierra Club, the Wilderness Society, and the NPA had the most direct stake in the issue, but they were small organizations and relied on the cooperation and clout of such large groups as the Izaak Walton League, the National Wildlife Federation, the National Audubon Society, and the Garden Club of America. The groups shared membership lists, coordinated mailings, and divided lobbying efforts to take advantage of each group's relative strength with different members of Congress.[18]

Olson's single most important contribution to the campaign was to help organize the strategy session and give the keynote talk at a major meeting in New York on November 17, 1954. Representatives of twenty-eight conservation groups attended the conference, held in the Baroque Suite of the Plaza Hotel. The meeting was especially important because division was beginning to appear in the ranks of the conservationists, with some saying the strategy should be to oppose the entire Colorado River Storage Project and others arguing that the fight should focus only on Echo Park Dam and the threat to Dinosaur National Monument. David Brower, executive director of the Sierra Club and the most visible conservationist in the fight, was among those who wanted to oppose the entire project. Olson disagreed. He wrote on November 5 to another conservationist:

I know what Dave Brower will think. Don't feel for an instant that I do not understand the broader implications or the need of a re-study. I feel, however, that the wisest strategy now is to make Dinosaur the major issue; that we should be in the position of fighting for a clear-cut principle, rather than get involved in the multitudinous ramifications of the entire Upper Colorado Project.[19]

He repeated this viewpoint in his keynote address at the conference and spoke about the values of such places as the wild canyons of Dinosaur National Monument:

The mere existence of [such wildlands] serves as a reminder of our past, gives us respect for the courage, hardship and vision of our forefathers, and serves as balance wheels to the speed and pressures of a high-powered civilization. It is good for moderns to experience the wilderness. It is part of the cultural background of America. . . . Any development in any national park or monument which destroys [this], is breaking faith with the original intent of Congress to pass these areas on unimpaired.[20]

Olson's view that conservationists should concentrate strictly on the threat to Dinosaur National Monument became the consensus, and the conference, which was covered by the national news media as well as regional media from the West, led to a reenergized and cohesive campaign. It also led to the creation of an umbrella group called the Council of Conservationists. Funded by a wealthy chemical manufacturer and Sierra Club member, Edward Mallinckrodt Jr., the council worked with two other lobbying groups, the Citizens Committee on Natural Resources and Trustees for Conservation, to build the largest-scale promotional campaign in conservation history. They produced letters to editors, articles, pamphlets, books, and films and distributed them on a massive scale, building a steady stream of favorable editorials and articles in national publications that then were reprinted and distributed as an indication of the campaign's growing support. The campaign generated ten thousand letters to the administration and Congress protesting the Echo Park Dam.

Victory came on April 11, 1956, when a bill approving the Colorado River Storage Project became law. The bill not only excluded the Echo Park Dam but included the statement that "no dam or reservoir constructed under the authorization of the Act shall be within

any National Park or Monument." This protective wording, negoti-
ated by the Wilderness Society's executive secretary, Howard Zahniser,
expressly indicated the government's commitment to the national
park system and to the principle of keeping dedicated natural areas
intact, a principle essential to the future establishment of a national
wilderness preservation system.

Despite Olson's role in the New York conference that reinvigorated
the campaign to save Dinosaur National Monument, he felt frustrated with the NPA. Like Devereux Butcher, who had lobbied Olson
to take the presidency, Olson had experienced at first hand the timid-
ity of the group's board of trustees. One of the issues the board raised
stemmed from a 1954 Supreme Court decision that affirmed the federal government's power to revoke the tax-exempt status of any organization that spent a substantial portion of its funds or time on lobbying. This was a major problem for all of the national conservation
groups, but they figured out ways to deal with it. The Sierra Club
chose to solve the problem by creating the group Trustees for Conservation to take charge of its lobbying activities. Other groups cooperated to form an umbrella organization for lobbying purposes; this was
one rationale behind the creation of the Council of Conservationists.

Typically, leaders of conservation groups also played leadership
roles in the lobbying organizations, making sure that any time they
were engaged in lobbying the funds came from the non-tax-exempt
organization. The NPA's board, however, was so concerned about
preserving the group's tax-exempt status that Olson, invited to serve
on the executive committee of the Council of Conservationists, had
to say no. The most he could agree to was to serve on a committee
that prepared informational material for the Dinosaur campaign.

Olson also received complaints from trustees when they felt the
organization's magazine was attacking too hard. He regularly pre-
viewed articles that might be controversial and occasionally asked for
changes when he thought a tough word or phrase was unnecessarily
antagonistic, but that did not prevent the complaints.

Devereux Butcher made the problem more difficult for Olson,
complaining about what he called the NPA's "yellow streak." On December 23, 1954, for example, a month after the New York conference,
Butcher wrote to Olson about an article he planned for *National Parks
Magazine*:

I am going to point out that we are losing ground in the fight for the parks, and the item will be an unsigned one, so that it will reflect the Association's thinking. If the Board does not like what I say, all they will have to do after that will be to ask me to surrender my editorship of the magazine—and when they do that, it will be the end. I'll find a fighting organization to tie in with.

Such incidents left Olson feeling stuck in a no-win situation.

Butcher also complained about the day-to-day management of the organization by Fred Packard, who had replaced Butcher as executive director so that Butcher could give more time to the organization's magazine. He said Packard too often was absent from the office and that he was never on top of correspondence. He also thought Packard was not hard-hitting enough in dealing with the Park Service and Interior Department.

Butcher's comments in part reflected different personalities. Although Butcher had brought Packard into the organization and had picked him as his successor in the position of executive director, they were true opposites. As William Wharton wrote to Olson in 1952, "Dev is a fellow who takes things very seriously, and to some extent is always looking for trouble. Fred, on the other hand, while throwing himself wholeheartedly into his job, can laugh things off and not become too seriously involved emotionally."[21] And part of the office problem simply was a matter of not enough people to handle all the work. But Olson, who enjoyed Packard as a person and believed that few people understood national park managment issues better than Packard, nevertheless realized that much of what Butcher said was true.

"Being a stickler for order and attention to detail, it is a constant source of irritation and worry to me too," Sigurd wrote to Butcher on July 26, 1954. "I feel as you do that his office reflects on all of us. As President of the organization believe me I am not happy to have a poorly run Washington office."

The Dinosaur campaign, in particular, had illustrated the problems in the front office. There was the time, for example, when Packard had told David Brower, his counterpart in the Sierra Club, that the NPA would pay the cost of $14.25 to send letters to five hundred newspaper editors. But he failed to follow through, and Brower, who was dipping into his organization's permanent funds, exploded. He told the NPA's western field representative to charge the mailing to the Sierra Club. When the representative informed Olson about the incident, Sigurd was upset. "In the future," he responded, "when you come up against something like this, wire me and I'll be glad to absorb the cost personally. A small expenditure such as this should not be allowed to jeopardize an important move."[22]

Even the New York conference in November 1954 was something of an embarrassment to Olson. The NPA was the sponsor, but most of the work was done by Howard Zahniser of the Wilderness Society and Fred Smith, a public relations executive who served as director of the Council of Conservationists. After the Dinosaur campaign ended, Olson wrote to Packard that the NPA "followed along and at no time showed any real leadership." He continued:

> There is one thing that has bothered me very much and that is the general feeling among allied groups that NPA is not carrying its weight as it should. This began during the Dinosaur effort where the Wilderness Society, the Sierra Club and others carried the brunt of the fight. . . . We lost ground during that effort and I have been constantly on the defensive ever since trying to explain that we did the best we could, we did not have the funds or the person-nel, etc. etc. but at the same time I smarted under the inference. . . . WHERE [ISSUES] CONCERN THE NATIONAL PARKS AND MONUMENTS OR ANY PART OF THE SYSTEM WE SHOULD TAKE THE LEAD. Let the Wilder-ness Society fight for wilderness wherever it may be but if any unit of the NPS [National Park System] is threatened or needs help, that is our sphere of influence. . . . It is a sad reflection on the NPA to play second fiddle on any issues that are ours.[23]

Olson's letter showed the frustration that would build over the next few years and lead to his resignation. Yet while the Dinosaur campaign illustrated the difficulties of leading the NPA, Olson con-tinued to make new friends and contacts. And while his organization was seen by others as not pulling its load, Olson himself was gaining respect. Unknown to him, in August 1954 the Wilderness Society seri-ously considered him for a seat on its governing council, deciding against it because the NPA already was represented on the council in the person of Charley Woodbury, the NPA's vice president.[24]

Even the New York conference, in which the NPA did not perform to Olson's satisfaction, proved personally valuable, for sitting in the audience during his keynote address was a man who went home believing that Sigurd should write a book. The man had more than just a little knowledge of the book world. He was an expert. His name was Alfred A. Knopf.

❖ Twelve ❖

The Singing Wilderness

1950–1956

At first, Sigurd Olson's professional conservation career dovetailed quite well with his desire to write. In 1948 and 1949 magazines published fifteen of his articles, more than in his last six years as dean of Ely Junior College. Nearly all of them were about the current battles over the Quetico-Superior and so were not in the essay style he most enjoyed, but he was able at times to slip in some of his feeling for wilderness, and the articles had given him new contacts and greater visibility as a writer.

After December 1949, when President Truman signed the order creating an airspace reservation over the Superior Roadless Areas, Olson's writing came almost to a halt. In 1950 four magazines published Olson articles or editorials celebrating the airspace reservation and promoting the Quetico-Superior program, but these were merely updates and reformulations of previously published articles. In earlier years such a decline in his writing would have been accompanied by journal entries in which Sigurd poured out his frustrations. But not this time. He had found a new project to excite him: the launching of a regional magazine called *North Country*.

The magazine was the inspiration of Grant Halladay, the outdoor photographer and lecturer who had shot the footage for "Wilderness Canoe Country." He envisioned *North Country* as the *Arizona Highways* of the central Great Lakes region, covering Wisconsin, Michigan, Minnesota, and Ontario, and in 1950 asked Olson to help plan it and to serve as editor. Sigurd asked Halladay to assume the main editorial responsibility until he could wind up his work with the Quetico-Superior program. At the time, Sigurd thought prospects for the treaty were favorable and that he soon would have to look for other paying work. Halladay agreed to let Olson sign on as associate editor; Sigurd would help line up stories and edit them.

North Country debuted with a Spring 1951 issue that promised readers it would rekindle their memories of the region "through magnificent color photography, through sketches and articles by the finest artists and writers in the north." Olson wrote three short essays for the issue, one about the coming of spring, another about the canoe country, and a third about the roughed grouse. Historian Grace Lee Nute contributed an essay on the fur trade era and a poem about Lake Superior. Sam Campbell, a popular Wisconsin nature writer and photographer who was a good friend of Olson and a mentor to Halladay, wrote "Autumn in Wisconsin," which Olson and Halladay included in this issue supposedly devoted to spring.

While there may have been some confusion in the content, the issue contained beautiful color photographs, mostly scenes from the canoe country and Lake Superior, and there were reproductions of wildlife art by a Michigan artist and by the widely known Francis Lee Jaques of Minnesota. Raymond Carlson, editor of *Arizona Highways*, wrote his congratulations, saying, "It seems to me that you have grasped the spirit of your north country, and I do want you to know that we wish you every success in the world." The issue also received praise from readers across the region, including the governors of Minnesota and Wisconsin. Paul Herbert, director of the Division of Conservation at Michigan State College in East Lansing, said the issue contained "some of the most beautiful and authentically colored photographs that has ever been my pleasure to see. . . . If future issues have the quality of your first, I predict great success for 'NORTH COUNTRY.'"[1]

The second issue, which came out in the summer of 1951, was better designed and contained a wider group of contributors, including several Canadians and a Wisconsin woman who was married to a Menominee Indian and wrote about Indian culture. By then the magazine had three thousand subscribers in three dozen states and eight countries, and Sigurd wanted to assume the major editorial responsibilities. Charles Kelly of the Quetico-Superior Council, however, did not approve, writing on June 7 that "our situation may become such that you couldn't give *North Country* the required time. . . .

You are already active in the Park Service organization [the NPA] and if you take on other major responsibilities those who make our funds available may later become restive."

The issue soon was moot, for *North Country,* which promised readers five issues a year, never came out again. Publishing a high-quality color magazine was expensive, and, while Halladay had put together an impressive list of subscribers on short notice, he had generated almost no advertising revenue. The second issue contained no ads at all, and Olson, who had no share in the magazine's ownership and who had been donating his services to help the magazine get on its feet, loaned Halladay two thousand dollars to cover production costs. But Halladay failed to get sufficient funds for future issues, and *North Country* folded. Olson never got his money back and was embarrassed to have been associated with the magazine.

Sigurd never was and never would be a shrewd money manager. "I am woefully ignorant," he confessed in 1951. "In fact I know nothing about making money. Even as manager of the Border Lakes, I simply hated to collect payment for services rendered. I always felt as though our parties were guests, not paying ones either."[2] Even by Sigurd's mediocre standards, 1951 proved to be a bad year for financial decision making. In June he sold his one-third share of the Border Lakes Outfitting Company to his longtime partner and neighbor, M. W. Peterson. The company had barely been profitable in the previous several years, and Sigurd hoped to invest in something with a greater return that, when combined with his earnings from freelance writing and from his expected future salary as an editor of *North Country,* would provide him and Elizabeth with an acceptable income.[3]

The Border Lakes brought him five thousand dollars; his capital gain on this twenty-two-year investment was less than nine hundred dollars. That summer, while he was deciding how to invest it, a friend from Pennsylvania told him about an oil and gas development near his home that promised to bring in a lot of money. "Overall," the friend wrote, "I don't see how we can miss and those of us on the ground had a chance to pick the best locations. . . . I'd hate to have you lose money but would feel sick if we hit big and you were not in, so count ten and roll the bones."[4]

At the urging of a close and trusted colleague, and with encouragement from Elizabeth, Sigurd invested four thousand dollars in Pamaco Gas and Oil in October 1951. It is possible that he invested more after this initial plunge; forty years later, Elizabeth thought the total investment amounted to ten thousand dollars. In any event, the oil and gas development did not pan out, and the Olsons eventually lost their money.

By the summer of 1952, when it was clear that *North Country* was finished, Olson began to experience dark moods reminiscent of his days at the junior college. Financial worry was not the main source; his investment with Pamaco had not yet given him serious cause for concern, and his two thousand dollar loan to Halladay made him more angry than worried. The real problem was that he was not writing. Once again he took up his journal. "These old signs of depression and loss of hope are familiar," he wrote on August 9:

> They have happened many times in the past. As soon as I get at my writing, anything at all, it will pass just as it has before. Money troubles, investments, complications, QS do not seem important compared to the joy of again pounding something off. That is your one anchor to windward as it has always been. . . . Sure, you have done nothing but talk about it, but the truth is there just the same.

That summer Sigurd resurrected an idea he had first thought of in the 1930s: he would write interpretive essays incorporating the joy and wonder that he felt in the outdoors, his experiences of connectedness with all life and the whole universe, and put them together in book form. "If people reading it can catch that then it is enough," he wrote on August 9, "then everything you write will have a solid core of worthwhileness."

But summer passed into fall, and the mallard-filled marshes near home occupied much of Sigurd's relatively little time free from conservation work. Before long the first white flakes of winter drifted quietly down, and Sigurd's idea once more seemed to fade away like the grass and pine needles on the snow-covered ground outside his writing shack.

Olson's January thaw arrived in the person of his younger son's wife, Yvonne. She and Robert came from San Francisco for a holiday visit, and Yvonne stayed for another month. She and Robert had been married for nearly six years but had spent little time in Ely, and to Sigurd it seemed as though he was really getting to meet Yvonne for the first time. She quickly won his heart.

"I can't tell you how much this month has meant to us in fun and laughter and music and poetry and companionship," Sigurd wrote to Robert on February 10, 1953, the day Yvonne left for home. "Your Vonnie has a beautiful mind. Her sense of awareness, understanding, wit and appreciation are something precious. . . . What I am trying to tell you clumsily is that we love your Vonnie very much and always will and so shall always bless you for finding her."

Sigurd found in Yvonne what he had never found in Elizabeth or in any of his friends in Ely: someone who read and enjoyed discussing articles, poems, and books about the human condition. It was a release for him, and possibly a relief, to have someone he could talk to about the search for meaning, that driving force of his life that few seemed to understand. And Yvonne had two other qualities Sigurd greatly admired. One was her assertiveness: she was quite willing to tell him off when he needed it. ("He loved it," Robert recalled. "Everybody else would hunker down. She wasn't being browbeaten by him.") The other was her sense of humor, which like Sigurd's, included a silly streak. ("In fact," Yvonne recalled with a smile, "he could be downright childish. When he'd get on something he thought was funny he'd repeat it to the point where it was worn out.")

After Yvonne's visit to Ely, she and Sigurd wrote to each other frequently, addressing each other with nicknames based on a popular song: Sigurd was "Papa Mia," and Yvonne was "Vonnie Mia." They would mark up and exchange articles from magazines such as the *Atlantic Monthly* and *Saturday Review* and would write their thoughts about what they were reading. Sigurd tried to convince Yvonne of the value of Gerard Manley Hopkins, and she tried to persuade him to give T. S. Eliot a chance. They wrote about Jacques Maritain and John Masefield and Ryo Nen, about Thoreau and Goethe. Through Yvonne, Sigurd belatedly discovered that Robert shared his philosophical and cultural interests, and he began opening up intellectually to his son as well. The three even started a joint collection of classical music recordings. (At the time, Sigurd especially enjoyed clarinet quintets.)

At some point in 1953, possibly during Yvonne's visit in January, Sigurd talked about his own writing. Yvonne had never read any of his essays and asked him to show her some. He went into his writing shack, pulled out a few of the essays, and gave them to her. She thought they were wonderful and told him he should put them into a book.

Coming from another family member or close friend, such a remark might not have had much impact—*of course* they will praise the work—but Yvonne's intellectual interests and respect for writing gave her enthusiastic response more weight. Sigurd took it to heart, and during 1953—the year of his father's death, the year of the FBI raid on the canoe country, the year of Sigurd's induction as president of the National Parks Association and of his monthlong summertime swing through the West, and the year of his first canoe trip with the Voyageurs—he quietly began writing a book manuscript. On January 16, 1954, a bitterly cold day that by night would reach nearly forty degrees below zero, leading to a broken furnace, a frozen pipe, and a blown stove fuse, Sigurd cheerfully confessed the truth to Yvonne:

> Yes I am working on a book and it will be finished sometime in 1954 and I AM NOT COPYING STUFF OUT OF A OTHER BOOK SEE. I am writing one of my own and next summer if you are here I want you to help me make clean copies of the rough MSS so that we can submit it somewhere in the fall. It is a compilation of essays I have written and now in the light of my mature knowledge (I hope) rather drastically rewritten. I have written some new ones and made a lot of additions to the old ones. . . . I have been working on it steadily since I got home and have some 20 chapters taking shape.[5]

Yvonne Olson arrived in Ely early in May 1954 to spend the summer. (She and Robert were in transition; he was in Minneapolis, looking for a place for them to live and beginning a doctoral program in history at the University of Minnesota.) While a crew of carpenters sawed and hammered away, adding an enclosed porch to the house, Yvonne pounded the typewriter, making fresh copies of Sigurd's essays.

By June the manuscript was far enough along to submit a portion of it. While he was in Washington, D.C., on National Parks Association business, Sigurd sought advice from his friend and workplace neighbor Howard Zahniser. The balding and bespectacled Wilderness Society executive secretary not only *looked* bookish, he *was* bookish. He had a huge personal library of nature books and rarely seemed to be without one. Theodor R. "Ted" Swem, a Park Service official and eventual Wilderness Society president who came to know Zahniser early in the 1960s, recalled a time in Denver when he was supposed to pick up Zahniser outside a downtown hotel. Zahniser was sitting on the sidewalk with his back resting against the hotel wall, so immersed in a book that he did not look up when Swem honked his car horn. Swem had to drive around the block three times before he caught Zahniser's attention. Seven years younger than Sigurd and a quiet, gentle, and tremendously effective conservationist, Zahniser was a perfect source for the kind of advice Sigurd needed.[6]

"Have just finished talking to Zahnie about the book," Sigurd wrote afterward to family members. "He is enthusiastic and thinks it might go big. . . . He thinks it might be best to contact a good agent, because an agent can best decide the question of pre-book publication of chapters and can place them where they will do the most good as a sort of advance publicity stunt." Zahniser recommended Marie Rodell, a widely respected New York agent who, he said, had done great promotional work for the nature writings of scientists Rachel Carson and Durwood Allen. On June 10 Olson sent the introduction, four sample chapters, and the table of contents to Rodell. "These essays and sketches . . . might be the answer for many to the gnawing ennui of today," he wrote. "If they can bring some joy to those who seem to have lost their capacity to see the world of nature in a fresh, clear light, the book will be justified." Using words from a poem by Oscar Fay Adams, he called the book "The Pipes of Pan."[7]

Rodell was interested but brought up an issue raised by others over the years. "There are some very pleasant passages in this sample material," she responded on June 16, but she wondered how much of the final version would be lively anecdotes and how much would be "straight lyrical appreciation." She said that Olson's wilderness adventures would interest readers more than "the more abstract pages of philosophy and feeling."

But Olson was not about to back down. For twenty years agents and editors had told him there was no market for his essays, but after six years of traveling the country as a professional conservationist, he was convinced they were wrong. Too many people had come up to him after his speeches and told him how much they enjoyed his discussions of the spiritual values of wilderness. By this time Yvonne had typed and retyped all of the essays (she later said that she and her father-in-law had some "royal battles" over punctuation) and Sigurd sent the rest of the manuscript to Rodell, saying:

> There are many books of adventure and factual accounts of observations in the out of doors. It was not my wish to do another. The value of my book as I see it is in my interpretation of the wilderness, its meaning, and my reactions to it. . . . You may not agree with me at all but I feel very strongly about this.

Rodell read the rest of Olson's manuscript, and on July 13, 1954, said she wanted to try to sell it. "I'm not at all certain of the sort of reception it will get," she wrote, "since the essay type of writing is not too popular these days; but let's try and see what we can do."

Later in Olson's life, the myth would develop—a myth he encouraged—that his manuscript was rejected by eight, even ten publishers. His own papers and Rodell's files document just three, and the timing is such that other, undocumented rejections seem extremely unlikely. But that does not mean it was not painful. Dodd, Mead said little in its rejection, the first of the three. But George Brockway, writing for W. W. Norton on October 29, 1954, called the book "too diffuse, too self-conscious, and too sentimental." And Paul Brooks, an editor at Houghton Mifflin, wrote a rejection letter to Rodell on November 23 that was difficult for both him and Sigurd, because they were friends:

> Of course I'm wholly sympathetic with the philosophy expressed in [the essays]—and sometimes he expresses it very well. However, as I told him, there is nothing tougher to sell than essays collected in book form. . . . It would have to be superbly written to have a chance, and Sig Olson's prose is not on that level. . . . Sig is a wonderful man and I hope to see more of him. But we'd all be disappointed if we tried to publish this.

Rodell forwarded Brooks's letter to Olson, who had just returned to Ely from New York, where he had played a key role in the conference that reunited conservationists in their strategy to fight the proposed Echo Park Dam in Dinosaur National Monument. But the sting of the new rejection was lessened somewhat by a letter Olson had just received from Alfred Knopf. The prestigious publisher and conservationist—he was a member of the National Park Service's advisory board—said he had attended Sigurd's keynote speech at the New York conference and was greatly impressed. "I am wondering if you are not going to have a book for us one of these days?" Knopf wrote. Olson wrote to Rodell on November 29, enclosing Knopf's letter and asking if she was getting pessimistic about the book's chances. "If you are, I don't blame you," he wrote. "Perhaps Alfred Knopf will in a moment of weakness decide to take a gambling chance."[8]

He did. "I don't know how much success we will have with such a book," Knopf wrote to Olson on January 6, 1955, "but I am happy to have it on our list." Rodell worked out the contract details. Knopf wanted Olson to change the title and the accompanying "pipes of Pan" theme in the introduction, to regroup the essays, and to write half a dozen or so additional essays. He agreed with Olson's request to use Francis Lee Jaques as the book's illustrator, but the cost of the black-and-white sketches—which would receive praise in the years ahead—was to come out of Olson's royalties. Rodell later convinced the publisher to split the illustration costs if the book sold eight thousand copies in the United States.[9]

Sigurd set to work in his writing shack, sketching out new essays. He had liked the "pipes of Pan" theme; the metaphor of music and wilderness strongly resonated with him. In fact, his original title choice in 1952 was "Wilderness Music." Perhaps his decision to use the metaphor as a theme for his first book arose from his reading of Aldo Leopold's *A Sand County Almanac,* which he had received as a gift in 1950. In the essay "Song of the Gavilan," Leopold wrote, "This song of the waters is audible to every ear, but there is other music in these hills . . . a vast pulsing harmony—its score inscribed on a thousand hills, its notes the lives and deaths of plants and animals, its rhythms spanning the seconds and the centuries."[10]

Then again, the idea could have arisen from an essay called "Wilderness Symphony," which Olson edited for the Summer 1951 issue of *North Country.* We may never know for sure, but that essay, by Sigurd's friend Sam Campbell, must have stirred Olson: "Who can write the symphony of the wilderness?" Campbell began. "What master can catch that elusive melody to whose rhythm all nature moves? Who can gather into notes and measures the song of the forest, the cyclic tides of verdure, the dance of the hills and mountains, the metric march of the seasons?" Olson had long believed *he* was that person, and in 1952, as he began thinking seriously about writing a book, his journal entries once again raised the theme of his uniqueness. On July 6, for example, he wrote, "You have something different—no one in your acquaintance feels as you do—no one at all." And on October 25, he wrote, "You are a poet. That is where your power lies. . . . You are emerging as a poet of the out-of-doors."

By early February 1955, Olson had decided on a new way to express the metaphor of wilderness music that would please Alfred Knopf. The idea came from Jean Packard, a good friend whose husband, Fred, served as executive secretary of the National Parks Association. She told Sigurd of a book about John James Audubon by nature writer Donald Culross Peattie. Published in 1935, it was called *Singing in the Wilderness*. Olson liked the title so much he decided to use a variation of it for his own manuscript. On February 7 he sat down at the desk in his writing shack, put a sheet of canary yellow paper in his manual Royal typewriter, and began a new introduction: "The Singing Wilderness has to do with perspective, a certain element of timelessness, and the need for tranquility. It is an open challenge to mechanization, to unlimited industrial expansion and the striving for material things." The introduction would go through a number of rewrites before he was happy with it, but he had found his metaphor and his new title: *The Singing Wilderness*.

Olson soon began writing new essays for the book, typing them on legal-sized, lined yellow paper. He quickly wrote drafts of such essays as "Loons of Lac La Croix," "The Last Mallard," "Birds of the Ski Trails," and "Scrub Oak." But he did not write free of distraction. Minnesota conservationists were campaigning to get Governor Orville Freeman to name Olson the state's conservation commissioner, and Freeman was interested. On January 6 the *Minneapolis Tribune* listed Olson as one of four contenders.

Sigurd was gratified by the attention. "In fact after some of the brutal criticism that came my way during the Air Ban fight, it warms the cockles of my heart," he wrote to a friend. And it would be incorrect to say that he had no interest. He told another friend he would have liked to have been able to at least consider it. But he knew he had far too many other things to do, and he told those who were leading the campaign on his behalf that he could not accept the position if it were offered.[11]

One of the chapters for *The Singing Wilderness* added an ironic epilogue to this distraction from his writing. When Marie Rodell had sent the book manuscript to publishers in 1954, she also had sent individual chapters to magazines, and *Sports Illustrated* had bought two of them. One, called "Dark House," the magazine renamed "Fishing at 20 Below" and published on February 28, 1955. The article was not about ordinary ice fishing; Olson wrote about spearing, which had long been controversial among Minnesota sportsmen. Those in the northern part of the state typically had supported it; those in the southern counties often had vigorously opposed it. Within the state division of the Izaak Walton League the issue had created such dissension in the late 1940s that the northern chapters had threatened to secede.

A number of biologists in the Minnesota Department of Conservation opposed spearing, saying that northern pike would disappear from the state if the practice continued. After the *Sports Illustrated* article appeared, state Izaak Walton League president George Laing wrote to Olson that his article had resurrected old wounds and that Twin Cities outdoor writers "have actually pointed to your article as evidence of your disinterest in the state's complete conservation program."[12] "Fishing at 20 Below" demonstrated to his critics that Olson was unfit for the job of conservation commissioner.

Sigurd responded on March 24 that he simply had not thought about the potential reaction when he submitted the article: "I guess the fact of the matter is that I have become so embroiled in controversial problems all over the country that I had forgotten how it might affect the Minnesota issue." He said he was willing to "accept the opinions of those who know the score," the researchers who believed spearing must end to save the northern pike.[13]

It was a minor storm that quickly passed, but it is surprising that Olson, the Izaak Walton League's wilderness ecologist, active in the organization since its inception three decades earlier, would be so unaware of an issue that deeply divided the league in his own state. Perhaps the outdoor writers that Laing referred to were correct, if by "disinterested" they meant that Olson had become so involved in conservation at a national level that he was losing touch with state issues. His response to Laing gives some support to such a charge.

Another possibility—and it would not necessarily preclude the other—is that Olson tended to separate his creative desires as a writer and interpreter of outdoor experiences from the political aspects of the conservation world. In his March 24 letter to Laing, Sigurd wrote that he did not write the essay to give support to spearing:

> I wrote this little piece some years ago as a pure interpretation of the feelings of a man when he sits in a dark house and looks down through a hole in the ice waiting for something to come along. I still think it is a wonderful experience. . . . And so I make no apologies for the way I feel about it and the joys I tried to point up in my story.

The controversy did not keep Olson from using the essay in *The Singing Wilderness* under its original title, "Dark House." He made but one significant change in the story: in the first sentence, he changed the timing of the episode from "two years ago" to "ten years ago," undoubtedly to distance himself from charges of supporting the practice in the mid-1950s.

Throughout the spring and summer of 1955 Sigurd continued working on the book as much as possible while keeping up with his conservation duties. He also made time for his first canoe expedition into the far north, the publicity-generating Voyageurs trip along five hundred miles of the Churchill River in Saskatchewan. The trip fulfilled a dream that went all the way back to 1921, when Al Kennedy had asked Sigurd to go prospect for gold in the Flin Flon and Sigurd had said no to keep from losing Elizabeth. He thought about that on July 23, after the group made its first camp on a sand point along the northern reaches of Lac Ile a la Crosse. He wrote in his notebook, "Here at last I am in the North Country, where I wanted to go thirty years ago. It is good to have seen it—good at last to have part of it under my belt."

Returning from the north in mid-August, Olson finished his manuscript and sent it to his editor. The final draft contained thirty-four essays, organized by seasons. At least nineteen of the essays were rewrites of pieces dating back ten years or more, many of them rejected by magazines. Three of them—"Easter on the Prairie," "Grandmother's Trout," and "Farewell to Saganaga"—had their origins in the 1930s, and shared a total of eighteen rejections. But whatever Alfred Knopf's original reservations were, he took a personal interest in the book and on February 13, 1956, after reading the final draft, he wrote to Sigurd, "I think you have done a fine job."

❖

Sigurd Olson wanted *The Singing Wilderness* to capture the joy, the wonder, and the sense of connectedness he had experienced outdoors. As he was working on the manuscript in January 1954 he read a recent book by John Masefield called *So Long to Learn* and took it as a sign that he was on the right track. Masefield had experienced the kind of epiphanies that Olson had known so well, and that, in Sigurd's mind, W. H. Hudson had come closest to capturing in print. Olson typically called these moments "flashes of insight," while Masefield described them as entering "into that greater life," but Olson could agree completely with Masefield's description of the importance of these experiences to modern society: "I believe that life [the greater life] to be the source of all that is of glory or goodness in this world; and that modern man, not knowing that life, is dwelling in death."[14]

Masefield also lamented that "fewer and fewer men are taking the discipline of the arts as qualifications for the attempt to know that glory and to bring from it something shining for man." Olson seized on that thought as he fleshed out the manuscript early in 1954:

> In the essays I am working on, each one must bring through it something shining for man. Each must tap somehow, enable men to touch that "greater life," the source of all glory, beauty, goodness in this world. . . . If each thing I write will somehow have this illumination, this glow, this transcendent beauty, the feeling of having touched the absolute, it will be enough. I can do this by bringing in somehow my feeling for the primeval, the origins of things, the Pipes of Pan, the glory, the sense of wonder, awe, oneness with all life and the universe itself, the childlike quality soon lost of being part of that greater life.

The Singing Wilderness follows most of the standard expectations for nature writing that had evolved since 1789, when the English clergyman Gilbert White produced the genre's prototype, *The Natural His-*

tory of Selborne. Like most books of the sort, *The Singing Wilderness* imparts a vivid sense of place, contains affectionate descriptions of flora and fauna, and is organized episodically, employing a standard seasonal format. But *The Singing Wilderness* differs from traditional nature writing in that the essays, while they are highly personal and strongly evocative of a particular place, are at the same time meant to be representative of experiences readers have already known, or can know if they try. The introduction concludes:

> In the chapters that follow I tell of my experiences in the north, but far more important than the places I have seen or what I have done or thought about is the possibility of hearing the singing wilderness and catching perhaps its real meaning. You may not hear it exactly as I did, but somewhere along the trails I have followed, you too may know the glory.[15]

It is useful to compare the book to Leopold's *A Sand County Almanac,* often referred to as the bible of the modern environmental movement, although there are important differences between the two works. Some of them are stylistic. Leopold, for example, wrote with a tightly controlled pen, taking great care with the most minute details of his narrative and using extremely precise language. Olson, interested much more in abstract feelings, painted word pictures with a broad brush. The tone of the books also differed, reflecting distinct personalities. *A Sand County Almanac,* despite passages of beautiful description and entertaining wit, is a much darker book than *The Singing Wilderness.* A theme of loss, sometimes depicted with biting sarcasm, pervades Leopold's narrative. Olson, while he is critical of modern society, uses a narrative voice that most often is optimistic, and never sarcastic.[16]

The most important difference between the two books, however, lies in their goals. Leopold wanted *A Sand County Almanac* primarily to do two things: to present fundamental ecological principles in a way that would hold the interest of a nonscientific audience, and to inculcate love and respect for natural communities through what he called "the land ethic." Because the book serves as a warning to modern culture as well as a doctrine for change, and because of the charismatic power of Leopold's text, *A Sand County Almanac* has been described as "the utterance of an American Isaiah."[17]

If the Leopold of *A Sand County Almanac* is an Old Testament prophet, then the Olson of *The Singing Wilderness* is a New Testament evangelist. Where Leopold invokes the God of power and wrath, preaching proper ethical behavior toward the land and prophesying doom if society disobeys, Olson invites his readers to experience the God of love, as made manifest in nature.

But *A Sand County Almanac* and *The Singing Wilderness* are no more incompatible for environmentalists than the Old and New Testaments are for Christians. Olson echoes Leopold's critique of and prescription for modern society, and Leopold echoes Olson's sense of wonder and joy. The authors give shared goals different emphasis. And it is this difference that makes comparing these works especially valuable, because the major contribution of *The Singing Wilderness* is its sustained treatment of a theme that was important to Leopold but strewn here and there in *A Sand County Almanac,* a theme that philosopher J. Baird Callicott has labeled "the land aesthetic."

It was a new, in fact revolutionary, aesthetic based in part upon full use of the senses. In Western culture, the dominant perspective on the beauty of nature—conceived, created, distributed, and perpetuated by artists—was based almost entirely on visual stimulation. Out of this picturesque aesthetic in art arose such terms as *landscape* and *scenery* as we use them today. Natural beauty was perceived as a function of composition as judged by the human eye according to standards of landscape painting and, eventually, photography. The national parks were selected according to this picturesque aesthetic; they were monuments of scenic beauty. By and large, the standard remains to this day. There is the story, for example, of how the famous landscape photographer Edward Weston would sleep in the car while his wife drove around the countryside, searching for scenes with a "Weston look." When she found one, she would wake him to photograph it.[18]

In *A Sand County Almanac*, Leopold describes the picturesque aesthetic as merely a beginning and claims that appreciation of beauty is greatly enhanced by such nonvisual sensory stimuli as the trumpeting of a sandhill crane, the rich smell of soil after a rain, the taste of ripe blackberries, the warmth of sun on the skin. What was revolutionary was his declaration that, in addition to full use of the senses, a true land aesthetic requires a mind informed by knowledge of evolution and ecology. In the essay "Marshland Elegy" he writes:

Our appreciation of the crane grows with the slow unraveling of earthly history. His tribe, we now know, stems out of the remote Eocene. The other members of the fauna in which he originated are long since entombed within the hills. When we hear his call we hear no mere bird. We hear the trumpet in the orchestra of evolution. He is the symbol of our untamable past, of the incredible sweep of millennia which underlies and conditions the daily affairs of birds and men.[19]

Leopold professes that knowledge of evolution deepens human perception and that an understanding of ecology—of communities and interdependencies—broadens perception. (As Callicott points out, "We cannot love cranes and hate marshes.") A marsh does not conform to the picturesque aesthetic, but a mind informed by evolutionary and ecological biology will perceive it as beautiful and precious. "Amid the endless mediocrity of the commonplace," writes Leopold, "a crane marsh holds a paleontological patent of nobility, won in the march of aeons."[20]

In a culture where aesthetic taste is still dominated by the picturesque, it is difficult to convey what a land aesthetic *experience* feels like. Just as Aldo Leopold did—and Sam Campbell, too—Sigurd Olson sensed that an aural metaphor, rather than a visual one, best captured its essence. Olson was less direct than Leopold, but the land aesthetic permeates *The Singing Wilderness*, from its aural-based title through each of its thirty-four essays.

Like Leopold, Olson uses knowledge of geology and evolution to add depth to perception. A piece of greenstone is much more than a rock—it is "part of the original crust formed when the molten lavas and gases first cooled," a symbol of the planet's enormous time span, which dwarfs human history. Caribou moss is beautiful and precious in part because it is an evolved combination of two different plants, "one whose rootlets can break down the rock [on which it grows], the other embedded deep within its tissues, a green and globular alga."[21] Referring to frogs calling in a bog at night, Olson writes:

This is a primeval chorus, the sort of wilderness music which reigned over the earth millions of years ago. That sound floated across the pools of the carboniferous era. You can still hear it in the Everglades: the throaty, rasping roar of the alligators and, above that, the frightened calls and screams of innumerable birds. One of the most ancient sounds on earth, it is a continuation of music from the past, and, no matter where I listen to a bog at night, strange feelings stir within me.[22]

Like Leopold, Olson uses ecological knowledge to broaden perception. The caribou moss, for example, not only has an interesting evolutionary background but also plays an important ecological role: "Those silvery little tufts before me are the shock troops of the north, the commandos with which the plant kingdom made a beachhead on a barren, rocky ridge. Surviving where other types would die, needing nothing but crystalline rocks and air, they prepare the way for occupation and for the communities to come." The lesson is clear: to paraphrase Callicott, we cannot love pines, cedars, and junipers and hate caribou moss. Olson, not surprisingly, often displays a special fondness for elements of the natural world that do not fit traditional notions of beauty: he enjoys scrub oaks and rocks and tamaracks, and he declares that "swamps are always a pleasure."[23]

But Olson's land aesthetic is not a clone of Leopold's. One important difference is their attitude toward science. Leopold often criticized the tunnel vision resulting from overspecialization, and he was angered by the ways in which tunnel-vision science led to damaged ecosystems, but he still maintained a deep faith in the scientific method: "Science has . . . made one contribution to culture which seems to me permanent and good: the critical approach to questions of fact." Olson used "facts" and theories generated by scientific research, but, more than Leopold, he feared that scientific rationalism had gained far too much power in society. Time and again he stated that scientific knowledge is an aid to understanding and appreciation, nothing more. "To be sure," he writes in "The River," an essay about weasels, "the ecological factors are important—the endless cycle of carnivores and herbivores, the inevitable assimilation of vegetable matter to flesh and blood and back again. . . . but what really counts is how [weasels] make me feel and how they contribute to the character and quality of wilderness."[24]

In fact, Olson worried that scientific knowledge, because of its claims to objectivity, could overrun less empirical beliefs that contained genuine truths of equal or even greater importance to humans.

In the essay "Northern Lights," for example, after giving the standard scientific explanation for the aurora borealis, Olson presents a competing description, based on American Indian mythology he learned as a child. He could believe what the scientists had discovered but expresses regret for the personal and cultural cost of scientific knowledge, which diminishes "the wonderment that only a child can know and a beauty that is enhanced by mystery."[25]

Olson's land aesthetic also goes further than Leopold's in incorporating humans. In the essay "Pools of the Isabella," for example, Olson shows how appreciation of a wild place can deepen through human associations. "During the many years I have fished the Isabella," Olson says, "it has become a part of me." Why? Not because it is picturesque, not because he knows its ecological history, but because each pool along the river brings back specific memories. "When I wade the Isabella," he says, "I am never alone. I always hear forgotten banter in the sounds of the rapids, the soft rhythmic swish of familiar rods. These things are as much a part of the river as the trout themselves."[26]

Human *history* also plays an important role in Olson's land aesthetic. His enjoyment of Lac la Croix was enhanced by his knowledge of the location where Ojibwe warriors long ago staged races and by the reddish-brown pictographs along the cliffs of Shortiss Island. Knowing that European fur traders traveled the same waters a hundred and fifty years earlier adds to his appreciation of human interaction with the land, and Olson writes that one who successfully navigates a stretch of spuming whitewater can hear "all the voyageurs of the past join the rapids in their shouting."[27]

The human aspects of Olson's landscape aesthetic are not limited to the past. Several times in *The Singing Wilderness* Olson describes encounters with primitive trappers' cabins in the canoe country, and, taking care to distinguish these one-room shacks from a "modern mouseproof cabin," he praises them: "Trappers' cabins are as natural as tents or teepees. They are part of the solitudes and as much a part of the wilderness as the trees and rocks themselves."[28] And in "Pools of the Isabella," Olson, in recalling his friend and former Ely grade school principal Glenn Powers, shows that the human act of fly-fishing can be beautiful, and in harmony with the land.

Olson's inclusion of humans in the land aesthetic stems from his concern for the spiritual and psychological health of modern society. Restating his long-held belief in what he called "racial memory," he writes in the introduction that "uncounted centuries of the primitive have left their mark upon us, and civilization has not changed emotional needs that were ours before the dawn of history." Modern society, in distancing itself from the natural world to which it belongs, has left these needs unfilled, and the result is widespread disillusionment:

> We sense intuitively that there must be something more, search for panaceas we hope will give us a sense of reality, fill our days and nights with such activity and our minds with such busyness that there is little time to think. When the pace stops we are often lost, and we plunge once more into the maelstrom hoping that if we move fast enough, somehow we may fill the void within us.[29]

In writing *The Singing Wilderness,* Olson did not set out to create a land aesthetic; that he *did* create one is simply a by-product of his primary goal, which was to show that the unmet needs of the civilized world could be met through regular and simple interaction with the *non*civilized world. Picking berries, looking for pine knots, fly-fishing, paddling a canoe, and many other activities not only are fulfilling in themselves, but even have "ritualistic significance," as Olson points out in "Campfires." Such activities, he says, give people "an opportunity to participate in an act hallowed by the devotion of forgotten generations."[30]

Olson implies, in fact, that the most deeply fulfilling human acts are those that are most in harmony with natural processes. Paddling a canoe thus becomes much more than a way to get from one point to another. "The movement of a canoe," he says in one of the book's most poetic passages, "is like a reed in the wind. Silence is part of it, and the sounds of lapping water, bird songs, and wind in the trees. It is part of the medium through which it floats, the sky, the water, the shores."[31]

This sense of communion is the distinguishing characteristic of *The Singing Wilderness* and marks the fulfillment of the land aesthetic. Olson describes it best in his essay titled "Silence," which, when he began working on the manuscript in 1952, he thought set the tone for the entire book. The essay is about the kind of deep communion that yields what Olson described as "flashes of insight." The three core paragraphs of the essay, which had their origins in a January 1930 journal entry, form the centerpiece of the book:

> I once climbed a great ridge called Robinson Peak to watch the sunset and to get a view of the lakes and rivers below, the rugged hills and valleys of the Quetico-Superior. When I reached the bald knob of the peak the sun was just above the horizon, a flaming ball ready to drop into the dusk below. Far beneath me on a point of pines reaching into the lake was the white inverted V of my tent. It looked very tiny down there where it was almost night.
>
> As I watched and listened, I became conscious of the slow, steady hum of millions of insects and through it the calling of the white-throats and the violin notes of the hermit thrushes. But it all seemed very vague from that height and very far away, and gradually they merged one with another, blending in a great enveloping softness of sound no louder, it seemed, than my breathing.
>
> The sun was trembling now on the edge of the ridge. It was alive, almost fluid and pulsating, and as I watched it sink I thought that I could feel the earth turning from it, actually feel its rotation. Over all was the silence of the wilderness, that sense of oneness which comes only when there are no distracting sights or sounds, when we listen with inward ears and see with inward eyes, when we feel and are aware with our entire beings rather than our senses. I thought as I sat there of the ancient admonition, "Be still and know that I am God," and knew that without stillness there can be no knowing, without divorcement from outside influences man cannot know what spirit means.[32]

This passage demonstrates how Olson's land aesthetic is intimately connected to what Leopold called the "land ethic"; just as certain norms of behavior are required if patrons of an art museum are to have a full aesthetic experience, so are they required if "patrons"— the better word is *pilgrims*—of the wilderness are to achieve the complete land aesthetic experience of communion with the cosmos. Olson's purpose in *The Singing Wilderness* is not to define a proper land ethic, but he sometimes states clear preferences. Later in "Silence," for example, he writes, "At times on quiet waters one does not speak aloud but only in whispers, for then all noise is sacrilege."[33]

The land aesthetic of *The Singing Wilderness* does not always provide clear guidelines for behavior. In the essay "Forest Pool," for example, Olson traces the history of a pond from its wilderness origins through the dramatic changes wrought by humans over the course of several generations without clearly indicating his approval or disapproval of the end result: destruction of the pond, which is replaced by a field of corn. In his next book, *Listening Point*, Olson would spend more time examining behavioral issues and would reach a clearer conclusion about the proper relationship between the civilized and noncivilized worlds, between culture and wilderness.

❖

The Singing Wilderness was published on April 16, 1956, twelve days after Sigurd Olson's fifty-seventh birthday. Publicity began earlier. Olson appeared on television in Minneapolis and St. Paul the evening of April 12, and the next day he signed copies of the book at Dayton's department store in downtown Minneapolis. The first major review was published on April 15 in *Saturday Review*. The prominent literary critic Bruce Hutchison wrote:

> A day with such a man in the woods must be an education. Even with the abbreviated compass of a book written rather like a casual yarn around the evening campfire, he manages to mix an extraordinary amount of information with a picture of the wilderness whole. For to him it is a whole thing, an organic body of which all life, from the lichen to the man, is interdependent, logical, and in timeless rhythm.

Hutchison established the tone for reviews in many other publications, both large and small. Renowned naturalist Roger Tory Peterson told readers of the *New York Herald Tribune Book Review* that *The Singing Wilderness* "is unequivocally the best series of essays on the northwoods country I have ever read." Nationally known outdoor writer Gordon MacQuarrie told *Milwaukee Journal* readers that Olson's work was an "inspiring book . . . of Leopold quality." The *Christian Science Monitor* called the book "as pleasing to the eye and ear as a whitethroat in a full burst of song." The *Chicago Sunday Tribune* said that while readers may not be able to regularly visit wild places, they "can hear the song of the wilderness in the overtones of such a book as this."[34]

One piece of good news followed another. On May 13, 1956, *The*

Singing Wilderness made the *New York Times* best-seller list, weighing in at sixteenth place. On May 21, Marie Rodell wrote that nearly forty-four hundred copies of the book had sold and that Knopf had ordered a second printing. ("All in all, not too bad," Knopf wrote dryly to Rodell on May 22.)[35] In June *The Singing Wilderness* made the *Philadelphia Inquirer*'s best-seller list. In July the Lutheran Book Club bought eighteen hundred copies to sell to its members. By year's end Olson's book had sold more than six thousand copies, and the American Library Association, saying that *The Singing Wilderness* made "a signal contribution to the literary world," included it in the group's annual list of notable books.[36]

Congratulatory letters poured in to Ely from friends and family. Fellow Voyageur Eric Morse wrote, "Sig, long have I heard you discourse around the campfire, and spout wisdom from the stern of a canoe—but you have kept your light under that shot-up hat of yours. You are a poet, man!" Wilderness Society director Olaus Murie wrote that he and his wife read a chapter aloud each night and discussed it. "Sig, it is marvelous," he said. Benton MacKaye, one of the Wilderness Society's founders, wrote that "never via talk or reading have I heard or seen any such insight on natural harmony as you display." Another of the group's founders, Harvey Broome, joked that Sigurd wrote so well that people might see his book as a substitute for the outdoors. *The Singing Wilderness*, in fact, cemented the Wilderness Society's decision to add Olson to its governing council in 1956. "He has the words and feelings of a poet and deep understanding," said council member George Marshall on April 13. "I am more enthusiastic about him than ever." Sigurd officially joined the council during its annual meeting in August.[37]

After laboring so long under the shadow of his older brother, the highly acclaimed dean of Northwestern University's journalism school, Sigurd must have been especially pleased by the letter Kenneth wrote on April 9, 1956: "Brother, I never appreciated how you can write. This is pure prose poetry—the pictures you paint with words. Someday English classes are going to study this as literature. It's better than Thoreau ever did. . . . Brother, am I proud to even know you!" (The competition between them had not quite ended, however. A few years later, after Sigurd had joined Kenneth in *Who's Who in America*, written several more books, and received a number of awards, Kenneth would say, "Well, Sigurd, I guess you're the most famous of us.")[38]

But what must have delighted Olson even more than the letters from friends and family were those that came from people he had never met. "At last," wrote a North Dakota man, "I now have found a modern pen which evokes moods and thoughts that far transcend our mundane day-to-day existence." A woman whose letter had no return address said that whenever she read bits of The Singing Wilderness "all of life seems to come into the proper focus again." Kathy Beaumont wrote from California that she and her husband, Hugh—an actor who played Ward Cleaver in the popular television series Leave It to Beaver—placed Sigurd's book "with a few special bedside volumes."[39]

Many readers described their personal memories of places where they had heard "the singing wilderness," and many took up the theme voiced by a Maryland man who had been reading the book to his bedridden wife: "You have found expression for all the urges that have driven us, all our lives, to take up our packs and search out the far places—feelings beyond our power of expression that have welled up in us as we have camped many places in the wilderness." One of Sigurd's favorites came from a Connecticut book publisher, John Howland Snow, who said he read part of the book "to the accompaniment of the Beethoven Ninth" and added, "Thank you for adding a depth to my horizon, and some comprehension of things which, unlived, otherwise might have remained unknown. Thank you for your enrichment of our symphonic literature."[40]

The letters were the beginning of a steady stream that continued for the rest of Sigurd's life. While most were from people in the Midwest, they came from all over; an unscientific sample of roughly a hundred written between 1956 and 1961 originated in nearly two dozen states and three Canadian provinces. Sometimes they came from eccentrics, such as the man who said he spoke to spirits and wanted Sigurd to endorse his booklet, "A Personal Testimony to Life after Death." Some of them must have brought a smile to his face for other reasons, as when a young woman wrote as a matchmaker for her widowed mother. (Women, in fact, wrote nearly 40 percent of the letters in the sample.) Some letters came from prospective writers and artists and conservationists, seeking advice. Some came from people who wanted to know where they should go on their canoe trips, or what they should take. Most, however, simply expressed admiration and gratitude for Olson's writing. He, in turn, made it a practice to answer every letter that came his way; if he was home when one arrived, he nearly always responded within a few days.[41]

Olson had developed his land aesthetic independent of Aldo Leopold's version in *A Sand County Almanac*. He had written drafts of many of the essays in *The Singing Wilderness* a full decade or more before he saw Leopold's book, and some of the key ideas were present in Olson articles published in the 1930s and 1940s. Olson's land aesthetic also differed from Leopold's in some important respects. But Olson's writing style was more accessible to a wider audience, and *The Singing Wilderness* sold at roughly twice the rate of *A Sand County Almanac* until the mid-1960s. In 1966 Oxford University Press reached an agreement with Ballantine Books to issue an inexpensive paperback edition of *A Sand County Almanac* (including several essays from another Leopold book, *Round River*), and sales skyrocketed as the new, more affordable edition made its way into university classrooms and caught the wave of the nation's burgeoning interest in the environment. *The Singing Wilderness* played an important role in sowing the cultural field that *A Sand County Almanac* later reaped, for without a sense of beauty, joy, connectedness, and wonder, there is little motivation to pay heed to, much less live, a land ethic. And the book remained Olson's most popular, with hardcover sales approaching seventy thousand by its fortieth anniversary in 1996. Excerpts were printed in a variety of publications in several languages, including Arabic and Russian, and portions of the book were read on radio and television programs.[42]

On a personal level, the publication and success of *The Singing Wilderness* was an immensely satisfying culmination of a long and hard-fought dream. For thirty years Sigurd Olson had been obsessed with writing, had felt it was his ordained mission in life, that success was his destiny. The odds often had seemed insurmountable: the kind of writing he was best at and loved most editors said had no market, and the kind that editors said was marketable yielded scathing rejection letters when Sigurd attempted it. He had felt trapped in an unfulfilling career, stuck in a community full of people who could not relate to him intellectually, and had sealed off his deepest beliefs, thoughts, and fears from his own family. Succumbing to periods of despair, he had bewildered his wife and damaged his health. He could not explain these things. He had not *wanted* to make life hard for Elizabeth or for their children or for himself. His dream went beyond want; it was a fire burning within him, a consuming flame that had the potential to fulfill or destroy him. Somehow, despite the many rejections, despite the self-torture—despite the genuinely long odds of succeeding as a writer of essays—he had held fast to his dream, and had triumphed.

❖ Thirteen ❖

The Search for Balance

1956–1960

Sigurd Olson was president of the National Parks Association during three landmark events in conservation history. The first of them, the fight to save Dinosaur National Monument, came to a successful conclusion in April 1956, just as *The Singing Wilderness* was making it onto the shelves of the nation's bookstores. By then the other two events were just beginning to take shape. One was a massive infusion of funds into the National Park Service under a program called Mission 66. The other was the introduction of legislation to create a national wilderness preservation system. Both campaigns were controversial. Between 1956 and 1958 Olson often found himself caught in the crossfire, and the essays he wrote reflected a search for a proper balance in the relationship between civilization and wilderness.

The goal of Mission 66 was to restore the damage done to the park system by years of fiscal neglect, improving access, facilities, and staffing so that by 1966, the fiftieth anniversary of the National Park Service, the system would be equipped to accommodate a projected eighty million visitors. Park Service director Conrad Wirth convinced President Eisenhower to support the program in February 1955, a month after *Reader's Digest* published an exposé called "The Shocking Truth about Our National Parks." The author warned those planning to visit a national park that their trip was "likely to be fraught with discomfort, disappointment, even danger."[1]

The article said little that had not been published in other magazines over the previous six years, but *Reader's Digest* reached a massive audience. Eisenhower was beginning to be concerned about the negative publicity he was receiving on conservation issues. Wirth's proposal, which called for large-scale spending on the parks beginning in 1956, a presidential election year, certainly was timely. And, by and large, Eisenhower probably agreed with it in principle. He gave it his immediate, unqualified support, and Congress soon authorized the program.

Sigurd Olson had known Conrad Wirth, whose father was a city park planner in Minneapolis, since at least 1940. When Wirth became Park Service director in 1951 Olson was vice president of the National Parks Association, and the two quickly formed a good working relationship. At the end of the 1970s, Wirth called Olson one of the top three professional conservationists of the postwar era and recalled:

> When I became director . . . he was the one person that did more than anybody else in aiding me to formulate policy and review our conservation and public use programs. This trusting and informal relationship had more effect on the expanding nationwide parks and open space program during the last forty years than can be measured by any system that I know of.[2]

Olson was an early supporter of Mission 66. "I am all for it and think a great deal of good may come from it," he wrote on January 15, 1956. Nevertheless, he had concerns. In the same letter, written to his friend Max Gilstrap, central news bureau chief of the *Christian Science Monitor*, Olson listed some of them.

"I have been concerned for some time at the trend toward increasing commercialization of the parks," he wrote, "the idea of making them summer or winter resorts by bringing in entertainment features that violate the basic premise of the whole national park concept." He singled out ski facilities in Mount Rainier and Rocky Mountain National Parks as setting bad precedents, and he said that local residents and the concession industry had achieved too much clout. "The concessions have held the whip hand over the Park Service for so long that the present administration as well as those in the past have been unable to do much about it," he said. Olson told Gilstrap that "a clear and dynamic statement of policy" from the Park Service was needed to keep development under control. Olson thought Conrad Wirth's plans were good but could be improved:

> I am encouraged to know that Connie Wirth favors the construction of additional facilities outside the park boundaries. That is a

move in the right direction, but I feel that he has not gone far enough, that instead of more construction in the parks under the new rehabilitation program, a definite start should be made now to move facilities outside the boundaries.

A number of conservationists were skeptical of Mission 66 from the very beginning. They believed that Eisenhower's support for it was insincere and that large areas of wild land would be destroyed by development. One of the most hostile was Devereux Butcher, editor of the National Parks Association bimonthly magazine. He saw Mission 66 as a wholesale assault on national park standards. "Sig, this whole thing is bigger than you or me . . . or any group of us," he wrote on April 9, 1956, "and it is bigger than the Association itself. Can we, dare we, let this situation continue?" He thought the NPA should replace executive secretary Fred Packard, whom he accused of "weak thinking," with someone "who has resigned from the [Park] Service in disgust at allowing policy to slip."

Olson, who had come to the NPA at Butcher's prodding, had learned early on that, as he put it, "Dev is so completely immersed in his ideals for the national parks, he is a crusader and absolutely intolerant of anyone who does not think exactly as he." Butcher at one point told Olson that he did not trust NPA vice president Charley Woodbury, and by the time Mission 66 was proposed in 1955, Sigurd wrote to a friend that "for that matter Dev I believe suspects me. . . . He hates Connie [Wirth] and others in the NPS who have deviated from the Standards."[3]

Olson could tolerate Butcher's excesses because Butcher was a tireless worker who did much for the NPA; for a while Olson could even joke about it, as in a note to Packard on October 5, 1955: "Dear Dev if he would only learn to smile and not take himself and the whole world so damned seriously." But by early 1956, as Butcher became even more strident, Sigurd sometimes grew testy. On January 10, 1956, after receiving another letter from Butcher complaining about Packard, Olson pointed out that Butcher had groomed Packard for the position and had voted for him. "If you had your doubts then, you should have spoken out as forcibly as you are now doing," he said. Sigurd even took umbrage at a comment by Butcher that teased Olson for catching the flu:

As far as your statement that with our wonderful outdoor life neither of us should ever get laid up—my friend if you had hit the
schedule I did for the last three weeks I was east, you would understand. You seem to forget that I am doing about four jobs of which
NPA is only one, that when I am gone I get along on about three to
four hours sleep a nite. The last trip was worse than that.

Olaus Murie, director of the Wilderness Society, also was becoming a strong critic of national park management. On October 30,
1956, after months of watching Mission 66 develop from the vantage
point of his home in Moose, Wyoming, he wrote a confidential letter
to Olson and Howard Zahniser. The letter was so long and negative
he decided not to send it. The next day he tried again:

> There is a decided cleavage in the Service over the question of qual-
> ity—I know you know this—but the opinion of those humble de-
> voted people, employees of the Service, do not reach to the surface
> of high officialdom. Several employees have told me that the fa-
> mous Mission 66 is really an appropriation drive, to spend a lot of
> money; to enhance the status of a bureau.
>
> Well, I need say no more on that, except that in view of what I see
> and learn in the west, I am faced with an ethical dilemma. Thou-
> sands of people, who do not have the opportunity to have the facts,
> depend on what some of us say. Shall I give lip service to principle,
> praise everybody and everything, and say "everything is fine, let's go
> right along?" Or shall I tell the truth.

Murie's answer was to "tell the truth" in a series of strongly worded
letters to Wirth; the letters at times exasperated the Park Service director, but not as much as the public attacks by Devereux Butcher in
the pages of *National Parks Magazine*. The attacks reached their peak
in his January 1957 article "Sunshine or Blizzard," which railed against
a new lodge at Jackson Hole National Monument in Wyoming. The
article's bitterness was summed up in the caption to a photograph of
the lodge: "Would this Alcatraz win first prize as the ugliest building
in the park system?"

Olson had read the article ahead of time and thought Butcher was
entitled to write critically of the building, but Sigurd apparently had
not seen the photo captions before publication. On January 30, 1957,
he wrote to Butcher and said the caption "makes the NPA lose dig-

nity and become vindictive and abusive. The building is there and nothing can be done about it. It would have been enough to publish the photos without the slurring captions."

Wirth was livid and sent Olson samples from letters he had received that condemned the article. One was from an NPA member who said, "I sort of begrudge the $10.00 a year that it costs me because it seems to be run by little men who would force their opinion on people in public places who have to actually run things instead of dreaming about how they would run them." A writer who took issue with Butcher's use of the word *sanctuaries* said, "That's an awful word which *sacrosanct* people fall back on whenever they find themselves floundering." A third writer said that "it is pure presumptuousness that leads Butcher to do it and I think that has led him into a frame of mind where he finds it necessary to make himself obnoxious in a number of places."[4]

Butcher, meanwhile, was unrepentant.

> Let me tell you, Sig, as I have a number of times, the parks are in the most serious plight they ever have been in in all time. We are going to have to take a much more vigorous stand to save them—that is, if we *intend* to save them. We will have to decide which is more important, personalities, whom we never attack anyway, or the parks and monuments. Today, the parks are being sold out to chambers of commerce, concessioners and others like the automobile clubs. . . . You will never learn all these things by talking to Connie. You need to meet some of the wonderful dedicated men in the field, and not only superintendents, but rangers and naturalists.

Butcher claimed that former Park Service director Horace Albright, who was part of the agency hierarchy from its inception in 1916 to his retirement in 1933, was telling Wirth what to do. Albright had always emphasized mass recreation over preservation and was a prominent supporter of Mission 66. He also was an NPA trustee who, as Butcher knew, was on good terms with Olson. "He is one of the most dangerous people with whom we must cope," wrote Butcher. "I believe he is the real director of the Service today, and the ski resorts and perhaps a lot of other things are going on with his approval. I know this to be true. Watch out for Albright!"[5]

In effect, Butcher's letter attempted to force Olson to choose sides.

"Always remember, Sig," he wrote, "that whenever the Association loses confidence in me, and would prefer another person to edit the magazine, you may make the change without notice beforehand to me. Just tell me you no longer need my service, and I'll gladly stop."

Hoping to clear the air and maintain an effective relationship with the Park Service, Olson arranged a February 18 luncheon in Washington between top NPA and Park Service officials. He began the meeting by saying that the NPA supported Mission 66, but he and others were disturbed by trends in park management. He cited a number of them—ski lifts and unneeded roads and obtrusive buildings, for example—and said that the service needed to make sure that any new facilities did not unnecessarily intrude upon the wilderness character of the parks.[6]

Wirth responded to each issue that was raised. He did not deny that his agency had made some mistakes, but maintained that some mistakes were inevitable in a program with the scope of Mission 66. (The National Park Service ultimately spent a billion dollars under the program.) He disagreed with the NPA's opposition to all ski lifts but said he thought that was the only significant difference of opinion. He agreed that facilities in Yosemite Valley should be removed from the park and hoped to do the same in other areas. What bothered him was that some of the developments the NPA was attacking in its magazine were based on historical circumstances that preceded Mission 66, and others were merely proposals that had been abandoned. He also was upset that the magazine did not cite the instances in which he had stopped the kind of developments the magazine attacked. He had, for example, opposed the construction of a road into Everglades National Park, was trying to remove overnight lodging facilities from Mesa Verde National Park, and had stopped construction of a poorly planned road in Grand Canyon National Park. In short, he hoped the NPA would publicize the positive aspects of park management as well as the negative.

Olson fully agreed on that point. He had said much the same thing himself a number of times over the years. On January 26, 1953, for example, he told William Wharton that "the swiftest way to nullify our effectiveness is to become known as a group of fanatical gadflies." And on January 30, 1955, he wrote to Butcher, "I have found that only when it is possible to sit down with individuals and talk things out can progress be made over a long period of time. There do come times when diplomacy must be thrown out the window, but only when all else has failed. When a shooting war starts then it is anyone's guess as to the outcome."

Both Olson and Wirth thought the meeting helped restore trust between the Park Service and the NPA. Olson soon organized regular meetings between Park Service officials and leaders of the other major conservation groups. "Really, Sig, I believe that we accomplished a lot at the luncheon and I am grateful to you and your associates for making it possible," Wirth wrote on February 27. "We must work closer together and we must understand each other's problems."

Two weeks after the luncheon, on March 7, Olson met with a number of NPA trustees and with Butcher, who had been out of town during the meeting with Wirth. The meeting's purpose, Olson wrote a day earlier, was "to see if we can arrive at a program, as far as the Magazine is concerned, that will be a step in the right direction." For Butcher, it was the final straw. Two months later he resigned from his position as editor and wrote to Olaus Murie, "The NPA is now little more than a rubber stamp for the Service. Our leadership, at a meeting held during my absence from town a couple of months ago or so, sold the NPA down the river. . . . The Association is today at the crossroads, and the parks are on the skids."[7]

❖

Olson, meanwhile, was being drawn into another battle. Congressional protection of wilderness had long been discussed by conservationists, many of whom believed that federal land management agencies had neither the will nor the ability to stand up to the logging, mining, and recreation industries. But the time did not seem ripe to introduce a bill until 1956, when the successful Dinosaur National Monument campaign gave conservationists new strength and a sense of broad public support. Howard Zahniser, executive secretary of the Wilderness Society, drafted a bill and enlisted comments from leading conservationists. He also began seeking congressional sponsors, including Minnesota Senator Hubert Humphrey. At the end of March 1956, Humphrey asked Olson for his opinion of the bill. On April 3, Olson advised the senator to sponsor it:

I have worked closely with Howard Zahniser and others for some time on this measure and feel that in view of the mounting pressures of population, commercialization, and industrial expansion, that the only way to assure future generations that there will be any wilderness left for them to enjoy is to give such areas congressional sanction now. . . . I feel strongly that this is the last chance to preserve the wilderness on this continent, for we are on the verge of an era where the pressures to destroy or change it will become greater than anything we have ever experienced.

Humphrey had joined the Senate in 1949, during the final stages of the conservation campaign to establish the airspace reservation over Superior National Forest's roadless areas. Olson first met him at the end of April that year and thought right away that the former Minneapolis mayor would be quite helpful to Quetico-Superior proponents. "Later on we can use him to good advantage," Olson wrote to Charles Kelly on May 2, 1949. "He is a climber and wants *national publicity* and fast." During the following months Olson began to establish a working relationship with Humphrey that progressed over the years from cordial to friendly, even warm. Olson's commitment to the wilderness bill was one of the factors that led Humphrey to introduce it in the Senate during the spring of 1956.

Not all conservationists supported the bill. Devereux Butcher and Olaus Murie, for example, feared disaster for the national park system. They worried that if the Park Service were forced to divide the parks into wilderness and nonwilderness zones, development-minded directors (surely Conrad Wirth and Mission 66 weighed in their thinking) would have a free hand in the nonwilderness zones. No sooner had Olson written to Humphrey than he began receiving letters from conservationists urging him to backtrack.[8]

One of these letters came from Arthur Carhart, a former Forest Service landscape architect who was one of the first to convince his agency to preserve remnants of the national forests for wilderness recreation. In 1919 he persuaded the Forest Service to keep cabins and roads away from the shoreline of Trapper's Lake in Colorado, and in 1922 he wrote a management plan for Superior National Forest that emphasized canoe-based recreation. The Superior plan was largely ignored, however; it called for a motorboat trunk line connecting a string of rustic hotels along the international border and for a series of chalets along two canoe routes, neither of which the agency wished to do.[9] Carhart left the Forest Service at the end of 1922 but remained active in wilderness issues and occasionally corresponded with Olson. On May 9, 1956, he told Olson that the wilderness bill was sure to backfire in the West, giving ranchers and other resource users even more power. He also thought that forest managers should have more, not less, latitude:

> On my part, I feel strongly that no more mandatory uses should be fixed in the national forests than timber production and watershed protection as they now exist. All others should remain permissive and administratively flexible. I hope you may keep this movement from precipitating the trouble I see may flare if it does result in a bill in Congress.

Frank Hubachek also was concerned about the bill, not so much for its broad goals and provisions, but for the political ramifications relating to the Quetico-Superior program. His most immediate concern was the fate of an appropriation bill before Congress that would give the Forest Service two million dollars to buy out private inholdings in the roadless areas. On April 6 he told Olson that, at the very least, the wilderness bill should be delayed until after the Superior National Forest appropriation bill passed.

Olson contacted Zahniser and arranged a postponement of the wilderness bill. On June 7, after Congress had authorized the two million dollars for Superior National Forest, Humphrey introduced the wilderness bill in the Senate; in July, Representative John Saylor of Pennsylvania introduced it in the House.

The first legislative hearings were not held until 1957, and it was then that Olson's real troubles began. On April 22, two months before the hearings began in Washington, Hubachek told Olson and Charles Kelly he still thought the bill was a bad idea that would backfire, and he wanted the President's Quetico-Superior Committee to keep out of the debate. "Likewise," he added, "I urge that all of us who are personally identified with the Q-S program as such, stay out of the lists. I hope we can let other knights in shining armor carry on this particular joust. I know this will hurt and possibly aggravate Sig but that's the way I feel just the same."

Sigurd did not want to be put in the position of choosing between the wilderness bill and his professional relationship with the Quetico-Superior program, and he responded to Hubachek on April 27, trying to make clear his predicament: "As far as my personal role is concerned, being wilderness ecologist of the [Izaak Walton] League, a member of the Wilderness Society Council, and having identified myself with the cause of wilderness preservation generally, I cannot refuse to lend my support as I have done in the past."

Hubachek appreciated Olson's difficult balancing act and moderated his stand on May 6, saying:

> When your position must be expressed, you have no alternative but to favor the measure and I do not counsel or request that you remain in hiding on matters of this kind. But I do very strongly counsel (almost request) that you stay out of the fight just as much as you possibly can and still preserve your conscientious convictions and your technical standing. . . . Please, Sig, try to withhold your punches and stay as far out of this fight as you can until we have made much more progress on the Q-S program.

But Olson soon was drawn right into the middle of the fight, with no choice but to respond. The fight involved his hometown neighbors, and they were not withholding *their* punches.

Word of the wilderness bill had only recently reached Ely. Many people were upset that their own Senator Humphrey would sponsor such a bill without first consulting or even informing them. It was a particularly bad time for such a surprise; the Chandler South Mine had announced that it was closing, leaving this mining city with two working mines where once half a dozen had thrived. Residents were worried that the wilderness bill would weaken their economy even more, by striking at their healthiest industry, tourism. But no community leaders had seen the bill or knew its details.

The undercurrent of worry exploded into anger and wild charges at a banquet in Ely on July 10. A local lawyer told the group that he had written to Humphrey asking for information about the bill but had received no response. A banker then stood to say he had written to Representative John Blatnik and to the state's other senator, Edward Thye, but had received only evasive replies. Soon the banquet hall was buzzing with rumors that the bill would condemn local resorts, ban outboard motors, and even expand the roadless areas to include lakes and woods and homes right on the edge of town. The rumors spread quickly, and the weekly *Ely Miner* voiced outrage in its next issue. Publisher Fred Childers called Humphrey a "Brutus or Judas" and asked residents to write the senator in protest. "Again we wonder if the senator will listen to the voice of his constituents," Childers wrote, "or is he subject to pressure groups operating under the cloak of conservation." Childers said Humphrey needed to visit Ely as soon as the current session of Congress was over and hear the concerns of those who lived and worked next to the wilderness.[10]

Humphrey was not going to let the publisher get the upper hand. "This fellow Childers is a reactionary editor in Ely," he wrote to one of his staff. "He hates my guts, and he has been after me for years. He feels he has a good issue now, so I want to take him on—head on—so let's give it to him." Humphrey also refused to visit the area. "I am not going to come to Ely when the session is over in order to be abused," he wrote on July 20. "There are a handful of people in that city that seem to feel that I am their mortal enemy.... I repeat, there are a few resort owners who have been determined and stubborn and have refused to cooperate with the will of the Congress and the Government. I cannot compromise with them."[11]

Childers kept up the attacks, denouncing the wilderness bill in front-page editorials. He charged that the bill would turn Ely into a "ghost town" and said, "The curtailment of our three basic industries—mining, lumbering and tourist business—without hope of replacement leaves no other alternative.... Who wants to take the risk of investment with the hard work it entails in a town that offers NO POTENTIAL for a reasonable return?"[12]

It was a difficult time for the Olsons. People stopped talking and turned away when Sigurd or Elizabeth entered a gathering. Ely Chamber of Commerce secretary Stan Pechaver expressed the breach in a letter to Humphrey: "Sig Olson (of Ely, we're sorry to say), is not a member of any organization active in local affairs.... He does not speak for any of our organizations." Even the Olsons' First Presbyterian Church turned a cold shoulder. The minister supported Sigurd and asked Elizabeth if he could post a quote from Olson's writings, but he said the congregation's governing board would not let Olson's name be attached to the quote. Elizabeth refused to accept the restriction. "Anything that happens up here I get blamed for," Sigurd wrote to a friend.[13]

Robert Olson, looking back on the opposition that his parents faced in Ely, said, "I don't know how they stood it." Yvonne agreed, adding, "Dad took it professionally—but Mom took it all personally. Mom would get personally angry at individuals."

Elizabeth also came to her husband's defense, without letting him know. On August 3, 1957, while she was staying at her childhood home in Seeley, Wisconsin, she sent Zahniser clippings from the *Miner* to show "how rough the going is." She criticized Zahniser for not including Ely residents in the discussions leading to the bill (in her defensive frame of mind it apparently did not occur to her that her husband, even more than Zahniser, should have thought of this) and said hearings needed to be held in the area, not just in Washington, D.C. "Sig is in the soup now," she said.[14]

When Elizabeth wrote to Zahniser, Sigurd also was away from home, the farthest north he had ever been. He and the Voyageurs spent July 20 to August 9 paddling canoes for four hundred miles along northern Saskatchewan, following a route from Reindeer Lake to Lake Athabasca explored by David Thompson in 1796. While they were camped on Reindeer Lake early in the trip, Olson joked in his notebook about undertaking such a rugged expedition at the age of fifty-eight. "I have lived backward. I should have done this or so I thought in my youth and now at last I am doing it and am satisfied." But he also thought it might be his last expedition and a couple of times wrote that his mind often was elsewhere, thinking of the wilderness bill and his writing, among other things. And of his wife. "I think of Elizabeth . . . and our remaining years together and how much I love her and how much she means to me. All—everything is E."[15]

While the Olsons were gone, another event escalated the tension in Ely. For several years residents had been excited about the possible development of a new mine by International Nickel Company. Test drilling along the Kawishiwi River near town had shown a potentially large deposit of low-grade copper and nickel sulfides, and the company had applied for a hundred-year mining lease on eight thousand acres of land at the edge of the wilderness. On August 8 the *Miner* reported that the U.S. Department of the Interior refused to approve the lease. Childers blamed the decision on the wilderness bill and on conservationist pressure to stall development until passage of the wilderness bill outlawed it.

In reality, the decision had nothing to do with the wilderness bill. It did, however, have a lot to do with Sigurd Olson and his relationship with a new secretary of the interior. Fred Seaton had replaced Douglas McKay in the election year of 1956, as the Eisenhower administration scrambled to improve the public's perception of its resource management policies. Seaton, owner of a chain of newspapers in the Midwest, had been serving as White House liaison to the Interior Department and had developed a reputation for tact and moderation. "It does us no good whatever at the polls to cry 'Socialism' every time a measure is offered to combat or correct an evil," he said. As interior secretary he performed admirably at balancing competing interests, and the news media reported on the "new look" in the department, saying Seaton's leadership meant "goodbye giveaway."[16]

Olson, who had had little contact with McKay, met with Seaton several times during the secretary's first few months in office. Sigurd reported that Seaton was a "fine chap" who "will not repeat the mistakes of McKay."[17] Over the next couple of years the two became friends, and Olson assumed an important role as a consultant to the Interior Department and to the National Park Service. His first official ties to the department were established in May 1957; Seaton created an advisory committee on fish and wildlife and appointed Olson one of its seven members.[18]

When Olson asked Seaton to deny a mining permit to International Nickel, explaining the dangers to the canoe country wilderness should mining occur, the request carried a lot of weight. Olson undoubtedly played the most important role in bringing the issue to Seaton's attention and in convincing Seaton that mining should not be allowed along the Kawishiwi River. At the same time, the ultimate decision was relatively easy for Seaton. As he explained to Olson after investigating the matter, International Nickel was in no hurry to develop the deposit; the company had discovered more important reserves in Canada and Cuba, and had a huge stockpile of nickel. Seaton said the company was content, however, to let northeastern Minnesotans believe that Hubert Humphrey, the wilderness bill, and conservationists such as Olson were responsible for the denial.[19]

When Sigurd arrived back in Ely from his expedition with the Voyageurs, the story about the permit denial had just been published and a new round of acrimony had begun. "Welcome back from the wilds of Canada, my friend," Humphrey wrote. "I am sure that the temperature around Ely has been somewhat warmer than you found in the Canadian wilds!" The senator added a handwritten postscript: "I need your help!"[20]

Olson told Humphrey on August 14 that fighting "the hysterical outcries" would not be easy. "The statement that people could lose their homes in Ely should the bill go through is actually believed by many people," he wrote. "It will take time to repair the damage that has been done. Eventually the truth will prevail."

The task was made even more difficult on September 5, when the *Miner* published an article about the wilderness bill that accused Olson of "openly and vigorously advocating the prohibition of the use of outboard motors" and claimed that he had "made the boast and prediction that he will effectuate such a ban to follow the air-plane ban effectuated by Presidential Order."

The *Miner* had distorted the truth. On August 20 Olson had told members of the Lutheran Men's Club, "I feel personally that it would not be too much to consider setting aside some of the interior lakes for canoe use only, allowing the use as now of motors on the larger waters adjacent to the resort areas."[21] But he made a point of telling the group that the wilderness bill specifically allowed motorboat use to continue in the canoe country. What he told the Ely group also was consistent with what he had told Howard Zahniser three years earlier. "The Quetico-Superior Committee," Olson wrote on May 28, 1954, "has never taken a stand against outboard motors because we have decided to wait and see what public use is made of them. You can only fight one battle at a time. It may be that public opinion will demand their elimination if it gets too bad. Time will tell."

Olson responded to the *Miner's* charges on September 10, calling the accusation that he was working to eliminate outboard motors "an absolute falsehood." "The bill states specifically," he continued, "that present regulations and established uses will not be changed in this area. In its application to this region the Superior National Forest is specifically exempted. Canoeists and resort people may use outboards as they always have."[22]

Olson's comments clearly were intended to apply to the wilderness bill before Congress, not as a promise that Congress would never in the future consider different legislation that might curtail outboard motors in the canoe country. It is a measure of the hostility Olson's name generated in Ely that this letter would still be cited nearly forty years later (and more than a decade after his death) as evidence that he had lied. By the 1990s, much of the outboard motor use *had* been prohibited, but the changes were the result of an act of Congress passed in 1978, twenty-one years after Olson wrote his letter to the *Miner*. By that time public opinion, as Olson had written to Zahniser in 1954, demanded the change.

At the time Olson wrote his letter to the *Miner*, he also was editing the latest draft of the wilderness bill, making comments in red pencil. Others worked on the same manuscript: David Brower made suggestions on the draft in green pencil, and Zahniser used a lead pencil to make minor editorial changes. Zahniser also wrote on the draft in blue ink, to direct the attention of Olson and of George Marshall to ideas he wanted them to consider.

Olson said the bill's major problem was its legalistic prose. "As it reads even a crack corporation lawyer cannot understand it," he told Zahniser on September 17. This made it possible for the already skeptical Ely residents to misinterpret the bill in a variety of ways. Olson wanted Zahniser to make it crystal clear that: "1. Outboard motors will not be banned; 2. Other uses will be continued; 3. The government will not seize private properties on well-developed lakes outside the roadless areas and in such towns as Ely. It sounds ridiculous but this is being said." Sigurd also said Zahniser should eliminate the bill's creation of a national wilderness preservation council, which many people feared would give conservationists control over federal management decisions relating to wilderness.

Zahniser was not yet willing to give up the council; a few years later, when it became clear that its elimination was necessary for the bill to make it through Congress, he would change his mind. He did, however, write a special provision for the Superior Roadless Areas. It went through several revisions, with key input from Olson, Charles Kelly, and Humphrey, but the purpose was to assure northeastern Minnesotans that the canoe country would be managed according to regulations established by the secretary of agriculture, "in accordance," as the final draft stated, "with the general purpose of maintaining, without unnecessary restrictions on other uses, including that of timber, the primitive character of the area, particularly in the vicinity of lakes, streams, and portages." At Humphrey's insistence, the following sentence was added: "*Provided*, That nothing in this Act shall preclude the continuance within the area of any already established use of motorboats."

From Olson's point of view, the new language was not a compromise, but merely an explicit statement of the bill's original intent. Even so, it was an immense help to him as he met with the heads of Ely organizations on September 26, 1957. Olson explained the bill, passed a draft of it around the room, and asked community leaders to send suggestions to Humphrey. Later, he felt that the air had been cleared. "I may be wrong in my hunch," he wrote to Zahniser the next day, "but I feel today that we are over the hump." Still, he realized that much of the furor could have been avoided if the proper groundwork had been laid:

> Much has been made of the fact that the Ely people were not kept informed and that is a fault of mine and ours generally. In the future let's try to remedy this not only in this area but in others. . . . Local groups like to feel they are part of the big picture, would like to have a hand in the development of ideas, resent bitterly coming in the back door. Time and again mention was made of the need of local opinion to influence national policies that might affect them. Hard to do I know, but let's give it serious thought.

Hubert Humphrey, who received a copy of Olson's letter to Zahniser, wrote back on October 2. "You are doing a wonderful job of getting across the true provisions of this bill to the people of the Ely area," he said. Humphrey also agreed with Olson's diagnosis of their mistakes: "You are a hundred percent correct in saying that much of our trouble is a direct result from our lack of ground work in the local area. Keep up the great work Sig, and let me know if there is anything I should be doing."

❖

A major source of stress relief for Olson during this period of conflict over national park management and the wilderness bill was a piece of land he had purchased a few miles west of Ely. For decades he had dreamed of owning a small cabin, and by the end of 1955 he had saved up just enough money to do something about it. When he heard that the owner of a large amount of undeveloped lakeshore property surrounding Sha Wa Nok Beach on the south arm of Burntside Lake had divided it into lots for sale, Sigurd bought six of them, totaling twenty-six acres. He and Elizabeth came into possession of a small but pleasant strip of beach, a cove bordered with alder and willow, upland stands of second-growth birch and pine, and huge, lichen-covered boulders left behind when the glaciers melted at the end of the last ice age ten thousand years ago. Most important, there was a glaciated, westward-facing greenstone point, fringed with weathered pines and partly covered with a patch of bearberry and juniper. From there he could see the wide-open spaces of Burntside Lake and some of its many islands, could feel the wind on his face, could watch sunsets and northern lights, and could hear gulls and loons and the wind in the trees.[23]

Sigurd did not want to build a new cabin, nor did he want anything fancy. He did not even want running water or electricity; after all, he had all of those comforts at his home less than ten miles away. He wanted a one-room, unpainted, hewn-log cabin built by Finnish or Scandinavian settlers decades earlier, so he spent some of his spare time in 1956 driving the back roads of the north woods looking for one. In October he finally found just the right structure about seven miles south of Ely, at a farm that had been condemned to make way for Ely's airport.

That was not the last of the work; after getting the cabin situated at the base of the point on a new stone and masonry foundation, windows needed to be cut into the north and south walls and a fireplace built along the short wall to the east. A picnic table and benches and beds needed to be built, and a bookshelf high on each wall. All of this was done in 1957, as Sigurd was making peace with the Park Service and working on the wilderness bill. Urho Salminen, a retired game warden who had helped Sigurd gather data in 1930 for his master's thesis on the wolf, helped with the general construction and foundation. Otto Tjader, whose daughter Esther was married to Sigurd Jr., built the table and beds and benches. A skilled craftsman and a perfectionist, Tjader did not approve of the rough look Olson wanted for the furniture. He said he would build the pieces as Sigurd asked, but told him not to tell anyone that he had made them.

The construction of the fireplace led to a story that Sigurd loved to tell long afterward. The fireplace was built by another local craftsman, John Brown, out of rocks that Sigurd had gathered on the property and piled near the cabin. When Brown was nearly done with the chimney, most of the rocks had been used up, and he needed to plug a hole. He sent his apprentice to the pile to look for just the right rock. The young man searched and searched, but eventually gave up and said he could not find one. Brown was an excellent stonemason but very particular and something of a crank. Stomping down the ladder, he gave the apprentice a withering look and shouted, "You're a damn fool! There's *always* a rock that fits!" He stormed down to the pile, looked it over briefly, found the stone he wanted, returned to the chimney, and plopped it into the spot. "See!" he shouted.

The point became Sigurd's getaway from the stress of his multifaceted career as an author and conservationist, with its associated chaotic travel and work schedule. "I think he spent a lot of therapeutic time there," said his son Sigurd Jr. At the point, he could completely unwind and regain a sense of balance. And seldom was a sense of balance needed more than in 1956 and 1957, as Sigurd was buffeted by charges that, on the one hand, he was caving in to a development-minded National Park Service, and, on the other hand, that he was a wilderness fanatic who cared nothing about the livelihood of his neighbors.

Balance weighed heavy on his mind during these two years as he wrote a new book of essays; it became an underlying theme of the book. And his beloved point provided the organizational structure. Each of the twenty-eight essays was tied somehow to the point, although they frequently digressed far afield from Burntside Lake (enough so that at least one critic would question the book's unity). Like the essays in *The Singing Wilderness*, the new ones were steeped in Olson's land aesthetic. But it is the search for balance—sometimes successful, sometimes not, frequently painful, occasionally self-contradicting—that distinguishes Olson's second book from *The Singing Wilderness* as well as from those he would write later.

In "The Cabin," for example, Olson discusses the care that went into choosing the best place on the property for the small, weathered cabin. He writes that he thought of putting it right on the point but decided that "nothing must ever change the point itself; it must remain a sanctuary forever, a place reserved for vistas and dreams and long thoughts."[24] Instead of placing the cabin where the view was best, he located it below the point in a less obtrusive spot behind an immense boulder.

In "The Breaking," Olson writes about the day he paid a man to bulldoze a rough driveway into the property from the main road. As the man began his work, Sigurd worried about the trees and the bushes and even the soil. Watching was painful:

> A huge boulder lay in the way, a rounded granite mass of many tons. Dropped by glacial ice, it had lain there for thousands of years. Its top was covered with gray and green lichens, and a squirrel had peeled a cone there. The cat moved its enormous bulk against it, and it rolled easily to one side and the white raw granite underneath lay exposed to the light for the first time since its deposition. If only it could be turned up again so the lichens would show, but the engine roared on and I followed helplessly behind. . . . More boulders were moved out of the trail, and the din of screeching steel, the crash of stone against stone deafened all sounds of the forest. More trees went down, and it ground them into the duff. This was my road too, and I was appalled at what I had done.[25]

The essay is ambivalent; Olson seems unsure if in this case he *has* found a proper balance. "Perhaps it was wrong to build the road," he writes. He seems anxious to justify it, saying that he had no choice because those who had bought the adjacent lots would build one if he did not. But such a rationale merely avoids the real and uncomfortable question: was it *right* to build a road there? In the context of the book as a whole, it is clear that Olson thought there was nothing inherently wrong about cutting a car-width trail on an undeveloped piece of property situated on a lake that already had resorts and cabins. But in this essay he gives a rationale that comes across as facile. (It also proved incorrect, for the neighbors eventually built their *own* roads.) Whether or not he was aware of his evasiveness is an open question. Either way, his justification illustrates what he describes in the latter part of his essay: just how rooted in the human psyche is the desire to alter the earth to suit human needs. He ends the essay by wondering if "all places of quiet and beauty [will] be altered by our unlimited ingenuity and enthusiasm for changing the face of the land."[26]

The heart of the book is best expressed in an essay called "The Whistle." He wrote it during the summer of 1957, after Devereux Butcher had resigned from what he saw as a traitorous National Parks Association, and during the height of controversy in Ely over the wilderness bill. It epitomizes the way in which Olson sought to balance wilderness and civilization.

The essay begins with Olson sitting on the end of the point shortly before sunset, absorbed in the stillness of the lake and trees, "one of those times when all seems in suspension and even the birds are hushed." But then, off in the distance and barely perceptible at first, he hears something, "a soft undercurrent of sound like the coming of the wind." He does not know what to make of it, but then he hears "the long-drawn wail of a steam locomotive" and realizes he has been listening to the train's progress over the distant tracks.[27]

The train whistles several more times, and Olson is disturbed:

> I had chosen the point fully aware of its closeness to civilization. All I had actually wanted there was a window through which I might glimpse at times the wilderness I had known. . . . I had accepted my road, motor boats and near-by cabins, and the realization that many times the silence would be shattered. I knew that, while the point was relatively unchanged and like ten thousand such points far to the north, it still was not the wilderness, did not have the element of isolation that only great distances could provide. Then why, I asked myself, was I troubled at hearing the sound of a train?[28]

Olson pauses to reflect on a group of Cree Indians he had met at a lonely campsite during the trip he had just completed with the Voyageurs in early August. He tries to imagine how *they* would react to the train whistle, and he concludes that they could not possibly interpret it in the same way as he did: "Only through my own personal contact with civilization had I learned to value the advantages of solitude. Without that experience they could not realize how man in an industrial age might need the very background of the life that was theirs."[29] That conclusion gave a new meaning to the sound of the train whistle,

> a deeper meaning than the train itself, one that encompassed man's inventive genius and all the realms of his exploring mind, a sound that was responsible for my own background and everything I knew and felt. And then the realization dawned on me that only because of its connotations and the contrasts that had been mine could I really appreciate the wilds and their importance to mankind. . . . Without that long lonesome wail and the culture that had produced it, many things would not be mine—recordings of the world's finest music, books holding the philosophy, the dreams and hopes of all mankind, a car that took me swiftly to the point whenever I felt the need.[30]

He might have added that the train whistle also symbolized a culture in which it was possible to make a living defending wild places and writing about them. In any case, Olson, who had long spoken and written about modern culture's need of wilderness, lends balance to a debate that, among conservationists, had not infrequently turned stridently antitechnology, antisociety, and at times antihuman. In the final essay of the collection he sent to Alfred Knopf in 1958, he speaks implicitly to those who, like Devereux Butcher, saw increased access to the national parks and forests as entirely bad:

> The many millions who drive through our national parks and forests, though they may never set foot on any of the back-country trails, never know the wilderness except from their automobiles, nevertheless are conscious of its power, a realization that gives significance to everything they see. The lure is more than scenery, varied vistas and magnificent lookout points; it is the consciousness of being at the threshold of the unknown.[31]

Olson wrote in an undated note that he wanted to keep his new book "as simple and non-intellectual as The Singing Wilderness." He jotted down nearly three dozen possible titles, including "The Sacred Place," "The Listening Place," and "The Secret Place," as well as many variations with the word *point:* "Point of the Winds," for example, and "Vantage Point" and "Discovery Point" and "Wanderer's Point" and "Solitude Point." He did not find one he was happy with until after a conversation with Yvonne Olson, who arrived in Ely in the spring of 1958. She had come from the Middle East, where Robert served as a U.S. Foreign Service officer in Benghazi, Libya, and Beirut, Lebanon.

Walking around the point with Sigurd and listening to him describe what it meant to him, Yvonne remarked on a similarity she saw between the point and the diplomatic community in Libya. Benghazi was referred to as a listening post, from which U.S. diplomats could stay in touch with the broader currents of life along the northern coast of Africa. She told Sigurd that the point, as he described it, was a listening post for the wilderness. Yvonne's comment led to the manuscript's final title, *Listening Point*.

Olson's search for balance, as described in *Listening Point*, is the search for a land ethic; in this book, more than in any of his others, he faces practical decisions about his relationship with nature. Unlike Leopold in *A Sand County Almanac*, however, Olson does not preach norms of behavior. Instead, to paraphrase one of Leopold's definitions of a conservationist, Olson shows with an ax rather than tells with a pen. "A conservationist," Leopold wrote, "is one who is humbly aware that with each stroke he is writing his signature on the face of his land. Signatures of course differ, whether written with axe or pen, and this is as it should be."[32] *Listening Point* shows Olson's thoughts and actions as he places his signature on six parcels of lakeshore property in northern Minnesota.

In doing this, the book also displays Olson's belief that land use issues are not always black and white, that knowledge of context is essential. Building a road to his undeveloped property on a partially developed lake is not the same as building a road into the heart of a wilderness area. Likewise, when a motorboat races by the islands near his point, disturbing his sense of harmony, he realizes that he is selfish to expect Burntside Lake to be completely free from such disturbances. "Knowing this," he writes, "I was ashamed at my resentment at intrusions no matter what they might be. I should be able to listen to all of them with equanimity."

On the other hand, Olson does not mean to imply that canoeists in the Quetico-Superior wilderness should simply tune out motorboats, for the context is entirely different. Sigurd could go to Listening Point any time he was home, and so he knows that "there would be many times in the months to come when the lake would be completely undisturbed." A wilderness area, on the other hand, is meant especially for those coming from far away who have just a few days or maybe a week or two to find a similar closeness to the natural world. Olson could write, as he did in the book's second to last paragraph, that "most will content themselves with a fleeting look at places that are still wild and unchanged." But he strongly believed that these wild and unchanged places served an essential balancing role in the modern world, that in fact modern culture could not truly be appreciated without the presence of its underlying context, wilderness. Even more, he believed a culture that denied this truth was a culture that, as Masefield had put it, was "dwelling in death."[33]

But *Listening Point* does not directly state this last conviction, which was rooted in Olson's still-developing spiritual philosophy. As we will see, his beliefs about the necessity of wilderness were intimately connected to his beliefs about the nature of God and of the human spiritual role in the universe. Olson was developing, in essence, a wilderness theology, which would assume its final shape after a period of study and reflection in 1959 and 1960. He would share his beliefs in talks before a variety of audiences in the United States and Canada, and in the 1970s would convert these speeches into essays for a book called *Reflections from the North Country*, which would join his first two in forming the core of his written work. All nine of the books Olson ultimately produced would sell well, but these three may be singled out as the most important: *Reflections from the North Country*, which best describes his spiritual beliefs; *The Singing Wilderness*, which contains the most consistently poetic writing and best captures his land aesthetic; and *Listening Point*, which best illustrates the land ethic of a man who believed that one could hold true to ideals without being an ideologue.

Beginning with the manuscript that became *Listening Point* and continuing for all of the manuscripts that followed, Olson received typing and editorial assistance from a longtime friend, Ann Langen. She lived with her husband and children just down the hill from the Olsons on Boundary Street. The Olsons had gotten to know the Langens during Sigurd's years at Ely Junior College; Ann's husband, Bill, was Ely's high school principal. The families grew close, going on picnics, canoeing, and snowshoeing together.

The Langens' daughter Pat later recalled many visits with the Olsons during her childhood in the 1950s and early 1960s, including fireplace sing-alongs with Mitch Miller music. She grew familiar with the sight of her mother and Sigurd sitting on a davenport in the living room, going over Sigurd's manuscripts. Sigurd would finish a chapter draft and bring it over, she said, and then he and Ann would read it together, word by word. Ann would point out when Sigurd was repeating himself, would spot problems with punctuation and grammar, and sometimes would question his choice of words. If Sigurd disagreed with her, he would send it to Knopf as it was and let his editor decide if there was a problem. After Ann and Sigurd finished discussing a chapter, Ann would type a clean copy on onionskin paper. Sigurd would take it back to his writing shack, make more revisions, and then they would repeat the process until Sigurd was happy with it and Ann would type the final draft for Knopf.

The Langen children learned to tiptoe through the room during these sessions. "We knew that when those two were working on the couch we were not to make a noise," Pat said. Sigurd typically smoked a pipe as he and Ann worked, unknowingly providing a spectacle that became part of Langen family lore. "Sig could not keep his pipe lit," recalled Pat:

> He was constantly relighting it. And then his matches—he'd be talking and putting his matches down, and you never knew where they would end up: next to the ash tray on the table, on the mantel by the fireplace. And he didn't always put the match out. It was kind of a joke that my mother would always follow his hand with an ash tray.

Listening Point was published in September 1958 after heavy advance publicity, capped when the State of Minnesota chose the book for a special edition in honor of the state's centennial. (Sigurd nursed a cramped hand after signing three thousand title page sheets for inclusion in the centennial edition.) It received enthusiastic reviews in the *New York Times,* the *San Francisco Chronicle,* and the *Atlantic.* Some other reviews were mixed. *Booklist,* for example, recommended it but called it "more repetitious and uneven in quality" than *The Singing Wilderness.* The *Chicago Tribune* called the book "a series of short essays, with bursts of good writing, but very little unity or cadence." The reviewer said reading *Listening Point* was "a difficult journey thru a forest of redundancies to reach a few chapters that are breathtakingly beautiful."[34]

Olson's reaction to such criticisms—or even if he saw them—is unknown. The *Chicago Tribune*'s complaint about unity seems to be a case of missing the forest for the trees: the essays *did* frequently stray from the piece of land known as Listening Point, but the search for balance between people, civilization, and nature is the theme that unites the essays. The point itself merely provides an organizational structure. The criticisms about repetition and uneven writing, on the other hand, have some merit. The fact that Olson wrote *Listening Point* over a far shorter period of time than *The Singing Wilderness* undoubtedly is a major reason for these faults. But Sigurd's impressionistic writing style, which worked so well at capturing human emotions in the presence of nature, also had a tendency toward vagueness and repetition. As Alfred Knopf himself put it in a letter to Marie Rodell on March 10, 1959, "Sig's writing has, of course, the defects of its virtues and I suppose vice versa. My feeling is that he, from time to time, lets his enthusiasm get away with him and the result is rhetoric which doesn't contribute very much to the impression he is trying to convey to the reader."

Nevertheless, *Listening Point* sold nearly eight thousand copies in its first two months and remained popular among the kinds of people who enjoyed *The Singing Wilderness*. Over the years Olson would receive hundreds of letters from readers who would describe—even send photos of—their own special places from which they listened to nature's rhythms.

❖

Early in 1958, as Sigurd was putting the finishing touches to his book manuscript, the National Parks Association board of trustees voted to give executive secretary Fred Packard one year to improve his performance. Olson hoped Packard would take the warning to heart and told him to write a report documenting his accomplishments. Packard wrote a seven-page report in April, but on May 22 the organization's executive committee voted to fire him. The vote sent the NPA into a crisis that would lead to Olson's resignation, as well as that of his successor.

Sigurd was livid about the vote to fire Packard, which came just four months into the year Packard had been given to improve his performance. Loyalty was a quality Olson cherished almost to a fault, and he saw the executive committee's vote as a terrible breach of faith. Sigurd organized an emergency meeting of the board of trustees on June 25 at the Cosmos Club. He prepared a word-for-word statement on note cards—highly unusual for him—and allowed no note taking.

It did no good. Packard was out. In August the NPA appointed Washington attorney Tony Smith its new executive director. Smith, who was on the organization's executive committee and board of trustees, had headed conservation work for the CIO and had served as secretary to Gifford Pinchot when the former U.S. Forest Service chief was governor of Pennsylvania. But Olson, along with those in whom he confided, including Howard Zahniser and Conrad Wirth, worried about Smith's temper and his ability to get along with others.

The worries proved well-founded. Smith was a hard worker and far more efficient than Packard, but he was an autocrat who did not like to take direction. By October Olson was complaining to Charley Woodbury: "Since Tony took over I have not had one scrap of news about NPA. I have been completely ignored, know nothing about what has been going on."[35] Smith even refused to send executive committee minutes to members of the committee or to board members. Former NPA president William Wharton complained to Smith on October 23, "If these decisions are strictly adhered to, how can the Board be in a position to approve or disapprove actions of the Executive Committee?" Wharton sent a copy of his letter to Olson, who responded, "I too am disturbed at the 'hush hush' business. . . . We have always stood for open discussion and truth. If what we do cannot stand the light of day, something is wrong. I will stand with you on this."

For Olson, the last straw came the following spring. Joe Carrithers, who worked in the NPA's western office, happened to have personal reasons to be in Washington at the time of the annual meeting in May and offered to attend at his own expense. Olson told Smith to send Carrithers an invitation. Instead, Smith sent a telegram telling Carrithers to stay away. Carrithers quit his job over the incident, and so did the NPA's other Western representative, Ned Graves.[36]

It was clear that Olson and Smith had come to an impasse, and on May 21, 1959, during the NPA's annual meeting, Sigurd resigned. Hoping to keep the transition smooth, he said nothing during the meeting about his relationship with Smith, but he did turn down the executive committee's suggestion of a dinner in honor of his six years as NPA president.[37]

Victor Cahalane, a former National Park Service biologist who was assistant director of the New York State Museum, succeeded Olson. By fall he was exasperated. Charles Stoddard, an NPA trustee who would become director of the Bureau of Land Management during the Kennedy administration, told Olson on October 30, "I understand Tony is running the office like a little Caesar and the situation is deteriorating rapidly." Cahalane resigned in April 1960, a month before the annual meeting and after less than a year in office, saying he was in a situation that "no self-respecting person would tolerate."[38] William Wharton sent Olson a telegram on April 20, saying, "The Association . . . greatly needs your help in restoring the cooperative spirit of former days."

But there was little Olson could do. The NPA, which had nearly tripled its membership to almost twelve thousand during Sigurd's presidency, surpassing that of the Wilderness Society, was becoming essentially a one-man organization. Tony Smith would remain as its executive director until 1979, an unusually long tenure. While he was effective for a time, his autocratic style eventually made the organization impotent in the face of changing circumstances. For Olson, once again, it was a question of balance. "I have a great deal of respect for Tony's ability and for his sense of dedication," he wrote on April 28, 1960, "but without humanity, basic courtesy, and a willingness to see the viewpoints of others any accomplishment is impossible."[39]

❖ Fourteen ❖

From Contemplation to Action: Sigurd Olson's Wilderness Theology
1959-1964

L ate in 1959, Sigurd Olson was ready to begin a new writing project. He had just completed a draft of a book about his 1955
Churchill River expedition with the Voyageurs (Knopf would publish
it in 1961 as *The Lonely Land*) and felt that, at the age of sixty, it was
time for him to write a book that described the underpinnings of his
philosophy. He planned to base the title on a line from the Finnish
epic poem *Kalevala*: "The frost squeaked out verses to me, and the
rain chanted runes." Writing to himself in an undated journal entry,
Sigurd said, "In *Runes of the North*—somehow must come in all of your
mature reflections on life in general, what we are, where we are going,
and why."

To prepare for the project, Sigurd entered his most intensive phase
of reading since the mid-1940s. Between December 1959 and February 1960 he read works by Harrison Brown, Joseph Wood Krutch,
Loren Eiseley, Lewis Mumford, Philip Wylie, Owen Barfield, Bertrand
Russell, Julian Huxley, Pierre Lecomte du Noüy, and Pierre Teilhard
de Chardin. He also typed some sixty pages of quotes, paraphrases,
and his own reflections. As it turned out, he did not use any of this
material in *Runes of the North*, which Knopf published in 1963, but he
did use it in speeches that he gave around the United States and
Canada and returned to it again in the 1970s when he finally did describe his philosophy in the book *Reflections from the North Country*. It
is clear from *Reflections*, published in 1976, that the final significant
development in Olson's thoughts about wilderness and the human
spirit occurred during this intense period of reading at the dawn of
the 1960s.[1]

Of the ten works Olson read between December 1959 and February 1960, five loomed large in his thinking: books by Julian and Aldous Huxley, Mumford, Lecomte du Noüy, and Teilhard de Chardin. Olson had read *The Perennial Philosophy* by Aldous Huxley and *Human Destiny* by Lecomte du Noüy more than a decade earlier, but he was encountering the other three books and their authors for the first time.

The Perennial Philosophy, as chapter 10 shows, argues that all the world's major religions share certain principles. By the time Olson first read the book in 1945, he already had concluded that all faiths are equivalent. In an undated letter from 1943, for example, he wrote to his two sons about Buddhism:

> There are so many things in Buddha that resemble Christianity, the working philosophy is the same—the main idea being to align oneself with the great spiritual forces of the universe, to be in tune with the universe and God, that only by being cognizant of spiritual forces and in agreement with the best thought and idealism of the ages can a man ever achieve serenity and tolerance and peace, to practice humility and understanding.

But a statement Huxley made early in his book caught Olson's attention and encouraged him to think of God in a new way. Writing about the nature of God, Huxley quoted the fourteenth-century German mystic Meister Eckhart, who said that God "becomes and disbecomes." To Huxley, this meant that God exists in time: "He might be an emergent God, starting unspiritually at Alpha and becoming gradually more divine as the aeons rolled on towards some hypothetical Omega."[2] Huxley's speculation made intuitive sense to Olson, who ultimately tied the idea of an emergent God into his wilderness philosophy, even using it as a chapter title in *Reflections from the North Country*.

More important to Olson's thought was *Human Destiny*, which he first read with fascination in 1947. In the book, Lecomte du Noüy, a pioneering French biophysicist and skeptic of religion who had converted to Roman Catholicism, wrote that "evolution continues in our time, *no longer on the physiological or anatomical plane but on the spiritual and moral plane*" (the emphasis is his). *Human Destiny* was the first book of what Julian Huxley came to label "evolutionary humanism." The central belief of evolutionary humanists is that the development of the human species started a whole new phase of evolution. As Julian Huxley put it in his 1957 book *Religion without Revelation*, which Olson read with care and appreciation in January 1960:

> The present is the first period in the long history of the earth in which the evolutionary process, through the instrumentality of man, has taken the first step towards self-consciousness. In becoming aware of his own destiny, man has become aware of that of the entire evolutionary process on this planet: the two are interlocked.[3]

Lewis Mumford took a similar perspective in *The Conduct of Life,* which was published in 1951 and read by Olson for the first time early in 1960. Mumford, however, went a step further than Julian Huxley: he tied the "evolutionary awareness" that Huxley spoke of to the idea of an emergent God: "The universe does not issue out of God, in conformity with his fiat: it is rather God who in the long processes of time emerges from the universe, as the far-off event of creation and the ultimate realization of the person toward which creation seems to move."[4]

Olson readily agreed with the basic belief of evolutionary humanism, the idea that the evolution of *Homo sapiens* has introduced a self-consciousness to the evolutionary process. He also agreed that the destiny of humanity is to spiritualize this process, to lead evolution along the path toward an emergent God. The spiritual growth of each individual, from this perspective, plays a key role in realizing human destiny and fulfilling evolution's end product of the emergent God. But Olson, unlike most evolutionary humanists, perceived this emergent God as also somehow directing or at least organizing the entire process, from beginning to end. "I may have to be content knowing there is some logic and reason behind the framework of the universe," he wrote in *Reflections*.[5]

Olson, in other words, believed in the idea of teleology, or purpose, in evolution and in human existence. This helps to explain his special interest in the mystical theory of evolution described by French paleontologist and Jesuit priest Pierre Teilhard de Chardin in a book published in English in 1959 under the title *The Phenomenon of Man.* Of all the books that Olson read early in 1960, this one had the greatest influence on his thought.

A central concept in the book is "convergence," which Teilhard described as a human tendency throughout evolution to prevent differentiation among races from leading to the kind of biological separation, seen among, for example, species of birds or insects. Another evolutionary process, "complexification," has led to increasingly complex patterns of organization: progressing, for example, from subatomic units to atoms to inorganic molecules to organic molecules, then to subcellular life, then to cells, and so on.

Teilhard wrote not just about evolution in the biosphere or the inorganic lithosphere; he coined the term *noosphere* to refer to the sphere of mind, a "thinking layer" superimposed on the other spheres, consisting of the total thought patterns of humans and the patterns of their activities: in other words, the summation of human experience. Teilhard believed that large increases in human population and rapid advances in human communications were producing a more complex noosphere and at the same time a convergence in mental activity, a global psychosocial unification. The end result, he wrote, would be an intensely unified, "hyperpersonal" noosphere, what he called "point Omega"—by implication, union with God.

Teilhard once wrote in his journal that his goal was to show to a skeptical modern world a God who was "as vast and mysterious as the cosmos" and yet "as immediate and all-embracing as life." Sigurd Olson did not believe in all of the major tenets of Christianity; in December 1959, for example, he wrote to one of his fans that "physical immortality is a juvenile conception of frightened man." Yet his idea of God, while it was free from any specific doctrine or creed, was very much like that described by Teilhard. And while for the most part Teilhard confirmed what Olson already had come to believe through his own experience, Teilhard's concept of the noosphere stuck with Olson for the rest of his life. In an interview published in 1980, two years before his death, Olson said, "I *do believe* . . . that no one can understand the cosmos without first being convinced there is a power behind all things. There is an energy, a thought spectrum, like a Van Allen Belt, in which all ideas and spiritual beliefs surround the earth like the belt of matter surrounding earth. We in our consciousness flow with this mythical thought."[6]

The fact that Teilhard had such an impact on Olson's views about God, human destiny, and evolution; the fact that Lecomte du Noüy also played an important role; and the fact that Sigurd later was drawn to works by other Roman Catholic authors such as Jacques Maritain, Josef Pieper, and Thomas Merton do not mean that he was a potential convert to Catholicism. Despite his rejection of Baptist dogma he undoubtedly would have been shocked at such a suggestion.[7] He did have something in common with a strand of Catholicism in which contemplative *experience* plays a major role. For Olson's philosophy grew directly out of the epiphanies, or flashes of insight, that he had experienced so many times in the wilderness. His rejection of Baptist dogma during his college years at Madison had left him with a painful inner void, but as a guide in the Quetico-Superior wilderness during the 1920s he had found moments of deep understanding and peace that had given him a sense of purpose and an intuitive grasp of the answers that he later found affirmed in the writings of Lecomte du Noüy, Teilhard de Chardin, and others.

A genuine mystical experience is difficult to describe, because such words as *oneness* often convey a sense of ethereal distance from the physical world. But while such experiences *are* accompanied by a feeling of *detachment*—a broadened perspective in which current problems, questions, and issues recede in importance—they also are accompanied by a feeling of *complete participation*. In *The Singing Wilderness*, Olson described his mystical experience on Robinson Peak in terms of listening "with inward ears" and seeing "with inward eyes," of an awareness that seemed to involve his entire being. He said he thought of the phrase from the Bible "Be still and know that I am God."[8]

This, ultimately, was why he fought for wilderness, and this was his message in countless speeches across the United States and Canada as well as in nine books and many magazine and newspaper articles: in wilderness people can find the *silence* and the *solitude* and the *noncivilized surroundings* that can connect them once again to their evolutionary heritage and, through an experience of the eternal mystery, can give them a sense of the *sacredness* of all creation. If, as Olson believed, evolution was proceeding toward an emergent God, and if, as he also believed, individual spiritual growth played an essential role in this evolutionary process, then a wilderness experience could be considered a sacramental experience, of benefit not just to the individual but to all of creation. Olson's wilderness philosophy may well be considered a theology, because it was deeply connected with his beliefs about the nature of God.

Olson was not a systematic philosopher who built rigorous arguments out of empirical evidence. Nor was he a scholar or a professional intellectual. He read very selectively, and his understanding of the great thinkers of modern civilization was as likely to come from the *Saturday Evening Post* or the *Atlantic* as from scholarly books. Yet he was a profoundly philosophical person who lived for ideas and who was engaged in a lifelong search for meaning.

Olson wanted to bring his message of wilderness salvation to people who would never think of reading a book by Lecomte du Noüy or Teilhard de Chardin or even Loren Eiseley. In August 1960, for example, he wrote in a note to himself, "I must bridge the gap between Eiseley and my audience of common people, the non-intellectuals . . . who feel deeply but are groping for ideas."[9] Because of this goal, and because he gave far more weight to intuitive experience than to building a coherent framework of logically consistent statements about the nature of such experience, he rarely was explicit about the details of his wilderness theology. His vagueness sometimes caused his readers to misinterpret him and quite likely will lead to disagreements among scholars.

Some of Olson's readers, for example, wrote letters asking if he was a pantheist. Sometimes, in fact, they *accused* him of it. "I'm amazed at your lack of understanding—forgive me—of the Bible and God's true relation as Creator," wrote one reader in 1957. But he was no pantheist. "God is not in nature," he told his son Robert; "God is in the human spirit."[10]

The heart of Sigurd Olson's environmental ethic and of his wilderness theology was what Loren Eiseley described in *The Unexpected Universe* as "the expression of love projected beyond the species boundary by a creature born of Darwinian struggle, in the silent war under the tangled bank." Love was the most important element in Olson's environmentalism. "There can be no real, lasting land ethic without love," he said. But Olson's idea of love went beyond the anthropocentrism common to both Christian and humanistic worldviews. While he often spoke of stewardship, a concept that is based in love yet implies human domination over the rest of nature, his essential philosophy went deeper: "What civilization needs today," he wrote, "is a culture of sensitivity and tolerance and an abiding love of all creatures, including mankind."[11]

To Olson, this meant love of all of the individual manifestations of creation within the context of an awareness of the evolutionary process. Behind that process, moreover, was an absolute mystery that was impossible for science to analyze, but that he had felt many times in the wilderness. Olson's wilderness theology was, in essence, a sacramental vision of life and of evolution. If the whole of the earth and the universe beyond is an extension of God, then humans are obliged to love all life, human and nonhuman, because all life is intertwined in the cosmic adventure.

Olson's argument for wilderness preservation focused on the human psychological and spiritual benefits, but he believed that these individual benefits would in turn lead to a more biocentric perspective. In wilderness humans could rediscover the timeless, creative force of the universe, regain a sense of being part of that force, and, in so doing, find salvation. Such an experience would make it impossible to maintain a purely anthropocentric worldview. Not only was this reason enough for preserving wilderness, according to Olson, it was the *essential* reason. In 1966 he went so far as to say that wilderness preservation could not be justified by appealing to outdoor recreational needs, "but only as a stepping stone to cosmic understanding. In a world confused and strident, a world where all the old verities are being questioned, this is the final answer."[12]

❖

Sigurd Olson's wilderness theology tied directly to his work as a professional conservationist. If, as he believed, the experience of wild nature plays an important role in individual spiritual growth, which in turn plays an essential role in directing evolution, then preserving wild nature can be seen as a moral duty. And in the late 1950s and early 1960s, few people worked as hard as Olson on as many different fronts, and still fewer were as influential. He was reaching his peak years as a conservation leader at a time when the National Park Service was undergoing a major shift in philosophy that led to a vast expansion of territory under the agency's jurisdiction. As a former president of the National Parks Association who was on close terms with the top personnel in the Interior Department and the National Park Service, Olson was in an ideal position to promote park expansion and to influence its direction.

In September 1959, four months after Sigurd resigned as president of the National Parks Association, he accepted an invitation from Interior Secretary Fred Seaton to join the Advisory Board on National Parks, Historic Sites, Buildings and Monuments. Consisting of eleven members serving staggered six-year terms, the board advised the secretary of the interior on park management and on proposed additions to the national park system. Until the late 1960s, when President Richard Nixon began filling the board with political appointees, it was the most prestigious advisory board in conservation, and its views carried a lot of weight in the Park Service, the Interior Department, and Congress.[13]

The board met twice a year, usually once in Washington, D.C., and once at a national park. When Olson joined the group its chairman was Frank Masland, who owned a carpet company in Carlisle, Pennsylvania. Masland was a former vice president of the National Association of Manufacturers and a delegate to the World Council of Churches. A big man with a big voice, he combined intense anticommunist views (he was a member of the John Birch Society) with just as deeply held convictions about the spiritual values of nature, and he had traveled to Asia to help the poor. A strong leader, he formed the board's nucleus along with two other men: *New York Times* columnist John Oakes, one of the nation's leading environmental journalists, and Stanley Cain, a respected wildlife biologist who later became an assistant secretary of the interior.

Olson quickly joined these three as a key member of the board. "Everybody looked to Sig," recalled Terry Wood, who attended Olson's first meeting in September 1960 at Isle Royale National Park. In 1961, when the new administration of President John F. Kennedy replaced Seaton with Stewart Udall, the new secretary of the interior asked the widely respected author and conservationist Wallace Stegner to observe the board in action and report back. Stegner responded:

> The strong members of the Board, as I saw them, were Frank Masland, a good chairman and very well informed; Sigurd Olson, who doesn't speak much but who is listened to when he does, and for cause; Stanley Cain, who struck me as being one of the sharpest and best trained people there, and who was invariably sure on his intellectual feet; and John Oakes, who adopted the role of conservation purist and did it well.[14]

Before Olson joined the board, he had talked a number of times with National Park Service director Conrad Wirth about expanding the size of the national park system. Traditionally, national parks had been created around monumental scenery, "natural wonders" such as the geysers at Yellowstone. By the late 1950s there was little acreage left that could meet these standards. Wirth's conversations with Olson about "remnant shopping" convinced both of them the standards needed to be changed. They knew millions of acres of irreplaceable wildlands were at stake, believed public pressure could be brought to bear on Congress to purchase new lands, and feared much of the land could be lost to development unless the current generation of Americans acted. "I am for any device that will get lands into recreational public status while there is time," Olson wrote.[15]

This was a hard message for purists to swallow. The National Parks Association clung to the old standards, as did some leading conservationists in the other major organizations. A number of National Park Service employees and advisory board members also found it hard to abandon the traditional requirement of monumental scenery. But Olson, along with Frank Masland, repeated the plea for new standards at meeting after meeting.

At times it was frustrating. Writing to Masland on July 27, 1962, Olson said:

> I, like you, have no patience with people who are afraid the system is going down the drain with dilutions of areas which may not measure at the moment up to the highest standards. You and I see so much alike on this that we don't have to explain to each other. I have another letter on my desk from Art Carhart of Denver, raising much the same question. I cannot answer him now but again it riles me to think people cannot see the importance of giving areas some protection—some designation NOW and letting the future dictate exactly what must be done. These people act as though this was still a virgin continent with a century to put our house in order.

When Kennedy took office in 1961 and named Udall secretary of the interior, the new administration made the expansionist perspective a cornerstone of its conservation program. Masland, who as chairman of the National Parks Advisory Board was one of the first to meet Udall, came away feeling that the atmosphere in the Interior Department had undergone a remarkable change. "Eager youth is on the move and at this stage of the game unwilling to admit for one moment that any desirable objective can't be accomplished," he wrote to Olson on March 13, 1961. "I don't think I have ever known anyone to move so far in so many directions in such a short period of time as the secretary. If anything, he moves faster than Kennedy."

Olson, who met with Udall for the first time on February 9, 1961, was even more impressed than his friend. Masland expressed concern that Udall's busyness could indicate a lack of focus, but Sigurd reminded him that the secretary and his staff were just getting settled: "We have seen that before and there is bound to be a lot of strange and unpredictable maneuvering, but we have this consolation during these first trying months that in Udall we have a man who feels strongly about the out of doors and wilderness." When the National Parks Advisory Board met in Washington in May, Olson predicted to his fellow board members that Udall would be the greatest secretary of the interior in U.S. history.[16]

It appears that Udall was similarly impressed with Olson. On April 29, 1961, Senator Hubert Humphrey wrote to Sigurd that he was being considered for appointment as director of the National Park Service. On May 31 Humphrey repeated the claim, saying, "I know this has been given some consideration. I shall try to be of help." Olson's response was noncommittal: "No doubt you are right as always."

Several decades later, Udall could not remember considering Olson for Park Service director. Ted Swem, however, who at the time was the service's chief of planning for new parks, recalled Olson's telling him that Udall had offered him the job. Olson said the secretary had called him twice at his home in Ely, trying to persuade him to become director. Elizabeth Olson in a separate interview told the same story.

Whatever the truth of the matter—and the only documentation discovered so far is the letters between Humphrey and Olson—it is fair to say that Sigurd would have hated being an administrator in Washington as much as, or even more than, he hated being an administrator at Ely Junior College. He not only would have complained once again about the meetings and schedules and paperwork, but he would have been lost in the world of Washington politics. Charles Stoddard, who served on Udall's staff in the early 1960s and developed a friendship with Olson, said in 1992, "Sig wasn't a political in-fighter. He didn't understand all the forces at work—he was an inno-cent abroad."[17]

Not everyone who knew Olson would have gone so far as to call him an innocent abroad, but the clear consensus among friends and family is that he did not care for politics. "I think he always kept his eye on the star, and he didn't get down here where we more common folks deal more with personalities," said Swem.[18] Sigurd certainly would not have been the kind of Park Service director that Stewart Udall, a consummate politician, wanted or needed. But Sigurd was exactly the kind of person Udall wanted to help plan and give per-spective to the expansionist goals of the Park Service during the 1960s, and in May 1962 Udall appointed Olson his consultant on wilderness and national parks.

Olson already was a consultant to the National Park Service and had worked for several years on issues that became major planks in Udall's conservation program. He had, for example, worked behind the scenes to arrange the transfer of lands and timber rights in a key portion of the proposed Point Reyes National Seashore in California. He also had inspected Cape Cod, Massachusetts, and wrote a report advocating national park status for the area. He knew full well that congressional authorization for a park at Cape Cod would set a precedent in committing the federal government to purchase private land in order to create the park and that the proposed park did not meet traditional standards. His 1958 report was very much in keeping with the perspective that made Cape Cod the top conservation prior-ity in the Kennedy administration:

> Most of our national parks are in the far West, and in spite of high annual visitation there will always be millions who cannot visit them. . . . What people need in an expanding industrial complex such as ours are areas close enough to be lived with and enjoyed without great expenditure of time or money. It is not enough to see them once a year. They should become a part of people's lives. Their very existence close to urban areas would exert a stabilizing and en-riching influence.[19]

In 1961 Congress authorized not a national park but a national seashore at Cape Cod. Nevertheless, the precedent was set, and the classification was not as important to Olson as was the goal of protecting the land from unregulated development. As consultant to Udall and to the director of the National Park Service, Olson continued to travel across the United States to study potential additions to the national park system. He paddled the Allagash River in Maine and the Suwannee in Georgia and Florida; he walked the beaches of Cumberland Island in Georgia and Padre Island in Texas; he traveled the Missouri River in Montana and the Current and Eleven Point Rivers in Missouri. Nearly everyplace he went the proposal was for a national seashore or lakeshore or river. Most of the exceptions to this rule were in Alaska, where Olson played an important role in selecting millions of acres of land that ultimately received congressional protection under the Alaska National Interest Lands Conservation Act of 1980.

Sigurd's interest in Alaska undoubtedly was first stirred by the frontier novels he read in his youth and then renewed in the late 1930s through his friendship with Bob Marshall, who had lived there and urged preservation of everything north of the Yukon River (nearly half of the future state). But his personal involvement began after 1951, when his son Sigurd Jr. moved to Alaska to work as a wildlife biologist for the U.S. Fish and Wildlife Service. By that time the National Park Service was studying the recreational potential of the territory, and the major conservation organizations, which until then had given only occasional attention to Alaska, were beginning to make it a long-term commitment. Sigurd Sr., as an official of both the National Parks Association and the Izaak Walton League, began working on Alaskan conservation issues as early as 1952; it was near the end of the decade, however, in his role as a consultant to the National Park Service and the secretary of the interior, that he began to play an important role.

Among the early priorities shared by conservationists and the Interior Department was the creation of three wildlife ranges. By far the largest and most prominent was the proposed Arctic National Wildlife Range, consisting of nearly nine million acres in the Brooks Range of northern Alaska. It was a key nesting ground for migratory waterfowl and provided essential habitat for caribou. The second largest proposal was for a 1.8 million-acre reserve in southwest Alaska between the Yukon and Kuskokwim Rivers, the nesting site for nearly half of the ducks and geese on the Pacific flyway. The third proposal was to set aside another key waterfowl breeding and concentration area of a little more than four hundred thousand square miles at Izembek Bay on the Alaska Peninsula. Some Alaskan hunting and conservation groups joined the national organizations in expressing support for the ranges; the context of the times, however, in a territory advocating statehood, was not favorable for federal land withdrawal. And after statehood was granted in 1959, Alaskan officials blocked congressional action.[20]

In the summer of 1960 Olson traveled to Alaska for the first time on behalf of the Interior Department, examining the proposed Arctic National Wildlife Range as well as a number of other areas. Some of these, such as Mount McKinley National Park and Glacier Bay National Monument, already had federal designation, while others, such as the Wrangell Mountains of south central Alaska, so far had received little attention.[21] Sigurd spent two months in Alaska. He flew through the Valley of Ten Thousand Smokes the day after a volcano erupted; the sky was full of swirling smoke and the acrid odor of sulfur. Another day he stood in the center of a plateau with glaciers and mountains on all sides and counted 191 Dall sheep without moving from his spot. Elizabeth accompanied him part of the time; they watched whales mate at Glacier Bay and took the frontier-era "Trail of '98" between Skagway and Whitehorse.

Sigurd Jr. also showed them some of the sights of his adopted state and took his father into the neighboring Yukon on a side trip before dropping him off at Anchorage to begin the official portion of his trip. He recalled his father shaking his head in amazement a few days after he arrived, saying, "I've been traveling for three or four days, and it's just been one national park after another."

The excitement never left him. After Olson returned home he wrote to friends:

> Alaska—what a big, bold, beautiful country. Our West has mountain ranges and glaciers and rolling tundra-covered high country, but nothing like Alaska. There everything seems to be on a monumental scale dwarfing everything below. I stood on one plateau one morning and could see for 75 to 100 miles in all directions to four immense mountain ranges with snow-capped peaks. Such a sense of immensity and distance, I had never known before.[22]

Olson was not among the key players in the early stages of the campaign to create the Arctic, Izembek, and Kuskokwim wildlife ranges, but his personal influence with Interior Secretary Seaton, combined with his convert's enthusiasm about Alaska, gave him an important role at the end. Conservationists hoped Seaton would establish the wildlife ranges by executive order if Congress refused to act on the proposals. Seaton, in fact, had told Olson and others he would do so if need be. And in November 1960, after Vice President Richard Nixon lost the presidential election to Massachusetts senator John F. Kennedy, it became much more politically feasible for him to make what certainly would be a controversial decision. Seaton, a Republican appointee, soon would be stepping down. He could establish the wildlife ranges and leave. But early in December he called Olson to his office and said he was under immense pressure from Alaskan officials and the mining industry to reject the Arctic National Wildlife Range, and was unsure of his decision.

Olson provided the steady hand that Seaton needed, telling him that years later people would not remember the controversy.[23] Undoubtedly he reiterated a point he had made in a letter to Seaton on October 6: "I realize that there are many conflicting interests to consider, but I am confident that, should it be done, in a short time all Alaska [will] embrace the Arctic Wildlife Range with enthusiastic support."

On December 7, 1960, Seaton established all three ranges by executive order: the Arctic National Wildlife Range, larger than the combined states of Connecticut and Massachusetts; the Izembek National Wildlife Range, and the Kuskokwim National Wildlife Range; (later renamed after Clarence Rhode, an Alaskan who played a key role in the campaign's success but died in an airplane crash before the areas were set aside).

The State of Alaska tried to get Seaton's successor, Stewart Udall, to rescind the executive order. Udall refused, and instead encouraged federal planning for additional reserves in the state. The National Park Service sent Ted Swem to Alaska in 1962 to begin the new initiative, and in 1963 he returned, this time with Sigurd Olson. Their work, in turn, helped prepare the way for a major Park Service study in 1964 conducted by a group called the Alaska Task Force. Chaired by retired senior Park Service planner George Collins, who had played a key role in developing the proposals for the wildlife ranges established by Seaton, the team included two active Park Service employees with Alaskan experience and two consultants, one of whom was Sigurd Olson. Their assignment, according to a Park Service memorandum of November 12, 1964, was "to prepare an analysis of the best remaining possibilities for the National Park Service within Alaska."

The Alaska Task Force completed its report in January 1965. Titled "Operation Great Land," the report recommended withdrawing roughly seventy-six million acres of outstanding wildlands in thirty-nine locations spread across the state. "Alaska must not succumb to the modern or it will lose much," the report stated in Olsonesque language. "What it has must be known and made available while still maintaining its integrity. . . . Alaska is our last great opportunity to set aside 'reserves of significant size and grandeur,' and to save those intangible values of wilderness which it now has. The challenge is before us. The time to begin is now."[24]

It was a landmark report, but potentially explosive at a time when half of the Alaskan labor force was employed for just six months out of the year. In addition, the report recommended Park Service management of some lands that were then under the jurisdiction of other federal agencies; these agencies could not be expected to give up territory without a fight. The Park Service buried the report and kept the copies in Ted Swem's office. Fifteen years later, however, the recommendations of the Alaska Task Force formed the core of what historian Roderick Nash has called "the greatest single act of wilderness preservation in world history."[25] Signed into law by President Jimmy Carter on December 2, 1980, the Alaska National Interest Lands Conservation Act protected one hundred and four million acres, more than a quarter of the state.

Olson's efforts to get as much wild land as possible set aside before it was too late extended into Canada. Indeed, an important element of Olson's influence with Interior Secretary Seaton when Seaton was unsure about establishing the Arctic National Wildlife Range was the fact that Olson also had been working with Canadian officials to set aside five million adjoining acres of Yukon Territory.

Olson's Yukon connection was provided by two of his favorite canoeing partners, Denis Coolican and Omond Solandt of the Voyageurs. They were friends of Gordon Robertson, Canada's deputy minister for northern affairs and natural resources. In January 1958 they arranged a meeting in Ottawa involving Olson, Robertson, and Ross Leffler, U.S. assistant secretary of the interior, to begin discussing a proposal for a joint U.S.-Canada reserve in the Brooks Range of Alaska and the Yukon. By December 1960, when Seaton was faltering over the issue of protecting the American portion by executive order, an agreement seemed possible. Olson, who had been back and forth between Ottawa and Washington so often that Leffler referred to him as an ambassador without portfolio, undoubtedly told Seaton that Canada would not create a reserve in the Yukon portion of the Brooks Range if Seaton failed to create the Arctic National Wildlife Range.[26]

Ultimately, however, the same pressures that nearly stopped Seaton stalled the Yukon initiative. The Yukon Mining Congress fought the reserve, and nothing was done for two decades, but in 1984 Canada established the Northern Yukon National Park of about four thousand square miles in the area envisioned by Olson and Robertson.[27]

Sigurd also helped Canadian conservationists draw their government's attention to the Kluane region along the Alaskan border of the southwestern Yukon, and to the Nahanni River in the Northwest Territories. Olson visited the Kluane area with Sigurd Jr. during his trip to Alaska in 1960. The St. Elias Mountains, which run through the area, include Canada's highest peak and one of the world's largest nonpolar icefields. Olson came to know of the Nahanni during his 1959 expedition with the Voyageurs in the Northwest Territories. They met a man who was trying to protect the river, which flows through tundra-covered mountains and has a falls twice the height of Niagara. Olson and the Voyageurs promised to help preserve the Nahanni, which Sigurd called a second Yellowstone. As an American citizen, he did not play a major role in these Canadian campaigns, but his ties to Robertson and other key Canadian officials allowed him to help draw government attention to these areas and to put in a word at opportune times. In 1972 Canada established national parks at Kluane and Nahanni.

In addition to scouting out lands for federal protection, Olson served on the master planning teams for the management of Mount McKinley National Park and Katmai National Monument in Alaska, and Yellowstone and Grand Teton National Parks in Wyoming. He also worked with the Park Service's long-range planning team and regularly attended Park Service training sessions and superintendent conferences to give inspirational talks steeped in his wilderness theology. He often ended with a call to action of some sort, as in this talk to a gathering of Park Service master plan teams:

> No matter what we are called, no matter what political pressures are brought to bear on you, every time a new development is proposed, look at it carefully and don't be too tolerant. Give in, if you have to, but only as a last resort. What you have is a sacred trust, a trust that future generations will hold you accountable for. Let's not look ahead just the next ten years with a definite use graph. Let's give it the broad, long vision. Let's think of a hundred years, five hundred years, a thousand years. . . . Look ahead to the time when our people will be clamoring for these areas as they have never clamored before. Look ahead to the time when, due to the Service itself and its ideals, these places will remain intact.[28]

Olson's talks, as much as anything else, made him extremely popular with Park Service employees. "He was better at giving a keynote talk to conservationists than anyone I ever heard," said Ted Swem, "probably because he was so knowledgeable and always seemed to sense what was needed for a particular occasion."[29]

On one occasion Olson's sense of "what was needed" helped save a major Park Service conference marred by controversy. It was October 1963, and the Park Service was holding its annual conference for superintendents at Yosemite National Park. No more than a handful of those attending knew that it would be the last conference under Park Service director Conrad Wirth. Interior Secretary Stewart Udall wanted a young director with strong political skills and interests; Udall did not fire Wirth, but it was clear to Wirth that he was not wanted, and he gave Udall his letter of resignation. It was to be made public during the conference.

While a number of conservationists had attacked Wirth's Mission 66 program over the years as being heavily skewed toward construction of roads and buildings in the parks, Wirth had many loyal supporters. Among them was Sigurd Olson, who always maintained that critics exaggerated the amount of construction conducted under Mission 66. In a letter to the editor of the *Atlantic Monthly*, which in

February 1963 had published three articles critical of park management, Olson gave the response he had given many other times: "What is missing in these articles is any recognition of the all-important fact that close to 95 percent of the park areas are still in wilderness condition."[30] Olson did not always agree with Wirth, but he believed that the director deserved praise for many of his efforts and that Mission 66 by and large was a program that successfully met urgent needs. Olson was one of relatively few people who knew that much of the vast expansion of federally protected wildlands between 1963 and 1980—including the Alaska lands—originated in studies funded under Mission 66. Olson knew it because he worked with the man in charge of Park Service planning, Ted Swem, whose position was funded with Mission 66 money.

Wirth's resignation in itself would have made the conference a delicate one for the Park Service and the Interior Department. Not only had Wirth made many friends in his dozen years as director, but his successor, George Hartzog, was viewed by some in the agency as being more prodevelopment than Wirth and made others nervous simply because they knew he would shake things up. Early in the conference, however, before the announcement was made, John Carver, assistant interior secretary, gave a speech that deeply angered nearly everyone there, turning a difficult situation into a real threat to Park Service morale. Carver's main point—that the Park Service had become too rigid and unresponsive to changing times—was something that many outside the agency agreed with. But to make the case to park superintendents right before the announcement of their boss's departure was poor timing, and Carver seemed to attack the very heart of the service itself.[31]

"When all else fails," he said, "the Park Service seems always able to fall back upon mysticism, its own private mystique." Carver criticized a recent Park Service memorandum, saying it had "the mystic, quasi-religious sound of a manual for the Hitler Youth Movement." He called this "simply intolerable" and added, "The National Park Service is a bureau of the Department of the Interior, which is a Department of the United States government's executive branch. It isn't a religion, and it should not be thought of as such."[32]

Carver left an auditorium full of furious people, and the subsequent announcement of Wirth's resignation and his replacement by

Hartzog made matters worse. Udall tried to smooth things over, praising the Park Service for its "dedication and esprit," but his sincerity at that moment was questionable to Wirth supporters.[33] According to Ted Swem, it was Sigurd Olson who saved the conference:

> Sig gave a talk that did more to pull things together than anyone else at this conference. In fact, I think it was within an hour or two or three after the announcement, and Sig just sensed the feeling on the part of so many of the people in the Park Service, but he also knew what the secretary was trying to achieve, and of course he was also very close to Connie Wirth.[34]

Olson spoke for about twenty minutes. It was a sentimental speech, and, while he never mentioned Carver by name, he spoke right to the heart of Carver's message. Olson began by talking about Olaus Murie, beloved by many in the Park Service, who was near death. "I think Olaus epitomizes mystique," Sigurd said, picking up on the word Carver used to attack the agency:

> And by mystique I mean devotion, dedication and faith. I don't think there's a single man here—I haven't met a single man in the Service—who hasn't the guiding depth of devotion to this cause. . . . It's the thing that binds us together, it's the thing that makes us conquer all the difficulties, the ramifications of our jobs. It's the thing that keeps us going when the chips are down and we're surrounded by difficulties. . . . So often we are tempted to be ashamed of sentiment; at my age I'm no longer ashamed. I think we do not wear our sentiments on our sleeves as often as we should. We seldom pay tribute when it should be paid. We are afraid to admit that love is an important part of our being.[35]

Olson concluded his talk with a ringing endorsement of the very language and sentiment and spiritual philosophy that Carver had attacked: "In places such as this [Yosemite National Park] you preserve eternal perspectives, and I can think of no higher occupation, no higher goal, no higher aspiration than that to which this group here is dedicated—preserving the silent sanctuaries and the eternal perspectives which can be found there."

It was perhaps the most important speech of Sigurd's life, and when he stepped down from the podium, many in the audience had tears in their eyes. At Christmastime, A. Clark Stratton, Park Service acting director, sent a transcript of Olson's talk to all of the agency's field offices, tweaking Carver once again and adding to Sigurd's glowing reputation among Park Service employees.

The Yosemite incident embarrassed Stewart Udall but did not damage the secretary's relationship with Olson. Indeed, Olson's talk greatly helped Udall, who was very professional but not known for his warmth. Not long after the conference Udall told an interviewer that Sigurd was "one of the most inspired, and inspiring, of America's conservation leaders." He and Olson sometimes disagreed; Olson fought Udall, for example, over a decision to build a power line across the Current River in the Ozark National Scenic Riverway, and over a proposal to build a road through Great Smoky Mountains National Park. Olson lost the first argument and won the second. But despite the occasional disagreements, they always remained friends. "I *love* that man!" Udall once exclaimed in a rare display of his feelings.[36]

❖

Olson's wilderness theology, which placed a premium on the experience of wild nature and, therefore, on the supply of wild nature, lent a moral edge to his efforts to expand the national park system. It also influenced his beliefs about the appropriate management of wildlands. While this can be demonstrated by referring to his statements about any number of parks and forests in the United States and Canada, there is no better example than the wilderness outside his home, the sparkling lakes and evergreen forest of the canoe country.

The Quetico-Superior movement, with its goal of an international treaty creating a vast zoning plan covering nearly fifteen thousand square miles of Ontario and northeastern Minnesota, had run aground late in 1957, just as Sigurd Olson and Hubert Humphrey were frantically trying to calm Ely residents about Humphrey's bill to create a national wilderness preservation system. Unhappy with what they felt was American interference in Canadian affairs, Ontario officials had rejected the proposal for a treaty. They had, however, agreed to a simple exchange of letters between Ontario and the United States, pledging collaboration in Quetico-Superior management. Charles Kelly and Frank Hubachek, along with Sigurd Olson and Ernest Oberholtzer and other conservationists, were greatly disappointed at first. But time proved that the two governments intended to practice what the letters pledged; in 1960 an international advisory committee was established, and soon joint research projects helped to build a high degree of cooperation.[37]

Meanwhile, developments on the American side of the border were bringing a new intensity to old issues. The Boundary Waters Canoe Area (a label given in 1958 to the old Superior Roadless Areas) was becoming the most heavily used wilderness in the country. Fishermen were driving all-terrain vehicles to reach some remote lakes and pulling motorboats into other lakes with a kind of dolly called portage wheels. Resort owners and guides cached as many as ten boats a portage along the most popular lake chains. Canoeists paddled over the wakes of water skiers several miles into the wilderness along the international border, and once they got past the large motorboats they encountered portage traffic jams and litter. Even the water was not as safe as it once had been: nearly two dozen lakes tested positive for high levels of coliform bacteria.

The ever greater numbers of people pouring into the Boundary Waters Canoe Area (BWCA) each summer made conflict over management of the area inevitable. There were essentially two kinds of tourists with quite different goals and expectations: those who primarily wanted to fish, and those who sought to experience a kind of quiet and connectedness to nature that often has spiritual connotations. The first group usually traveled by motorboat or motorized canoe and tended to be tolerant of both crowds and noise in the wilderness. The second group paddled canoes and often resented the sights and sounds of outboard motors and crowds, which represented the very qualities of civilization from which they were trying to escape.

Questions about management intensified after an Ely canoe outfitter wrote in a regional nature magazine late in 1963 that the BWCA was being destroyed by logging. "The lower fourth of the Canoe Country has been almost completely logged out in the past two decades," he wrote. "What was once a choice two-week canoe route in completely virgin wilderness, the Kawishiwi-Isabella loop, is now a cut over road-riddled shambles."[38]

Over the course of the next year, other magazines picked up the theme. Many canoeists had not realized the extent of the logging, which took place during the winter. Having been encouraged for many years through a steady stream of advertising, magazine articles, and Sigurd Olson's books to think of the area as an untouched wilderness, they were outraged to learn that a vast network of logging roads crisscrossed a large portion of the BWCA. Meanwhile, the bill to create a national wilderness preservation system was nearing passage after eight years of intense lobbying. Seizing the moment, the Izaak Walton League, the Wilderness Society, and other groups demanded an end to logging in the BWCA and a ban on outboard motor use except in areas where such use had been established by 1948.

Sigurd Olson joined the call for an end to logging, but it was not easy for him. As early as 1929 he had indicated his personal opposition to logging in the canoe country, but after he began working with Kelly and Hubachek and Oberholtzer in the 1930s he learned that trying to get too much too soon could jeopardize genuine progress in wilderness preservation. And as he became a spokesperson for the Quetico-Superior group, he was expected to represent the group's stated goals for the international treaty, not his own preferences. The Quetico-Superior program explicitly allowed for carefully controlled logging, and in May 1964, after Olson publicly supported the Izaak Walton League's call for a logging ban, Charles Kelly called him on the carpet.

"This is a serious challenge to the stature of the President's Committee and something that I intensely regret," Kelly wrote on May 26. "If you and we are to go in different directions, we should have this clearly established."

Olson responded that he had no choice:

After all I had written and said over the years, plus my long connection with the League . . . I simply could not refuse to stand up and be counted among those who plead for wilderness. . . .

I sincerely hope that this difference of opinion will not result in breaking up the old triumvirate with so many battles behind it. After all these years, that would break my heart. Both you and Hub are part of my life and loyalty and though we may differ, it will never change my feelings for you.[39]

Between May and July Olson and Hubachek and sometimes Kelly debated their philosophies of wilderness management. Olson argued that allowing logging in the name of preservation was not sound: "To me as an ecologist, it is not true wilderness if it is crisscrossed with logging roads, with only a fringe of trees along the lake shores. Scientifically as well as aesthetically, such interference in the name of harvest and management changes the entire concept of unchanged ancient wilderness."[40]

Hubachek responded that it was Olson's vision of an *unchanging* wilderness that was unsound:

> No forested area is ever stabilized. It is constantly changing. The forest cover . . . is a complex living structure, forever under the threat of wind, insects, and fire, and most positive of all, forever growing to maturity and dying. . . . To think that it [a beautiful forest] will remain in that condition without management is fatuous. Such a fallacy should be constantly and vigorously exposed.[41]

Olson did not directly answer Hubachek. Instead, he shifted the focus of his argument away from the ecological to the aesthetic:

> The old concept to me is permitting logging in the face of a growing mass use which makes it untenable. People today . . . are not willing to wait for the country to come back. Those who see these last pockets of red and white pine or even stands of spruce and jack feel they are as precious as museum pieces of the past and as worthy of cherishing and protecting as famous paintings.[42]

Sigurd was not entirely consistent, because while he referred to trees as "museum pieces" in arguing against logging, he also supported an emerging ecological perspective that recommended an end to the policy of total suppression of all wildfires, disease, and insect infestations. These natural processes, as Hubachek had indicated, eventually would destroy the museum pieces just as surely as would logging. Olson's inconsistency can be traced in part to his ecological training at the University of Illinois. As a student under Victor Shelford in the early 1930s, Olson had learned an organismic ecological perspective that lent itself to inductive reasoning rather than to the reductive methods of modern science. The organismic school taught that the whole is greater than the sum of the parts, and Shelford argued that plants and animals in a natural system interact in such a way as to create a stable, climax community.

Olson was taught to think that an ecosystem can reach a point in its development where change is minimal, and that nature is best managed by letting it manage itself. But in the years since Olson had received his master's degree in ecology, the field had moved away from the organismic perspective. It had grown far more reductive, increasingly relying upon quantitative analysis and rigorous scientific methodology. Hubachek, who funded forest research in the BWCA and had a strong lay interest in it, probably had a better understanding of forest ecology in the 1960s than did Olson.

Sigurd's organismic ecological perspective gave him intellectual support for the nostalgic ideal of a perpetual old-growth forest. But the inconsistency revealed in Olson's antilogging argument cannot be attributed solely to an out-of-favor theory; part of the problem is that he attempted to justify his position using language designed for credibility in the modern world. The validity of his original argument—"To me as an ecologist, it is not true wilderness if it is crisscrossed with logging roads"—rested on Olson's scientific knowledge. Olson knew that arguments based on science, which supposedly consisted of "facts" rather than "opinions," carried more weight in a technological era. But when Hubachek exposed the flaws in Olson's argument—even calling it "fatuous"—Olson fell back to a defense based on aesthetics, which had a long tradition in the conservation movement. Even this was somewhat clumsily stated, as Olson apparently did not think it through to the obvious conclusion: people who "are not willing to wait" for a logged-over area to come back are unlikely to be willing to wait for a burned-over area to come back.

Olson certainly understood just as well as Hubachek did that if the Forest Service stopped putting out all BWCA fires, some trees would burn, and the land would bear scars. The real issue for him, then, was how the scars were created. Olson's antilogging argument revealed not so much an inconsistency of thought as a choice among values, and his wilderness management preferences rested less upon his science than upon his wilderness theology. "Wilderness," he wrote for *Naturalist* magazine in 1964, "is more than lakes, rivers, and timber along the shores, more than fishing or just camping. It is the sense of the primeval, of space, solitude, silence, and the eternal mystery."[43]

Olson believed that the most important reason for preserving wilderness is to give people a chance to feel the presence of a universal power that science can never explain, but that brings meaning to their lives:

> Wilderness offers [a] sense of cosmic purpose if we open our hearts and minds to its possibilities. It may come in . . . burning instants of truth when everything stands clear. It may come as a slow realization after long periods of waiting. Whenever it comes, life is suddenly illumined, beautiful, and transcendent, and we are filled with awe and deep happiness.[44]

When the *primary purpose* of wilderness is defined in essentially sacramental terms, then the wilderness itself becomes a sacred temple, and anything that either violates the temple or disrupts the "service"—the cosmic communion at the heart of a wilderness experience—is out of place. In effect, Olson saw logging as a violation of sacred space and outboard motors as a disruption of a sacramental experience. And, while he certainly enjoyed singing around a campfire just as much as he loved singing the traditional Protestant hymns in church, he believed that canoeists, like churchgoers, need to learn and appreciate the proper times for silence. "At times in quiet waters," he wrote in *The Singing Wilderness*, "one does not speak aloud but only in whispers, for then all noise is sacrilege."[45]

Olson undoubtedly would feel uncomfortable to see himself and his philosophy described in terms ordinarily reserved for organized religion: "theology," "sacramental perspective," "service," and so on. He had, after all, rejected the dogma of his father's church and had never fully accepted the doctrine of any other. But regardless of his disagreements with organized religion, and regardless of whether scholars classify him as a liberal Christian or an agnostic humanist or a pantheist, it is clear that Sigurd never entirely abandoned the worldview that came with his Swedish Baptist heritage. His whole life was based on a faith in the existence of absolute values such as truth and duty and love. Maybe he did not believe in the threat of divine wrath for sinners, but he did believe in the golden rule and a conservative moral code. Maybe he did not believe in physical immortality, but he believed that an individual's thoughts live on in some mysterious way in the noosphere envisioned by Teilhard de Chardin. Maybe he did not believe in the Trinity, but he believed in an emergent God of love as real as the human heart, a God who to many was most accessible in the wild places of the world. This was the God whom Olson had known ever since he was a small child, the wilderness God whose singing he had first heard at an abandoned pier near Sister Bay, Wisconsin. And this was the faceless and nameless God whom Olson invoked throughout his adult life in his writings and speeches. Sigurd Olson may not have become the Baptist missionary that the Reverend L. J. Olson once hoped for, but a missionary he was, and late in life he would admit it in a statement that spoke both to the pain of a difficult father-son relationship and to the pride he took in his own success: "I've probably saved as many souls as my father did," he said.[46]

Olson was, in many respects, a second John Muir. A famous turn-of-the-century writer and conservationist, Muir founded the Sierra Club. The similarities are striking. Like Olson, Muir was raised by a grim fundamentalist preacher and as an adult turned away from religious dogma. Like Olson, Muir went through a frustrating period in which he kept his dreams at arm's length in order to make a living to support his family. (Muir spent most of the 1880s as a California fruit rancher.) He grew irritable, developed a persistent cough, and felt that life was passing him by. Like Olson, Muir eventually broke his self-imposed shackles and became a highly popular author as well as an influential conservation leader. Like Olson, Muir developed a true wilderness theology—and described it in such vague terms that scholars have been arguing about whether he was a pantheist or a liberal Christian. Muir's theology, like Olson's, arose out of direct, joy- and wonder-filled experiences in nature, with subsequent reflection and reading giving form and adding nuances to those experiences. And Muir's evangelism, like Olson's, was devoted to helping people discover the sacredness of creation and their own connectedness to it.[47]

Surprisingly, Olson seems to have read very little of Muir. In *Open Horizons,* he describes reading Muir during his youth, but there is no indication in his published writings or in his private papers that he read Muir as an adult. Muir is mentioned only in passing in Sigurd's journals.

Olson and Muir also share a common intellectual descent from the nineteenth-century Transcendentalist Henry David Thoreau, and it is important to briefly describe Olson's ties to the man he called "the Sage of Concord"; those ties were less essential to the development of

Olson's theology than some may expect, yet valuable to Olson on a more personal level, and to his development as a writer. He read *Walden* many times; it was the one book he chose to take overseas with him when he went to England in 1945, and he could quote from a number of the essays. He also read *A Week on the Concord and Merrimack Rivers* and *The Maine Woods*. Even so, when Sigurd wrote about or quoted Thoreau in his journals, the ideas did not refer to nature or nature-related philosophy, but to the necessity of breaking free from worldly expectations and fully living each moment.

Thoreau became an inspiration at a time when Olson wanted to quit his career at Ely Junior College and spend his time experiencing and writing about nature. And the inspiration was all the greater because Olson (like John Muir) shared Thoreau's key insights. Like Thoreau, Olson believed that the highest form of knowing is not scholarly research or theorizing, but a combination of direct sensory experience with nature and the mind's intuitive perception of the experience. Like Olson, Thoreau viewed nature-inspired epiphanies as the lodestone of everyday life: they bring joy and wonder and a sense of meaning. If Olson developed the key elements of his wilderness theology largely independent of his reading of Thoreau—and it appears that he did—the writer of *Walden* still played an important role in helping Olson begin to put his own feelings into words. (Indeed, when Olson began to write essays in the early 1930s he feared he might seem to be an imitator of Thoreau or of Olson's favorite American nature writer, John Burroughs.) While Olson was much more of an optimist about progress than Thoreau (or than Muir—optimism was another trait Sigurd had in common with Teilhard and the evolutionary humanists), and while he also was more sentimental, he clearly fits into the Thoreauvian tradition.

❖

The Wilderness Act, signed into law by President Lyndon Johnson in September 1964, gave the secretary of agriculture the power to determine the fate of logging in the BWCA. After appointing a commission to study the issue, former Minnesota governor Orville L. Freeman, Johnson's agriculture secretary, decided to greatly reduce the acreage open to logging. In addition, he created a zoning system for outboard motors. But the controversy made 1964 a difficult year for Olson. It nearly severed his thirty-plus-year connection to the Quetico-

Superior Council and the President's Quetico-Superior Committee, and once again he faced animosity at home. "As usual the Chamber of Commerce crowd are out to crucify me," he wrote to Charley Woodbury on June 5.

What upset him the most, however, was that Izaak Walton League activists questioned his dedication. Early in June, Olson told one of the activists in confidence of his talks with Kelly and Hubachek and said he was trying to sort out the various strategies. The activist took this as a sign that Olson was wavering. When Sigurd arrived at the Blackhawk Hotel in Davenport, Iowa, for the league's national convention later that month, seven telegrams and two letters were waiting for him, all urging him not to lose his resolve. One of them said, "I always thought canoe men represented a breed of quiet strength and determination." Hurt by the insinuation, Olson angrily wrote to the activist who had betrayed his confidence:

> For forty-two years I have fought threat after threat, any one of which could have destroyed the wilderness canoe country. We have not always achieved our objectives one hundred percent but have usually won substantially. In the process, I hope I have learned some wisdom and strategy on how best to get things done. Never before in all this time has anyone ever felt my hand and convictions must be bolstered. My record can stand.[48]

❖ Fifteen ❖

The Making of a Myth

1960–1982

Sigurd Olson once told a friend that despite his growing reputation as an author in the late 1950s and early 1960s, and despite his role in battles over the canoe country, many people in his hometown had little idea of how he spent his days. Sometimes a former student or another Ely acquaintance would come up to him at Zup's grocery store or the First Presbyterian Church or somewhere else downtown and, after exchanging a few pleasantries, would ask, "By the way, Mr. Olson, what do you do with your time now that you're retired from the junior college? You must find it boring." "Yes," Sigurd would answer, "but it isn't so bad."[1]

To the extent that such encounters actually occurred, they probably provided Olson with a healthy dose of humility at a time when his life was anything *but* boring. His books were read on public radio, his portrait was taken by Alfred Eisenstaedt for *Life* magazine, and awards almost routinely came his way. Among U.S. and Canadian conservationists, among members of Congress who sat on committees overseeing America's wildlands, among the federal employees who managed the lands and the journalists who wrote about them, and among the growing numbers of North Americans who enjoyed reading nature books, Sigurd Olson achieved celebrity status during the 1960s. By the 1970s he was an icon, his name and image a potent symbol for a new generation of Americans who called themselves environmentalists rather than conservationists.[2]

Sigurd's popularity was not simply due to his poetic writing style or his spiritual philosophy or his effective handling of conservation issues. These things were part of it, but there was something else, too. His friends recognized it, even if they found it hard to describe. "It's sometimes gnomeish, often mystical," said Charley Woodbury of the National Parks Association, "it's fleeting in and out, but it's there always."[3]

Careful biographers try to avoid the word *charisma;* it is overused and exposes them to the charge that they have become too close to their subject. But in Olson's case, the word seems to apply. There was something in his bearing—a combination of gracefulness, poise, confidence, and an engaging voice—that had a strong effect on people.

There are many examples of this. One comes from Jean Packard, whose husband, Fred, served as executive director of the National Parks Association during the years Olson was the group's president. "When I was working at American Airlines," she recalled, "[Olson] would call me at work when he came into town [Washington, D.C.]. When any woman would answer the phone she would practically swoon, and I got a long interrogation about who had that marvelous voice."[4]

A letter to Olaus Murie from a friend in Arizona provides another example:

> You may not yet know that [Howard] Zahniser and Sig stayed over two days after the ride so that Sig could speak at the American Game Protective Association banquet in Springerville Saturday night. He did and did a magnificent job. He spoke first and influenced every speaker afterwards to use similar words to his. . . . Lin thinks Sig is a combination of Raymond Massey and Lowell Thomas. He adored Sig too, and brought him out to the house . . . when the afternoon meeting settled to mundane matters of the day. Then we all three rode back to the banquet. . . . Who knows what ripples the pebble he cast will create? . . . Never will I be the same.[5]

Former Minnesota governor Elmer L. Andersen, who got to know Olson well during the 1960s, recalled, "Sig conveyed a religious fervor and a depth of conviction that no one else I know succeeded in generating. Others could win adherence; he produced disciples." The same could be said of a handful of other prominent conservationists and environmentalists after World War II, including David Brower, Ralph Nader, and Barry Commoner. But disciple producers, like Old Testament prophets, tend to be divisive, creating enemies and upsetting their friends. Olson had no enemies, except perhaps in Ely. There is no question that he stirred intense anger among those who hated wilderness restrictions in the canoe country, and that anger not infrequently led to ostracism and other forms of boorish behavior. At the same time, the only people in Ely who hated *him* because of his wilderness activism were people who did not know him personally. Ely's political leaders, who fought Olson many times over wilderness issues, at times even expressed warmth and admiration for him. In 1972, for example, Mayor J. P. Grahek, who had battled Olson for two decades, declared July 19 "Sig Olson Day," saying, "In many ways Sigurd Olson is a great man. You don't have to agree with some of the things he has advocated to recognize his quality and his worth as a writer."[6]

What separated Sigurd Olson from most disciple producers was his gentleness and warmth, which made him a master of diplomacy and drew affection from all quarters. George Marshall, who served as president of both the Wilderness Society and the Sierra Club, summed it up in six words: "He made wilderness and life sing."[7] Such affection goes a long way toward explaining why Olson is the only person to have received the highest honors of four leading citizen organizations that focus on the nation's public lands: the Izaak Walton League, the National Wildlife Federation, the Sierra Club, and the Wilderness Society.[8]

That accomplishment is even more extraordinary in light of the fact that Olson also received the John Burroughs Medal, the highest honor in nature writing. Of the more than sixty winners of the medal since it was first awarded in 1926, only a handful have played major leadership roles in national conservation organizations; only two others have received even one of the major conservation group awards.[9] This is not to disparage the Burroughs Medal winners, but to suggest that it is extremely difficult to achieve national recognition as a nature writer while also leading national conservation groups. Some might argue that writers tend to have a temperament that makes them uninterested in or even unsuited for organizational leadership, but the real obstacle is time. Both writing and national leadership require long, difficult hours of work, and to put in the hours that may lead to success in one area usually leaves little time for anything else.

Sigurd Olson ran smack into this conundrum in the 1960s. Because of his immense popularity, he was asked to do many things. His inborn sense of duty and his deep need for recognition, as well as his enjoyment of his popularity, made it extremely difficult for him to say no. To start with, he was a consultant to the Park Service and the secretary of the interior; this not only meant travel all over the country but also required him and Elizabeth to spend several winters in Washington, D.C. Then there was his ongoing Quetico-Superior work, a chronic source of tension-causing controversy.

But that was hardly the end of it. In 1962, for example, he was a member of the organizing committee for the First World Conference on National Parks as well as a speaker at the conference that July in Seattle. In 1963 he flew to Toronto to help create a major conservation group, the National and Provincial Parks Association. He helped design the group's structure, philosophy, and fund-raising strategy. Meanwhile, that same year, Wilderness Society leaders decided to persuade Olson to become their group's vice president. Richard Leonard, writing to Charley Woodbury on April 6, 1963, said it would be an ideal way "to get Sig to accept eventually the responsibility of president of the society." Woodbury, who was close to Olson and knew he wanted to spend more time writing, wrote back, "I'm not at all confident that Sig will agree. . . . I think however we should try."[10] Olson said yes.

And there was still more. Sigurd served as a consultant with Time-Life Books, Reader's Digest Books, and the National Geographic Society. He also gave advice to a number of local and regional conservation groups, such as the Committee for the Preservation of the Tule Elk (in California), the Save the Dunes Council (Indiana), and the Algonquin Wildlands League (Ontario). It was not unusual for him to fly to one of their meetings to give them encouragement when the chips were down. And, of course, Olson spoke about the spiritual values of wildlands to audiences across the United States and Canada—not just at conservation group meetings, but also before scout groups and garden clubs and historical societies, and at colleges and universities and even the Mayo Clinic.

Woodbury called Sigurd's schedule "insane," but Olson felt he had little choice. "It is very difficult to say no to everything," he wrote to Woodbury on September 21, 1965. "For instance I was called last night and asked if I could come down for a big meeting on Indiana Dunes, a cause I have fought for a long time. I could not say no for this is the most crucial time. And what applies to the Dunes applies to many other places."[11]

When Sigurd *was* at home, a steady stream of letters from fans and colleagues demanded his attention, and visitors frequently dropped in. A letter Olson wrote to Woodbury on July 8, 1965, before embarking on a month of almost solid travel, describes a typical summer day at home:

> Yesterday . . . a University of Wisconsin team came up to tape some of my reactions on wilderness to be inserted in a film the U is producing. Last night at 5:30 after they had gone a group of seventeen young people from Fargo came up for an hour session on wilderness before going out on a [canoe] trip. Then this morning the U team came back and have just left. What the rest of the day will bring we do not know but think we will run out to Listening Point for the rest of the day just to collect our wits.[12]

When Sigurd Jr. and Robert and their families managed a rare trip to Ely (Sigurd Jr. from Alaska and Robert from some far-flung diplomatic post), they often found visiting impossible. "He'd become so well known and he had all these visitors," said Robert. "The house was always in a turmoil, and mother would invite anybody in who showed up at the door." The only place they could talk uninterrupted was out at Listening Point.

The sons found this frustrating, but both Sigurd and Elizabeth genuinely enjoyed the visitors, who often arrived without warning. At times it was tiring or inconvenient, but the people who dropped in at 106 East Wilson Street tended to be true fans of Olson's books, and both Sigurd and Elizabeth took pleasure in the attention Sigurd received. Elizabeth would answer the door with a smile, usher the visitors into a three-season paneled porch with a picture window view of red pines and bird feeders, and introduce the guests to her husband. Then she would hurry off to the kitchen for coffee and some of her freshly made lemon cake or sugar cookies.

Sigurd did become frustrated in the 1960s, but not because his home had become a tourist destination. What bothered him was the huge amount of time he spent away from home as a professional conservationist. It was an irony in Olson's life that conservation work, which led him into the arms of Alfred Knopf and a successful writing career, came between him and his writing in the 1960s. Even as early as 1958 he found it necessary to write in hotel rooms and airplanes to keep his books moving along. But at least they *were* moving along: *Listening Point* in 1958, *The Lonely Land* in 1961, *Runes of the North* in 1963. By the time *Runes* was published, however, he was deep into his work as a consultant to the Park Service and to Stewart Udall, was vice president of the Wilderness Society, was involved in other conservation work, and found almost no time at all to write.

"He used to go to these meetings in Washington and he'd come back absolutely wrung out," said his son Robert. "It killed him. Not just the travel, but the exercise itself. It wasn't his cup of tea."

Sigurd once again began writing journal entries reminiscent of his days at the junior college in the 1930s and 1940s. Sitting in his office at the Interior Department one winter morning early in 1963, he wrote:

> This work here palls. . . . After the hitch this year, I am through and can see the end coming. All I want to do is get back to my writing and thinking. That is my forte, nothing else. The days even though I have been here only a month seem endless and I am doing nothing constructive. I can picture myself at home heading out to the cabin or the bush and the shack . . . taking a few speaking engagements, but being absolutely free of all practical conservation problems. It is the same old stalemate I have been up against before, back thirty years when I used to pound off a few paragraphs every morning and dream and hope for release. Never again shall I be caught in such an impasse.[13]

But what did he do? He accepted the vice presidency of the Wilderness Society, flew to Toronto to help launch the National and Provincial Parks Association, then spent a good portion of the summer scouting out Alaskan park possibilities with Ted Swem. In January 1964, three months short of his sixty-fifth birthday, he was back in Washington and writing gloomy notes:

> All of this leaves me cold, all these hearings [are as] boring as terminology. . . . Others should do this, not me. Wilderness preservation will go on but it engrosses me less and less. Others can carry on the fight. . . . This fall was bad. It must not happen again. I must make a decision soon. . . . I've got ten years left, I should put them all to the

best and not feel frustrated or fighting or feel torn—it is the feeling of being torn every which way that hurts.[14]

Sigurd finally began a new book in 1965—an autobiography. He also signed a contract with McGraw-Hill to write a book called *Rivers of the Shield* for a series on the American wilderness. He did not reduce his conservation workload, however, so he made very slow progress on the autobiography and none at all on the McGraw-Hill book.

Two more years passed. Olson's term on the National Park Service Advisory Board ended, but he continued to attend its meetings in a nonvoting capacity along with Frank Masland and other former members. He also continued his work as a consultant. In July 1967, at Yellowstone National Park as part of a team working to create a master management plan for the park, Olson chastised himself: "I have no right at my age to be wasting my time any more. Finish this job and then say no. You cannot clutter your mind if you are going to write."[15]

Eight months later, on March 8, 1968, Wilderness Society president and cofounder Harvey Broome died of a heart attack at his Knoxville, Tennessee, home while sawing a log to make a wren house. He was sixty-five, four years younger than Olson, who suddenly found himself president of a national conservation group for the second time.

By then it had been five years since the publication of *Runes of the North*. After three years of off-and-on writing, Sigurd was close to finishing his autobiography, which he called *Open Horizons*. Meanwhile, he signed a contract with Viking Press to provide the text for a coffee table book showcasing the work of a Minnesota friend, photographer Les Blacklock. Olson had promised Blacklock several years earlier that he would write the text if Blacklock found a publisher, but he could not have seen the timing as ideal. He had not even started *Rivers of the Shield,* which was due at McGraw-Hill in January 1969, and he had an autobiography to wrap up and an organization to lead. Sigurd focused first on *Open Horizons,* finishing it late in the summer. Then, perhaps thinking his work with Blacklock would not take long and assuming he could get a contract extension with McGraw-Hill (he did, but dropped the project two years later), he began dashing off some of the text for the photo book and preparing for the first Wilderness Society Council meeting of his presidency.

Olson's overbooked calendar caught up with him on November 22, 1968, at Sanibel Island, off the Gulf Coast of southwestern Florida. He and Elizabeth had flown down for the Wilderness Society Council meeting. During the opening dinner, Sigurd suddenly grew pale and clutched his chest. Frantic, Elizabeth called out for help. Wilderness Society executive director Stewart Brandborg helped Sigurd out of his chair and onto the floor, while others scrambled to get medical help. Hotel staff located a vacationing doctor from New York City, who came and cared for Olson until a rescue squad arrived.[16]

Sigurd had suffered a major heart attack. He spent three weeks in Lee Memorial Hospital at nearby Fort Myers, the first three days in intensive care. Letters and cards and flowers arrived from friends across the United States and Canada. After ten days in the hospital he was able to get out of bed long enough to walk to the bathroom, which he took as a sign that he was mending. But even after he left the hospital in mid-December, he was far too weak to travel home. Instead, he and Elizabeth leased an apartment at the Seacrest Motel in Sarasota, ninety miles to the north along the coast.

They stayed in Sarasota until February 1969. Sigurd gradually worked his way up to several slow walks a day along the beach and enjoyed an occasional restaurant dinner of shrimp rolled in flour and broiled in beer. His doctor told him he absolutely could not give any talks or go to any meetings for at least six months and warned him to change his lifestyle for good if he wanted to avoid a killing heart attack.

❖

Olson remained president of the Wilderness Society for three years, but he did not totally ignore the doctor's warning. He couldn't, really—his recovery took many months, and he did not regain all of his strength. His facial twitch, always a bother to him but somewhat under control with medication, grew worse, to the point where his entire head shook. (From then on, people often would mistakenly assume that he suffered from Parkinson's disease.) He walked slower and got tired faster. Nevertheless, in 1970 he gradually resumed travel to Washington on Wilderness Society business and attended the group's executive committee and council meetings.

During Olson's presidency the Wilderness Society was involved in a number of conservation issues, from the protection of the Florida

Everglades from a proposed airport to a long and unsuccessful fight to prevent construction of the Alaska Pipeline. But the one that meant the most to him was the campaign to establish a national park in the Rainy Lake region along his home state's northern border, just to the west of the Boundary Waters Canoe Area. As early as 1891 the Minnesota Legislature had lobbied for a national park there, but Congress had taken no action. The issue of federal protection was raised again in the late 1920s, when Ernest Oberholtzer drafted his ambitious proposal for an international treaty to carefully zone the entire Rainy Lake watershed. Oberholtzer's Quetico-Superior program called for public ownership of the Minnesota lands and waters along the international border from Lake Superior to Rainy Lake. A vast expansion of Superior National Forest in the 1930s and the 1951 establishment of Grand Portage National Historic Site along Lake Superior (later designated a national monument) achieved part of this goal, but federal designation for the final section to the west proved elusive.[17]

At the end of the 1950s, hopes for an international treaty to implement the Quetico-Superior program died. Olson, meanwhile, became a consultant to the Park Service and began traveling around the country to evaluate areas proposed for national park status. When Minnesota officials expressed interest in reopening the issue of a national park in the Rainy Lake area, Olson was the ideal intermediary. On October 6, 1961, he toured the area with personnel from the National Park Service and the Minnesota Department of Conservation. It was a gusty day, with rolling waves splashing over the bow as they motored for seventy miles around the Kabetogama Peninsula, which formed the heart of the proposed park. "You should have seen the color, it was absolutely magnificent," an exuberant Olson wrote the next day to his friend and fellow Voyageur Eric Morse. "What we are thinking of, shshsh—national park status. . . . Please keep this confidential for the time being."

The following June, Park Service director Conrad Wirth, who had received a favorable report from the officials who had visited the area the previous fall, as well as some heavy lobbying by Olson, came to see it for himself. He was joined by Olson, Minnesota governor Elmer Andersen, and several others. Wirth was convinced. Writing about the trip years later, Olson said that as they cruised toward the end of

Crane Lake they tried to think of a good name for the park. A number of names were suggested, none of which excited Wirth. Then Sigurd spoke. Recalling the eighteenth-century voyageurs who had traveled the border lakes between Lake Superior and Rainy Lake on their way to the far north, he suggested the name Voyageurs National Park. According to Olson, Wirth slapped his knee and said, "That's it!"[18]

Olson worked hard for Voyageurs National Park, getting the support of the Park Service's advisory board and engaging in endless discussions with federal and state officials and executives from the Minnesota and Ontario Paper Company, which was the largest property owner in the proposed park area. When George Hartzog replaced Wirth as director of the Park Service in 1964 and suggested that the area should receive a less prestigious designation, such as national historic waterway, Olson got the advisory board to reaffirm its stand and change Hartzog's mind. This was a departure from Sigurd's usual position, which was to get the land as soon as possible and worry about the details later. But he was determined to get a national park established in Minnesota.[19]

It took a long time. There were disagreements over the park boundaries, over hunting, over snowmobiling, over other issues. After legislation was introduced in 1968, Olson testified at a number of hearings, arguing not only for the national park but also for eventual wilderness status for the Kabetogama Peninsula. Many other Minnesotans also testified or worked behind the scenes, writing letters and generating publicity. Although statewide support was strong, the proposal drew intense opposition among some northeastern Minnesotans, who said the federal government already had far too much land and power in the region.

Nevertheless, the bill made it through both houses of Congress by the end of 1970, although it took some personal lobbying by Elmer Andersen and Sigurd Olson to shepherd it through the final stages in the Senate. On January 8, 1971, President Richard Nixon signed the act, and Minnesota had its national park. "I doubt very much if the Voyageurs National Park would have been established if it had not been for Sig," Conrad Wirth wrote later. "He not only explained and recommended it, but followed his concept through to its establishment. Of course he had help, but he was the spirit behind it."[20]

The campaign to establish Voyageurs National Park took place during a period of intense national interest in the environment. In 1962, the year Olson proposed the name for the park during his trip to the area with Conrad Wirth, Rachel Carson's *Silent Spring* created widespread concern about the use and misuse of pesticides. Between then and January 1971, when President Nixon signed the bill to create the park, urban power failures, oceanic oil spills, the licensing of nuclear power plants, and predictions of calamity from worldwide population growth were among the events and issues that generated increasing media coverage of the environment. The United States enacted a series of landmark legislation during this period, including the Clean Air Act, the Land and Water Conservation Fund Act, the Wilderness Act, the Wild and Scenic Rivers Act, the National Trail System Act, and the National Environmental Policy Act. New federal environmental organizations were created: the Bureau of Outdoor Recreation, the Environmental Protection Agency, the National Oceanic and Atmospheric Administration, and the President's Council on Environmental Quality. The first Earth Day, in April 1970, symbolized the heightened national interest as it approached its peak.

Outwardly, at least, it was a time of great prosperity for groups such as the Wilderness Society; during Olson's three years as president, membership in the society grew from forty-five thousand to seventy-five thousand. In fact, however, the very success of environmentalism posed immense challenges for the old-time conservation organizations, and the Wilderness Society was no exception.

Money was the most obvious, if not the most important, problem. After celebrating the passage of the Wilderness Act in 1964, the Wilderness Society soon realized the downside of success. The act initiated a long process of federal review of potential wilderness areas; if the society was to have any substantial say in the makeup of the national wilderness preservation system it had so long struggled to establish, it needed to participate in the review process in many areas around the country at the same time. This meant sending staff members to study these areas and write reports, testify at hearings, and enlist public support. Olson, who was vice president at the time, argued along with the majority of the governing council that the Wilderness Society had no choice but to engage in deficit spending to meet these new demands.

Soon another success story brought new opportunities and imposed more financial burdens on the society. A precedent-setting court decision in 1965 gave the Sierra Club legal standing to join a suit seeking to protect Storm King Mountain in New York from a power project; during the next few years other national organizations began hiring lawyers and filing lawsuits in other environmental disputes. The trend began in earnest during Olson's years as Wilderness Society president. In 1968 the society spent just $610 on litigation, about a tenth of 1 percent of all expenditures for that year. By 1970 the group was spending more than $64,000, 7 percent of the year's expenditures, on litigation. Meanwhile, the ongoing wilderness system debates continued to escalate costs. During Olson's presidency the group's total budget doubled, from just over half a million dollars in 1968 to more than a million dollars in 1971. The money brought in by the large numbers of new memberships did not meet the rapidly expanding costs. In the last year under Olson's leadership, 14 percent of the society's income came from the liquidation of capital assets.[21]

The new political, legal, and financial environment forced major changes on the national conservation groups. As they hired scientific and policy experts to analyze environmental impact statements and other government documents, lawyers to lead litigation, and managers to develop and implement new fund-raising strategies such as mass mail membership drives, they began to resemble the bureaucracies they challenged. Meanwhile, the older generation of leaders—the people who had led the groups for thirty years and had established and nurtured their philosophies—was dying. The Wilderness Society, for example, lost Olaus Murie in 1963, Howard Zahniser and Bernard Frank in 1964, Harold Anderson and William Zimmerman in 1967, Harvey Broome in 1968, and Charley Woodbury in 1971. These men had played major roles in the organization; Frank, Anderson, and Broome were among the group's eight founders. Benton MacKaye and Ernest Oberholtzer were the only founders still alive in 1971, and they were in frail health. Robert Marshall, Robert Sterling Yard, and Aldo Leopold had been gone a long time. Sigurd Olson and Robert Marshall's brothers Jim and George were the last active Wilderness Society leaders with ties to the group dating back to its inception in 1935.

After Sigurd resigned from the society's presidency in September

1971, citing his health and his desire to write, conversation and correspondence among the three took a nostalgic turn. George Marshall
succeeded Olson as president for a year and all three remained active
on the society's governing council, but they worried that the increasingly bureaucratic nature of the organization posed a subtle long-
term threat to the continuing development of the philosophy that
sustained wilderness preservation. George Marshall wrote to Sigurd:

> At present, our colleagues seem to be bogged under a deluge of im-
> mediate problems. These must be met and they are being handled
> with skill and devotion. However, it seems to me that almost all of
> the emphasis is being placed on land classification and manage-
> ment policy, and almost none on wilderness interpretation and
> those deeper qualities and understandings that make wilderness
> essential for a continuance of life and higher human values. There
> is too little consideration of the aesthetic, mystical, and inspira-
> tional aspects of wilderness. There is not enough of what you have
> called "the singing wilderness."[22]

Olson, exasperated by the increasingly legalistic approach to wilderness issues, passed a note of frustration to Jim Marshall during
the society's annual meeting in October 1972: "We strangle ourselves
with words, make mountains out of molehills, exchange simplicity
for complexity. God save us." That same day, Sigurd opened the blue
three-ring binder that contained the meeting's agenda and other
background information, took out his black felt tip pen, and began
doodling a picture of an elephant. At the top of the page, he wrote:
"Here I sit out of place as always, wasting time, hours and days and
months and years when I should be writing."[23]

❖

In 1970 officials in a Minneapolis suburb got Sigurd Olson's permission to name a new elementary school in his honor. Less than two
years later, but with some difficulty, he was persuaded to lend his
name to an environmental institute being established at Northland
College in Ashland, Wisconsin.[24] Both schools recognized that Olson's
name had gained potent symbolic power and hoped to use it to capture favorable attention during a time of tremendous public interest
in the environment. President Malcolm McLean of Northland College was explicit in a January 19, 1972, letter to Sigurd:

Now . . . let me tell you candidly that I think it is important that our environmental activity honor your name in its title. There are many reasons for this. One of them is that it is entirely appropriate for Northland to salute a distinguished son in this fashion. Another is that the impact of a name attracts attention; it calls forth an association to the college and to the institute from many, many persons who otherwise would have only a hazy concept of what and who we are here. Third, I realized something interesting in discussing this question with a good friend in Washington whom you don't know, but who knows and admires your work. He pointed out that many people, young and old alike, look up to the hero. In our days it is not the hero in the military sense who is the center of adulation, but increasingly it is the humanitarian man, free of false values and deeply enmeshed in an affectionate relationship with the environment, both human and physical, which surrounds him. One of the concepts of the hero is that others . . . want to be like him. . . . A person can aspire to "being like" Sigurd Olson in love of nature and concern for his fellows. Hence, having a Sigurd Olson Center or Sigurd Olson Institute evokes this kind of response while a Northland Center simply does not.

The creation of Sigurd F. Olson Elementary School and the Sigurd Olson Environmental Institute marked the completion of the final transformation of Sigurd's life: his emergence as a beloved figurehead whose name and image evoked strong feelings. Often photographed with a pipe in his hand and a warm yet reflective expression on his weathered face, he had become not just a hero, but an icon. "I look at the picture of Sigurd Olson," wrote Wisconsin journalist and nature writer George Vukelich, "and he gazes at me like some guru—wise, benign, his very being full of the knowledge that waits for us beyond the cities where the bush begins." Sierra Club president Edgar Wayburn said, "To many of us, he is the personification of the wilderness defender."[25]

Sigurd's fan mail began taking on a decided tone of veneration after 1972. The writer Annie Dillard, for example, excited that Olson had read and approved of the first portion of what would become her best-selling book *Pilgrim at Tinker Creek*, wrote: "It is an undreamed-of pleasure for me that you (Sigurd Olson!) should have taken the time to read a chapter of my first book of prose, let alone that you

should write me personally about it. . . . Your writing has been a joy—
and a beacon—to me for the last several years."[26] Many people saved
letters they received from Olson; some even framed them.

By the 1970s Olson routinely was described and treated as a prophet,
or, as Vukelich said, a guru. Arlys Utech, principal of Sigurd F. Olson
Elementary School, described him as being surrounded by a "beautiful aura" that led anyone he encountered to experience "inner
growth." Sister Noemi Weygant, an accomplished photographer and
an instructor at St. Scholastica College in Duluth, Minnesota, regularly took her students to Olson's house on what was essentially a pil-
grimage. "To have sat with him," she wrote, "watching him fill his
pipe, encouraging him to keep talking that I might hear his wisdom,
was truly to experience increase in living."[27]

When the Sigurd Olson Environmental Institute's new building
was dedicated in 1981, the ceremony had elements of religious ritual.
The audience read in unison a selection from *The Singing Wilderness,*
musician Douglas Wood performed a song he wrote about Olson,
and, at the end of the ceremony, Northland College students dressed
as French Canadian voyageurs carried Olson's wooden canoe into
the auditorium, slipped ropes under it, and hoisted it up to a permanent resting spot high on the wall. Then they stood under it and sang
some of the traditional voyageur chansons.

As early as 1970, Olson-as-icon began playing an important role in
conservation battles. At that time, Quetico Provincial Park was embroiled in a controversy over logging within its boundaries. Ontario
conservationists arranged what they called an "international summit"
at the edge of the park. About a hundred people attended the October 3 event: Canadian and American conservationists, Ontario government officials, logging industry representatives, and, most important of all, journalists from major Canadian newspapers, wire services,
and television networks. Sigurd Olson was the keynote speaker.[28]

He was the perfect choice, even though anti-American sentiment
was running strong in Canada at the time. Olson had made so many
public relations trips to Ontario in the 1950s and 1960s to talk about
wilderness canoeing and his expeditions with the Voyageurs, and his
book *The Lonely Land* was so popular in Canada, that he was as
revered among Canadian environmentalists as he was among their

American counterparts. "The wilderness appreciation and support in this part of Canada today owes much to the work done by Sig during his frequent trips, mainly here to Toronto, during the 1950s and 1960s," according to Fred Bodsworth, one of Canada's best-known nature writers.[29]

An early winter storm struck on the day of the summit, which made travel difficult but added to the effect of Olson's speech. Facing a fierce snowstorm on a bridge that spanned a historic fur trade route and talking about what he called the global spiritual significance of the Quetico, the elderly conservationist with the shaking head galvanized his listeners. The resulting media coverage was decidedly prowilderness. Olson's speech was the turning point of the campaign, which led to a ban on logging and reclassification of the Quetico as a primitive park.

Olson's opponents in Ely also understood his power as a symbol. During the late 1970s, in the wake of repeated court battles and in response to legislation that threatened to reclassify 40 percent of the Boundary Waters Canoe Area to allow logging and motorized recreation, environmentalists successfully campaigned to give the BWCA more protection as a federally designated wilderness area. Olson regularly conferred with the activists and offered advice and moral support, but was too frail to play a leading role. Nevertheless, as the issue began building to a peak in the summer of 1977, local residents disrupted Olson's testimony and hanged him in effigy during congressional hearings in Ely. The incident must be viewed not simply as a personal attack on Olson; those involved understood his symbolic importance and knew their actions would be viewed as a personal attack on *all* wilderness defenders. Similarly, the *Ely Echo* invoked the icon that summer in an editorial that sarcastically characterized environmentalists as saying, "The BWCA is our sacred place and you cannot enter in until you have been baptized in the name of Sigurd."[30]

Underlying Olson's emergence as an icon was the cultural upheaval of the 1960s and early 1970s. Race riots, Vietnam War protests, political assassinations, and the hippie movement all pointed toward disenchantment with society. Young people searching for new heroes and new prophets often found a home in the environmental movement.

Ironically, Olson never felt comfortable describing himself as an environmentalist; he preferred the term *conservationist*. Part of the reason undoubtedly was a matter of being used to the older term, but it also reflected his cultural conservatism. He disliked the male environmentalist fashion of wearing beards, for example, and he detested long hair. After a speech in San Francisco in 1967 or 1968, a group of long-haired students wearing beads approached Olson and said they wanted to help save the environment. Sigurd later recalled that he responded by saying, "Why don't you bathe? Cut your hair? Why don't you put on clean clothes once in a while?" They bristled, but he continued: "As an ecologist I look at you as a species doomed to extinction. Cleanliness is absolutely essential for survival. When animals befoul themselves they become diseased, vermin-ridden and die."[31]

Olson also complained about the era's sexual mores. "Magazines have changed," he said in an interview published in 1977. "They're becoming obsessed with sex. Past cultures that were obsessed with sex collapsed."[32]

But if the evolving culture contained elements that Sigurd deplored, it also expanded his readership, and of all the ingredients that made Sigurd into an environmental cult figure, his books were essential. Some two hundred thousand hardcover copies were in circulation by the end of 1972, and his 1976 book *Reflections from the North Country*, which summarized his philosophy, sold twenty thousand copies in three months. The people who wrote to him for advice, who framed and hung his letters, who dropped in at his house without warning in hopes of meeting him did not do these things because they knew he had been president of the Wilderness Society or because they had heard he was a warm and dynamic man. They did these things because they had been deeply touched by Olson's books, especially *The Singing Wilderness* and *Listening Point* and *Reflections from the North Country*.

The true fans read most or all of his nine books and quite naturally built their image of Olson out of what they could tell about him from his writings and from publicity about him. Sigurd, of course, like the vast majority of nature writers, tended to show his best personal qualities in his writing. Olson the storyteller is invariably optimistic and kind and thoughtful; he exudes peace and faith and connectedness. There is no sign of Olson's occasional temper, no indication that he suffered from stress (as indicated by, for example, his frequent bouts of insomnia and regular doses of antacids), no hint of his long and painful search for meaning and purpose. Inevitably, readers who based their impressions of Olson on his essays created an idealized image of him.

This romanticized image of Olson would have been shaken had they known some things that he did *not* write about. Mrs. C. J. Walker of LaGrange, Illinois, wrote to Sigurd on June 19, 1958, recounting how DDT had killed dozens of songbirds in her yard. *The Singing Wilderness,* she said, had been "a great balm to my sorely troubled spirit." What would she have said had she known that Olson and his Voyageurs used DDT at campsites on every one of their expeditions, including the trip to Hudson Bay in 1964—well after Rachel Carson's *Silent Spring* warned of the pesticide's dangers?

Others would have been surprised to know that Sigurd held stock in Homestake Mining, American Metal Climax, St. Joseph Light and Power, and Columbia Gas System, as well as a handful of other companies representing industries that many considered environmentally unfriendly. The point is not that he was wrong in making such investments; even today, when there is much more discussion about environmentally sound investing, well-meaning people disagree on many aspects of the issue. The point is that Olson's following probably included—and now includes—people who would disagree with his investments and would be disillusioned to discover that the real Olson was not fully compatible with the icon they created. The fact that Olson was a small investor would not lessen the disillusionment.

And then there are the nonhunters, a dominant category among readers of nature books. Not all of these readers oppose hunting, but many of them vehemently do, and many others are uncomfortable with it. They would be surprised, and possibly shocked, to learn the full extent of the role of hunting in Sigurd's life. The descriptions of hunting that appear in his books easily lead to false conclusions.

In *The Singing Wilderness,* for example, Olson wrote that a key motive for his taking up hunting and trapping as a child was his need to possess the wild beauty that brought out such deep emotions in him. This impulse caused him to catch and attempt to keep wild squirrels and made him want to shoot a goose. "The sound of wild geese on the move haunted me," he wrote, "and I felt that somehow I must capture some of their mystery, some of their freedom and of the blue distances into which they disappeared."[33]

But Sigurd went on to say that he never did kill a goose, that he no longer wanted to, and that "the sight and sound of them is enough." Such statements in this and other books easily give the impression that he had stopped hunting, that it was a phase of life he had long since outgrown. True, Olson did not apologize for killing birds and animals, and in *Open Horizons* portrayed his love for hunting in great detail. In describing his first mallard kill, for example, he admitted he had felt no regret, "only wild happiness and joy." But he wrote it as an admission, and he was writing about the past; never in his books did he write about hunting in the present tense.[34]

When it came to deer, past tense was accurate; he stopped regularly hunting them when he was in his forties. The reason, however, had little or nothing to do with regrets or "maturing" out of a youthful phase of life, as his books implied. He stopped because his deer hunting partners had died and it was not as much fun anymore. And, while he decided that the sight and sound of geese was enough for him, he continued to hunt ducks until he was well into his seventies. He did not mind if he came home empty-handed, but he still felt the old excitement when he brought one down. One of his last unpublished essays, written less than a year before he died, looked back nostalgically to the time he shot seventeen mallards in one hour on a northern Minnesota lake and "came back to camp with a look of triumph in [his] eyes."[35] One of his favorite stories to tell old friends was about the time he and Wilson Carlson brought down thirty mallards on the Sand River.

Sigurd Olson loved hunting—reveled in it—and did not see it as incompatible with any of his other beliefs about conservation or wilderness. His son Robert remembered how, after plucking and dismembering a bunch of ducks or grouse, Sigurd would plunge his arms into the bucket of bloody remains, searching for a prized gizzard, not only without any sign of squeamishness but actually relishing the moment. To Sigurd Olson, hunting—and trapping and fishing as well—was a natural human activity, one of the most ancient human connections to the world. He supported laws designed to sustain wildlife populations, but he did not have much patience for opponents of hunting.[36]

Both Sigurd and Elizabeth cared about his public image, but they focused on different aspects of it. Elizabeth wanted Sigurd to appear upper class and dignified. His fame mattered a great deal to her, as did his association with such VIPs as William O. Douglas and Hubert Humphrey. After all, she had a large personal investment in her husband's career. During the many difficult periods in the early years of their marriage, when Sigurd hated his job and suffered bouts of depression, she had resented his obsession with writing. She was not able to understand why he was not happy as dean of the junior college, a position of responsibility and status in the community. But if she had not always found the strength to encourage him to follow his dream, she found it often enough, and if there were times when she wished he would stay at home instead of traveling to Chicago or Toronto or Washington or some remote wilderness, there is no indication that she ever showed it. And once he found happiness and success, they became hers, too. Elizabeth found tremendous satisfaction in playing the role of Mrs. Sigurd F. Olson—traveling to conferences with him, being invited to dinners, entertaining senators and ambassadors and publishers and Supreme Court justices. She made sure Sigurd looked his best, tried to keep him healthy, and kept a sharp eye out for potential trouble.

On May 21, 1963, for example, Sigurd wrote to Alfred Knopf to ask that the publisher remove descriptions of Olson's guiding from future publicity: "I do not like to have my guiding constantly pointed out because it gives the impression I am still catering to tourists. Elizabeth, as shown by the attached personal note, called my attention to this and with her I never argue."

Elizabeth probably also was behind some self-censorship that Sigurd engaged in while he was writing *The Lonely Land,* which told of his 1955 Churchill River expedition with the Voyageurs. Concerned that knowledge of his group's regular evening round of rum would damage his image, especially as a role model, Sigurd nearly removed from the manuscript any mention of alcohol. His editor and agent persuaded him to merely reduce, rather than eliminate, depictions of drinking.

Sigurd placed much less importance than Elizabeth did on respectability, dignity, and social class. Instead, he wanted people to perceive him as a man of the out-of-doors who thought deeply and wrote movingly of his experiences. He clearly wanted people to receive his message of wilderness salvation with open arms, but at the same time he wanted them to perceive *him* not just as a guru, not just as someone who sat on a log and had deep thoughts, but as a *man of action* who lived what he wrote. He wanted to be seen as a modern-day voyageur, someone who laughed in the face of a storm.

This was not a false image, and it was very important to him. Ever since his youth, he had identified with frontier farmers and woodsmen, such as the people he met as a college student spending his summers working on the Uhrenholdt farm in Seeley, Wisconsin; with gold-seeking Al Kennedy in Nashwauk, Minnesota; with the woodsmen and guides he came to know during his early years in Ely. He had admired their toughness, had enjoyed their exaggerated tales of bravado, and even had been jealous of them—because they seemed to live a life that was both simple and very real. His obsession with writing had prevented him from living that simpler life, and he had felt that his work in Nashwauk and Ely was unreal, that he was watching life pass him by. The woodsmen and farmers of Sigurd Olson's youth and young adulthood, along with the fur-trading voyageurs and north country Indians of history, had inspired him during his long search for his own destiny. He had never quite fit in with the ones he had known, because of his education and career, but he had gained their respect by proving he could do the things they did, that he was indeed a woodsman, albeit one with a master's degree.

That was why, as a highly successful author, he continued to wear his beat-up, World War I–vintage felt hat. That was why he wore moccasins. That was why he was photographed only with a pipe, despite the fact that he also smoked cigarettes throughout his life. He enjoyed these things, but he also knew that they were an outward sign of his identity as a woodsman, "a man of action with the bark on," as his son Robert called him.

People in the public eye never have complete control over their image. Sigurd *wanted* to inspire others with his message and accepted his popularity and royal treatment as a matter of course, but the Olson icon constructed by his fans was more than he bargained for. An icon's full humanity is stripped away, leaving only the idealized image. Sigurd's rising fame in the 1960s and 1970s came during a period of great confusion and disillusion, a period in which thousands searched for new panaceas and new gurus. Olson's accessible, spiritual, and lyrical writing made him easy to idealize, and to some extent he felt he had to play the role. "The toughest thing with all the publicity I receive," he admitted in a November 1976 interview, "is that people expect me to have a certain image, which I'm supposed to maintain. It's hard to be myself when people expect me to be something like they imagine from my books."[37]

❖

Reflections from the North Country was published on September 30, 1976, with the usual fanfare.[38] Sigurd signed books in Minneapolis and St. Paul and Duluth, and gave interviews for radio and television stations. The *National Observer* ranked it as the top new book in the country, and fan mail poured in as always. Even Devereux Butcher, who so often had made life difficult for Olson in the National Parks Association, wrote on December 4 to say he thought it deserved a Nobel Prize.

When Sigurd began writing the book in 1973, Elizabeth tried to dissuade him. She remembered telling him, "You're so tired, Sig, you're so tired. How can you do more if you're so tired?" But he insisted, and as always went ahead and did it anyway. To give him time and energy, he dropped most of his remaining conservation commitments; he gave up his role as a Park Service adviser and a Citizens Committee on Natural Resources board member, and, in the fall of 1974, his position on the governing council and executive committee of the Wilderness Society. The society made him its first honorary president, a sign of the affection in which he was held and also of the fact that his days as an active conservation leader were over. He continued to stay on top of developments and to offer advice, and occasionally made brief trips to help out with a cause, but that was all.

Elizabeth was right—he *was* tired. And in the fall of 1976, in the midst of enjoying what turned out to be the last book published during his lifetime, he suffered an accident that left him in pain for the next several years. He was burning a brush pile at the Uhrenholdt farmstead in Seeley, Wisconsin, when the fire got away from him. It would not have amounted to anything if he had not been burning too close to a tree. But he was, and the flames charred some branches. Embarrassed, Sigurd decided to get rid of the evidence by pruning the burned limbs, so he propped a ladder against the tree, climbed up, and began cutting away with a hand saw. But he had not properly hooked the upper part of the ladder, and it collapsed. Sigurd crashed to the ground, injuring a foot.

He did not break the foot, but despite medical attention it did not get better. "For three years I was in a lot of pain," he recalled in 1980, "and I could hardly walk."[39] He added painkillers to his medical regimen, along with drugs for his heart and for his shaking head, antacids for his stomach, and sometimes pills to help him fall asleep.

Sigurd had thought that *Reflections,* which summarized a lifetime of insights and conclusions, would be his last book. But two years after its release he confronted once more the central truth of his life. "The fact remains," he wrote on August 25, 1978, "that unless I am writing, I'm not happy." So he began a new book called *Of Time and Place,* a nostalgic series of anecdotes describing treasured memories. He also planned a book to be called "Packsack Adventures," designed as a paperback to be taken on wilderness excursions, and a book of childhood memories to be called "Days of My Boyhood."

Meanwhile, in 1979 doctors discovered that the eighty-year-old author had cancer of the colon, and in December they operated. The surgery was successful, but Sigurd never regained his strength. On January 19, 1981, Elizabeth wrote to Ted and Helen Swem: "Sig feels healthy but gets very confused. We do not discuss this but there it is, and the illness and operation has had the effect of him growing out of his keen interests and his command of situations."[40] When the Sigurd Olson Environmental Institute dedicated its new building in May, Elizabeth wrote to the Swems two weeks later that Sigurd was just beginning to recover from the trip to Ashland and the excitement and stress of the event. That summer Sigurd finished the essays for *Of Time and Place* and began "Days of My Boyhood," but there was a noticeable decline in the quality of his writing.

In the fall of 1981, the U.S. Department of the Interior chose Sigurd for its highest civilian honor, the Conservation Service Award. Informed over the phone, and asked if he would accept it, he said yes. But soon afterward he had second thoughts. He did not want to seem to be endorsing the controversial James Watt, who as secretary of the interior appeared to represent nearly the opposite of everything Olson believed in. Sigurd decided to reject the award, but his health was so poor he was not able to write an adequate letter. He and Elizabeth discussed it over the phone several times with Ted

Swem, and Swem wrote a draft incorporating the ideas of all three. The letter said:

> I have decided that I cannot in good conscience accept [the award]. I have been greatly bothered over the past several months by many expressions from the Department of the Interior concerning its desire to open existing, as well as possible new wilderness, to oil and gas exploration. Just last week, oil leases were issued covering portions of the Capitan Wilderness in New Mexico. I have also been greatly concerned over several decisions affecting the National Park System, actions which could well compromise those priceless values that belong to all Americans. As you know, I have spent most of my life espousing the importance of wilderness and national parks to our society and the need to protect them at all costs. With this deep-felt personal philosophy, particularly in the context of the Department of the Interior today, there was only one way that I could go and that was to turn down the award.[41]

It was Olson's first act of political protest, and his last.

Sigurd and Elizabeth got each other new snowshoes for Christmas that year, a gesture of nostalgia and perhaps of denial. When they traveled to Seeley, Wisconsin, for a holiday visit with Robert and Yvonne, who recently had bought Elizabeth's childhood home, Sigurd was very weak. At times he did not even seem aware of what was going on around him.

January 1982 brought record-breaking cold to the canoe country. Elizabeth, writing to the Swems on January 12, said the wind chill index had struck a hundred degrees below zero a few days before, and Ely was just recovering from a blizzard. Sigurd was napping as she wrote. "Sometimes Sig is in good spirits but often he does tend to be very quiet," she said. At the end of the letter she said she had just wakened him and told him to get ready for a dinner of spare ribs and sauerkraut, "and that really sparked a quick interest!"[42]

The temperature inched above zero on January 13, a Wednesday. Twelve inches of new snow lay on the ground, and the sun was shining. Sigurd suggested that he and Elizabeth try out their new snowshoes, but just as they were about to get ready the kitchen phone rang. It was Ann Langen, the longtime friend who had helped copy edit and type Sigurd's books. While Elizabeth talked, Sigurd went outside and adjusted the straps on his snowshoes.[43]

Not wanting to keep Sigurd waiting, Elizabeth cut short the phone call and got her snowshoes. In a few minutes they were shuffling down a nearby esker, following a path that ran along the edge of a swamp, the birthplace of a little stream Sigurd called Caribou Creek. The clearing was crossed by power lines and led to a small stand of pine bordered by a residential street, but to Sigurd it was a sanctuary. He had written about the swamp and its creek just a few months earlier, in an essay probably intended for the "Packsack Adventures" book:

> I often walk to the ridge of the esker to enjoy a few moments of its beauty and to feel the quiet there, the sense of solitude always found in the wilderness. . . . Despised and avoided by man, the swamplands keep their old primordial ways free from intrusion, from cities and roads, from the sounds of industry. They are like forgotten islands in time where a man can still sense the ancient presence of nature absolute. For others, could they read their secrets and their history, they would become, as Caribou Creek swamp is to me, a sanctuary of the spirit.[44]

They had not gone far when Elizabeth's snowshoes started giving her trouble. In her haste to get off the phone and outside with her husband, she had not taken the time to adjust the straps properly. She decided to return home. Sigurd said he would go on to the bottom of the hill.

Along the residential street toward which Olson descended, the nearest home—about a block from the path—belonged to a friend, the Reverend Scott Pearson, pastor of Ely's Baptist church. Home that day with his wife, Beth, and their new baby, Pearson got up when the doorbell rang. It was Terry Anderson, a local elementary school teacher. Anderson asked Pearson to call an ambulance; he had just found Sigurd Olson lying face down in the snow. Beth Pearson called the ambulance, and her husband and Anderson ran back to Sigurd at the edge of the clearing. Pearson tried mouth-to-mouth resuscitation, to no avail. The ambulance soon arrived and took Sigurd to the Ely-Bloomenson Hospital. Pearson hurried to the Olsons' house, told Elizabeth, and took her to the hospital. Sigurd's heart gave out soon after they arrived.

The funeral, held at the Presbyterian church on January 16, was packed with family, friends, fans, and reporters, despite weather that was so cold—nearly ninety degrees below zero on the wind chill index—that people had to leave the service briefly to start their cars to ensure that they would run afterward. Services were held later in Duluth and St. Paul, and at the Sigurd Olson Environmental Institute in Ashland, Wisconsin. Over the next few weeks Elizabeth received hundreds of cards and letters from friends and fans in more than forty states and half a dozen countries.

The fact that Olson's fatal heart attack occurred while he was snowshoeing gave his death a romantic twist befitting his image. "What a way to go!" exclaimed Les Blacklock, whose statement was spread across the country in Associated Press reports. Later, after the funeral, romanticism merged with mysticism as Sigurd's fans learned about the last sentence he wrote.

The day after Sigurd died, Sigurd Jr., who had just arrived from Alaska, went out to the writing shack to see if the heat was on and to check things over. On a sheet of paper in the typewriter, along the top of the page, right of center, was one sentence, split across three lines, like a poem, each line centered under the previous one:

A New Adventure is coming up
and I'm sure it will be
A good one.

The next day, January 15, Sigurd Jr. or Elizabeth mentioned this during a visit with Malcolm McLean, president of Northland College. At the end of the eulogy McLean gave at the funeral on January 16, he described the sentence as Sigurd's "last testament of hope and encouragement to us." At least one newspaper, the Madison, Wisconsin, *Isthmus,* repeated the remarks, and Olson fans spread the story, interpreting it as proof that the spiritual philosopher of the wilderness had foreseen his death and had been looking forward to finding out what awaited him afterward.

Had he? It is impossible to be certain what was in Sigurd's mind when he wrote his last words, or even how long before his death he wrote them, but there is no evidence to indicate that he had experienced a premonition of his death. Elizabeth said she had no idea what he meant. His sons were openly skeptical about the popular opinion. Indeed, their viewpoints, expressed in separate interviews, lead to a much less mystical but still fascinating and plausible interpretation: Sigurd Olson may have intentionally gone out on his snowshoes knowing that he was risking death, and perhaps even hoping death would come.

Robert pointed out that his father was extremely frail during their holiday get-together in Seeley and at times was not mentally alert. Elizabeth's letters to the Swems confirm this. "He had no business going out on snowshoes in his condition," Robert said. Unless, of course, Sigurd didn't care what happened to him.

That theory does have a weak spot. It requires either Elizabeth's complicity or a letting down of her guard. People who knew her would find it hard to believe that she would have allowed Sigurd to go snowshoeing if she thought he might die. It is quite possible, however, that the day of Sigurd's death seemed to be one of his better days and that she let down her guard when he asked her to go snowshoeing.

At the same time, there is good reason to believe that Sigurd *would* place himself at risk. When he was in the hospital at the end of 1979, recovering from his colostomy, he told Sigurd Jr. that he did not want to die in a hospital. "When I have to pass away," he told his son, "I want to pass away outside someplace. I'll crawl outside and die in a snowbank before I'll stay in bed and die." Sigurd Jr. did not speculate that his father went out on his snowshoes seeking death, but his father's statement increases the plausibility of such an interpretation. And if Sigurd *was* having one of his increasingly rare good days, he might have seen it as one of his last chances—either to see his treasured Caribou Creek once again, or to die the way he wanted to die, if death came his way.

And that last sentence in the typewriter? "It is my guess," said Robert, "that this thought occurred to him one day, that he liked it and decided to leave it as his 'last words,' just in case." Sigurd Jr. said he thought his father might have been thinking of a trip to Hawaii that they had been talking about taking together. "People say, 'Do you think he had a premonition?' No way!" Like his brother, however, Sigurd Jr. recognized something else about those last words, how they seemed perfectly matched to the public image of Sigurd Olson. That last sentence, no matter its intent, remains intriguing not just because of the mystical interpretations of the faithful, but because it is one final instance in which Sigurd Olson the man satisfied the wishes of those who looked up to Sigurd Olson the icon. "Here he writes this," said Sigurd Jr., "and then he goes out and dies. You know, he did a lot of dramatic things in his life. It was almost as though that was part of the role, and he just kept with it right on up to the very end."

❖ Notes ❖

When I began this project in the fall of 1990, nearly all of Sigurd Olson's journals and many other important documents were still at his home in Ely. Much of this treasure trove was in his writing shack, but there was more in the house, including the first six years of his journal, discovered in 1993 by his son Robert when he opened an old, unplugged refrigerator in the Olsons' basement.

Sigurd was not an organizer. Any librarian or secretary would have declared his writing shack a disaster area—papers piled on tables and shelves, jammed at the back of an old cabinet, stuffed in disorganized file drawers. And his papers at the Minnesota Historical Society in St. Paul are no different. When I began my research, the Olson collection there consisted of eighty large boxes of material, all organized (to use the word loosely) according to the way they had been received. After Elizabeth Olson's death in August 1994, the society picked up most of the rest of the documents from the writing shack and the house, so the collection at St. Paul now is larger, but no better organized, unless and until the day that grant money is made available to perform the mind-boggling task. Many of Sigurd's file folders have several labels, depending on where you look, and the one on the folder's tab is not necessarily the one that best describes the contents. Documents that logically belong together often are in unrelated files, and many letters and other documents are simply loose. There also are duplicate box numbers.

All of this makes it difficult to use traditional methods for citing sources. When the source of a document is a manuscript collection for which it is possible to use box numbers, I do so. For the Olson Papers, however, that is impossible. For those who choose to do further research on him and are trying to find a specific document that I have cited, I can try to be of further help. I kept detailed records of where I found each document, and can try to give a road map. ("You're looking for a manuscript that he wrote in 1945 called "Wilderness Cure"? It's in Box 1—no, not the one donated in 1981, or the Box 1 donated in 1980, but the one donated in 1974. It's in a folder labeled 'Song of the Bush/1947.'")

In the following notes, any document that does not indicate a manuscript collection is from the Olson Papers. Any journal entry or letter that is mentioned in the narrative but not in the following chapter notes also is part of the Olson Papers. Unless otherwise documented, any quote from Olson family members came from my interviews with them.

One. Boyhood and Youth, 1899–1916

1. The opening anecdote about Ida May Olson's immigration experience is based on Sigurd's unpublished essay "Mother's Expedition" (ca. 1960s). (Sigurd claimed that Ida May was thrown off the top deck of the ship and caught by a sailor on the lower deck, which seems extremely unlikely.)

Sigurd did not start keeping a journal until 1930, and only a handful of letters from earlier years survive. The vast majority of information for the first thirty years of his life, then, relies on his own memories and on those of others. His autobiography, *Open Horizons* (New York, 1969), is the starting point for learning about his life, but it provides only an overview. Many details are missing, others are misleading, and events are often out of chronological order (which is difficult for the reader to know, because the book does not refer to dates).

The early drafts of *Open Horizons,* contained in his manuscript collection at the Minnesota Historical Society, contain many useful pieces of information not found in the book and clear up a number of questions about the timing and chronology of events. Olson's *The Singing Wilderness* (New York, 1956) and *Of Time and Place* (New York, 1982), also contain anecdotes relating to his childhood. Interviews with family members yielded other information and anecdotes about Sigurd and his family, some based on firsthand knowledge and others based on stories that Sigurd had told them. (Unless otherwise identified, quotes from family members came from these personal interviews.) Obituaries and a brief family history loaned to me by Robert K. Olson contained important details about L. J. Olson and Ida May Olson. The following additional sources made minor contributions to this chapter:

Frank Graham Jr., "Leave It to the Bourgeois: Sigurd Olson and His Wilderness Quest," *Audubon,* November 1980; Selma Hagg to Sigurd Olson, June 20, 1974 (a reminiscence about Ida May Olson as a Sunday school teacher); Elizabeth Olson to Sigurd Olson, November 28, 1945; Sigurd Olson, journal entry, January 23, 1930; Sigurd Olson to Walt Goldsworthy, May 15, 1973, copy in author's possession; Sigurd Olson, "Days of My Boyhood: My Love of Rabbits" (unpublished essay, ca. 1981). My own visits to Olson's childhood haunts helped me to describe them in the narrative.

2. For the background on Swedish Baptists (here and elsewhere in the chapter), I found George M. Stephenson, *The Religious Aspects of Swedish Immigration* (New York, 1969), especially useful. Also helpful, although written from the perspective of advocates, are J. O. Backlund, *Swedish Baptists in America: A History* (Chicago, 1933), and Gustavus W. Schroeder, *History of the Swedish Baptists in Sweden and America* (New York, 1898). Useful details about Swedish Baptists in Wisconsin and on the Sister Bay church in particular can be found in Edgar L. Killam, *The Centennial History of the Wisconsin Baptist State Convention* (n.p., 1944), and in *Fifty Years of the Baptist Church, Sister Bay, Wisconsin* (n.p., 1927).

In addition, I found the following helpful for understanding Swedish immigration and settlement patterns: Florence E. Janson, *The Background of Swedish Immigration, 1840–1930* (Chicago, 1931); Frederick Hale, *The Swedes in Wisconsin* (Madison, 1983); and Ulf Beijbom, *Swedes in Chicago: A Demographic and Social Study of the 1846–1880 Immigration* (Chicago, 1971).

3. Olson, *Singing Wilderness,* 8.

4. Olson, journal entry, March 4, 1935.

5. Sigurd writes about his first teacher in an unpublished essay called "My Education as It Was" (ca. 1981) and about the second in another unpublished essay, "The Days of My Boyhood: Spelling Bees" (ca. 1981).

6. Sigurd Olson, "The Old Ones Speak," *Open Horizons* chapter draft dated April 8, 1966.

7. Sigurd Olson, "Home from the Hill," *Open Horizons* chapter draft dated April 3, 1967.

8. Olson, *Singing Wilderness,* 219.

9. Quoted in Jim dale Vickery, *Wilderness Visionaries* (Merrillville, Ind., 1986), 195.

10. The information and quotes about Sigurd's grandmother, Anna Cederholm, come from 1930s-era drafts of his essay "Grandmother's Trout" and the final version published in *The Singing Wilderness,* supplemented by an obituary, cemetery records, and family interviews.

11. Nathaniel B. Dexter, *Northland College: A History* (Ashland, Wis., 1968), gives good background information about the college. Some yearbooks and issues of the student paper from the First World War era are available at the college library.

Two. College Years, 1916–1919

1. Interviews with Elizabeth Olson, as well as family documents shared by Robert K. Olson, provided background on the Uhrenholdts. See also Gordon MacQuarrie, "Farmer Philosopher Reaps as He Sowed," *Milwaukee Journal,* July 21, 1940.

2. For good background on the Wisconsin Cutover region, its people, and its politics, see Vernon Carstensen, *Evolution of a State Land Policy for Northern Wisconsin, 1850–1932* (Madison, Wis., 1958).

3. Sigurd Olson, *Open Horizons* (New York, 1969), 42.

4. Ibid., 59.

5. For the portions of this chapter referring to the First World War, I found especially helpful David M. Kennedy, *Over Here: The First World War and American Society* (New York, 1980); Carol S. Gruber, *Mars and Minerva: World War I and the Uses of the Higher Learning in America* (Baton Rouge, La., 1975); and Alfred W. Crosby Jr., *Epidemic and Peace, 1918* (Westport, Conn., 1976). Rev. Harry S. Ruth, ed., *Ashland County, Wisconsin in the World War, 1917–1919* (Boston, 1928), provided some details about Kenneth Olson's service that I had not found elsewhere.

6. Information about Northland College's production of *A Doll's House* comes from yearbooks and newspapers available at the college, and from Olson's recollections in manuscript drafts of *Open Horizons.*

7. For a detailed historical and literary analysis of the play, see Errol Durbach, *A Doll's House: Ibsen's Myth of Transformation* (Boston, 1991).

8. Henrik Ibsen, *The Collected Works of Henrik Ibsen*, vol. 7 (New York, 1929), 182–83.

9. Sigurd quotes his grandmother in an early, undated draft (ca. March 1938) of his essay "Grandmother's Trout."

10. Robert Service, "Over the Parapet," in *Collected Poems of Robert Service* (New York, 1940), 353–55.

11. About Ida May's "heart attack": Robert K. Olson is convinced that she feigned it and says she did this on more than one occasion as a means of controlling people. In addition to the evidence included in the text for this chapter, Sigurd's various sketchy references to the incident lend support to this theory. In a draft of an unpublished essay written in 1981, titled "The Days of My Boyhood: The Warrior Clan," Sigurd writes that his mother called the Uhrenholdt farm to say she was having a heart attack and asking for Sigurd to come home. If she really was having a heart attack, of course, it is unlikely that she would have made the call. In another unpublished essay written in 1977, titled "My Brother Ken," Sigurd simply says, "I too wanted to go over but mother rebelled and so I bowed to her wishes."

12. About the TNT factory: see *The First Fifty Years of Barksdale Works, Wisconsin's Pioneer Explosives Plant* (n.p., 1954). Sigurd Olson recalls his work here

briefly in a journal entry of February 3, 1939; the anecdote about the explosion he witnessed is in the 1977 essay "My Brother Ken."

13. The University of Wisconsin Archives records for the Office of Registrar contain primary source material related to the Students Army Training Corps.

14. Olson, "The Days of My Boyhood: The Warrior Clan," unpublished essay, ca. 1981.

15. These and the remaining Olson quotes in this chapter come from his journal entry of January 14, 1930.

16. Olson's University of Wisconsin transcripts, combined with catalogs in the university's archives, provided valuable background information.

17. Kenneth Olson to Sigurd Olson, January 3, 1961.

Three. A Rolling Stone, 1920–1923

1. Sigurd Olson, "Home from the Hill," *Open Horizons* chapter draft dated April 3, 1967.

2. For more on the iron mining industry in northern Minnesota, see David A. Walker, *Iron Frontier: The Discovery and Early Development of Minnesota's Three Ranges* (St. Paul, Minn., 1979).

3. From an *Open Horizons* chapter draft with two titles ("The Long Long Dances" and "The Maker of Dreams") and two dates (April 1 and April 4, 1966). Labeled "Chapter X" on the manuscript, it is a draft of what ultimately became chapter 9 in the published version.

4. Sigurd Olson, "The Old Ones Speak," *Open Horizons* chapter draft dated April 8, 1966.

5. James Oliver Curwood, *Steele of the Royal Mounted: A Story of the Great Canadian Northwest* (New York, 1911), 90–91.

6. Olson's published version of Al Kennedy's offer to go pan for gold in the Flin Flon, which appears in *Open Horizons*, is, like many anecdotes in the book, incorrectly placed in time. The version recounted here is based on interviews with Elizabeth Olson; Robert Olson also remembers learning this story in accord with the version included in this chapter.

7. All Uhrenholdt family correspondence cited throughout this book was provided by Robert K. Olson.

8. The section about the Olsons' wedding and honeymoon is based on interviews, photos, and an unpublished essay Sigurd wrote in about 1981, called "Honey Moon Trip." But Sigurd's recollections must be treated with caution. He claimed that shortly after the wedding dinner he and Elizabeth took the five o'clock train to Spooner, transferred to another coach that took them to Duluth, and then caught the Duluth and Iron Range Railroad line to Winton. When they arrived, they stored their wedding clothes at the

depot, bought supplies, and found a room at a nearby Finnish boarding-house. The food was delicious and plentiful—a full-sized roast served with a hunting knife plunged into it—but their bed was infested with bugs.

It is hard to believe that they could leave Seeley at 5:00 P.M. and arrive in Winton in time to buy supplies and have dinner. If they *did* stay at the board-inghouse, it must have been at the *end* of their canoe trip. The excerpted letter from Elizabeth to her parents suggests that they did not arrive in Winton until Saturday, August 13.

9. The section about Olson's graduate work in geology is based on interviews with Elizabeth Olson, Sigurd's drafts and final version of *Open Horizons,* University of Wisconsin course catalogs for the period, Sigurd's transcript, and the following secondary sources: Sturgess W. Bailey, ed., *The History of Geology and Geophysics at the University of Wisconsin-Madison, 1848–1980* (Madison, 1981), and Sylvia Wallace McGrath, *Charles Kenneth Leith: Scientific Adviser* (Madison, 1971). For more background on the university as a whole, see the two-volume history by Merle Curti and Vernon Carstensen, *The University of Wisconsin: A History* (Madison, 1949).

10. The anecdote about Sigurd's job offer from the high school in Ely, Minnesota, is based on interviews with Elizabeth Olson and Uhrenholdt family correspondence.

Four. Northwoods Guide, 1923–1929

1. For early Ely history, see two Ely-Winton Historical Society pamphlets: *A Souvenir Booklet: Centennial Roaring Stoney Days* and *Ely 100th Anniversary Scrapbook: 1888–1988.* See also Lee Brownell, *Pioneer Life in Ely* (Virginia, Minn., 1981).

2. Most of the recollections of Olson as a teacher are from interviews conducted by the author. The exceptions, two letters from the Olson Papers and a newspaper article, are: Eugene Laitala to Orville Freeman, January 7, 1955; Helen Denley Barnes to Olson, November 13, 1970; and Clarence W. Ivonen, "An EJC Student Remembers," *Mesabi Daily News* (Virginia, Minn.), January 14, 1982.

3. Sigurd Olson, *Open Horizons* (New York, 1969), 70.

4. Sigurd's official version of the story about the birth of Sigurd Jr. is contained in his article "Confessions of a Duck Hunter," *Sports Afield,* October 1930. The quote from Roland Erikson's manuscript and the quoted letter from Olson to Johanne Uhrenholdt were provided by Robert K. Olson. Elizabeth Olson provided additional details about the labor and delivery. (Sigurd Jr.'s middle name was an accidental misspelling of Elizabeth's mother's maiden name, which contained no *e.*)

5. For Olson's experiences as a guide, see *Open Horizons* and its drafts; his

journal entry for January 20, 1930; his early 1940s "Field Notes" essay called "Make Yourself a Pillow"; an unpublished mid-1950s essay called "Voyageurs Country"; and an unpublished 1981 essay called "Guiding Adventures."

6. Here and following, see Olson, "Guiding Adventures."

7. Olson *Open Horizons*, 97.

8. Olson, "Voyageurs Country."

9. Olson, *Open Horizons*, 116.

10. Here and following, ibid., 118.

11. The sources for the sections about Sigurd's early spiritual experiences in the Quetico-Superior while guiding during the 1920s come from Olson's journal entry for January 20, 1930, as well as several drafts of an unpublished essay called variously "The Supernatural Instinct" and "Sanctuary." The version quoted in the anecdote about the sunset on Robinson Lake is called "The Supernatural Instinct," dated 12/26/33, and labeled "Final Draft."

12. For information on Will Dilg and the early history of the Izaak Walton League, two sources are essential: Philip V. Scarpino, *Great River: An Environmental History of the Upper Mississippi, 1890–1950* (Columbia, Mo., 1985), and Stephen Fox, *John Muir and His Legacy: The American Conservation Movement* (Boston, 1981).

13. Two books cover the conservation history of the canoe country, both with an emphasis on the American side. R. Newell Searle's *Saving Quetico-Superior: A Land Set Apart* (St. Paul, Minn., 1977) focuses on the politics behind each battle for the wilderness, beginning with the fight over roads in the early 1920s and ending in 1960. Searle tells the story from the perspective of the small group of conservationists known as the Quetico Superior Council. The second book is my *Canoe Country: An Embattled Wilderness* (Minocqua, Wis., 1991), which focuses more on the cultural context of the battles over the canoe country than on the political details. It is especially concerned with the ways in which individuals and organizations created *images* of the canoe country in the mass media, and how they attempted to use these images to achieve their often conflicting goals for the region. The section of this chapter about the fight over roads relies on these two books, as well as on the Superior National Forest Records, on microfilm at the Minnesota Historical Society. Roll 9 of the records contains primary sources related to the road issue.

No book-length history of the canoe country emphasizing the Canadian side has yet been published. George Warecki's 1983 master's thesis at the University of Western Ontario, called "The Quetico-Superior Council and the Battle for Wilderness in Quetico Provincial Park, 1909–1960," is a key unpublished source. For published sources, see especially the following: Gerald Killan and George Warecki, "The Battle for Wilderness in Ontario: Saving Quetico-Superior, 1927 to 1960," in *Patterns of the Past: Interpreting Ontario's*

History, ed. Roger Hall, William Westfall, and Laurel Sefton MacDowell (Toronto, 1988); and Gerald Killan, *Protected Places: A History of Ontario's Provincial Parks System* (Toronto, 1993). Killan and Warecki also have published an article that examines Quetico Park logging policies in the context of provincial politics during the late 1960s and early 1970s. See "The Algonquin Wildlands League and the Emergence of Environmental Politics in Ontario, 1965–1974," *Environmental History Review,* Winter 1992.

For the early political history of wilderness preservation, a number of sources are essential. (For sources about the *philosophy* behind wilderness preservation—the "wilderness idea"—see the notes to chapter 14.) The third edition of Roderick Nash's *Wilderness and the American Mind* (New Haven, Conn., 1982) is rightfully considered a classic. While its focus is on the intellectual history of the wilderness idea, it also presents a basic political history of wilderness preservation. Stephen Fox's *John Muir and His Legacy* is an excellent general history of twentieth-century conservation in the United States, especially for information about organizations and their leaders. It contains a good deal about wilderness preservation.

For more detailed treatments of wilderness preservation in the 1920s and 1930s, an unpublished dissertation and three biographies are essential: James P. Gilligan, "The Development of Policy and Administration of Forest Service Primitive and Wilderness Areas in the Western United States" (Ph.D. dissertation, University of Michigan, 1953); Curt Meine, *Aldo Leopold: His Life and Work* (Madison, 1988); James M. Glover, *A Wilderness Original: The Life of Bob Marshall* (Seattle, 1986); and Donald N. Baldwin, *The Quiet Revolution: Grass Roots of Today's Wilderness Preservation Movement* (Boulder, Colo., 1972), a biography of Arthur Carhart, an early and important leader in wilderness preservation. Be forewarned, however: Baldwin was a devoted advocate of Carhart as *the* father of the modern wilderness movement and often overstates his case.

14. Olson, *Open Horizons,* 197.

15. *Field and Stream* published "Fishin' Jewelry" in November 1927.

16. Ray Christensen and Steve Kahlenbeck, *The Wilderness World of Sigurd F. Olson,* produced by Twin Cities Public Television in 1980, most recently distributed in VHS format by NorthWord Press Inc., Minocqua, Wis.

17. Olson, journal entry, January 22, 1930.

18. Sigurd Olson, "A Mountain Listens," ca. January 1968.

Five. The Reluctant Ecologist, 1930–1932

1. Any Olson quotes in this chapter not otherwise cited (either in the text or in the notes) come from his journal entries of January 1930.

2. Olson, journal entry, March 4, 1935.

3. W. H. Hudson, *Far Away and Long Ago: A History of My Early Life* (New York, 1918), 227–28, 231.

4. Olson, journal entry, ca. November 1942–February 1943.

5. For background, see Thomas R. Dunlap, *Saving America's Wildlife* (Princeton, N.J., 1988).

6. Ibid., 48.

7. In his thesis notes he wrote about a wolf killing a fawn. When he wrote about this incident for publication in *Open Horizons* nearly forty years later, he changed the details. The fawn became an old doe; he also said the wolf ran off as soon as it saw his canoe, and that he and his traveling companions bled the deer, cut off a haunch, and cooked it for supper. His thesis notes say that the wolf did not run until Olson and his friends went to shore and fired several shots. No note is made of cooking the haunch. Such differences are not important except to show again that Olson's autobiographical writings, in *Open Horizons* and elsewhere, must be interpreted cautiously rather than literally. He was less interested in presenting accurate recountings of events in his life than in telling a story with a particular message, and so he felt free to alter facts.

8. L. David Mech, *The Wolf: The Ecology and Behavior of an Endangered Species* (New York, 1970), provides some background on early wolf research methods.

9. The letter is undated, but is from the spring of 1930; like all Uhrenholdt family correspondence, it was made available by Robert K. Olson.

10. I am especially indebted to the following sources for the background information about the science of ecology that appears in this chapter: Robert A. Croker, *Pioneer Ecologist: The Life and Work of Victor Ernest Shelford, 1877–1968* (Washington, D.C., 1991); Donald Worster, *Nature's Economy: The Roots of Ecology* (New York, 1979); Robert P. McIntosh, *The Background of Ecology: Concept and Theory* (Cambridge, 1985); and Frank N. Egerton, ed., *History of American Ecology* (New York, 1977).

11. Olson, journal entry, December 9, 1931.

12. Olson, journal entry, December 28, 1931.

13. Quoted in Worster, *Nature's Economy*, 301.

14. Aldo Leopold, *A Sand County Almanac, with Other Essays on Conservation from Round River* (New York, 1966), 177.

15. Sigurd F. Olson, "Organization and Range of the Pack," *Ecology* 19 (January 1938): 168–70; and Sigurd F. Olson, "A Study in Predatory Relationship with Particular Reference to the Wolf," *Scientific Monthly* 46 (April 1938): 323–36.

16. Letter to the author, August 16, 1991.

Six. A Need for Recognition, 1932–1935

1. From Robert K. Olson's introduction to Mike Link, ed., *The Collected Works of Sigurd F. Olson: The Early Writings, 1921–1934* (Stillwater, Minn., 1988).

(All otherwise undocumented quotes from Olson family members are from interviews with the author.)

2. Olson, journal entry, September 27, 1934.

3. Leopold to Olson, November 10, 1933.

4. Here and next paragraph: Olson, journal entry, November 14, 1933.

5. Olson, journal entry, November 7, 1933.

6. Olson, journal entry, December 12, 1933.

7. For a detailed examination of the proposal, the conservationist response, and the International Joint Commission's role, see R. Newell Searle, *Saving Quetico-Superior: A Land Set Apart* (St. Paul, Minn., 1977).

8. *Minneapolis Star,* October 12, 1933.

9. Olson, journal entry, October 11, 1933.

10. The reference to Oberholtzer as "an elf" is from the author's interview with Michael Nadel, a former Wilderness Society officer, on December 7, 1992. For this section on Oberholtzer's background I also am indebted to Searle, *Saving Quetico-Superior.*

11. Ernest Oberholtzer, "President Roosevelt Acts to Save the People's Forest among the Border Lakes," *National Waltonian,* September 1934, and "The Ancient Game of Grab," *American Forests,* October 1929.

12. Sigurd F. Olson, "Roads or Planes in the Superior," *Minnesota Waltonian,* April 1934.

13. Sigurd F. Olson, "A New Policy Needed for the Superior," *Minnesota Conservationist,* May 1934.

14. About Bob Marshall: James M. Glover has written the only complete biography, *A Wilderness Original: The Life of Bob Marshall* (Seattle, 1986). Michael P. Cohen has added some important insights from a Jewish perspective in his informative but quirky article "The Bob: Confessions of a Fast-Talking Urban Wilderness Advocate," which appears in *Wilderness Tapestry: An Eclectic Approach to Preservation,* ed. Samuel I. Zeveloff, L. Mikel Vause, and William H. McVaugh (Reno, Nev., 1992). Cohen also briefly but usefully examines Marshall's intellectual background in his book *The History of the Sierra Club, 1892–1970* (San Francisco, 1988). Still useful as brief summaries of Marshall's career, but getting somewhat dated, are Stephen Fox, *John Muir and His Legacy: The American Conservation Movement* (Boston, 1981), and Roderick Nash, *Wilderness and the American Mind,* 3d ed. (New Haven, Conn., 1982).

15. Here and following: Robert Marshall, "The Problem of the Wilderness," *Scientific Monthly,* February 1930.

16. Robert Sterling Yard to Bernard Frank, September 13, 1937, quoted in Nash, *Wilderness and the American Mind,* 206.

17. Olson to Oberholtzer, December 10, 1934.

18. Glover, *Wilderness Original,* 57.

Seven. Storms of Life, 1934–1938

1. Olson to Ernest Holt, October 12, 1934.

2. Olson, journal entry, April 9, 1935.

3. The information in the section about Sigurd's writing trip to Bear Island Lake comes from his journal of January 1–3, 1935, with the exception of the quote beginning "No one has as yet developed a philosophy of the wilderness," which comes from his journal entry of November 21, 1934.

4. Olson, journal entries for October 5 and November 17, 1935.

5. From an undated journal entry, written sometime after 1934.

6. Olson, journal entry, December 9, 1935.

7. The information about Julius Santo in Mexico comes from Olson's unpublished essay "My Education Such as It Was" and interviews with Elizabeth Olson.

8. Here and following: Olson, journal entry, January 28, 1936.

9. Olson, journal entry, March 4, 1936.

10. Marshall to Olson, May 27, 1936.

11. Marshall, memorandum, June 3, 1936.

12. Sigurd F. Olson, "A Recreational Plan for the Red Lake Reservation," ca. July 1936.

13. The information about the history of Basswood Lake and the Four Mile Portage comes from Superior National Forest Records in Duluth, Minnesota, in a folder labeled "Proposed Road Fernberg to Basswood Lake," which is part of the 2320 Wilderness and Primitive Areas files; see also a letter from William H. Magie to Willard Watters, July 6, 1949, in the forest's Friends of the Wilderness files. A memorandum in the Olson Papers, written by Frank Hubachek, titled "Basswood Area," and dated March 25, 1952, also is helpful.

14. Oberholtzer to Olson, November 1, 1937.

15. About Olson's efforts to put the Border Lakes-Peterson's Fishing Camp relationship on more equal financial footing, see his letters to Wallie Hanson on September 9 and September 20, 1939.

16. Mueller to Olson, May 21, 1953.

17. Olson, journal entry, December 12, 1933.

18. The speech is untitled and undated.

19. Olson recounted his canoe trip with Bob Marshall in "Quetico Superior Elegy," *Living Wilderness*, Spring 1948.

Eight. The Hidden Life of a Dean, 1936–1940

1. The first section of this chapter, about Sigurd Olson as a dean and his frustrations with the job, is based primarily on interviews, letters, and his journals, and secondarily on issues of the college newspaper and yearbook.

2. Olson, journal entry, January 15, 1939.

3. Olson, journal entry, September 13, 1939.

4. Olson, journal entry, February 22, 1940.

5. Olson, journal entry, November 8, 1939.

6. Olson, journal entry, September 22, 1940.

7. Olson, journal entry, February 15, 1939.

8. Olson, journal entry, January 15, 1939.

9. The background on Kenneth Olson comes from interviews and from two published sources: Robert Nelson, "The Dean of Medill," *Christian Science Monitor,* June 26, 1963, and Olson's obituary in the *New York Times,* July 15, 1967. Sigurd's statement is from a journal entry on May 14, 1937.

10. Olson to Hough, March 3, 1939.

11. The version of Olson's short story "Beaver Time" that is quoted in this chapter is dated March 10, 1939.

12. Olson, journal entry, January 20, 1938.

13. In analyzing Olson's journal entries for insights into his mental state, I found very helpful the American Psychological Association's *Diagnostic and Statistical Manual of Mental Disorders,* 3d ed. (Washington, D.C., 1980), which gives the diagnostic criteria for major depressive episodes. I also benefited from Kay Redfield Jamison's *Touched with Fire: Manic-Depressive Illness and the Artistic Temperament* (New York, 1993).

Sigurd's letters from the 1930s only occasionally hint at his inner turmoil, so his journal provides the only useful source of evidence. I made calendars for each year and color coded each day for which Sigurd wrote a journal entry. I used blue when the entry showed signs of sadness, yellow when the entry showed happy feelings, and green when the entry seemed neither sad nor happy. This helped me to look for possible patterns.

14. Soren Uhrenholdt's after-dinner talk was recounted in "The Pines," an unpublished story Sigurd wrote three months later.

15. Olson, journal entry, November 28, 1938.

16. Olson, journal entry, February 23, 1939.

17. The statement about Ovid Butler was made by Irving Brant, a Midwestern journalist who in 1930 became treasurer of the Emergency Conservation Committee, formed for the purpose of reforming the Audubon Association. See Stephen Fox, *John Muir and His Legacy: The American Conservation Movement* (Boston, 1981).

Leopold's "The Last Stand of the Wilderness" was published in the October 1925 issue of *American Forests.* In July 1926, Howard Flint responded with an article titled "Wasted Wilderness."

18. Olson to Marshall, November 22, 1938.

19. Sigurd F. Olson, "The Spiritual Need," in *Wilderness in a Changing World,* ed. Bruce M. Kilgore (San Francisco, 1966), and Sigurd F. Olson, *Re-*

flections from the North Country (New York, 1976). Although Olson was not a devotee of John Muir (see chapter 14 for more on this), his "coming home" remark may have been based on the opening paragraph of John Muir's *Our National Parks* (Boston, 1901), in which Muir said that "going to the mountains is going home ... wildness is a necessity ... [and] mountain parks and reservations are useful not only as fountains of timber and irrigating rivers, but as fountains of life."

20. For the Carl Jung quotes, see volume 5 of *The Collected Works of C. G. Jung,* ed. Sir Herbert Read, Michael Fordham, Gerhard Adler, and William McGuire (Princeton, N.J., 1956); Olson's statement is from his "Search for the Wild," *Sports Afield,* May-June 1932.

21. *Ely Miner,* April 22, 1938.

22. Olson, journal entries for September 22, 1938, and February 7, 1939.

23. Elizabeth Olson provided useful background information on Kelly, Hubachek, and Winston. I also am indebted to R. Newell Searle, *Saving Quetico-Superior: A Land Set Apart* (St. Paul, Minn., 1977).

24. Hubachek to Olson, December 12, 1939.

25. The single most important source for background on the history of name changes in the canoe country, from "wilderness area" to "primitive area" to "roadless area" to "canoe area," is the Superior National Forest Records file called "Data Concerning Change of Name to BWCA." The quote from Bob Marshall about the hypocrisy of applying the label "wilderness" to the Basswood Lake area is reported in the file's most important document, a memo by J. W. White dated January 29, 1964.

26. Olson to Hubachek, November 20, 1939; Oberholtzer to Olson, December 8, 1939.

27. Olson to Hubachek, November 20, 1939.

28. Hubachek to Olson, December 12, 1939; Oberholtzer to Olson, December 8, 1939; and Oberholtzer to Winston, December 12, 1939, Box 4, Quetico-Superior Council Papers, Minnesota Historical Society, St. Paul.

29. Winston to Kelly, December 16, 1939; Olson, journal entry, December 18, 1939.

Nine. The War Years, 1940-1946

1. Hardy to Olson, May 8, 1939; Elmo to Olson, June 1, 1939.

2. Olson quotes Hough in a journal entry on January 7, 1940; he describes Elizabeth's opinion in his journal on May 2, 1940.

3. Olson, journal entry, May 2, 1940.

4. Olson, journal entry, September 17, 1940.

5. The information about logging in Quetico Park and Olson's role in establishing new restrictions comes from letters and documents in his per-

sonal papers, from the papers of the Quetico-Superior Council, and from two secondary sources: George Michael Warecki, "The Quetico-Superior Council and the Battle for Wilderness in Quetico Provincial Park, 1909–1960" (M.A. thesis, University of Western Ontario, 1983); and R. Newell Searle, *Saving Quetico-Superior: A Land Set Apart* (St. Paul, Minn., 1977).

6. My book *Canoe Country: An Embattled Wilderness* (Minocqua, Wis., 1991) also describes the smallmouth bass program, including a description of the ecological effects of introducing this new species to the Quetico-Superior ecosystem. The effects have been subtle. To put it simply, research indicates that when long-term weather patterns produce warmer temperatures, the competition for food between smallmouth and walleyed pike (native to the Quetico-Superior and another favorite of anglers) favors the bass; under long-term patterns of cooler weather, walleyes are favored. *Canoe Country* also describes in detail the publicity given to fishing in the boundary waters in general and Basswood Lake in particular.

7. The letter is undated, but written on a Sunday night in February 1941—probably February 2.

8. Walters to Olson, February 10, 1941.

9. Leo Marx's *The Machine in the Garden: Technology and the Pastoral Ideal in America* (New York, 1964) provides an excellent study of pastoralism that proved invaluable in my analysis of Olson's 1941 essay "Interval."

10. Meyers to Olson, March 22, 1941; April 11, 1941; and April 2, 1941.

11. Olson, journal entry, September 11, 1941.

12. Olson, journal entry, April 1, 1941.

13. Robert K. Olson's recollections (here and following) of the bombing of Pearl Harbor come from his introduction to Mike Link, ed., *The Collected Works of Sigurd F. Olson, The Early Writings: 1921–1934* (Stillwater, Minn., 1988), xvii. Sigurd Olson Jr.'s recollections come from interviews with the author.

14. Ely Junior College newspapers from the period provided much of the background for this section. Olson's letters and journals provided other details.

15. The letter to Sigurd Jr. is undated. For Sigurd's advice to young men going into war, see his "America Out of Doors" manuscript "Seventeen."

16. Otto to Olson, September 8, 1942.

17. Olson, journal entry, July 23, 1945.

18. Like all Uhrenholdt family correspondence, this letter, written in February 1944 (but undated), was provided by Robert K. Olson.

19. In addition to letters and diaries, there are several other important sources for Sigurd's memories of his year in Europe. One is a speech, "A Midwesterner's Impressions of Post War Europe," that he wrote early in 1947. Another is an unpublished essay, "What England Means to Me," he wrote soon after arriving in England. A third key source is an unpublished essay, "My Education in Europe," written in the 1960s but not dated.

20. Sigurd Olson to Elizabeth Olson, September 15, 1945.

21. The section on Lady Grogan relies on the following sources: letters from Sigurd to Elizabeth on September 15 and 18, 1945; a letter from Ellinor Grogan to Sigurd on October 2, no year given but presumably 1945 (other letters from Grogan also exist); a letter from Olson to Ted Swem, April 29, 1968; and a draft of *Open Horizons* called "The Old Ones Speak," dated April 8, 1966.

22. Diamant to Sigurd Olson, January 11, 1945; and to Elizabeth Olson, September 17, 1945.

23. Diamant to Olson, January 17, 1946.

24. Sigurd Olson to Elizabeth Olson, July 17, 1945.

25. Sigurd Olson to Elizabeth Olson, November 12, 1945; Elizabeth Olson to Sigurd Olson, November 30, 1945.

26. Elizabeth Olson to Sigurd Olson, November 30, 1945.

27. Here and following: Olson, "Midwesterner's Impressions of Post War Europe."

28. Sigurd Olson to Elizabeth Olson, March 8, 1946; Olson, "My Education in Europe."

29. Olson, "My Education in Europe."

30. Sigurd Olson to Elizabeth Olson, March 22, 1946.

31. Olson, undated journal entry, ca. April 1946.

32. Sigurd Olson to Elizabeth Olson, May 8, 1946.

Ten. A Professional Conservationist, 1946–1949

1. Olson to Ken Reid, August 22, 1946.

2. The anecdote about Olson's breaking up the gambling in the Ely Junior College attic was provided by retired Minneapolis *Star Tribune* columnist Jim Klobuchar, who was raised in Ely and was one of the card players present when Olson entered the room. The comments from Elizabeth and Robert Olson about the 1946–47 school year came from interviews with the author.

3. About Sigurd's eye problems: In a letter he wrote to Erling W. Hansen, a Minneapolis physician, on April 17, 1947, Sigurd said, "I am suffering from extreme sensitivity to light, a condition that began over in Germany in 1946 and became exaggerated upon my return to the states." The next day he wrote to Ken Reid, "I cannot stand bright light anymore and long reading or close work is impossible over protracted periods." He did not mention the involuntary twitch in either letter. Elizabeth Olson told me that Sigurd's eye twitch began during his last year as dean of Ely Junior College, and that doctors told him it was caused by stress. In any case, there is no more mention of light sensitivity in Sigurd's papers, but many references to the twitching, which grew worse over the years. He could have suffered from Meige's syn-

drome, a disorder in which the eyelids involuntarily close. It occurs in association with involuntary movements of the lower face, jaw, and neck—all of which Olson experienced as he aged.

4. Regarding Rabbi Joshua Loth Liebman, see Donald Meyer, *The Positive Thinkers: Religion as Pop Psychology from Mary Baker Eddy to Oral Roberts* (New York, 1980). The quotes come from Liebman's book *Peace of Mind* (New York, 1946).

5. About Olson's relief at not finding a Baptist church in Ely and how he and Elizabeth eventually joined the Presbyterian Church: this information came from Elizabeth during interviews with the author.

6. Olson, journal entry, November 7, 1933; Ida May Olson to Sigurd Olson, August 3, 1936.

7. Ralph Waldo Trine, *In Tune with the Infinite; or, Fullness of Peace, Power and Plenty* (New York, 1897), preface, 205–6.

8. The background on John Burroughs is from the fine biography by Edward J. Renehan Jr., *John Burroughs: An American Naturalist* (Post Mills, Vt., 1992). Burroughs's statements about God and religion come from his books *Accepting the Universe: Essays in Naturalism* (Boston, 1920) and *The Light of Day: Religious Discussions and Criticisms from the Naturalist's Point of View* (Boston, 1900).

9. Sigurd Olson, "The Supernatural Instinct," dated December 26, 1933.

10. Olson to Olaus Murie, November 11, 1956.

11. George Gould's letter was dated May 3, 1947, and addressed to Zella Richter, an elderly grade school teacher who was very fond of Sigurd. She apparently gave the letter to Olson, for it is in his papers at the Minnesota Historical Society.

12. Litten to Olson, August 7, 1947; Blassingame to Olson, August 1, 1947.

13. Olson's two journal entries quoted here are both undated. Both are from 1947, and one was written the day after he received a letter Litten wrote on August 7.

14. Regarding Sigurd's best twelve-month sales record before he resigned as dean in 1947: he sold six articles between the summer of 1930 and the summer of 1931. Five were published by *Sports Afield,* the other by *Outdoor Life.*

15. Kelly's comment is from a 1986 interview that is part of the Minnesota Environmental Issues Oral History Project, available at the Minnesota Historical Society in St. Paul. For background on Oberholtzer, I also found useful R. Newell Searle, *Saving Quetico-Superior: A Land Set Apart* (St. Paul, Minn., 1977), and George Warecki, "The Quetico-Superior Council and the Battle for Wilderness in Quetico Provincial Park, 1909–1960" (M.A. thesis, University of Western Ontario, 1983).

16. Hubachek and Kelly to Oberholtzer, August 8, 1946, Charles Kelly fold-

ers, Quetico-Superior Council Papers, Minnesota Historical Society, St. Paul. These papers hereafter will be abbreviated QSC.

17. Olson to Ken Reid, August 22, 1946; Kelly to Winston, Kelly folders, QSC; Kelly to Oberholtzer, August 15, 1946, Resumption of Efforts to Organize Canadian Support files, QSC.

18. Kelly to Oberholtzer, August 15, 1946, Resumption of Efforts to Organize Canadian Support files, QSC.

19. This letter is in the Olson Activities folder, QSC.

20. Olson to John Ainley, January 15, 1948.

21. Olson's role in the campaign to give the Forest Service authority to buy land in Superior National Forest, which ended with the passage of Public Law 733 in June 1948, is documented primarily in the following manuscript collections: the Quetico-Superior files of the Sigurd Olson Papers; the Olson Activities folder, QSC; the Charles S. Kelly folders, QSC; and the PL 733 folders of the Superior National Forest Records, Duluth, Minn. All three collections also contain newspaper clippings, but the QSC Papers are the best source for comprehensiveness and organization.

22. Blatnik to Olson, June 8, 1948; Winston to Olson, May 22, 1948, Winston folders, QSC.

23. Untitled editorial, *Living Wilderness*, Summer 1948.

24. The story of the airplane conflict has been told in greatest detail in my master's thesis, "The Air Ban War: Sigurd F. Olson and the Fight to Ban Airplanes from the Roadless Area of Minnesota's Superior National Forest" (University of Wisconsin-Madison, 1983). In addition to the Olson Papers, the major manuscript sources for this issue are the following: the 2320 Use of Airplanes folders, Superior National Forest Records, Duluth; the Olson Activities folder and the Control of the Use of Airplanes files, QSC; and the Friends of the Wilderness Papers, also at the Minnesota Historical Society (hereafter cited as FOW).

25. Olson's magazine articles in 1948 and 1949 that drew attention to the Quetico-Superior's wilderness problems consist of the following, in chronological order: "Let's Finish What We Started," *Outdoor America*, February 1948; "Quetico-Superior Elegy," *Living Wilderness*, Spring 1948; "Quetico-Superior Challenge," *Sports Afield*, May 1948; "Voyageur's Return," *Nature Magazine*, June 1948; "Wings over the Wilderness," *American Forests*, June 1948 (reprinted in *Minnesota Sportsmen's Digest*, July–August 1948); "The Preservation of Wilderness," *Living Wilderness*, Autumn 1948; "Airspace Reservations over Wilderness," *Sports Afield*, January 1949; "Battle for a Wilderness," *Forest and Outdoors*, March 1949; "Voyageur's Country," *National Home Monthly*, October 1949; and "Swift as the Wild Goose Flies," *National Parks Magazine*, October–December 1949.

26. The letter is in the Olson Papers.

27. On April 10, 1954, Olson wrote to Ken Reid, "I wrote the original story but Harold Martin wrote the final, using what he could out of mine."

28. About the threats of violence during the airplane conflict, see Charles W. Ingersoll to Friends of the Wilderness, August 29, 1949, Correspondence and Miscellaneous files, FOW; Bill Trygg to Bill Magie, July 2, 1949, Correspondence and Miscellaneous files, FOW; Bill Rom to Sigurd Olson, March 9, 1949, Olson Papers; Rom to Olson, March 29, 1949, Control of the Use of Airplanes file 6, QSC; and "F. B. Hubachek Makes Statement," *Ely Miner*, August 25, 1949. Bill Rom is the outfitter who claimed in the letters cited here that his house was "bombed." In an interview with the author on May 16, 1992, he made it clear that the explosive was really a potent firecracker; he called it a "police firecracker."

29. For more details about the northeastern Minnesota economy during this period and its relationship to wilderness issues, and for more on local efforts to build a tourism industry, see my book *Canoe Country: An Embattled Wilderness* (Minocqua, Wis.: NorthWord Press, 1991).

30. The film is at the Minnesota Historical Society, and the script is in the Olson Papers.

31. The anecdote about President Truman's signing the executive order for an airspace reservation over the Superior Roadless Areas is based on two sources: an undated and unpublished essay Olson wrote in the 1960s titled "In Perspective—President Harry Truman," and Russell P. Andrews, *Wilderness Sanctuary*, Inter-University Case Program #13 (Indianapolis, Ind., 1953).

32. Regarding the attacks on Olson's character: Jack Connor wrote a seven-article series that appeared between June 26 and July 3, 1949; the series attacked the airspace reservation proposal in general and Olson and Frank Hubachek in particular. Other important sources include Roland Ericson to Olson, March 26, 1949, Airplanes file 6, QSC (quoted in the text); Olson to Ericson, April 1, 1949, Airplanes file 6, QSC; Kenneth Reid to Elizabeth Olson, June 29, 1948, Olson Activities folder, QSC; Hubachek to Olson, July 15, 1948; Olson Activities folder, QSC. Bill Rom's statement quoted in the text is from an interview with the author on May 16, 1992.

33. Olson to Hubachek, July 12, 1948, Olson Activities folder, QSC; Olson to Roland Ericson, April 1, 1949, Control of the Use of Airplanes files, QSC.

34. Sigurd Olson, "On Getting Close to Things," September 3, 1940.

35. The November 1943 column draft was titled "On Flying."

36. On Olson's work to get the Border Lakes and other outfitting companies to stop using airplanes, see the following from the Olson Papers: Olson to M. W. Peterson, April 29, 1949; Peterson to Olson, May 9, 1949; Olson to Peterson, May 16, 1949; Olson to Elizabeth Olson, July 22, 1949; Olson, "Sigurd F. Olson's answer to Commissioner Floyd's charges reported in 'County Courthouse Comments'" (undated, printed by Friends of the Wilderness).

Notes to Chapter 11

Eleven. Widening Horizons, 1950–1954

1. Butcher to Olson, March 26, 1947.
2. The letter from Eisenhower to Massey, dated March 19, 1949, is in the Canadian QSC folder, QSC. Oberholtzer asked Karl Compton, an original Quetico-Superior Council board member who was a friend of Eisenhower's, to tell Eisenhower about the Quetico-Superior program and to encourage the general to write to Massey. See R. Newell Searle, *Saving Quetico-Superior: A Land Set Apart* (St. Paul, Minn., 1977), 198–99. For further background on the Canadian Quetico-Superior Committee and the treaty proposal from a Canadian perspective, see George Warecki, "The Quetico-Superior Council and the Battle for Wilderness in Quetico Provincial Park, 1909–1960" (M.A. thesis, University of Western Ontario, 1983); and Gerald Killan and George Warecki, "The Battle for Wilderness in Ontario: Saving Quetico-Superior, 1927 to 1960," in *Patterns of the Past: Interpreting Ontario's History*, ed. Roger Hall, William Westfall, and Laurel Sefton MacDowell (Toronto, 1988).
3. Here and following: Bodsworth to the author, March 25, 1992.
4. Bodsworth to Olson, August 14, 1950.
5. Omond Solandt, "Sigurd Olson: Mister Voyageur," *Che-Mun*, Summer 1992 (*Che-Mun* is "The Newsletter of Canadian Wilderness Canoeing").
6. Ibid.
7. Regarding "the Voyageurs," the key published sources for background information are Eric W. Morse, *Freshwater Saga: Memoirs of a Lifetime of Wilderness Canoeing in Canada* (Toronto, 1987); Solandt, "Sigurd Olson: Mister Voyageur"; Blair Fraser, "We Went La Vérendrye's Way," *Maclean's*, October 1, 1954; and two books by Sigurd Olson, *The Lonely Land* (New York, 1961) and *Runes of the North* (New York, 1963). Letters and diaries in the Olson Papers, as well as interviews and media accounts of the journeys, provided additional information.
8. Solandt, "Sigurd Olson."
9. Information on the trial before Judge Nordbye comes from the *Duluth News Tribune*, the Autumn 1952 issue of *Living Wilderness*, and two letters from the Olson Papers: Olson to Kelly, August 1, 1952; and Arthur M. Clure to Kelly, August 8, 1952. The rest of the section about the Quetico-Superior airplane issue in 1953 and 1954 relies primarily on Olson's papers and secondarily on the Control of the Use of Airplanes files, QSC.
10. For the discussion of conservation and politics during the Eisenhower administration, I am especially indebted to Elmo Richardson, *Dams, Parks and Politics: Resource Development and Preservation in the Truman/Eisenhower Era* (Lexington, Ky., 1973), and Mark W. T. Harvey, *A Symbol of Wilderness: Echo Park and the American Conservation Movement* (Albuquerque, N.M., 1994).
11. The key documents regarding Olson's role in the Olympic strip annexation, all in his papers, are: Olson to Kelly, January 7, 1954 (misdated

1953); Olson to Bob Beatty, April 8, 1954; Olson to Burt Marston, June 28, 1966; and Rita Shemesh to Clark MacGregor, April 23, 1970.

12. Bernard DeVoto, "Let's Close the National Parks," *Harper's Magazine*, October 1953.

13. On the benefits to the NPA of DeVoto's article, see Olson to Ned Graves, May 31, 1955. In addition to DeVoto's article, key sources for understanding National Park Service issues and problems during the 1950s include Ronald A. Foresta, *America's National Parks and Their Keepers* (Washington, D.C., 1984); John Ise, *Our National Park Policy: A Critical History* (Baltimore, 1961); Alfred Runte, *National Parks: The American Experience*, 2d ed., rev. (Lincoln, Neb., 1987); and Conrad L. Wirth, *Parks, Politics, and the People* (Norman, Okla., 1980).

14. Sigurd Olson to Elizabeth Olson, November 5, 1949; and Sigurd Olson to Elizabeth Olson, undated, ca. February 1952. For information about Sigurd's facial twitch, I relied on interviews with Elizabeth, Robert, and Yvonne Olson, in addition to such documents as the letters cited.

15. Douglas to editor, *Washington Post,* January 15, 1954.

16. Olson's account of the C&O Canal hike was misdated December 28, 1954; since he wrote it the day after the hike, the actual date was *March* 28, 1954.

17. Olson to Ken Reid, April 10, 1954.

18. The battle for Dinosaur National Monument has been documented in a number of publications, but the definitive work is Mark Harvey's *A Symbol of Wilderness.*

19. Olson to Fred Packard, November 5, 1954.

20. Quoted in Harvey, *Symbol of Wilderness.* Harvey found the speech in the Sierra Club Papers, which I did not examine.

21. Wharton to Olson, August 30, 1952.

22. Olson to C. Edward "Ned" Graves, January 5, 1954.

23. Olson to Packard, January 5, 1957.

24. Regarding Olson as a finalist for the Wilderness Society Council, see George Marshall to TWS Council, August 6, 1954, Box 79, Wilderness Society Papers, Denver.

Twelve. The Singing Wilderness, 1950–1956

1. The quotes come from letters printed in the magazine's Summer 1951 issue.

2. Olson to Ed Haase, June 18, 1951.

3. While the evidence indicates that Olson sold his part of the Border Lakes Outfitting Company primarily so he could find a better return on his investment, there is no question but that his partial ownership had compli-

cated his Quetico-Superior work. Northeastern Minnesotans had long tried to make Olson's role in the company an issue, saying it proved that his Quetico-Superior work was motivated by money, but by 1949 the issue also was being raised in Ontario. See, for example, Harold Walker to Charles Kelly, November 22, 1949. Then there was the additional embarrassment of discovering that his company was flying people into the border lakes wilderness at the same time he was trying to get such flying banned (see chapter 10).

4. The quote, from a friend named John Brown, was repeated in a letter from Olson to Ken Reid, September 16, 1951. I did not find Brown's original letter.

5. This letter is part of Robert and Yvonne Olson's personal files, along with a number of other letters from Sigurd.

6. Swem related the anecdote in an interview with the author on January 12, 1993.

7. Olson to "Dearest friends and kindly people," undated, ca. June 1954, Robert K. Olson's personal collection; Olson to Rodell, June 10, 1954. The Oscar Fay Adams poem "Where Are the Pipes of Pan?" was in an old book that Olson treasured: *Ballades and Rondeaus, Chants Royal, Sestinas, Villanelles &c*, compiled by Gleeson White (New York, 1888).

8. Olson quotes Knopf in his November 29 letter to Rodell: "By the way, isn't the attached letter from Alfred Knopf also of interest—'I am wondering if . . .'" etc. Rodell's files, sent to Robert K. Olson in 1995, contain Olson's original letter, but not the letter from Knopf that Olson said he attached.

9. The letter from Knopf is in Olson's papers. Rodell's files provide more complete contract negotiation details than do Olson's files.

10. Aldo Leopold, *A Sand County Almanac, with Other Essays on Conservation from Round River* (New York, 1966), 149.

11. Olson to Gene Laitala, January 31, 1955; Olson to Bill Magie, January 13, 1955.

12. George Laing to Olson, March 14, 1955.

13. Olson to Laing, March 24, 1955.

14. Here and following: Olson records passages from Masefield, and his own reactions, in an undated series of notes, ca. February 1954, titled "Suggestions for the Book."

15. Sigurd Olson, *The Singing Wilderness* (New York, 1956), 10.

16. For my discussion of *The Singing Wilderness*, I am deeply indebted to J. Baird Callicott's "The Land Aesthetic" in *Companion to "A Sand County Almanac": Interpretive and Critical Essays*, ed. J. Baird Callicott (Madison, Wis., 1987). Also helpful, and from the same source, was John Tallmadge's "Anatomy of a Classic." Peter A. Fritzell, *Nature Writing and America: Essays upon a Cultural Type* (Ames, Iowa, 1990), is an excellent discussion of what Fritzell describes as the essential characteristics of the best American nature writ-

ing, as well as comparisons of a wide variety of authors and their works; it includes brief references to Olson.

17. Wallace Stegner, "The Legacy of Aldo Leopold," in Callicott, ed., *Companion to "A Sand County Almanac."*

18. Alfred Runte's *National Parks: The American Experience,* 2d ed., rev. (Lincoln, Neb., 1987), contains valuable material on the relationship between art and the national parks. Hans Huth, *Nature and the American: Three Centuries of Changing Attitudes* (Berkeley, Calif., 1957), while dated, is still useful for its analysis of art's role in shaping attitudes toward nature. The Weston anecdote is from Susan Sontag, *On Photography* (New York, 1977).

19. Leopold, *Sand County Almanac,* 96.

20. Callicott, "The Land Aesthetic," 162; Leopold, *Sand County Almanac,* 97.

21. Olson, *Singing Wilderness,* 126, 162.

22. Ibid., 202.

23. Ibid., 160–61, 41.

24. Leopold quoted in Curt Meine, *Aldo Leopold: His Life and Work* (Madison, Wis., 1988), 490; Olson, *Singing Wilderness,* 223–24.

25. Olson, *Singing Wilderness,* 187.

26. Ibid., 90, 91.

27. Ibid., 80.

28. Ibid., 206, 208.

29. Ibid., 7, 6.

30. Ibid., 108.

31. Ibid., 77.

32. Ibid., 130–31.

33. Ibid., 133.

34. Reviews of *The Singing Wilderness* (all 1956) include: *Kirkus,* February 15; *Library Journal,* March 15; *Chicago Sunday Tribune,* April 15; *Milwaukee Journal,* April 15; *Capital Times* (Madison, Wis.), April 19; *New York Times,* April 22; *New York Herald Tribune Book Review,* April 29; *Christian Science Monitor,* May 3; *New Yorker,* May 5; *San Francisco Chronicle,* May 6; *Ottawa Journal,* May 11; *Booklist,* May 15; *Toronto Telegram,* June 2; *Carmel* (Calif.) *Pine Cone,* June 21; *Atlantic,* June; *Minnesota Naturalist,* June; *Winnipeg Free Press,* July 1; *Canadian Geographic Journal,* November.

35. From Rodell's files, loaned to me by Robert K. Olson.

36. *ALA Bulletin,* February 1957, 98.

37. Morse to Olson, April 22, 1956; Murie to Olson, October 31, 1956; MacKaye to Olson, May 19, 1956; Broome to Olson, May 2, 1956. George Marshall's letter in support of adding Olson to the Wilderness Society's governing council, written to Charley Woodbury on April 13, 1956, is in Box 64, Wilderness Society Papers, Denver. Other related letters are in this box and in Box 71.

38. Kenneth Olson to Sigurd Olson, April 9, 1956. Kenneth Olson's later comment was recalled by Robert K. Olson.

39. William A. Strutz to Olson, March 3, 1962; Mrs. Richard C. Karstad to Olson, July 18, 1960; Beaumont to Olson, ca. February 1962.

40. Howard Higbee to Olson, June 9, 1956 (misdated 1955); Snow to Olson, January 19, 1961.

41. The man who conversed with spirits, Edward Cope Wood, wrote to Olson on many occasions, and Olson seemed to enjoy the exchanges; he did not, however, endorse Wood's pamphlet. The matchmaker was Lyn Comins, a Massachusetts woman who wrote on December 29, 1961, after seeing Olson's picture in *Life* magazine.

42. Regarding relative sales of *The Singing Wilderness* and *A Sand County Almanac:* Curt Meine, in *Aldo Leopold: His Life and Work* (Madison, Wis., 1988), says that Leopold's book had sold about twenty thousand copies by 1966, seventeen years after its publication. Royalty statements in Olson's papers indicate that *The Singing Wilderness* sold twenty thousand copies by 1964 or 1965, or in about half the time as *A Sand County Almanac.* A more precise date in Olson's case is not possible, because there is not a complete collection of royalty statements. The total sales over the book's first forty years were provided by Alfred Knopf Inc.

Regarding the Russian and Arabic translations of *Singing Wilderness* excerpts, see Garrett K. Sias to Olson, April 21, 1959. The book's first radio appearance was on Wisconsin Public Radio's *Chapter a Day* program in 1958. Part of the essay "Timber Wolves" was included in a *CBS Sports Spectacular* episode in the 1970s.

Thirteen. The Search for Balance, 1956–1960

1. Charles Stevenson, "The Shocking Truth about Our National Parks," *Reader's Digest,* January 1955.

2. Wirth to Thomas Bacig, December 15, 1978.

3. Olson to C. Edward "Ned" Graves, May 20, 1955. Graves was the NPA's western field representative, based in Carmel, California.

4. Wirth to Olson, February 27, 1957.

5. Here and following: Butcher to Olson, February 9, 1957.

6. The description of the meeting between NPA and NPS officials is from a memo from Fred Packard to the NPA board of trustees, February 20, 1957.

7. Olson to Theodore Wirth (Conrad's son), March 6, 1957; Butcher to Murie, May 11, 1957, Olaus J. Murie Papers, Denver Public Library.

8. The Murie Papers and the Wilderness Society Papers, located in the Denver Public Library's Conservation Collection, both document the opposition of Murie and Butcher to the wilderness bill. See, for example, Butcher

to Zahniser, July 26, 1958, and Murie to Butcher, undated, ca. 1958, both in the Murie Papers. By September 1958 Murie's opposition to the bill and criticism of Zahniser's efforts, voiced during the governing council's annual meeting, left Zahniser for a full year debating resignation from the society. See Zahniser to Murie, September 21, 1959, Box 2, Wilderness Society Papers (hereafter TWS).

9. The details of Arthur Carhart's plan for the canoe country are discussed in my article "Wilderness Visions: Arthur Carhart's 1922 Proposal for the Quetico-Superior Wilderness," *Forest and Conservation History* 35 (July 1991): 128–37.

10. *Ely Miner,* July 18, 1957. Details of the July 10, 1957, banquet in Ely at which the wilderness bill became a major local issue are contained in a letter from Olson to Zahniser, July 17, 1957, Olson files, Friends of the Wilderness Papers (hereafter FOW), Minnesota Historical Society.

11. Humphrey, memo to Herb Waters, July 20, 1957, Box 146, Hubert H. Humphrey Papers, Minnesota Historical Society; Humphrey to Gerald Heaney, July 20, 1957, Box 146, Humphrey Papers.

12. *Ely Miner,* July 25, 1957.

13. Pechaver to Humphrey, August 3, 1957, Box 146, Hubert H. Humphrey Papers; Olson to Magie, ca. July 17, 1957, Olson files, FOW. Elizabeth Olson told me the anecdote about the First Presbyterian Church.

14. The letter is in Box 58, TWS.

15. Olson, journal entries, ca. July 22 and 26, 1957.

16. Background on Fred Seaton, including his statement about "crying socialism," comes from Elmo Richardson, *Dams, Parks & Politics: Resource Development and Preservation in the Truman-Eisenhower Era* (Lexington, Ky., 1973).

17. Olson to Bill Magie, November 9, 1956.

18. The original Interior Department Advisory Committee on Fish and Wildlife included, besides Olson, the following well-known conservationists: Ira Gabrielson, Michael Hudoba, Thomas Kimball, J. W. Penfold, Ernest Swift, and Howard Zahniser.

19. The details about Seaton's conversation with Olson regarding International Nickel are from the notes taken by Michael Nadel of the Wilderness Society during a phone call with Olson on December 5, 1957, right after the talk with Seaton. The notes are in Box 57, TWS.

20. Humphrey to Olson, August 22, 1957.

21. Olson's comments to the Lutheran Men's Club are taken from his prepared draft of the talk, titled "The Meaning of the Wilderness Bill." The text is in the Olson files, FOW.

22. Olson to editor, *Ely Miner,* September 10, 1957.

23. Information about Olson's property and cabin on Burntside Lake

comes from documents in the Olson Papers, documents in the possession of Robert K. Olson, and interviews with Elizabeth, Robert, and Sigurd T. Olson. Sigurd Sr. eventually bought four more adjoining lots and part of a fifth, adding approximately ten acres to the twenty-six he initially purchased.

24. Sigurd F. Olson, *Listening Point* (New York, 1958), 19.

25. Ibid., 27–28.

26. Ibid., 27, 34.

27. Ibid., 147.

28. Ibid., 150.

29. Ibid., 151.

30. Ibid., 153.

31. Ibid., 239–40.

32. Aldo Leopold, *A Sand County Almanac, with Other Essays on Conservation from Round River* (New York, 1966), 68.

33. Olson, *Listening Point,* 152, 243.

34. Reviews of *Listening Point* (all 1958) include: *Atlantic,* December; *Booklist,* December 1; *Chicago Sunday Tribune,* September 24; *Library Journal,* September 1, *New York Herald Tribune Book Review,* November 16; *New York Times,* September 28; *San Francisco Chronicle,* November 23.

35. The letter is not dated. It is worth noting that Olson's papers contain extensive correspondence relating to the National Parks Association.

36. See Olson to Carrithers, August 27, 1959.

37. Regarding the dinner, see Fred Packard to Olson, May 16, 1959. Olson did agree to a reception following the annual meeting. See *National Parks Magazine,* July 1959.

38. Cahalane to Wharton, April 26, 1960.

39. Olson to Ira Gabrielson, April 28, 1960. John C. Miles does an excellent job of describing the Tony Smith years in his *Guardians of the Parks: A History of the National Parks and Conservation Association* (Washington, D.C., 1995).

Fourteen. From Contemplation to Action:
Sigurd Olson's Wilderness Theology, 1959–1964

1. For my discussion of Olson's wilderness theology, a number of sources were invaluable. Lawrence S. Cunningham, *The Catholic Experience* (New York, 1987), and Max Oelschlaeger, *Caring for Creation: An Ecumenical Approach to the Environmental Crisis* (New Haven, Conn., 1994), helped me the most in my attempt to understand and describe Teilhard's complex perspective, which played an important role in Olson's thought. George N. Shuster and Ralph E. Thorson, eds., *Evolution in Perspective: Commentaries in Honor of Pierre Lecomte du Noüy* (Notre Dame, Ind., 1970), provides solid background for understanding the author of *Human Destiny.*

2. Aldous Huxley, *The Perennial Philosophy* (New York, 1945), 29.

3. Pierre Lecomte du Noüy, *Human Destiny* (New York, 1947), 104; Julian Huxley, *Religion without Revelation* (New York, 1957), 212. For more on Lecomte du Noüy, see George N. Shuster and Ralph E. Thorson, eds., *Evolution in Perspective: Commentaries in Honor of Pierre Lecomte du Noüy* (Notre Dame, Ind. 1970). For more on Huxley, see H. James Birx's introduction to Julian Huxley, *Evolutionary Humanism* (Buffalo, N.Y., 1992).

4. Lewis Mumford, *The Conduct of Life* (New York, 1951), 71. When Lewis Mumford is quoted in Olson's later writings and speeches, *The Conduct of Life* invariably is the source.

5. Sigurd F. Olson, *Reflections from the North Country* (New York, 1976), 57.

6. For the quotes from Teilhard's journal, see Cunningham, *The Catholic Experience,* 126. For the Olson quotes, see Olson to Robert H. Day, December 29, 1959, and Jim dale Vickery, "A Bluejay Calling," *Canoe,* February 1980. Max Oelschlaeger, *Caring for Creation: An Ecumenical Approach to the Environmental Crisis* (New Haven, Conn., 1994), provides—along with Cunningham's book—a good, concise summary of Teilhard's thought.

7. Olson read Maritain's *A Preface to Metaphysics: Seven Lectures on Being,* Merton's *Seeds of Contemplation,* and Pieper's *Leisure: The Basis of Culture.* Of these three writers, Pieper seems to have had the biggest impact on Olson. Olson's copy of *Leisure,* a Mentor Omega paperback published in 1963, is full of underlined passages, and Pieper's words creep into one of Olson's speeches and two of his books. The speech is "The Spiritual Need," which Olson presented at the Sierra Club-sponsored Ninth Wilderness Conference in April 1965. (It was published in Bruce M. Kilgore, ed., *Wilderness in a Changing World* [San Francisco, 1966].) It was his first major speech after reading *Leisure,* and Olson quoted Pieper during the presentation. He also used Pieper's language without attribution at the end of his speech. Olson ended by saying, "Unless we can preserve places where the endless spiritual needs of man can be fulfilled and nourished, we will destroy our culture and ourselves." The opening epigraph of Pieper's book contains the following, which Olson underlined: "Unless we regain the art of silence and insight, the ability for nonactivity, unless we substitute true leisure for our hectic amusements, we will destroy our culture and ourselves."

In the speech, Olson also attributed to Thomas Aquinas a statement made by Pieper in *Leisure* (p. 91) in his discussion of Aquinas. After a short quote from Aquinas, Pieper writes, "To know the universal essence of things is to reach a point of view from which the whole of being and all existing things become visible; at the same time the spiritual outpost thus reached by knowing the essence of things enables man to look upon the landscape of the whole universe." Olson used this sentence in his speech and attributed it to Aquinas. He later made the same mistake in the final chapter of *Open*

Horizons, and in *Reflections,* he paraphrased the sentence, again attributing it to Aquinas (p. 48).

8. Sigurd F. Olson, *The Singing Wilderness* (New York, 1956), 131.

9. The note is not dated.

10. Mark Greer to Olson, November 11, 1957; Robert K. Olson, interview.

11. Loren Eiseley, *The Unexpected Universe* (New York, 1964), 87; Olson to George Laing, June 30, 1955; Olson, *Reflections,* 49.

12. Sigurd F. Olson, "The Long Long Dances," chapter draft for *Open Horizons,* dated April 15, 1966.

13. About the National Park Service's advisory board: Ronald A. Foresta, in *America's National Parks and Their Keepers* (Washington, D.C., 1984), calls it a "prestigious 'bucket of fog,'" a public relations tool of the Park Service that simply said yes to whatever the agency wanted. George Hartzog, who served as director of the National Park Service from 1964 to 1972, contradicts this view in his book *Battling for the National Parks* (Mt. Kisco, N.Y., 1988). My own interviews with Hartzog, with Stewart Udall, secretary of the interior in the Kennedy and Johnson administrations, and with former NPS assistant director Ted Swem—as well as examination of advisory board minutes and letters in the Olson Papers—give little credence to Foresta's opinion. While the evidence indicates that from the late 1950s to the mid-1960s the board most often supported agency policies and initiatives, members were well enough informed and independent enough to challenge the agency when they felt it was necessary.

14. Terry Wood, interview with the author, March 2, 1992; Stegner to Udall, September 25, 1961, Box 190, Stewart L. Udall Papers, University of Arizona, Tucson. Stegner's perception of Olson was similar thirty years later. He wrote to me on August 23, 1991, that "Sig was always a major presence. He loved company, loved friends, liked a drink, liked to sing when he had had a drink; but his was an essentially serious mind: he never lost track of why we were visiting these exotic places, or what we had to keep our eyes out for. He was a wheelhorse, a tower of strength, to the Park Service and to the forces that were trying to establish new parks, seashores, canoe wildernesses, and other reservations during the Kennedy and Johnson years. But his heart was always out at Listening Point in Ely. He somehow looked as if he felt the need of a canoe paddle in his hand, and his greatest love was the Voyageurs park that he was very instrumental in establishing. I have worked with him on master plans for Yellowstone and other parks, and he was always—he and Stan Cain—the best informed, wisest, and sanest of the committee."

15. Olson to Burton Marton, March 16, 1961. For a full treatment of the importance of "monumentalism" in national park history, see Alfred Runte, *National Parks: The American Experience,* 2d ed., rev. (Lincoln, Neb., 1987).

16. Olson's first impressions of Udall are from a letter he wrote to Frank

Masland on March 16, 1961. Regarding his prediction of Udall's greatness, see Olson to Udall, February 9, 1969.

17. Interview with the author, July 2, 1992.

18. Interview with the author, May 18, 1992.

19. Sigurd Olson, report, "Cape Cod National Park," ca. March 1958.

20. For background on conservation in Alaska during the 1950s and 1960s, I found John M. Kauffmann, *Alaska's Brooks Range: The Ultimate Mountains* (Seattle, 1992), quite helpful, and also Hartzog's *Battling for the National Parks*.

21. Information about Olson's 1960 Alaska trip comes primarily from his papers, supplemented by interviews with Sigurd T. Olson and Ted Swem. See also Olson's article "Alaska: Land of Scenic Grandeur," *Living Wilderness*, Winter 1971–72.

22. Olson to Mary and Walter Tisdale, September 7, 1960, lent to the author by Robert K. Olson.

23. Information about Olson's intervention with Seaton on behalf of the Arctic National Wildlife Range comes from an interview with Ted Swem and from a letter Olson wrote to Wilbur Mills on May 3, 1969, in Swem's personal files. The minutes of the Wilderness Society's Governing Council meeting of September 2, 1971, also contain a reference to it.

24. A copy of the Alaska Task Force's "Operation Great Land" report was provided to me by John Kauffmann, a member of the task force and the editorial assistant for the report.

25. Roderick Nash, *Wilderness and the American Mind*, 3d ed. (New Haven, Conn., 1982), 272.

26. The documentation regarding Olson's work in Canada comes from the Olson Papers, except for the reference to Olson as an "ambassador without portfolio." That quote is in a letter Olson wrote to Wilbur Mills on May 3, 1969, which is part of Ted Swem's personal files.

27. For background on Canadian conservation, I found the following very useful: Marilyn Dubasak, *Wilderness Preservation: A Cross-Cultural Comparison of Canada and the United States* (New York, 1990); C. J. Taylor, *Negotiating the Past: The Making of Canada's National Historic Parks and Sites* (Montreal, 1990); Robert Page, *Northern Development: The Canadian Dilemma* (Toronto, 1986); Geoffrey Wall and John S. Marsh, eds., *Recreational Land Use: Perspectives on Its Evolution in Canada* (Ottawa, 1982); and Gerald Killan, *Protected Places: A History of Ontario's Provincial Parks System* (Toronto, 1993).

28. The transcript of Olson's talk to Park Service master plan teams is untitled and undated; the talk was given sometime after George Hartzog became director of the service in 1964.

29. Theodor R. Swem, "Sigurd F. Olson," *Cosmos Club Bulletin*, April 1984.

30. Olson to Edward Weeks, February 25, 1961.

31. Conrad Wirth, in *Parks, Politics and the People* (Norman, Okla., 1980), and

George Hartzog, in *Battling for the National Parks* (Mt. Kisco, N.Y., 1988), give their perspectives on the circumstances surrounding Wirth's resignation and the conference at Yosemite National Park. Correspondence in the Udall Papers at the University of Arizona, the Wilderness Society Papers at the Denver Public Library, and the Olson Papers, along with interviews of Udall and Ted Swem, provided additional background for this section.

32. Quoted in Wirth, *Parks, Politics, and the People,* 308–10.

33. Udall's speech is in Box 111 of the Udall Papers.

34. Interview with the author, May 18, 1992.

35. Olson's speech, titled "The Conservation Ethic and the NPS," is in the Olson Papers.

36. The first Udall quote is from Dorothy Boyle Huyck, "Sig Olson: Wilderness Philosopher," *American Forests,* May 1965; the source of the second is Robert K. Olson, to whom Udall said it.

37. The background on Quetico-Superior issues and problems during the early 1960s comes primarily from my earlier research, published in my book *Canoe Country: An Embattled Wilderness* (Minocqua, Wis., 1991). See also R. Newell Searle's *Saving Quetico-Superior: A Land Set Apart* (St. Paul, Minn., 1977), especially for details about the demise of the international treaty.

38. Bill Rom, "Latest Threat to the Canoe Country," *Naturalist,* Winter 1963.

39. The letter is undated.

40. Olson, statement prepared for a committee hearing in St. Paul, May 23, 1964.

41. Hubachek to Kelly, May 12, 1964.

42. Olson to Hubachek, July 11, 1964.

43. Sigurd Olson, "Wilderness Preservation," *Naturalist,* Winter 1964.

44. The quote comes from a talk Olson gave in April 1965 at the Sierra Club sponsored Ninth Biennial Wilderness Conference. Titled "The Spiritual Need," it was published in Bruce M. Kilgore, ed., *Wilderness in a Changing World* (San Francisco, 1966).

45. Sigurd F. Olson, *The Singing Wilderness* (New York, 1956), 133.

46. Olson's statement about saving more souls than his father did is from an oral history interview conducted in 1976 for the Minnesota Historical Society by Robert Herbst, John McKane, and R. Newell Searle. The interview lasts just over four hours; a forty-six-page transcript also is available at the society.

47. For helping me to tie Olson's thoughts about God and evolution to his thoughts about wilderness, and to place him in the intellectual tradition of Thoreau and Muir, I am deeply indebted to the following: Max Oelschlaeger, *The Idea of Wilderness: From Prehistory to the Age of Ecology* (New Haven, Conn., 1991); Frederick Turner, *Rediscovering America: John Muir in His Time and Ours* (New York, 1985); Michael Cohen, *The Pathless Way: John Muir*

and American Wilderness (Madison, Wis., 1984); Sally M. Miller, ed., *John Muir: Life and Work* (Albuquerque, N.M., 1993); and Joel Porte, *Emerson and Thoreau: Transcendentalists in Conflict* (Middletown, Conn., 1965). Other essential sources for comparing Olson's perspective to those of other key wilderness thinkers and activists are Curt Meine, *Aldo Leopold: His Life and Work* (Madison, Wis., 1988); J. Baird Callicott, ed., *Companion to "A Sand County Almanac"* (Madison, Wis., 1987); and James M. Glover, *A Wilderness Original: The Life of Bob Marshall* (Seattle, 1986).

48. Olson to Clayton Rudd, July 1, 1964.

Fifteen. The Making of a Myth, 1960–1982

1. The opening anecdote was provided by Simon Bourgin.

2. Olson appeared in the December 22, 1961, issue of *Life* magazine, which was devoted to America's outdoors and conservation leaders.

Olson had friends at a number of the major newspapers and magazines in Canada and the United States, and could count on access when he needed it. A letter that the highly respected journalist Harrison Salisbury of the *New York Times* wrote to Olson on February 13, 1964, is indicative of the esteem in which he was held. "Please remember that you have the strongest of allies right here on the Times," Salisbury wrote, "and at any time when there is something which we can do which would be constructive and would advance the cause, do let us know. I myself will make it a point to keep in touch with you constantly, every few months, in hopes that there is some kind of story we can carry which will repel the hordes."

3. Woodbury to Olson, September 14, 1963.

4. Packard to Robert and Yvonne Olson, September 4, 1995. Used with Packard's permission.

5. Betty (no last name) to Olaus and Mardy Murie, September 14, 1959, Box 264, Olaus J. Murie Papers, Denver Public Library.

6. Andersen quoted in Robert B. Oetting, "Sigurd Olson, Environmentalist," *Naturalist*, Autumn 1981; Grahek quoted by Jim Klobuchar in the *Minneapolis Star*, July 19, 1972.

7. Marshall to Elizabeth Olson, January 26, 1982.

8. Olson's highest awards from the major conservation groups are as follows: the John Muir Award (Sierra Club, 1967); the Founder's Award (Izaak Walton League, 1969); the Robert Marshall Award (Wilderness Society, 1981, the first year the award was given); and induction into the National Wildlife Federation Hall of Fame (1991). The Izaak Walton League also presented Olson with its Conservation Award in 1959 and inducted him into its Hall of Fame in 1963. Of the six oldest and most important national conservation groups with a major interest in public lands issues (in other words, exclud-

ing large international organizations such as the World Wildlife Fund, as well as groups that do not get actively involved in public lands management issues, such as the Nature Conservancy), only the Audubon Society and the National Parks Association have not given him their highest award.

9. Olson received the Burroughs Medal in 1974. Only Aldo Leopold (an inductee into the National Wildlife Hall of Fame) and Paul Brooks (a recipient of the Sierra Club's John Muir Award) have received both a Burroughs Medal and the highest honors of one of the six major American conservation groups.

10. The letters are in Box 64, Wilderness Society Papers, Denver Public Library.

11. Olson to Woodbury, September 21, 1965, Box 54, Wilderness Society Papers. This letter also is the source of the Woodbury quote.

12. In Box 64, Wilderness Society Papers.

13. The loose-leaf note is undated.

14. Olson, loose-leaf note, January 27, 1964.

15. Olson, loose-leaf note, July 26, 1967.

16. Details of Olson's heart attack come from correspondence from the time and from interviews with Elizabeth Olson and Michael Nadel, who was editor of the Wilderness Society's magazine and was sitting near the Olsons when Sigurd suffered his heart attack.

17. Background for the following section on Voyageurs National Park comes from Robert Treuer, *Voyageur Country: A Park in the Wilderness* (Minneapolis, 1979), and Fred T. Witzig, "The Crane Lake Issue in the Establishment of Voyageurs National Park," *Upper Midwest History* 3 (1983): 41–53.

18. Olson's recollection of his June 27, 1962, trip through the area with Wirth is in an undated, unpublished 1981 essay called "Voyageur's [*sic*] National Park."

19. Olson's effort to get the National Parks Advisory Board to reaffirm the proposal after Hartzog raised questions is documented in the minutes of the board's fiftieth meeting, April 14, 1964, in the Olson Papers. The other details here and following also come primarily from Olson's papers, although I also studied the papers of the Voyageurs National Park Association, a Minnesota-based group that played a major role in the lobbying effort for the park. Any full story of the park's creation will require extensive use of these papers, located at the Minnesota Historical Society. Box 18 of the Minnesota Division of the Izaak Walton League Papers at the Minnesota Historical Society also contains documents related to the park's creation.

20. Wirth to Thomas D. Bacig, December 15, 1978.

21. The Wilderness Society financed its deficit by drawing on an endowment established when cofounder Robert Marshall died in 1939. At the end of 1964, the Robert Marshall Wilderness Fund held stocks in fourteen com-

panies valued at a total of a little less than $800,000. Three-fourths of the monetary value consisted of stock in three companies: Monsanto Chemical, and Kennecott Copper, and Sears, Roebuck. A group of six trustees controlled the fund; Olson served as a trustee from 1964 to 1975. The trustees began dipping into the capital in earnest in 1969. At a meeting on November 20, 1968, which Olson attended (it was held on Sanibel Island in Florida, two days before Olson's heart attack), the trustees voted to grant the Wilderness Society $75,000 for 1969. About $50,000 of that had to be raised by selling securities, including 500 shares of United Fruit Co., valued at $38,000. By the end of 1974 the fund's total value had dropped to $425,000. The details come from Olson's papers and from Boxes 54 and 75 of the Wilderness Society Papers in Denver.

22. Marshall to Olson, March 6, 1973.

23. Both notes were written on October 10, 1972.

24. Sigurd F. Olson Elementary School in Golden Valley, Minnesota, was dedicated on October 24, 1971. In a 1975 commemorative album made by the school for the Olsons, Leroy Hood makes it clear that, like Northland College and its Sigurd Olson Environmental Institute, the grade school saw Olson's name as a perfect symbol for the environmental perspective at the heart of the school's curriculum.

According to his son Robert, Sigurd finally agreed to lend his name to the Sigurd Olson Environmental Institute at Northland College after intense pressure from Harriet Dexter, a longtime family friend who had served Northland College for many years as a faculty member and, for a brief period in 1971, as acting president. Sigurd had been trying to say no but gave in after Dexter asked him if he thought he was too good for Northland College.

25. The George Vukelich quote comes from his "North Country Notebook" column in the Madison, Wisconsin, newspaper *Isthmus,* January 22, 1982. Edgar Wayburn called Sigurd "the personification of the wilderness defender" on April 8, 1972, while presenting Olson with an honorary life membership in the Sierra Club, the thirty-fifth such award in the club's eighty years of existence.

26. Dillard to Olson, June 28, 1973.

27. Arlys Utech's comment about Olson's "beautiful aura" is included in the school's 1975 "Commemorative Album for Sigurd F. Olson." Sister Noemi Weygant's comment is contained in her "Course on Sigurd Olson" file, which she made available to me.

28. For more details on the logging controversy in Quetico Provincial Park, see Gerald Killan and George Warecki, "The Algonquin Wildlands League and the Emergence of Environmental Politics in Ontario, 1965–1974," *Environmental History Review,* Winter 1992, and George Warecki, "Protecting Ontar-

io's Wilderness: A History of Wilderness Conservation in Ontario, 1927–1973"
(unpublished Ph.D. thesis, McMaster University, 1989).

29. Bodsworth to the author, March 25, 1992.

30. *Ely Echo*, June 8, 1977. The congressional hearing was on July 8.

31. Olson's recollection of his confrontation with the long-haired youths
in San Francisco is contained in the transcript of his speech "The Revolution in Environmental Concern," written about 1969.

32. Quoted in Jim Vickery, "Profile of a Pioneer: Sigurd F. Olson," *Back-
packing Journal*, Summer 1977.

33. Sigurd F. Olson, *The Singing Wilderness* (New York, 1956), 147.

34. Ibid.; Sigurd F. Olson, *Open Horizons* (New York, 1969), 33.

35. Sigurd F. Olson, "Duck Hunting Adventures," ca. 1981.

36. The full story of Olson's hunting comes primarily from interviews
with his sons and with Chuck Wick, a longtime friend. Occasional references to hunting in his letters and unpublished manuscripts also proved
useful. As president of the National Parks Association, for example, he battled Devereux Butcher and Fred Packard over virulent antihunting statements in NPA publications. Olson deleted such words as *killers* and *butchers*,
and wrote to Ken Reid of the Izaak Walton League on May 6, 1954, that
"both Fred and Dev go off the deep end" when it came to hunting. "I shall
never forget how shocked Dev was," he added, "when I mentioned at one
time that I liked to hunt ducks. Imagine I have been damned ever since. It is
absolutely impossible for those chaps to understand people who hunt or for
that matter people who fish. All are killers." In case anyone concludes that
my intention is to criticize Olson for his hunting, I should state that this is
not the case. I have never hunted, but I am not opposed to hunting and have
enjoyed meals of wild game prepared by friends who are hunters.

37. Quoted in Jim Vickery, "Profile of a Pioneer: Sigurd F. Olson," *Back-
packing Journal*, Summer 1977.

38. The title *Reflections from the North Country* was suggested by Sigurd
Olson Jr.'s wife, Esther. Sigurd wrote a good portion of the book while he
was staying with his son and daughter-in-law in Douglas, Alaska. Sigurd
dedicated the book to Ann Langen, who typed his manuscripts.

39. Quoted in Frank Graham Jr., "Leave It to the Bourgeois: Sigurd Olson
and His Wilderness Quest," *Audubon*, November 1980.

40. The letter is part of Ted Swem's personal files.

41. Olson's letter rejecting the Department of the Interior's Conservation
Service Award was sent in November 1981 to Park Service director Russell E.
Dickenson. Copies of several drafts are in Ted Swem's personal files. Swem
also provided the other details about the incident.

42. The letter is part of Ted Swem's personal files.

43. The details about Sigurd's last hours come from interviews with his

wife and sons, from a letter Elizabeth wrote to the Swems on February 24, 1982 (in Ted Swem's personal files), and from interviews with Scott and Beth Pearson. Sigurd was introduced to the Pearsons by longtime friend Chuck Wick after Ann Langen became ill and could not finish typing Olson's *Of Time and Place* manuscript. Beth Pearson finished the job. Wick now owns and lives in Olson's house at 106 East Wilson Street.

44. "Caribou Creek" was published in *Audubon*, March 1982.

❖ Index ❖

Index

Index

Index

Index

David Backes met Sigurd and Elizabeth Olson while an undergraduate at the University of Wisconsin in Madison. He later lived for a short time near Ely, Minnesota and visited with the Olsons at their home on several occasions. Their encouragement helped convince him to go to graduate school at Madison, where, shortly after Olson's death, he wrote a master's thesis about his key role in banning airplanes from the area known today as the Boundary Waters Canoe Area Wilderness. By 1990 Elizabeth Olson, who had carefully guarded her husband's image and was often reluctant to provide access to his papers and diaries, granted David permission to write Olson's biography. David not only had the opportunity to read and study his private journals, he also extensively interviewed other members of the Olson family and many others who knew Sigurd Olson, including such major figures in conservation history as former Interior Secretary Stewart Udall and Park Service Director George Hartzog.

David is professor in the Department of Journalism and Mass Communication at the University of Wisconsin-Milwaukee. He is also the author of *Canoe Country: An Embattled Wilderness* and *The Wilderness Companion.*